The
NORMANS
and the
NORMAN CONQUEST

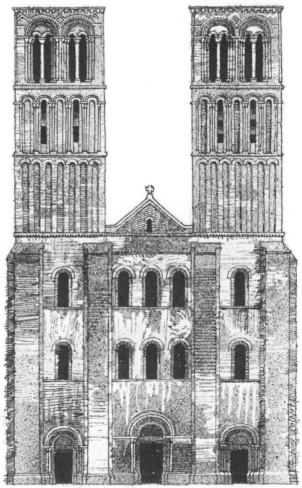

The abbey church of St. Stephen at Caen, founded by William the Conqueror, and also his burial-place. (West end, omitting the later spires.)

The
NORMANS
and the
NORMAN CONQUEST

R. Allen Brown

THOMAS Y. CROWELL COMPANY, INC.

New York   Established 1834

To the Lady Mary

Contents

Preface

It might perhaps be thought that anyone writing another book on the Norman Conquest just now should begin with an apology. In fact, I do not feel apologetic, though I should perhaps begin with the explanation that when, some years ago, I was invited to undertake this work, it did not occur to me, in my innocence, that the nine-hundredth anniversary in 1966 would call forth a number of other publications on the subject. In those days it could still be said that no book on the Norman Conquest *per se* had been written since Freeman's volumes a century before. And now, in the event, I have enjoyed myself and the subject far too much to feel any regrets. It may also be thought that this book still fills a gap, for it has been written especially for students, both in colleges and schools, and seeks to answer as comprehensibly as possible, and in as much detail as my knowledge allows, those questions which they ought to ask, and certainly will be asked. Yet while intended to meet the needs of students, whom I am privileged to know and work with, I trust it is also written in such a way as to attract rather than repel the elusive general reader. The book takes a strong line, in stressing the importance of the Norman Conquest, and, again, this calls for no apology since, as it seems to me, that fundamental truth needs emphasising at the present time. Nor, finally, do I wish to apologise for the footnotes. It is a heresy, spreading among publishers and symptomatic of our 'instant' age, that footnotes put off even intelligent readers. Such readers should protest at the insult thus offered them behind their backs. Footnotes have an honourable place in history. They cite the authority for statements made, and they also lead all those who wish to follow into the deep woods, green pastures and rewarding byways which lie on either side of the motorway of the text.

Those, and she especially, who have helped most in the making of this book know well the deep obligation which I feel, without my making public what is essentially private. But I also have other obligations which something more than convention impels me to put on record here. To the publishers I am grateful, for inviting me to write the book, and for their patience when it was not finished when it should have been finished. To my college I am grateful, for enabling me to have the kind of life which still, just, allows books to be written—though if those who think that Universities should work double shifts and surrender their vacations have their way, there will be no more books like this. To my colleague Mr. Gerald Hodgett, and to Dr. Christopher Holdsworth of University College, London, I am grateful for reading the typescript which greatly benefited from their generosity. To my many pupils, past and present, I am grateful, even if it surprises them. I am grateful in particular to a former pupil, Mr. John Gooch of King's College, London, for reading the proofs, and to my research pupil, Miss V. M. Elsley, also of King's, for performing the same office, doing the typing (together with Miss I. R. Newman, formerly of the Public Record Office), and helping vastly with the index. Yet in spite of so much help it is again not only convention which necessitates the statement that I alone remain responsible for the text, and for the footnotes, and for any errors therein.

King's College, London   R.A.B.
September 1968

A LIST OF ABBREVIATIONS IN THE NOTES

B.S.A.N., Bulletin de la Société des Antiquaires de Normandie.
E.H.R., English Historical Review.
R.S., Rolls Series.
V.C.H., Victoria County History.
(Reference may also be made to the Bibliography, where all titles are given in full.)

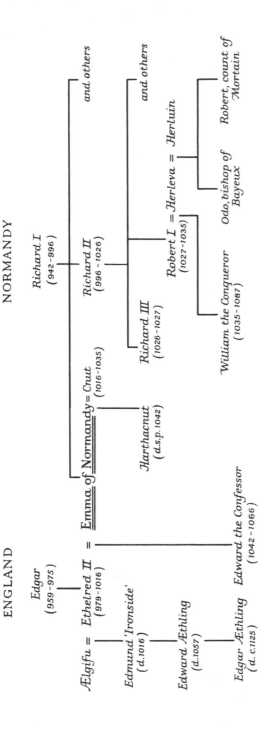

The ruling houses of England and Normandy in the late tenth and eleventh centuries with the dates of the reigns.

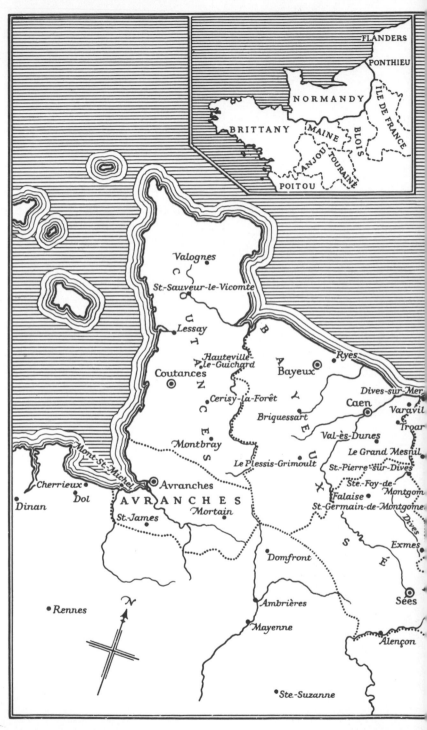

FLANDERS
PONTHIEU
NORMANDY
ÎLE DE FRANCE
BRITTANY
MAINE
BLOIS
ANJOU
TOURAINE
POITOU

Valognes
St.-Sauveur-le-Vicomte
C
O
T
E
N
T
I
N
Lessay
Hauteville-le-Guichard
Coutances
Cerisy-la-Forêt
Montbray
Le Plessis-Grimoult
Mont-St.-Michel
Cherrieux
Dol
Dinan
St.-James
AVRANCHES
Mortain
B
A
Y
E
U
X
Bayeux
Ryes
Briquessart
Val-ès-Dunes
Dives-sur-Mer
Caen
Varavil
Troarn
Le Grand Mesnil
St.-Pierre-sur-Dives
Ste.-Foy-de-Montgom
Falaise
St-Germain-de-Montgome
Dives
Exmes
S
É
E
S
Domfront
Sées
Ambrières
Mayenne
Alençon
Rennes
N
Ste.-Suzanne

Normandy and

Pevensey

Hastings

Boulogne

St.-Valery-sur-
Somme

Eu

Abbeville

Fécamp

Arques

St.-Aubin-le-Cauf

Varenne

Auffay

Amiens

Graville-Ste.-Honorine

R

Lillebonne

St.-Wandrille

Clères

Mortemer

O

Bonneville-
sur-Touques

Jumièges

U

Cormeilles

Rouen

Lisieux

Montfort-
sur-Risle

E

Vexin

N

Brionne

Bec

Bernay

Meules

Beaumont-
le-Roger

Tosny

La Croix-St.-Leufroy

Vernon

St.-Clair-sur-Epte

Evroult

Risle

Conches

Évreux

Échauffour

É

R

E

U

X

Breteuil

Mantes

Verneuil

Tillières

Ivry

Seine

Avre

Nonancourt

Bellême

0   Miles   50

Boundaries of Norman Bishoprics ....

England and Wales in 1066.

Introduction

England itself, in foolish quarters of England, still
howls and execrates lamentably over its William Conqueror, and rigorous line of Normans and Plantagenets;
but without them, if you will consider well, what had it
ever been?[1]

Few subjects in English history have been studied more and
for longer than the Norman Conquest, and few have been
more bent in the process by biased interpretations based
upon unhistorical prejudices.[2] While, therefore, modern
historians owe a great debt to the labours of their more remote
predecessors, the results of those labours have often been unhappy, not least when they have filtered through into public
consciousness to remain as common knowledge. As early as
the sixteenth century, significantly enough, Matthew Parker,
archbishop of Canterbury, sought both a justification for the
Elizabethan religious settlement and the origins of the Church
of England in the pre-Conquest English church. In the seventeenth century both the supporters of absolute monarchy and
the champions of liberty, in their earnest quest for precedent,
reached back to the Norman Conquest to remould it closer to
their heart's desire. Thereafter, in this as in so many matters,
the triumphant Whig view largely prevailed, the Anglo-
Saxons tended to become 'us', the Normans 'them', and
William the Conqueror to be cast in the role, which he is still
sometimes called upon to play, of a foreign tyrant winning a
regrettable victory over clean-limbed Englishmen with marked

[1] Thomas Carlyle, *Frederick the Great* (London, 1858), i, 415.
[2] See especially D. C. Douglas, *The Norman Conquest and British
Historians* (The David Murray Lecture for 1946, Glasgow, 1946), and
Christopher Hill, 'The Norman Yoke', in his *Puritanism and Revolution*
(London, 1958).

1

liberal and Protestant leanings. This interpretation of events in the interest of national, liberal and Protestant sympathies, reached its climax in the great work of Edward Augustus Freeman, whose five volumes of *The Norman Conquest*, first published between 1867 and 1879, though still a mine of information derived mainly from chronicle sources, are in this respect a positive embarrassment to read. Freeman, too, stood four-square in the Whig tradition of history, and allowed contemporary political sentiment to colour his vision of the past scarcely less than his seventeenth-century predecessors had done. Thus he was able to write on one occasion that 'We must recognise the spirit which dictated the Petition of Right as the same which gathered all England around the banners of returning Godwin,[3] and remember that "the good old cause" was truly that for which Harold died on the field, and Waltheof on the scaffold'.[4] He went further than his predecessors also in that, not content with seeing the struggle in terms of a 'national party' versus the Normans, he presented as the 'patriotic leaders' and champions of that party the unlikely figures of Godwin, earl of Wessex, and Harold his son[5] – with the result that to this day Harold is popularly regarded as a national hero rather than as an overmighty subject usurping the English throne. Since for Freeman, also, the Norman Conquest was 'only a temporary overthrow', by which England gained 'not so much by anything which our Norman conquerors brought with them, as through our own stores which it was an indirect result of the Conquest to preserve to us', and 'in a few generations we led captive our conquerors; England was England once again, and the descendants of the Norman invaders were found to be among the truest of Englishmen' [he has in mind the barons of Magna Carta, Simon de Montfort and Edward I],[6] one begins to appreciate the point of G. K. Chesterton's remark that

[3] For the political crisis of 1051–2 see pp. 82, 119 below.
[4] See *Life and Letters of E. A. Freeman*, ed. W. R. W. Stephens (London and New York, 1895), i, 125.
[5] See E. A. Freeman, *The Norman Conquest*, ii (2nd. edition, Oxford, 1870), and iii (Oxford, 1869), *passim*.
[6] Op. cit., i (2nd. edition, Oxford, 1870), p. 2, and v (Oxford, 1876), pp. 334, 709, 726–32.

'[A man] may end by maintaining that the Norman Conquest was a Saxon Conquest'.[7]

Since Freeman's day 'Anglo-Norman scholarship has been marked not so much by a development of his ideas as by a reaction from them',[8] and has at least succeeded in dismissing the anachronistic concept of the Norman Conquest as a national and bilateral struggle, both by questioning the very existence of an English nation in the mid-eleventh century and by emphasising the Scandinavian participation in the contest for the English kingdom, which reached its climax, but not its end, in 1066. And still, after the nine hundredth anniversary of the Conquest has passed, the interest of historians in the subject shows no signs of waning, and still, after nine hundred years, the outcome is controversy. Interest now has shifted from Freeman's preoccupation with political events and constitutional implications to more institutional, social and economic studies, to the nature of society and its cultural manifestations, to the church and its condition, to government and the state, and, above all, to the effects of the Norman Conquest upon these things. The controversy and debate which have arisen are concerned essentially with the results of the Norman Conquest, with the degree of continuity between pre-Conquest and post-Conquest England, and therefore with the basic question of how much the Conquest matters in the history of this country. To put it another way, no one now denies the precocious development of the kingdom of England in the post-Conquest period and in the twelfth century especially; the question is whether this is a case of *post hoc, propter hoc,* and of who, Anglo-Saxon or Norman, contributed the most to this undoubted achievement.

Within this context of modern historical enquiry, the most striking change of the last half-century has been the increasing realisation and appreciation of Old English, i.e. pre-Conquest, achievement in almost every sphere. The contrast, for it is scarcely less, may be best illustrated by comparing two books, *William the Conqueror,* first published in 1908, and *Anglo-Saxon England,* first published in 1943, both of them

---

[7] *Orthodoxy* (London and New York, 1909), p. 126.
[8] D. C. Douglas, op. cit., p. 22.

written by Professor Sir Frank Stenton, the most eminent scholar of the period and the principal architect of the change. In 1908 there seemed little that could be said in favour of England on the eve of the Norman Conquest – her kings, *rois fainéants*, incapable even of producing heirs, and hamstrung by their *witan* or consultative assembly; society weak in the absence both of good kingship and strong lordship; the kingdom disunited by provincial particularism and the cleavage of the Danelaw, dominated by the private interests of the great earls, and (retrospectively the most startling of condemnations in the light of subsequent research) 'with no administration worthy of the name'. To move from all this to contemporary Normandy seemed to pass 'from decadence to growth'[9] – an opinion which was currently being confirmed by the fundamental work of Charles Homer Haskins, later to be distilled in his *Norman Institutions* (Harvard, 1918). By 1943 the scene had changed on this side of the Channel, and therefore by degree upon the other. An informed and sympathetic appreciation of Anglo-Saxon achievement is evident at almost every turn, and not least in the creation of a strong monarchy ruling over a united kingdom. 'In comparison with England, Normandy in the mid-eleventh century was still a state in the making', and although England in Edward the Confessor's day, externally threatened and militarily weak, 'had ceased to count as a factor in European politics', the Normans who were to enter upon this inheritance had less to offer than before. They were 'a harsh and violent race. They were the closest of all western peoples to the barbarian strain in the continental order. They had produced little in art or learning, and nothing in literature, that could be set beside the work of Englishmen.'[10]

[9] F. M. Stenton, *William the Conqueror* (London, 1928 edition), pp. 5–23.
[10] F. M. Stenton, *Anglo-Saxon England* (Oxford, 1943), pp. 546, 678. For other appreciations of Anglo-Saxon achievement, roughly contemporary with Stenton's *Anglo-Saxon England*, see e.g. R. R. Darlington, 'Ecclesiastical Reform in the late Old-English period', *E.H.R.*, li (1936), and 'The last phase of Anglo-Saxon history', in *History*, xxii (1937); for pre-Conquest English achievement in the field of government especially, see V. H. Galbraith, *Studies in the Public Records* (London, 1948), Chapter II.

Sir Frank Stenton has thus brought us a long way from the contemptuous attitude which underlies Carlyle's famous and rhetorical question about the Normans – 'Without them . . . what had it ever been?'[11] – and there is no doubt that much of this advance represents a proper progress towards the attainment of historical truth and justice. For Stenton, also, is in no doubt about Norman strength and the profound effects of the Norman impact upon England in the mid-eleventh century: 'politically they were the masters of their world', and in spite of many points of continuity between pre-Conquest and post-Conquest England, 'the fact remains that sooner or later every aspect of English life was changed by the Norman Conquest'.[12] Unfortunately, however, matters have not remained where they were left by Stenton's magisterial and comprehensive study. In recent years, for example, a voice from Manchester has denied to the Normans even the credit for the introduction of feudalism into England, safely theirs since John Horace Round in 1891–2, and before that since the seventeenth century.[13] English feudalism, it proclaims, far from being a Norman importation in 1066 was already obsolete when the Normans came.[14] But the most extreme and generalised statement so far, seeming unnervingly to echo the pugnacious patriotism of Freeman in the 1860's

[11] His own answer ran as follows: 'A gluttonous race of Jutes and Angles, capable of no great combinations: lumbering about in pot-bellied equanimity; not dreaming of heroic toil and silence and endurance, such as leads to the high places of the Universe and the golden mountain-tops where dwell the Spirits of the Dawn' (Thomas Carlyle, *Frederick the Great*, i, 415). Cf. John Milton, *History of Britain* (ed. 1695), pp. 356, 357, and for an early twelfth-century estimate of the English on the eve of the Conquest not dissimilar in substance, see William of Malmesbury, *Gesta Regum Anglorum* (Rolls Series, ed. W. Stubbs, 1887–9), ii, 304–6, translated in *English Historical Documents*, ii, ed. D. C. Douglas (London, 1959), pp. 290–1.
[12] Op. cit., pp. 677, 678.
[13] See Round's great essay on 'The Introduction of Knight-Service into England', first published in the *English Historical Review*, vi and vii (1891–2), and subsequently reprinted in his *Feudal England* (London, 1895). Cf. Douglas, op. cit., p. 27.
[14] Eric John, *Land Tenure in Early England* (Leicester Univ. Press, 1960), Chapter VIII and p. 160.

and '70's, was made in 1963: 'for half a century or so from 1066 the English way of life was not sensibly altered. The Normans had very little to teach, even in the art of war, and they had very much to learn. They were barbarians who were becoming conscious of their insufficiency.'[15]

It may, indeed, be suggested that in historical studies in this country at the present time there is a marked tendency to over-praise pre-Conquest English achievement in almost every field from government to art and learning, and it is tempting to declare that upon English historians in the twentieth century the influence of the Anglo-Saxons has increased, is increasing, and ought to be diminished. The object of the present book is thus twofold, both to present some account, analysis and explanation of the Norman Conquest, and also to attempt some just assessment of its results, whereby it is hoped to redress the balance a little from what is surely an excessive favour shown to the Anglo-Saxons in our day. If it were necessary to take sides, I should be with duke William at Hastings,[16] but in this day and age it should be possible to appreciate the accomplishments of the Anglo-Saxons (who are not 'us'), without undertaking the manifest absurdity of decrying the fantastic achievements of the Normans (who are not 'them'). To do this, to strike a balance and attain at least an approximation of the truth, it is necessary to make as close and sympathetic an examination of Normandy as of England before 1066, and to remember also that Norman achievement in the eleventh century was confined to neither country, but that in the full history of this extraordinary race of men the conquest of England is but one chapter which can only be understood in relation to the whole.[17] The wider our view, the more we see, and it may be well to end these introductory

[15] H. G. Richardson and G. O. Sayles, *The Governance of Mediæval England.* . . . (Edinburgh, 1963), p. 27 – upon which page the Normans are denied even their outstanding military and administrative proficiency.

[16] Thus to find myself locked in mortal combat with E. A. Freeman, who declared he would gladly have fought upon the other side. See Douglas, op. cit., p. 21.

[17] Freeman (to do him justice, as one should) was aware of both these points. See *The Norman Conquest*, i (1870), pp. xii, 246.

remarks by reflecting upon the conclusion of a recent historian, concerned not with the single incident of the Norman Conquest of England but with the formation of the medieval world of Latin Christianity, no less, for whom 'true medieval society is unimaginable' without the impact and expansion of the Normans.[18]

[18] J. M. Wallace-Hadrill, *The Barbarian West* (London, 1946), p. 146.

CHAPTER I

The Emergent West

Present promise and wealth of the future beyond the
eye's scope.

BROWNING

Of all centuries in the history of the West, the eleventh is perhaps the most exciting and the most formative. There is much
to be said for the view that the decisive break between classical
antiquity and the medieval world comes not with the 'decline
and fall of the Roman Empire' in the West (whenever that
may have been) and the establishment of the barbarian successor states, but with the terrible and triple onslaught upon
Western Europe, by Saracens, Hungarians and Vikings,
which took place in the ninth century and early tenth. From
the south came the Saracens, the Moslems, who had absorbed
the Middle East and the southern shores of the Mediterranean
in the seventh century and had occupied Spain in the eighth.
In the ninth century they took Sicily and large areas of
southern Italy, and continued their raids deep into Gaul.
From the east, in the later ninth century, came the Hungarians, devastating into Germany, into Bavaria, Saxony and
Swabia, and on into Burgundy and Provence, their power not
finally broken until 955, at the decisive battle of Lechfeld, by
Otto the Great of Germany. Most serious of all, perhaps, and
certainly of most immediate relevance to the history of
England, of Normandy and of France, were the Vikings,
whose raids, by reason of their extreme mobility, seemed to
range over almost all Latin Christendom and to come from
every direction at once. Their first recorded attack was upon
England in 787; the ninth century was the century of the fury
of the Norsemen, especially for Britain and for France; and
only in the tenth century did their menace die away, though

England was to be conquered, by Swein Forkbeard and Cnut his son, as late as 1013–16.

The ninth and early tenth centuries thus have some claim to be the real 'Dark Ages' of Western Europe if such ever existed. But after the night came the morning; the challenge and destruction brought forth a response and a revival; the later tenth century, and the eleventh century especially, saw the establishment of a Brave New World, which differed from the Old, and which was centred increasingly on northern France. In it the origins of medieval civilisation, and therefore of the modern world, are largely to be found. It was an age of progress and expansion in almost every sphere of human activity. Revival, and with it change, came first to the church, with the new monasticism of the tenth century, which was followed by a general reformation of the whole church in the eleventh century. This great reform movement in the Western, Latin church, increasingly directed by the revived Papacy (and labelled by historians 'Hildebrandine' or 'Gregorian' after its principal champion, Hildebrand, who became Pope Gregory VII in 1073), brought a new and medieval dimension to the plenitude of papal power, altered the whole attitude of the official church to the world it sought to lead, and culminated in the Investiture Controversy with its revolutionary implications. The struggle which ensued between 'Church and State', between *regnum* and *sacerdotium*, being chiefly waged between the Papacy and the Western Empire of the German kings to the lasting damage of the latter, helped to ensure, moreover, that the political and cultural leadership of the West should pass to northern France. And there the outlines of a new and feudal society were being hammered out upon the anvil of incessant war. The break-up of the Carolingian Empire and of Carolingian Gaul or Francia in the ninth century meant the collapse of central authority, and society painfully rebuilt itself from the bottom upwards upon the basis of local authority, of local and feudal lordship. Remote control and centralised direction proved ineffective in that age, and everything favoured local action, self-help and private enterprise. Old concepts of the unity of Christendom were not forgotten, but were relegated to the realm of theory rather than of harsh political fact – 'It was agreed that it was God's will that his people should unite, but when the Vikings, the Moslems, and the Hungarians were abroad, the urgent necessity was a safe stronghold and a lord whose protection would be at hand'.[1] In Francia (which will be France) therefore, political reality ceased to be the large unit of the kingdom – upon whose throne in any case the ancient Carolingian line was replaced by the new dynasty of the Capetians in 987 – and became instead the emergent feudal principalities, Normandy and Anjou, Blois, Champagne and Chartres, Flanders and Brittany, Burgundy, Toulouse, and all those nascent states (the domain of the French kings in the Ile de France but one among them) which came to dominate the history of the times. In the formation of Anjou we may see, happening as it were before our eyes, a classic instance of the creation of such a feudal state.[2] In Normandy, though particular circumstances differ, we shall shortly see another.[3] Sometimes, of course, the process never reached completion, as the lords of Bellême in the eleventh century failed to coalesce their widely scattered castles, fiefs and rights into a viable entity.[4] At other times we may already see, as with the county of Maine in the same century (ground down between the upper and the nether mill-stones of neighbouring Normandy and Anjou),[5] that subsequent processes, centripetal and engulfing, of larger fiefs absorbing smaller – like Marx's concept of the last stages of capitalism – whereby this fragmented France of feudal principalities withered eventually away to be transmuted into the unified French monarchy of

[1] R. H. C. Davis, *A History of Medieval Europe* (London, 1957), p. 173.
[2] R. W. Southern, *The Making of the Middle Ages* (London, 1953), pp. 81 et seq.; L. Halphen, *Le Comté d'Anjou au xie siècle* (Paris, 1906).
[3] Below, Chapter II.
[4] For the house of Bellême, see e.g. H. Prentout, 'Les origines de la Maison de Bellême', in his *Etudes sur quelques points d'histoire de Normandie;* G. H. White, 'The First House of Bellême', *Transactions Royal Historical Society* (4th series), xxii (1940); J. Boussard, 'Le seigneurie de Bellême au xe et xie siècles', in *Mélanges d'histoire du moyen âge dédiés à la mémoire de Louis Halphen* (Paris, 1951).
[5] See R. Latouche, *Historie du Comté du Maine pendant les xe et xie siècles* (Paris, 1910).

the later Middle Ages. Meanwhile the political spirit of the
mid-eleventh century is portrayed, like so much else, upon
the Bayeux Tapestry, which shows the petty count of Ponthieu, Normandy's small northern neighbour, sitting in his
court enthroned in majesty like a sovereign prince.[6]

The princes, the comital families, who created and imposed
their will upon these new political entities arising from the
ashes of the Carolingian past, were themselves new men. 'War
made them conspicuous, grants of land established their position, marriage consolidated it, and the acquisition of ancient
titles of honour cloaked their usurpations.'[7] The great ruling
families round whom much of the history of the Middle Ages
must be written only emerge from obscurity in the late ninth
and tenth centuries, and even more recent in origin were most
of their vassals, local lords again, of lesser status, upon whom
they depended for further decentralisation of authority – and
who, with the princes, formed the new, military, militant and
feudal aristocracy of the West, given cohesion and identity
by the bonds of homage, fealty and service, and by the
developing concepts and techniques of knighthood. Here, then,
was a new world and a new society, military in origins and
ethics and often violent in practice, dominated by new men
who were also for the most part young men;[8] an open society
with as yet no hereditary nobility, where lordship and authority were largely a matter of the survival of the fittest; a world
also of open frontiers, since the new states were themselves
still in the process of formation, and almost everywhere
ancient administrative divisions, which were one source of
authority, were breached by the ties of personal lordship
which were the other. Meanwhile within these fluid frontiers
the foundations of modern government were being laid, on
the basis of new lordship, surviving rights of sovereignty

---

[6] *The Bayeux Tapestry*, ed. F. M. Stenton (2nd. edition, London, 1965),
Pl. 11.
[7] R. W. Southern, *The Making of the Middle Ages*, p. 82.
[8] It took the genius of Marc Bloch to extract, from the often repeated
gloomy statement that life in the Middle Ages was short by modern
standards, the exciting corollary that Western Europe was therefore
governed by young men. See *Feudal Society* (trans. L. A. Manyon,
London, 1961), p. 73.

from the past, and ancient Carolingian concepts of Christian kingship. The religion of these men, of course, was already ancient, as was their church; yet there were changes in the church, as we have seen; there were new manifestations of the old religion, in the cult of pilgrimages, for example, or in the sumptuous liturgy of Cluniac monasticism; and Latin Christianity itself now underwent a great extension, to north and east, as the formerly hostile Scandinavian and Slav peoples became converted, and settled down into respectability as the new kingdoms and principalities of Denmark, Norway and Sweden, Hungary, Bohemia and Poland. And yet the Universal Church of the eleventh century, in practice if not in theory, was still as local as its prelates and its patrons, the local saint recruited as the ally of the local bishop and the local count. For this was an intensely local world, in which lords temporal and spiritual, and therefore also many men of lesser rank, were constantly on the move, to govern, to administer and to fight.[9]

In the hearts and minds of men, confidence and hope replaced defeatism and despair, and a new, restless and enquiring spirit, avid for knowledge and its application, ensured that the material revival of the West would be accompanied by a revival of learning. The so-called Twelfth-Century Renaissance began in the eleventh, generated in the new cathedral and monastic schools of northern France, and fed upon rediscovered Greek learning. Art, too, revived, not least in its practical application as architecture, and the new building-styles of 'Romanesque', characteristically local in their minor differences, broke away at last from classical models to usher in the true Middle Ages. Some of the great churches of the eleventh century remain still to impress us,

[9] Cf. again Marc Bloch, who resolved the seeming paradox of localism and movement with a characteristic flash of insight – 'Where transport is difficult, man goes to something he wants more easily than he makes it come to him' (op. cit., p. 62). Bloch continued by observing in illustration that 'The kings of the first feudal age positively killed themselves by travel'. Cf. Lady Stenton, who remarked that life at the itinerant royal court in the earlier Middle Ages must have been like a grand but perpetual picnic (D. M. Stenton, *English Society in the Earlier Middle Ages*, London, 1952, p. 17).

but at the time, as they rose on every side in majesty above the surrounding countryside, they must have seemed to beggar all description, and the hyperbole is acceptable from the contemporary chronicler who wrote, 'One would have thought that the world was shaking itself to cast off its old age and was clothing itself in a white robe of churches'.[10]

Underlying all this achievement, as its prerequisite – and also, in the beginning, as cause as well as effect of the overcoming of the Viking, Saracen and Hungarian menaces – there was economic expansion, a growing prosperity, which, combined with an increasing population, manifested itself in new and improved agricultural techniques, the taking in of waste, new colonising ventures, urbanisation and the growth of towns, the revival of trade and commerce, and industrial growth – the last especially in Flanders where the cloth trade, a central factor in the Middle Ages, can be securely dated from the eleventh century. And then, prosperous, vital, virile and confident, the resurgent West, by means of its new chivalry, its knights, its surplus of younger sons, lordlings bred and trained for war, landless and land-hungry, embarked upon a remarkable territorial expansion. Moreover, while this expansion involved inevitably the expansion of Latin Christendom – for the Cross went with them – it was different in kind from the more or less spontaneous conversion of Viking and Slav already mentioned, and out of it was born a new concept of Holy War, of the Crusade. In Spain the Christian kingdoms which had perilously survived upon the northern fringes, Castille, Léon, Navarre, began in the eleventh century their militant expansion southward against the Moor, i.e. the Saracen, the Infidel. In the same century the Normans wrested first southern Italy and then Sicily not only from a Byzantine sphere of influence but also from Saracen, i.e. Infidel, occupation. In 1095 Pope Urban II at Clermont made his appeal for the rescue of the Holy Places from the Infidel, the First Crusade was launched, and the chivalry of France and Norman Italy broke out of the confines of Western Europe altogether to take Jerusalem and found the Latin

---

[10] *Raoul Glaber, Les cinq livres de ces histoires*, ed. M. Prou (Paris, 1886), p. 62.

crusading states of the Middle East, of Outremer. 'Thou shalt come from thy place out of the north parts, thou, and many people with thee, all of them riding upon horses, a great company, and a mighty army' (Ezekiel xxxviii, 15).

Though not themselves an original race, the Romans rather than the Greeks of medieval history, adopters and adapters *par excellence*, the Normans nevertheless had their share, which was often the lion's share, in all the achievements and developments of the eleventh century, and most notably by their own conquests, which formed the major part of the whole physical expansion of Western Europe at this time, greatly extended the influence of northern France from whence they came, and helped to bring Greek learning to the West from Arabic and formerly Byzantine Sicily. New men themselves, Vikings in origin and established in their province from 911 by the grant and 'treaty' of St. Clair-sur-Epte, they made of Normandy in the next one hundred and fifty years one of the most powerful states in Latin Christendom and the most potent feudal principality in France. Thus established, they conquered the far larger kingdom of England in 1066, and in due course rode out from there into Wales and southern Scotland, and ultimately into Ireland. Overlapping this achievement, and going forward at the same time, was their piecemeal conquest of southern Italy and Sicily, which in some respects was even more remarkable than their English enterprise. The Norman Conquest of England was, by contemporary standards, a state undertaking, centrally conceived and directed by duke William, with all the resources which as ruler he could command, to vindicate his right to the English throne. The Norman Conquest of southern Italy and Sicily, by contrast, was the achievement of individual Norman adventurers in one of the most dazzling examples of private enterprise the medieval and modern world has witnessed – only possible, one might say, in eleventh-century Western Europe or nineteenth-century North America.

The Italian enterprise[11] began, paradoxically yet character-

---

[11] For the Normans in Italy and Sicily, see especially F. Chalendon, *Histoire de la domination normande en Italie et en Sicile* (Paris, 1907); Claude Cahen, *Le régime féodal de l'Italie normande* (Paris, 1940); and

istically in this age of muscular Christianity, of violence mixed with piety, by pilgrimages, the fashion of the times, and one in which the Normans as always were pre-eminent. For pilgrimages to the Holy Land the route lay through Italy, and southern Italy was then a kind of political no-man's-land, torn by the competing claims of native Lombard princes and Saracen and Byzantine overlords. Here then was a situation ripe for exploitation by Norman knights willing to hire their swords to employers who were anxious to benefit from their irresistible military prowess (before them, said a Lombard prince, the enemy were 'as meat to the devouring lion'.[12]). The first Norman companies were evidently in action in 1017, aiding a Lombard rebellion in Apulia against the authority of the Byzantine Emperor. The price exacted was to prove prodigious, and by 1071, some fifty years later and five years after the Norman Conquest of England, all of southern Italy was under Norman domination. Meanwhile these dusty adventurers from the North had pressed on into Moslem Sicily, whose conquest, begun in 1061, was completed thirty years later. Southern Italy and Sicily thus became, at home in Normandy, the Promised Land for younger sons avid for fiefs, for political exiles in need of new fields of endeavour, and for prelates in search of funds to carry on the ambitious works of their great new churches,[13] and the new Norman kings established there, self-made men of near-incredible success, ruled in Oriental splendour over the richest, the most powerful, the most cultured and technically the most advanced state in all Latin Christendom.

This extraordinary accomplishment has somehow to be explained in terms of an expanding population in Normandy

C. H. Haskins, *The Normans in European History* (New York, 1915; reissued, New York and London, 1959).

[12] Aimé of Monte Cassino, *L'ystoire de li Normant* (ed. O. Delarc, Rouen, 1892), p. 124, cited by C. H. Haskins, op. cit., p. 200.

[13] For examples of political exiles, see p. 37 below and Ordericus Vitalis, *Historia Ecclesiastica*, ed. A. Le Prévost (5 volumes, Paris, 1838–55), ii, 81 et seq., 93–4; for the collection of alms, ibid., ii, 56–7, and *E.H.R.*, lix (1944), pp. 136–7. An unusual recruit for Norman Italy was Edgar aethling in 1086 (F. M. Stenton, *Anglo-Saxon England*, p. 611 and below p. 140).

as elsewhere in the West, land-hunger and a shortage of fiefs at home as the feudal solution reached saturation point, the restless existence of a military aristocracy in search of war as well as gain, the cult of knighthood and the cult of violence – these and other factors, combined with the remarkable spirit of expansionist adventurism which permeates the upper ranks of Norman society at this time, and the no less remarkable abilities of the individual participants, all working within the context of the opportunities which Apulia and Calabria then offered to the unscrupulously bold. Spurred on by the lust for land and lordship, the love of fighting and the lure of Mediterranean riches, the Norman knights came flocking to southern Italy, and the chronicler at Monte Cassino gives us a glimpse of them cantering 'through the fields and gardens . . . happy and joyful on their horses, as they rode up and down to seek their fortunes'.[14] There were few, if any, magnates of established position amongst them, and typical of them all were the brothers Hauteville, who won for themselves the leadership of the enterprise and thus became exceptional only in the enormity of their success. According to Ordericus Vitalis, writing in the early twelfth century, Tancred of Hauteville, a minor lord in Normandy, had twelve sons, eleven of whom went off to Italy. They included Robert, surnamed Guiscard (the Wary), who by 1059, with papal recognition and true Norman effrontery, was able to proclaim himself 'by the grace of God and St. Peter duke of Apulia and Calabria and, with their help, hereafter of Sicily'.[15] When he died at the age of seventy, he was described as 'the terror of the world' upon his epitaph,[16] but meanwhile the conquest of Sicily had chiefly been the work of his younger brother, Roger, whose son, Roger II, in 1130, having brought all the Norman lordships in Italy under his rule, was crowned and anointed at Palermo king of Sicily, Apulia and Calabria – and as such he, and his descendants after him, remained. The Hautevilles had come a long way from their undistinguished manor, now Hauteville-

---

[14] Aimé of Monte Cassino, op. cit., p. 70.
[15] Haskins, op. cit., p. 204.
[16] Ibid., p. 206; William of Malmesbury, *Gesta Regum* (Rolls Series, ed. W. Stubbs, London, 1887–9, 2 volumes), ii, 322.

le-Guichard (Manche) in Lower Normandy, though one of them, as we shall see, was to go further, if not higher, yet.

It is some measure of Norman military potential in the eleventh century that their conquests of southern Italy and Sicily were carried out both in the teeth of the greatest lay power of the age, the Byzantine or Eastern Roman Empire, and at the expense of the potent Moslem world. There is, moreover, another aspect of this achievement. In Italy the Normans had become the allies of the Papacy, and the subsequent campaigns in Italy against the Infidel, to 'win back to the worship of the true God a land given over to infidelity',[17] were undertaken with papal blessing. There were also, at this time, individual Norman adventurers fighting the Infidel in Spain, and others in the service of the Eastern Emperor against the Turk.[18] Even the Norman Conquest of England took on a religious colouring, and duke William received the papal blessing and a papal banner for his expedition which included in its published aims a necessary reformation of the English Church.[19] In short, the Normans in the eleventh century were becoming the self-appointed champions of a new concept of Holy War,[20] and when this growing concept had been given explicit expression by the appeal of Pope Urban II at Clermont in 1095, the Normans were in the vanguard of the First Crusade, with a powerful contingent from Normandy under duke Robert 'Curthose', the Conqueror's eldest son, and another, even more powerful, from Norman Italy and Sicily, under Bohemond of Hauteville, a son of Robert Guiscard, and Bohemond's nephew Tancred. Jerusalem was

[17] Geoffrey Malaterra, *De Gestis Guiscardi et Rogerii principum Normannorum*, ii, 1, ed. J. G. Graevius, in *Thesaurus Antiquitatum et Historiarum Siciliae*, v (Leyden, 1723–5), p. 19, cited by Haskins, op. cit., p. 207.

[18] For Roger de Tosny, called 'de Hispania', who returned from Spain to Normandy to meet his death during the minority of duke William the Bastard, see Ordericus Vitalis, ed. Le Prévost, i, 180–1 and note. Cf. Haskins, op. cit., pp. 195–6; D. C. Douglas, *William the Conqueror* (London, 1964), pp. 85, 260.

[19] See below, pp. 148–9.

[20] The point was frequently noted by Freeman, though scarcely with favour, and has been re-emphasised by Douglas (see e.g. *Norman Conquest*, i (1870), 459; ii (1870), 169, 232; iii (1869), 271–2, 280, 306, 321. Cf. Douglas, op. cit., pp. 188, 260).

taken from the Infidel in 1098, and meanwhile another Norman lordship was established by Bohemond at Antioch, which characteristically became the strongest and best governed of the Latin states of Outremer.

The eleventh century was in many ways the Norman century, and by the end of it a chain of Norman states had been established from the Atlantic to the eastern shores of the Mediterranean, all strong, all efficient, and all ruled by a potent mixture of borrowed institutions, new feudal customs, and dynamic energy. In such a context the single incident of the Norman Conquest of England comes more sharply into focus. Yet we can scarcely understand it fully by posing the far greater problem of Norman political achievement as a whole, and therefore we must turn next to a more detailed examination of Normandy, and of England.

CHAPTER II

Normandy

Boot, saddle, to horse and away!

BROWNING

The history of the future duchy of Normandy, and the explanation of its subsequent achievements, begin in or about the year 911 at the so-called Treaty of St. Clair-sur-Epte. At that time and place Charles the Simple, king of the West Franks, granted to a band of Vikings, operating in the Seine valley under Rollo their leader, territory corresponding to Upper or Eastern Normandy, bounded by the rivers Bresle, Epte, Avre and Dives. To this original concession Lower Normandy was subsequently added by two further grants, first the Bessin (the district of Bayeux) and the districts of Exmes (l'Hiémois) and Séez in 924, and second the Cotentin and the Avranchin (the districts of Coutances and Avranches) in 933 in the time of William Longsword, son and successor of Rollo.[1] At once, therefore, some of the distinguishing features of the duchy are apparent. Like the Danelaw in England (but with a very different future) it was the direct result of the Viking onslaught upon Western Europe in the ninth and tenth centuries. But though its origins were violent, they were also tidy and precise. While other feudal principalities in France tended to be the gradual and piecemeal creations of centripetal local lordship, here a little, there a little, and the edges left untidy, Normandy was created by the three consecutive grants of 911, 924 and 933 within frontiers which, for the most part, were both ancient and defined. The territorial extent of Normandy, more or less established by 933, coincided not with Carolingian Neustria (whose name is, and

[1] See especially J. F. Lemarignier, *Recherches sur l'hommage en marche et les frontières féodales* (Lille, 1945), pp. 9–10 and notes.

was, sometimes loosely applied to it) but with the former Roman province of the Second Lyonnaise, which had been perpetuated and projected into the future as the ecclesiastical, metropolitan province of Rouen.[2] The fact is doubly important both for the future relations of church and state in Normandy,[3] and also and more immediately as a fundamental cause of that exceptional coherence and unity of the duchy which contributed greatly to its strength.[4] Whereas elsewhere frontiers and administrative divisions were obliterated or made hazy by the shifting tides of lordship and feudal dependency, in Normandy you knew where you were in a quite modern political sense. The point may perhaps be driven home by citing an exception. According to Ordericus Vitalis, after the battle of Mortemer in 1054, Roger de Mortemer, because he had previously done him homage, sheltered and helped to escape Ralph, count of Valois and Amiens, a leader of the French king's defeated army. It is the kind of incident characteristic of the age elsewhere but rare in Norman history, and in Normandy the outcome was the banishment of Roger de Mortemer and the confiscation of his lands and castle.[5] There was, it is true, for long an increasingly dangerous dichotomy within the confines of the duchy itself between Upper Normandy, favoured by the dukes and rapidly becoming more Frankish or 'French', and Lower Normandy, where the Scandinavian influence and custom remained stronger; but this division was to be ended by William the Conqueror, not least by his victory at Val-ès-Dunes and his development of

---

[2] H. Prentout, *Essai sur les origines et la fondation du duché de Normandie* (Paris, 1911), pp. 32–3.
[3] Below, pp. 32–5.
[4] This is the accepted thesis of Lemarignier, op. cit. There were certain discrepancies. The province of Rouen included the French Vexin, which was not permanently a part of Normandy, and excluded *le Passais*, the district about Domfront, which William the Conqueror appropriated in 1052. The Norman frontier to the south-west was rendered hazy until duke William's reign by the presence of the great marcher family of Bellême (Lemarignier, op. cit., pp. 18–19, 39 ff., 60 ff.). For William's expansion and stabilisation of his frontiers, see p. 58 below.
[5] Ordericus Vitalis, *Historia Ecclesiastica*, ed. A. Le Prévost (5 vols., Paris, 1838–55), iii, 237. Roger was subsequently reconciled with duke William, but never recovered his castle of Mortemer.

the town of Caen as a new centre of ducal control in the west.[6]

The origins of Normandy in the first decades of the tenth century also reveal the double inheritance of the Normans, from the Scandinavian world from whence they came and from the ancient province of Roman, Frankish and Carolingian Gaul which now they colonised. Doubtless their most important heritage from Gaul was those surviving administrative divisions which formed their frontiers without and, within, gave them the *pagi* as the basis of their future *comtés* and *vicomtés* and of the revived organisation of their church.[7] From the Carolingian past Rollo and his successors, as rulers of Normandy, also obtained lingering concepts of sovereignty, the title of count which gave them respectability and status,[8] valuable rights such as the monopoly of coinage,[9] or the right of calling in emergency on the military service of all free men through the *arrière-ban*,[10] and still more valuable assets in their widespread domains and fiscs which assured their increasing dominance and which, after the fashion of the age,

---

[6] See especially M. de Boüard, 'De la Neustrie Carolingienne à la Normandie féodale: continuité ou discontinuité', *Bulletin of the Institute of Historical Research*, xxviii (1955), pp. 10–12. See also pp. 52, 59 below.

[7] The *pagus* was the 'characteristic subdivision of Carolingian Neustria'. Cf. D. C. Douglas, *William the Conqueror* (London, 1964), p. 27; de Boüard, 'Le duché de Normandie' in F. Lot and R. Fawtier, *Histoire des Institutions Françaises au Moyen Age*, tome i, *Institutions Seigneuriales* (Paris, 1957), pp. 10–11.

[8] Cf. again R. W. Southern on the new men of the age—'War made them conspicuous, grants of land established their position, marriage consolidated it, and the acquisition of ancient titles of honour cloaked their usurpations' (*The Making of the Middle Ages*, p. 82). 'Count' remained the usual and favourite title of the rulers of Normandy until well into the reign of William the Conqueror (1035–1087). See Douglas op. cit., pp. 23–4; Marie Fauroux, *Recueil des Actes des Ducs de Normandie (911–1066)*, (Caen, 1961), pp. 49–50.

[9] For ducal control of coinage and mints, see C. H. Haskins, *Norman Institutions* (1918), pp. 38–9, 280 ; de Boüard, 'Le duché de Normandie', loc. cit. pp. 5, 9, 21; D. C. Douglas, op. cit., pp. 135–6; D. J. A. Matthew, *The Norman Conquest* (London, 1966), p. 53.

[10] For the *arrière-ban*, see C. W. Hollister, *The Military Organisation of Norman England* (Oxford, 1965), pp. 77 et seq.; P. Guilhiermoz, *Essai sur l'origine de la noblesse en France* (Paris, 1902), pp. 289 et seq.

they used to create their new world of great abbeys and lay vassals.[11] Yet the degree of continuity between Carolingian Neustria and feudal Normandy can be, and often is, exaggerated,[12] and the sheer destruction which the Vikings had perpetrated before the settlement of 911 cannot be denied.[13] Scandinavian settlement in Normandy and close connections between the duchy and the Scandinavian world of which it long formed an outpost continued for a century after St. Clairsur-Epte,[14] and it seems impossible not to attribute the very difference and pre-eminence of Normandy among its neighbours to the Scandinavian elements within it. Viking blood flowed in the veins of the individuals who made its history,[15] and from this Scandinavian inheritance the Normans derived their sea-faring, much of their trade and commercial prosperity which they shared with the Nordic world,[16] their love of adventure, their wanderlust which led to the great period of Norman emigration in the eleventh century, their dynamic energy, and, above all perhaps, their powers of assimilation, of adoption and adaptation, which mark and yet obscure their achievements in Normandy, in England, in Italy and in Antioch. The ultimate paradox of the history of the Normans, it could be argued, is that in the end they adapted themselves out of existence, but meanwhile in Normandy before the mideleventh century and in little more than a hundred years after St. Clair-sur-Epte, they had adopted Frankish religion and law, Frankish social customs, political organisation and warfare, the new monasticism, the new learning and the new

[11] De Boüard, 'Le duché de Normandie', ut supra, p. 5.
[12] Ibid., p. 1, and see especially the same author's 'De la Neustrie Carolingienne à la Normandie féodale: continuité ou discontinuité', *Bulletin Institute Historical Research*, xxviii (1955).
[13] 'L'hiatus est certain', de Boüard; 'Le duché de Normandie', ut supra, p. 3.
[14] De Boüard, *Bulletin Institute Historical Research*, xxviii, 5–6; D. C. Douglas, 'The Rise of Normandy', *Proceedings of the British Academy*, xxxiii (1947), pp. 107–9. See also L. Musset, 'Relations et échanges d'influences dans l'Europe du Nord-Ouest (x^e–xie siècles)', *Cahiers de Civilisation Médiévale*, i (1958), pp. 63 et seq.
[15] See especially de Boüard, *Bulletin Institute Historical Research*, xxviii, 13.
[16] Ibid., and below, p. 51.

architecture, to become, as it were, more French than the French,[17] and to play a dominant role in the new feudal world which they helped to create.

Through sheer lack of evidence, few subjects are more obscure than the early history of Normandy in the tenth century.[18] Nevertheless, certain developments can be distinguished – economic prosperity, ecclesiastical revival, the establishment of a new aristocracy, the growth of ducal power and pre-eminence in warfare – all of which reach their apogee in the mid-eleventh century and, combined, go far to explain the dominance of Normandy at that time and the remarkable achievement of the Norman Conquest of England. For the latter crucial period, moreover, we have evidence which – though historians, rightly, are never satisfied – is ample at any rate by comparison with the past. Norman sources alone provide, amongst others, the contemporary and well-informed chroniclers, William of Poitiers,[19] a knight turned priest and chaplain to duke William, William of Jumièges,[20] a monk at one of the principal ducal abbeys, close to Rouen, and Ordericus Vitalis,[21] the English-born monk of St. Evroul who,

---

[17] 'Ce qu'il y a de plus remarquable chez les Scandinaves de Normandie, c'est leur faculté d'assimilation . . . les Normands ont été à l'avant-garde de la France et de la civilisation française', H. Prentout, Essai sur les origines . . . de Normandie, p. 270.

[18] The Norman sources for the period consist almost solely of the chronicle of Dudo of St. Quentin, compiled in the early eleventh century and unreliable. The last word on Dudo was written by Henri Prentout, Etude critique sur Dudon de Saint-Quentin (Paris, 1916), and his conclusions are usefully summarised in his Essai sur les origines . . . de Normandie, pp. 126 et seq. The latter work remains the most comprehensive survey of early Norman history and the origins of the duchy. To it should be added de Boüard, 'Le duché de Normandie' (loc. cit. This essay deals chiefly with institutions because of the nature of the larger work of which it forms a part) and the important essays of de Boüard and D. C. Douglas respectively in Bulletin Institute Historical Research, xxviii and Proceedings of the British Academy, xxxiii, already cited.

[19] Histoire de Guillaume le Conquérant (written c. 1073–1074), ed. and trans. Raymonde Foreville (Paris, 1952).

[20] Gesta Normannorum Ducum (written c. 1071), ed. J. Marx (Rouen and Paris, 1914), with interpolations by Ordericus Vitalis and Robert of Torigny.

[21] Historia Ecclesiastica, ed. A. Le Prévost (Paris, 5 volumes, 1838–55).

though writing (with immense industry)[22] in the early twelfth century, had at his finger-tips an endless fund of knowledge which describes in depth, as does no other source, the feudal society of eleventh-century Normandy and its neighbours. To these are added a rapidly growing body of contemporary charters and other analagous business documents,[23] the records of provincial ecclesiastical councils,[24] and – by no means to be neglected as a direct link with the past – surviving architectural monuments and archaeological remains.[25] We even have, in the Bayeux Tapestry, contemporary and accurate illustrations of many of the events which will concern us most, and of that society which peoples the pages of Orderic's chronicle.[26]

It is by no means paradoxical for the historian of the

[22] Thirteen books of the *Historia Ecclesiastica* alone, which occupy, (with the editor's notes and indexes) five substantial volumes of printed text.

[23] Of which the ducal charters and other *acta* have recently been printed for the period 911 to 1066 by Marie Faroux (*Recueil des Actes des Ducs de Normandie*, Caen, 1961.)

[24] *Concilia Rotomagensis Provinciae*, ed. G. Bessin (Rouen, 1717).

[25] See the magnificent volumes of V. Ruprich-Robert, *L'Architecture Normande aux xie et xiie siècles en Normandie et en Angleterre* (2 vols., Paris 1899). The most convenient survey of the greater Norman churches of this period is still A. W. Clapham, *English Romanesque Architecture after the Conquest* (Oxford, 1934: reissued 1964). The castles still await their historian, at least in print, but see Raymond Ritter, *Châteaux, Donjons et Places Fortes* (Paris, 1953), and E. S. Armitage, *Early Norman Castles of the British Isles* (London, 1912).

[26] *The Bayeux Tapestry*, ed. F. M. Stenton (London, 1957; second edition 1965). The Tapestry, and the chronicles listed above, are each discussed by their editors in their introductions to the respective editions cited. A full, but somewhat negative and pessimistic discussion of all these sources, together with contemporary English chronicles, will also be found in S. Körner, *The Battle of Hastings, England, and Europe 1035–1066* (Lund, 1964). The Norman literary sources, together with the Tapestry, may be prejudiced in their presentation and interpretation of events, and to some degree interdependent, but they are very full and well informed, and for that reason alone are often more valuable than the sparse and thin English literary sources which themselves are scarcely neutral. For Ordericus Vitalis, see also H. Wolter, *Ordericus Vitalis: ein Beitrag zur kluniazensischen Geschichtsschreibung* (Wiesbaden, 1955).

Norman Conquest, seeking to explain the power of mid-eleventh-century Normandy, to begin with the church and the ecclesiastical revival in the duchy which commenced in the tenth century and reached its apogee under duke William.[27] Latin Christianity, of which the Normans were to become the champions, was the instrument of their civilisation, their cloak of respectability, the inspiration of many of their deeds, and the Norman church was to contribute largely to the unity and power of the duchy and to the success of the Norman Conquest of England. No institution had suffered more than the church in Carolingian Neustria by the depredations of the Vikings, and by 911 its organisation was broken and its monasteries destroyed.[28] But the baptism of Rollo was a condition of St. Clair-sur-Epte, and thereafter, with whatever reluctance, under the example of their dukes the Seine Vikings became Christian Normans, the poachers turned gamekeepers. Revival, characteristically in this monastic age, came first to the monasteries. Jumièges was restored by William Longsword (927–43), son of Rollo, who is said to have wanted to become a monk there himself.[29] By his successor, Richard I, the Fearless (943–96), the ancient houses of Mont-St.-Michel, St. Wandrille or Fontanelle, and St. Ouen at Rouen were likewise restored, under the influence of the reformed Lotharingian monasticism from Ghent. 'The decisive moment in the history of Norman monasticism'[30] came in the year 1001, in the reign of Richard II, the Good (996–1026), who persuaded *le grand Clunisien*,[31] William of Volpiano, a Cluniac monk and reformer, then abbot of St. Bénigne at Dijon, to undertake the reforma-

[27] Good accounts of the Norman church will be found in H. Prentout, *Guillaume le Conquérant* (Caen, 1936), Chapter VII; D. C. Douglas, *William the Conqueror*, Chapter V; and, for all that concerns monasticism, Dom David Knowles, *The Monastic Order in England* (Cambridge, 1940; second edition 1963), Chapter V and Appdx.V. See also Douglas, 'The Norman Episcopate before the Norman Conquest', *Cambridge Historical Journal*, xiii (1957).

[28] For the pre-Norman monasteries, see Prentout, *Essai sur les origines . . . de Normandie*, pp. 86 ff.

[29] William of Jumièges, pp. 38–41, which evidently contains a Jumièges tradition.

[30] Knowles, op. cit., p. 84.

[31] Prentout, op. cit., pp. 4–5.

tion of his father's foundation at Fécamp.[32] Cluny, whose
second great church was completed about the year 981,[33] was
at this time the principal source of the revived monasticism of
Western Europe, and from Fécamp the influence of Cluny,
and the particular influence of William of Volpiano, spread
throughout Normandy, not only to the few monasteries
already founded, but also to almost all those yet to come –
including Bernay, founded by the Countess Judith, wife of
Richard II, and Cérisy-le-Forêt and the Holy Trinity at Rouen,
founded by Robert I (1028–35), father of William the Conqueror. The movement thus began, and so far monopolised,
by the ducal family, continued in the reign of duke William
and spread to the new Norman aristocracy who, with the
duke's encouragement and patronage, then undertook a series
of foundations and refoundations outstanding even in this age
of revival in the Latin church. Between the accession of duke
William in 1035 and the Norman Conquest of England in 1066,
at least twenty religious houses were established,[34] and while
these include the great foundations of the duke and duchess
respectively at St. Stephen's and The Trinity at Caen, as
penance for their marriage, a list of the founders of the others
reads like a roll-call of Norman feudal lordship – Tosny and
Beaumont, Montgomery and fitz Osbern, Grentemesnil and
Tesson, Robert, count of Eu (with the countess Lesceline his
mother, and Hugh, bishop of Lisieux, his brother), Robert,
count of Mortain (with his mother and father, respectively the

[32] Richard I had tried and failed to get Cluniac monks for Fécamp
which had remained a house of secular canons. William is said at first
to have been reluctant to come, remarking that he understood the
Normans to be more apt to destroy than to build the temples of the
Lord (see Porée, *Histoire de l'abbaye du Bec*, Evreux, 1901, i, 26; cf.,
however, René Herval, in *L'Abbaye Bénédictine de Fécamp*, p. 34, cited
below). For his church of St. Bénigne at Dijon, begun also in 1001 and
which must have influenced subsequent church building in Normandy,
see the important paper by K. J. Conant, 'Cluny II and St. Bénigne at
Dijon', in *Archaeologia*, xcix (1965). For Fécamp see the volumes issued
to commemorate the abbey's thirteenth centenary in 1958, *L'Abbaye
Bénédictine de Fécamp* (2 vols. Fécamp, 1959–60), and for William of
Volpiano, see the paper by René Herval, therein, i, 27 et seq.

[33] *Archaeologia*, xcix, 183.

[34] Douglas, *William the Conqueror*, p. 111.

mother and step-father of duke William the Bastard), and Neal of St. Sauveur, *vicomte* of the Cotentin.[35] Ordericus Vitalis, writing of these years, observed in a famous passage that 'the barons of Normandy, seeing the great zeal of their princes for holy religion, urged themselves and their friends to similar undertakings for the good of their souls. They vied with each other in taking the lead in such good works, and in the liberality with which they made ample endowments. The most powerful nobles held themselves cheap if they had not on their domains some establishment of monks or clerks provided by them with whatever was necessary for the service of God.'[36] In the dying speech which the same author puts into the mouth of William the Conqueror, the duke and king refers, in a metaphor beloved of contemporary clerical writers, to the castles of God with which he has defended his duchy.[37]

Mere numbers, though certainly a measure of the enthusiasm for monasticism in eleventh-century Normandy, are not a test of quality. But the Norman monasteries were, by and large, distinguished in an age distinguished by its monasticism. They were new, and thus vibrant with the first, fine, careless rapture of spiritual endeavour – and John of Fécamp, who succeeded William of Volpiano as abbot there in 1028, has been called 'the greatest spiritual writer of the epoch before St. Bernard'.[38] They were reformist in an age increasingly

[35] Ibid., pp. 112 ff., and cf. Knowles, op. cit., Appdx. V. The information is chiefly drawn from the twelfth-century lists of Robert of Torigny in his *De Immutione Ordinis Monachorum* and in his interpolations to the chronicle of William of Jumièges (the latter at pp. 252–6 of Marx's edition; the former, volume ii, pp. 181–206, of L. Delisle, *Chronique de Robert de Torigny . . ., S.H.N.*, 2 volumes, 1872–3).

[36] *Historia Ecclesiastica*, ii, 12. Cf. his interpolation to William of Jumièges (ed. Marx, p. 173), '*In diebus illis maxima pacis tranquillitas fovebat habitantes in Normannia et servi Dei a cunctis habebantur in summa reverentia. Unusquisque optimatum certabat in predio suo ecclesias fabricare et monachos, qui pro se Deum rogarent, rebus suis locupletare*'.

[37] *Historia Ecclesiastica*, iii, 241. '*Hujusmodi castris munita est Normannia.*'

[38] See Knowles, op. cit., p. 86, quoting Dom A. Wilmart in *Auteurs spirituels et Textes dévots du Moyen-Age Latin* (Paris, 1932). For John of Fécamp see also Dom J. Leclerq et J. P. Bonnes, *Un maître de la vie spirituelle au xi⁰ siècle, Jean de Fécamp* (Paris, 1946).

anxious for reform. Their new buildings, and especially their great churches rising on every side, could often rival anything to be found in Latin Christendom. They were, above all, up to date. And they were, in many cases, distinguished for their learning, their teaching, and their schools (at Fécamp, St. Wandrille, Holy Trinity at Rouen, Jumièges, St. Evroul, Cormeilles, and Bec especially)[39] which they derived, not from Cluny herself, increasingly absorbed in her elaborate versions of the *Opus Dei*, but from the particular example and influence of William of Volpiano and Fécamp. Occasionally we can penetrate within their walls, and Ordericus Vitalis has left us an agreeable, and no doubt typical, picture of abbot Thierry of St. Evroul encouraging his monks to work harder,[40] as Gilbert Crispin tells us that abbot Herluin did at Bec ('Of what use is a man who is ignorant of letters and of the commandments of God?')[41]. And Bec, different from the rest in its undistinguished beginnings, in the independence, the austerity and the humility of its foundation (in 1034 by Herluin, a knight formerly in the service and *familia* of count Gilbert of Brionne) rose in a few short years to be the most outstanding, the most influential and the most famous of all the Norman monasteries.[42] Its pre-eminent distinction resulted from its learning and its schools, opened by Lanfranc, one of the foremost scholars of his age, and producing amongst its pupils Anselm, 'the most luminous and penetrating intellect between Augustine and Aquinas'.[43] Of Lanfranc's teaching at Bec Ordericus wrote that 'His reputation for learning spread throughout all Europe, and many hastened to receive lessons from him out

[39] Cf. Prentout, *Guillaume le Conquérant*, p. 93.
[40] *Historia Ecclesiastica*, ii, 49–50. He was accustomed to tell them the story of a certain monk who, at the Day of Judgement, had his many transgressions balanced against the number of letters which he had transcribed, and was saved by one unit.
[41] *Vita Herluini* in J. Armitage Robinson, *Gilbert Crispin* (Cambridge, 1911), p. 104; Knowles, op. cit., pp. 96–7.
[42] For all that concerns the history of Bec see le Chanoine Porée's labour of love, *Histoire de l'abbaye du Bec* (2 volumes, Evreux, 1911), and J. Armitage Robinson, *Gilbert Crispin*, which contains the text of the *Vita Herluini*.
[43] Knowles, op. cit., p. 96.

of France, Gascony, Brittany and Flanders', and of the monks of Bec under first Lanfranc and then Anselm that they 'are thus become so devoted to literary pursuits, and so exercised in raising and solving difficult questions of divinity, that they seem to be almost all philosophers'.[44]

Revival in the sense of moral and spiritual reform came later to the secular church, and though the beneficial effect of the monastic schools and the monastic control of many parishes must have been felt before, scarcely begins as a centrally directed policy before the reforming councils of duke William's reign and his appointment of the reforming Maurillius to the archiepiscopal throne of Rouen in 1055.[45] But the wonder is, as with the monasteries, that so much was done so soon, for the Normans were pagans when they came (and they continued to come long after 911), and in Normandy after St. Clair-sur-Epte it was necessary to recreate a clergy.[46] Of the lower clergy we have little information save the calumnies of Ordericus Vitalis,[47] but the Norman dioceses of the metropolitan province of Rouen were evidently fully re-established by 990, though the bishops of Coutances were unable to return to their cathedral city for some decades thereafter.[48] The bishops who subsequently take their appointed places in the Norman history of the earlier eleventh century have until recently received a bad press, but they were, as D. C. Douglas says of them, 'among the makers of medieval Normandy'.[49] Intensely aristocratic – 'cette galerie de seigneurs-évêques, issus de la haute aristocratie normande'[50] – they shared, to a degree which might shock contemporary reformers but should

[44] *Historia Ecclesiastica*, ii, 210, 246.
[45] De Boüard, 'Le duché de Normandie', loc. cit., pp. 12, 23; Prentout, *Guillaume le Conquérant*, pp. 101, ff.
[46] Prentout, op. cit., p. 93.
[47] *Historia Ecclesiastica*, ii, 397–8. He speaks of the early priests of Danish extraction with their addiction to arms and concubines, and of how when reform came they proved more willing to give up the former than the latter.
[48] De Boüard, *Bulletin Institute Historical Research*, xxviii, 4–5; J. H. Le Patourel, 'Geoffrey of Montbray, Bishop of Coutances, 1049–93', *E.H.R.*, lix (1944), pp. 134–7.
[49] *Cambridge Historical Journal*, xiii, 115.
[50] De Boüard, *Guillaume le Conquérant*, p. 67.

not surprise historians, the secular interests, and sometimes the secular morals, of the great but *parvenu* families from whence they sprang. They were men, in short, of the old and pre-Gregorian school, and not so very different from their episcopal colleagues in the Universal Church elsewhere in France. Perhaps they were what the time and place required.[51] Certainly they shared the dynamic energy of their class and race, and what as a group they lacked in spirituality they made up for in organising ability. They reorganised their dioceses – in the case of bishop Geoffrey of Coutances re-creating what had practically ceased to exist – and the establishment of archdeaconries and cathedral chapters in Normandy can be traced back to the middle years of the eleventh century.[52] In due course they cooperated with the duke in his reforming synods as they already cooperated in his secular government and especially in the maintenance of his peace.[53] Not only archbishop Maurillius but also three bishops of pre-Conquest Normandy passed the critical scrutiny of a later generation – William, bishop of Evreux, Hugh, bishop of Lisieux, and Ives, bishop of Séez, albeit the last two were members of the highest aristocracy.[54] Some, like Odo, bishop of Bayeux, half-brother to the Conqueror, Geoffrey de Mowbray (or Montbrai), bishop of Coutances, and Hugh, bishop of Avranches, were patrons of the arts and scholarship,[55] and almost all of them were mighty builders. To the monastic churches rising in Normandy at this time, notably at Jumièges, Mont-St-Michel, Bernay, Cérisy-le-Forêt, Bec, St. Pierre-sur-Dives and the twin churches of

[51] Cf. the remark of C. R. Cheney, applied by him to the twelfth century but certainly no less applicable to the eleventh, '[The Church's] government, as then constituted, required the service of sinners as well as of saints' (*From Becket to Langton*, Manchester, 1956, p. 41).

[52] Douglas, *Cambridge Hist. Journ.*, xiii, p. 113.

[53] For the Truce of God, see below.

[54] Ordericus Vitalis, *Historia Ecclesiastica*, ii, 71–2. There is much information about Ives de Bellême in Ordericus and see also Prentout, op. cit., pp. 87–9; for Hugh bishop of Lisieux, son of William count of Eu and grandson of duke Richard I, see especially William of Poitiers (archdeacon of Lisieux at the end of his career), ed. Foreville, pp. 136–42.

[55] Douglas, op. cit., pp. 105–6.

Caen, they added their cathedrals at Rouen, Bayeux, Evreux, Lisieux, Séez and Coutances. Many of these major works of Norman Romanesque architecture survive in whole or part and stamp the duchy to this day with the imprint of its eleventh-century ecclesiastical revival.

If now, from our point of view of Norman power, politics and the ability to conquer England, we survey the Norman church on the eve of the Conquest, we shall find that its con-tribution to that achievement was very great. First and fore-most it had been the principal means whereby the Normans were accepted into the community of Western Europe. Next, it was a principal cause of the remarkable unity and coherence, and therefore strength, of Normandy. Almost everywhere, as we have seen, the frontiers of the duchy coincided with the limits of the metropolitan province of Rouen – one duke and one archbishop, often enough side by side at Rouen, where the former had his fortified palace[56] and the latter his cathedral church. Further, the duke controlled the church, both secular and regular.[57] He appointed, and invested, his bishops who, already before 1066, owed him military service for their lands;[58] also he could upon occasion dismiss them, as archbishop Mauger was deposed, with papal sanction, in 1054 or 1055.[59] The greatest abbeys, of which those established before about 1050 also owed him military service,[60] were ducal foundations, and thus their abbots were appointed and invested by him, while Ordericus Vitalis' account of the early history of St. Evroul strongly suggests that duke William had scarcely less control over appointments to private foundations which, like

[56] For the ducal palace at Rouen, see P. Héliot, 'Sur les résidences princières bâties en France du xe au xiie siècle', *Le Moyen Age*, lxi (1955), p. 47; R. Allen Brown in *The Bayeux Tapestry*, ed. F. M. Stenton (2nd edition, 1965), pp. 80–1.

[57] 'an ecclesiastical supremacy to which the eleventh century affords no parallel', C. H. Haskins, *Norman Institutions* (New York, 1918; 1960), pp. 35–6.

[58] See below.

[59] Douglas, *William the Conqueror*, p. 69. The words used by William of Jumièges to record Mauger's deposition may be worth noting in this connection – *Malgerius . . . insipientia ductus, archipresulatum reddidit duci* (ed. Marx, p. 129).

[60] See below.

St. Evroul, were under his protection.[61] Robert de Grente-mesnil, second abbot and co-founder of St. Evroul, was de-posed by William – *sine reatu et judicio synodi* – who imposed another abbot on the community,[62] and the *Vita Herluini* of Gilbert Crispin contains the well-known story of the duke's intended banishment of Lanfranc, then prior of Bec.[63] Duke William was accustomed to summon, and preside over, the provincial synods of his church, and a familiar passage of William of Poitiers refers both to this and to his intervention in ecclesiastical justice where this appeared to him too lenient.[64] But if the Conqueror, by 1066, stood out among contemporary rulers as the champion of the new wave of ecclesiastical reform, he subscribed not at all to the new ideas of centralised direction by the Papacy, and it was with good reason that in the next century Henry II began his great struggle with the church by appealing back to the provisions of his ancestor's Council of Lillebonne in 1080.[65] At every point the Norman church was integrated with, and helped to integrate, the society of which it formed a part. Many of the bishops were members and close relatives of the ducal family – Robert (989–1037)[66] and Mauger (1037–54),[67] successively archbishops of Rouen, Hugh (1015–49) and Odo (1049–99),[68] successively bishops of Bayeux, John, bishop of Avranches (1060–7),[69] Hugh, bishop of Lisieux (1049–77) – or members of the new Norman aristocracy, like Ives de Bellême, bishop of Séez (1035–70) and Geoffrey de Mowbray, bishop of Coutances (1049–93). The monasteries likewise contained a high pro-

[61] *Historia Ecclesiastica*, ii, 18, 38–9, 68–9, 81–2, 125–6.
[62] Ordericus Vitalis, interpolation in William of Jumièges, ed. Marx, p. 185; *Historia Ecclesiastica*, ii, 81–2. In the latter work Ordericus' language is even stronger – *sine probabilibus culpis non per judicium synodi, sed per tyrannidem furentis Marchisi* [i.e. duke William].
[63] J. A. Robinson, *Gilbert Crispin*, pp. 97–8; Porée, op. cit., 61–2.
[64] Ed. Foreville, pp. 124–5.
[65] Haskins, *Norman Institutions*, pp. 31, 170–1. Cf. de Boüard, 'Le duché de Normandie', loc. cit., p. 23, who remarks that William's 'politique ecclésiastique s'inspire d'une sorte de césaropapisme éclairé'.
[66] Also count of Evreux.
[67] For the date of Mauger's deposition, see Douglas, op. cit., p. 69.
[68] Subsequently also earl of Kent.
[69] Subsequently archbishop of Rouen, 1067–87.

portion of the same ruling class who founded and protected them, offered in early youth as oblates by their parents, like Gilbert Crispin, Ordericus Vitalis himself, or Cecilia, the daughter of duke William and Matilda, at the Trinity at Caen,[70] or barons and knights who wearied of the world and fighting, like Robert of Grentemesnil at St. Evroul or Herluin at Bec,[71] or many others whose own exploits frightened them,[72] or who were too badly wounded to fight again, or who, a common practice, made their professions upon their deathbed.[73] The church also, through its prelates in council and in their local franchises, assisted in ducal government, while in Normandy the Truce of God, introduced by duke William after Val-ès-Dunes at Caen, was an effective combination of secular and ecclesiastical powers.[74] The great abbeys brought prestige, and while they inspired that sense of communal identity and well-being which nowadays we seem to get only from success-ful sports teams (athletes as well as knights of Christ were popular synonyms for monks), their schools, open to all, trained the future servants of both church and state, and the list of the *alumni* of Bec, that Balliol of the age, is so long and so distinguished as to transcend the history of Normandy and her daughter states beyond the seas.[75] From Bec, also, duke William obtained the services of Lanfranc, to make of him his principal ecclesiastical adviser.[76] Through Lanfranc, the scholar, teacher and vanquisher of Berengar of Tours, even more than by his own considerable efforts, the Conqueror won his reputation as the champion both of orthodoxy and reform, so that, when the time came, the Papacy was the chief prize of

[70] J. A. Robinson, op. cit., pp. 1, 15; Ordericus Vitalis, *Historia Ecclesiastica*, ii, 303, 419–20 and cf. 1, xxxiii–iv

[71] Ibid., ii, 40; J. A. Robinson, op. cit., pp. 2–4, 88–93.

[72] According to Ordericus Vitalis, Herluin himself made his vow when in peril of his life in an unsuccessful action led by his lord, count Gilbert of Brionne, against Ingelran, count of Ponthieu (*Historia Ecclesiastica*, ii, 13).

[73] E.g., ibid., ii, 114, 457–61.

[74] See de Boüard, 'Trève de Dieu', *Annales de Normandie*, October, 1959; *Guillaume le Conquérant*, pp. 29–31; 'Le duché de Normandie', p. 19; D. C. Douglas, *William the Conqueror*, pp. 51–2.

[75] See Porée, op. cit., i, 103, 121, 164, 185.

[76] See especially William of Poitiers, ed. Foreville, p. 126.

Norman diplomacy, and the expedition to England was undertaken by this favoured son of Holy Church with papal blessing and a papal banner.[77]

The contribution of the Norman aristocracy to the power and political achievements of mid-eleventh-century Normandy is more obvious and, in the last resort, even more important. Contemporaries, especially monastic chroniclers, might describe monks as knights of Christ and monasteries as castles of God, but in the event it was by real knights and real castles that the defence of Normandy and the Conquest of England were assured. The most outstanding feature of the Norman aristocracy of duke William's day, after its ability and its energy, was its newness.[78] In a world dominated by new men, the great feudal families of Normandy only appear in the late tenth and early eleventh centuries, a full century, that is to say, after their peers in neighbouring lands.[79] The houses of Montgomery, Montfort and Beaumont, Ferrers[80] and fitz Osbern, Mortemer and Mowbray[81] Tosny, Warenne and the sons of count Gilbert of Brionne (who will be Clare in England), emerge from the mists of the tenth century during the reigns of Richard (II) the Good, Robert the Magnificent and William the Bastard. The counts at the head of this new aristocracy were likewise new in the sense that the title which gave them distinction was only conferred upon them in the eleventh century,[82] though they themselves were close members of the ducal family which alone could show unbroken continuity from 911 – a fact which must have added greatly to its prestige in a society then, as always, anxious to have ancient origins.

After the initial and inevitable troubles of his minority,

---

[77] See below p. 149. For the Berengar affair see Prentout, op. cit., pp. 98–100; R. W. Southern, 'Lanfranc of Bec and Berengar of Tours', *Studies in Medieval History presented to F. M. Powicke* (Oxford, 1948).

[78] For what follows see especially D. C. Douglas, 'The Earliest Norman Counts', *E.H.R.*, lxi (1946); cf. L. C. Loyd, *The Origins of Some Anglo-Norman Families* (Harleian Soc., ciii, 1951).

[79] Cf. p. 12 above.

[80] I.e. Ferrières.

[81] I.e. Montbrai, Manche, arr. St.-Lo.

[82] Douglas, op. cit., pp. 130–1 and cf. p. 12 above.

the 'anarchy' of 1035–47, during which Normandy lacked the strong, personal, adult rule essential in this age for any state in Latin Christendom[83,] duke William the Bastard was able to establish an ascendancy over the military and militant lay aristocracy within his duchy which by 1066 was no less complete than his control over the Norman church and its prelates. Personal leadership and personal example, mutual interests and a common outlook, were powerful elements in this ascendancy, yet also no aspect of ducal power as wielded by duke William is more impressive than his capacity to make or break the magnates who shared at his will the lordship of the duchy with him. Compounded, no doubt, of elements of Scandinavian banishment,[84] of Carolingian rights of confiscation,[85] still more of the rights of feudal suzerains, and with at least a touch of sheer autocracy, this capacity was exercised upon occasions of rebellion and disloyalty, and sometimes of mere suspicion. Counts were amongst its victims, as William of Arques for his rebellion[86] and William Warlenc of Mortain for a vague report of his intentions;[87] Roger of Mortemer was exiled for his disloyalty after the battle of Mortemer,[88] and the family of Giroie was broken largely by the Conqueror's will, incited, we are told, by Mabel of Bellême and Roger of Montgomery, her husband.[89] Many of these political exiles,

---

[83] Though he had been recognised as his father's heir before the departure of duke Robert the Magnificent on his ill-fated pilgrimage, William's succession in 1035 at the age of some seven years was open to challenge on the grounds of both youth and illegitimacy. Convenient accounts of his minority and the attendant anarchy will be found in de Boüard, *Guillaume le Conquérant*, Chapter I, and⁻ Douglas, *William the Conqueror*, Chapter II. Cf. also p. 58 below.

[84] Prentout, *Guillaume le Conquérant*, p. 46.

[85] Lemarignier, *L'hommage en marche*, p. 30; de Boüard, 'Le duché de Normandie', loc. cit., pp. 9, 15.

[86] William of Poitiers, ed. Foreville, pp. 50–64; Ordericus Vitalis, *Historia Ecclesiastica*, e.g. iii, 232–3.

[87] Ibid., ii, 259, *pro uno verbo exhaeredavit*; iii, 246, *pro minimis occasionibus*. Cf. the interpolation of Ordericus in William of Jumièges, ed. Marx, pp. 171–3.

[88] Ordericus Vitalis, *Historia Ecclesiastica*, iii, 237. Cf. p. 21 above.

[89] Ibid., ii, 80–1, 93, 106–8, 410. At p. 108, after the poisoning of Arnold d'Echaufour, at that time back in Normandy and reconciled with the duke, Ordericus observes, '*tota Geroianorum nobilitas pene*

like William Warlenc, abbot Robert of St. Evroul[90] and
Arnold d'Echaufour his cousin, went off to Apulia to join in
the Norman colonisation of southern Italy and remake their
fortunes there;[91] some were later reconciled with the duke and
reinstated, like Hugh de Grentemesnil and Ralph of Tosny on the
eve of the conquest of Maine in 1063, when the Conqueror had
need of amity and knights.[92] St. Anselm, in a parable of the
different kinds of knights to be found at the courts of princes,
listed those who serve him in return for their fiefs, those who
serve for pay, and those who serve in the hope of regaining
the inheritance lost by their fathers,[93] and the last category
appear no less than the first two at the court of duke William
in the pages of Ordericus Vitalis.[94] For what the duke took
away, the duke also could bestow. William of Poitiers remarks
how the young William sought to dismiss from his presence
those who were incapable or evil, and to profit from the counsel
of the best and wisest,[95] and Ordericus observed how he put
down his overmighty paternal relatives, i.e. the '*Richardides*',
the descendants of dukes Richard I and II,[96] and exalted the
humble issue of his mother, Arlette, and her husband, Herluin

*corruit, nec ullus posterorum stemma priorum ex integro usque hodie
adipisci potuit'.* For the banishment of abbot Robert de Grentemesnil,
nephew of William fitz Giroie, see p. 33 above. His brother, Hugh de
Grentemesnil, another nephew and co-founder with him of St. Evroul,
was reconciled with the duke in 1063 and fought at Hastings to win a
great fortune in England.

[90] Also his two sisters, both nuns, who, hearing of their brother's good
fortune in Apulia, cast off their veils, went out there themselves, and
married very well. Ordericus adds that God made them barren as a
punishment (*Historia Ecclesiastica*, ii, 91–2).

[91] A point that mitigates a little the criticism that ducal power in
Normandy must have been weak to allow the emigration (Stenton,
Anglo-Saxon England, p. 551).

[92] Ordericus Vitalis, *Historia Ecclesiastica*, ii, 93, 106–8.

[93] *The Life of St. Anselm . . . by Eadmer*, ed. R. W. Southern (London,
1962), p. 94.

[94] *Historia Ecclesiastica*, ii, 106–8; cf. ibid., ii, 104–5, or the slightly
later example of the sons of Roger of Breteuil at the court of Henry I
(ibid., ii, 264–5).

[95] Ed. Foreville, p. 14; cf. William of Jumièges, ed. Marx, p. 122.

[96] See Prentout, *Guillaume le Conquérant*, pp. 17–18; Douglas, *William
the Conqueror*, pp. 38, 40–1.

de Conteville.[97] The *comté* of Mortain, taken from William Warlenc in 1055 or 1056, was thus bestowed upon Robert, William's half-brother, as the bishopric of Bayeux had already been bestowed upon the other brother, Odo, in 1049, and both, until the latter's fall in 1082, were high in the duke's confidence and counsels. Echaufour, lost by Arnold d'Echaufour, passed to Roger of Montgomery,[98] and the castle of Mortemer, taken from Roger of Mortemer, passed to the rising house of Warenne.[99] The duke also had much to give of his own from his vast domain, and his liberal enfeoffments can be seen as a cardinal factor in his reign,[100] creating new vassals and knight-service and securing the predominance of those he trusted and liked best. By these means the Norman aristocracy in duke William's time became almost a hand-picked group, and those who rose highest in the duchy, and afterwards in England, were his companions in arms, relatives and friends or both, like his two half-brothers, Robert, count of Mortain, and Odo, bishop of Bayeux, or Roger of Montgomery or William fitz Osbern[101] 'whom of all his intimates he had loved the most since their childhood together'.[102] It was all very personal, and it is sad to see – but also perhaps inevitable in a world so dependent upon personal relationships – as William grew old and a new generation came to restless manhood, the sons and nephews of the companions of his youth supporting his own rebellious eldest son in Normandy,[103] or Roger of Breteuil, son and heir of William fitz Osbern now dead, rebelling against the king in England.[104]

[97] Interpolation to William of Jumièges, ed. Marx, p. 172.
[98] *Historia Ecclesiastica*, ii, 410.
[99] Ibid., iii, 237. See Douglas, *William the Conqueror*, pp. 99–100.
[100] Cf. de Boüard, *Guillaume le Conquérant*, p. 43; 'Le duché de Normandie', loc. cit., p. 14.
[101] Marie Fauroux finds that of all the Norman magnates, ecclesiastical and lay, William fitz Osbern and Roger of Montgomery appear most frequently among the attestations of William's formal acts in Normandy before 1066. '*L'un et l'autre semblent inséparables de Guillaume le Batârd, car nul ne figure plus souvent qu'eux au bas des actes de ce prince*' (*Recueil des Actes des Ducs de Normandie*, p. 62).
[102] William of Poitiers, ed. Foreville, p. 240.
[103] Ordericus Vitalis, *Historia Ecclesiastica*, ii, 377, 380–1, 388.
[104] Ibid., ii, 258, cf. p. 199 below.

Important as were personal relationships in this age of immense power concentrated in the hands of the few, there is no doubt that in Normandy in the mid-eleventh century the relations between the duke and his magnates were also formalised by the feudal bonds of fealty and homage – themselves as solemn as society could make them – and, increasingly, by dependent tenure in return for military service. The Normans were new and alien arrivals in the developing feudal world of late Carolingian France, but they adopted the organisation, customs, and habits of that society as they adopted its religion and its laws, with 'an astonishing facility',[105] and we need not doubt the reality of Norman feudalism in 1066 just because it had not then attained the further stage of development to be found a century later, or was less tidy and comprehensive than Anglo-Norman feudalism in England established in the very different and artificial circumstances of the Norman Conquest. Haskins wrote of Normandy on the eve of the Conquest that it was 'one of the most fully developed feudal societies in Europe', and his conclusion has been confirmed by the most recent Norman historian in almost the same words – 'dès avant 1066, la Normandie était l'un des Etats féodaux les mieux constitués que l'on pût voir en Europe'.[106] At the highest level, the duke became the vassal of the French king from 940 if not from 911,[107] and it seems likely that the various revolts within Normandy in the tenth century, at both magnate and peasant level, were in part a reaction against the imposition of feudal services of which, at

[105] 'Ils s'y adaptèrent avec une facilité étonnante, et adoptèrent sans hésiter des moeurs, des coutumes, des usages tout-à-fait inconnus dans leur pays d'origine. Ils surent même developper le régime, le perfectionner, si l'on peut dire, bien avant les autres provinces françaises, qu'ils devancèrent de près d'un siècle à ce point de vue.' H. Navel, 'Récherches sur les institutions féodales en Normandie (region de Caen)', B.S.A.N., li (1952). These are strong words from an historian who, it must be emphasised, has studied Norman feudalism and its origins more closely than any other.
[106] C. H. Haskins, Norman Institutions, p. 5; de Boüard, Guillaume le Conquérant, p. 61.
[107] De Boüard, 'Le duché de Normandie', loc. cit., p. 4. Cf. Lemarignier, L'hommage en marche, pp. 80 et seq.

that time, there is scarcely any other evidence.[108] As for the
eleventh century, before the accession of duke William in 1035
the ducal abbeys rendered knight-service for their lands, and
after about 1050 such service was explicitly reserved by those
endowing monasteries.[109] It is clear that by 1066 most of the
bishoprics and many of the great lay lords also owed military
service to the duke for their 'benefice' or 'fief',[110] and if such
service had not yet in all cases been precisely fixed in amount it
follows neither that service was not rendered, nor that precise
assessment when it came was in the interests of the duke.[111]
It is in any case also clear that in Normandy, where feudalism
was a natural growth in an initially egalitarian society of
Scandinavian extraction, subinfeudation frequently preceded
the recognition of military service to the duke.[112] The basic
unit of the knight's fee, the *fief de haubert*, varying in value
and extent but owing the service of a knight, mounted and
fully armed,[113] was already established by the beginning of the
eleventh century, and the Norman peculiarity of the *vavasseurs*, half-way between the noble and the peasant, reflects an
earlier form of tenure moulded untidily into feudal form at
what must have been an early date.[114] The elaborate feudal
arrangements revealed in the bishopric of Bayeux by the

[108] Prentout, *Guillaume le Conquérant*, p. 6.
[109] Haskins, op cit., pp. 8–14; de Boüard, op. cit., pp. 7, 14; Navel,
op. cit., p. 164.
[110] E.g. Douglas, *William the Conqueror*, p. 103.
[111] Ibid., p. 101. Definition of service was most frequently not in the
interests of the lord, and the whole history of the feudal 'incidents' of
aid, relief, wardship and marriage in Anglo-Norman England between
1066 and 1215 (and after) is of definition reluctantly conceded by the
king in place of arbitrary exactions at his will.
[112] This is the implication of the consistent discrepancy between the
number of knights owed to the duke and the far larger number of
knights'-fees held of the tenants-in-chief shown by the returns to the
Norman inquisition of 1172 (Haskins, op. cit., 8–9; *Red Book of the
Exchequer*, Rolls Series, London, 1896, ii, 624 et seq.; cf. Douglas, *Proceedings British Academy*, xxxiii, 118–19), and in particular by the wording of the Bayeux Inquest of 1133 in this matter (Navel, 'L'enquête de 1133
sur les fiefs de l'Evêché de Bayeux', *B.S.A.N.*, xlii, 1934, pp. 14, 44).
[113] For the distinction between *plena arma* and *plana arma* see ibid.,
pp. 51–2.
[114] Ibid., 60, 77 et seq.

Inquest of 1133[115] relate to arrangements already made in the second half of the eleventh century and in some instances at least before 1066, and the inescapable implication of the feudal society established by the Normans in southern Italy and Sicily (and, one may surely add, in England[116]) is that its customs and arrangements were already prevalent in Normandy in the mid-eleventh century and before.[117] H. Navel, in his fundamental work upon early Norman feudalism, concluded that the feudalisation of the Caen region was a gradual process taking place between the reigns of Richard I (942–96) and Robert the Magnificent (1028–35)[118] – i.e. before the advent of William the Conqueror – and it is certainly worth adding that, if anything, the Caen region is likely to have been more backward in these matters than Upper Normandy.[119] Nor can a study of the sources of Norman history in the mid-eleventh century leave any doubt of the nature of the society which produced them. 'Vassalage and dependent tenure', as Haskins said, 'meet us on every hand',[120] and so do the language and assumptions of feudalism. William of Jumièges says that Robert archbishop of Rouen held Evreux *in dominio* in 1027, and that William de Bellême held the castle of Alençon as a *beneficium* in the same year.[121] He also says that William of Arques had obtained the *comté* of Talou from his young nephew duke William as a 'benefice', *ut inde illi*

---

[115] Navel, *B.S.A.N.*, xlii; cf. Haskins, op. cit., p. 15.

[116] See pp. 216–36 below.

[117] De Boüard, 'L duché de Normandie', loc. cit., p. 14. See Claude Cahen, *Le Régime féodal de l'Italie Normande* (Paris, 1940), especially p. 91.

[118] 'Recherches sur les institutions féodales en Normandie' (Région de Caen),' *B.S.A.N.*, li, p. 173.

[119] Lower Normandy was for long the more 'Scandinavian', and Upper Normandy the more 'French', part of Normandy, and the breach, which had strong political implications, was scarcely closed before the earlier years of duke William. Cf. p. 59 below, and p. 20 above.

[120] Haskins, op. cit., p. 6.

[121] William of Jumièges, ed. Marx, pp. 100, 101 (writing, it is true, of events which took place nearly fifty years earlier). '*Beneficium*' in Normandy and elsewhere was at this time the usual word for what will later be the fief (*feodum*): see F. L. Ganshof, *Feudalism* (London, 1952), pp. 96–7.

existeret fidelis,[122] while William of Poitiers lists among the
causes of the later breach between the count and duke the
fact that the former had left the siege of Domfront (1051–2)
without the duke's licence and had thus withdrawn the
[military] service of a vassal which he owed him (*satelliti
debitum . . . detrectans*).[123] A charter of duke Robert of *c.* 1030
refers to the land which Neal of St. Sauveur, *fidelis noster*,
holds *in beneficio*,[124] and the same Neal, exiled and disinherited for his part at Val-ès-Dunes, refers wistfully in a charter of *c.* 1048 to his confiscated *honor* which he hopes, God
willing, to recover, while it is clear from the attestations of
this charter and another of *c.* 1060 after his restoration that
certain members of his household, his *familia*, had accompanied him in exile,[125] as Ordericus Vitalis says that the
barones of Ralph de Tosny, Hugh de Grentemesnil and Arnold
d'Echaufour were exiled by duke William together with their
lords.[126] Examples dating from before 1066, carefully and
accurately described, of fealty, homage and investiture are to
be found in the pages of the former knight, William of
Poitiers.[127] Ordericus Vitalis, writing in the earlier twelfth
century, but knowing his facts and with the relevant charter
before him, describes how, some time between 1061 and 1066,
a certain knight, Richard de Heudicourt, mortally wounded
as it was thought, decided with the counsel of his lord, Hugh
de Grentemesnil, in whose household he served, to become a
monk at St. Evroul, and how the same Richard then gave

[122] William of Jumièges, p. 119.
[123] William of Poitiers, p. 52.
[124] L. Delisle, *Histoire du château et des sires de Saint-Sauveur-le-
Vicomte* (Paris, Caen, 1867), Pièces Justificatives, no. 9, p. 10; M.
Fauroux, *Recueil des Actes des Ducs de Normandie*, no. 73.
[125] Delisle, op. cit., nos. 21, 31, pp. 25, 35. For the *familia* and the
military household, see below.
[126] *Historia Ecclesiastica*, ii, 81. The word *baro* (baron) also occurs in pre-
Conquest charters (Fauroux, op. cit., p. 56).
[127] E.g. ed. Foreville, pp. 78–80, Geoffrey of Mayenne to duke William,
*sibi manus perdomitas daret, fidelitatem quam satelles domino debet,
jurans*; p. 88, Herbert count of Maine to duke William, *manibus ei sese
dedit, cuncta sua ab eo, ut miles a domino, recepit*. Cf. the careful assertion
(whether true or false) of Harold's fealty and homage to, and investment
by, William, ibid., p. 104 (for which see also p. 130 below).

his land to the abbey, having first obtained the consent of his closest relatives and of Hugh Pincerna, the chief lord of the fee (*qui capitalis dominus erat*).[128] Attention has been drawn before now to Roger de Clères who, in the anarchical years of the Conqueror's minority, slew Robert de Beaumont in vengeance for the murder of his lord, Roger de Tosny, slain by Robert's brother Roger.[129] Though such illustrative examples of feudal society in pre-Conquest Normandy might be multiplied almost indefinitely, one more must suffice. There can be little doubt that the reason why Herluin, the founder of Bec, a few years before the dramatic incident just described, soldiered on with increasing reluctance as a knight in the service and the household of count Gilbert of Brionne for some considerable time after his conversion to religion in *c.* 1032, was because as vassal he could not, without great difficulty and the consent of his lord, release himself and his lands for that higher service of God which he had come so ardently to desire.[130]

Feudal society in its upper levels was essentially a military society – and it is the upper levels which are the test of feudalism, itself an affair of lordship, tenurial lordship, of lords and would-be lords and the relationships between them. In Normandy the characteristic products of this society, knights and castles, were very evident before 1066. Castles,[131] the

[128] *Historia Ecclesiastica*, ii, 114. Richard subsequently recovered and as a monk at St. Evroul was put in charge of the building of the new church by abbot Osbern.

[129] Douglas, *William the Conqueror*, p. 96. The story, like most of the best stories, is in Ordericus, i, 180 and ii, 40, 41.

[130] *Vita Herluini* in J. Armitage Robinson, *Gilbert Crispin*, pp. 88–91.

[131] For Norman castles see especially J. Yver, 'Les châteaux-forts en Normandie jusqu'au milieu du xii⁰ siècle. Contribution à l'étude du pouvoir ducale', *B.S.A.N.*, liii (1957). It must however be emphasised that negative conclusions drawn from the negative evidence of Norman chroniclers only, as to the number of castles in existence in this early period, are to be treated with considerable caution. A thorough search of all types of the more plentiful written sources of the kingdom of England for the following century still does not produce evidence for all castles known to have existed (R. Allen Brown, 'A List of Castles, 1154–1216', *E.H.R.*, lxxiv, 1959). An additional hazard for the historian of early castles is the ambiguity of the contemporary vocabulary used to describe

private and residential fortresses of lords and thus to be contrasted with the public and communal fortifications surviving from an earlier age, are mentioned from the tenth century, and in the eleventh there is ample evidence of new ones being built both by the duke and by his magnates.[132] Some incorporated stone-built defences, including great towers or donjons such as those at Rouen,[133] Ivry[134] and Brionne;[135] others were simpler, but effective, strongholds of earthwork and timber, often, but not always, of the 'motte-and-bailey' type shown on the Bayeux Tapestry.[136] In the

them—see E. S. Armitage, *Early Norman Castles of the British Isles* (London, 1912), p. 69 (a most remarkable book which seems to contain or anticipate all more recent work).

[132] E.g. Tillières by duke Richard II; Cherruiex by Robert the Magnificent; Ambrières, Bretueil, Caen, St. James and others by William the Conqueror; Arques by count William of Talou after 1035. See Yver, op. cit., 38–9, 50, 58–9.

[133] The tower at Rouen was built by Richard I (943–96) and is glimpsed from time to time in the reign of his successor and thereafter (Robert of Torigny, in *Chronicles . . . of Stephen, Henry II, and Richard I*, Rolls Series, ed. R. Howlett, iv, 106; William of Jumièges, ed. Marx, pp. 74–5, 89; Ordericus Vitalis, ii, 296, iii, 192). It may have been the prototype for the great Norman towers at Colchester and London (*The Bayeux Tapestry*, ed. F. M. Stenton, 2nd ed., 1965, p. 81).

[134] The donjon at Ivry is attributed to Aubrey, wife of Raoul comte d'Ivry who held the castle in the late tenth century. She is said afterwards to have beheaded the architect lest he should subsequently build another like it for anyone else. See Ordericus Vitalis, *Historia Ecclesiastica*, iii, 416.

[135] The *aula lapidea* at Brionne, which evidently formed the strong-point of the castle and may therefore have resembled the keep of Fulk Nerra at Langeais, is mentioned by William of Poitiers when duke William besieged the castle in 1047 after Val-ès-Dunes (ed. Foreville, pp. 18, 19, passage badly mistranslated). Recent excavation, however, has revealed no trace of it (*ex inform.* de Boüard). For Langeais see *Congrès Archéologique de France*, cvi (Tours 1948) pp. 378 et seq.

[136] Mottes of this date in Normandy survive, for example, at Briquessart (de Boüard, *Guillaume le Conquérant*, p. 33) and one may recall how, according to Wace, Hubert of Ryes was standing between the church and his motte ('*Entre le mostier et sa mote*') as the young duke galloped up on his great ride from Valognes to Falaise in 1047 (*Roman de Rou*, ed. H. Andresen, Heilbronn, 1879, ii, 178, 1.3704 (and *passim*) – which seems an authentic snap-shot of the past). The alternative form of early earthwork and timber castle, the so-called 'ring-work' consisting of a simple

eleventh century, sieges take their place along with battles in the chronicles of Norman warfare,[137] and castles were, without doubt, introduced by the Normans into England and were one of the principal means of effective occupation after Hastings.[138] But, like the church and the lay aristocracy, fortification, which could add effectively to the political power of both,[139] was closely controlled in Normandy by the duke. In 1035 the death of Robert the Magnificent and the accession of the minor and the bastard William was the signal for the wide-spread construction of unauthorised castles.[140] After the triumph of the young duke William at Val-ès-Dunes in 1047 such strongholds were demolished,[141] and thereafter the two principles essential in a well-ordered feudal state were rigorously maintained – that castles could not be raised without the licence of the ruler, and that all baronial castles must, in case of need, be made available to him.[142]

bailey or enclosure of ditch and bank with no motte, is currently being investigated in Normandy as elsewhere (cf. p. 237 below). A contemporary example is evidently to be found at le Plessis-Grimoult (Calvados), which can be securely dated to before 1047 and is a circular earthwork whose stone perimeter wall and entrance may be a later addition. (See de Boüard, 'Les petites enceintes circulaires d'origine médiévale en Normandie', in *Château-Gaillard, Etudes de Castellologie européenne*, i, 1964, especially p. 33. Cf. B. K. Davison, 'The Origins of the Castle in England', *Archaeological Journal*, cxxiv, 1967).

[137] The sieges of the castles of Brionne, Domfront and Arques are landmarks in the early reign of William the Conqueror scarcely less important than Val-ès-Dunes, Mortemer and Varaville. Cf. Yver, op. cit., p. 49. There had, of course, been sieges in Norman history before Brionne.

[138] See below p. 234.

[139] Prelates, of course, were also barons in feudal Normandy. For the relatively few episcopal castles in the duchy, see Yver, op. cit., p. 51.

[140] William of Jumièges, ed. Marx, pp. 115–16.

[141] Ibid., pp. 123, 124; William of Poitiers, ed. Foreville, pp. 18–20.

[142] The *Consuetudines et Justicie* of 1091, relating to ducal rights in the time of William the Conqueror, clause 6 (Haskins, *Norman Institutions*, p. 282): – '*nulli licuit in Normannia castellum facere, et nulli licuit in Normannia fortitudinem castelli sui vetare domino Normannie si ipse eam in manu sua voluit habere.*' Yver seems to me to misinterpret the first part of the passage, and exaggerate the extent of the ducal garrisoning of baronial castles referred to in the second (op. cit., pp. 60 et seq.) The same clause prohibits ditches and stockades beyond a certain strength for normal domestic and agricultural security in the open country, and

Normandy in 1066 was full of knights and had indeed been 'exporting' them, especially as younger sons, for over a generation – to Spain, Italy and beyond.[143] In war knights[144] were the heavy cavalry and the *corps d'élite*, whose hauberk or full coat of mail distinguished them from lesser men,[145] and in society at large they were the ruling class. Already the expense of the knight's equipment and the necessity to be free from other commitments for the long apprenticeship to arms and subsequent dedication to the art of war, combined with ancient Frankish and Teutonic notions of the honourable nature of military service to a lord, and the evolution of feudal notions of vassalage and lordship, had brought social and military distinction together in the concept of knighthood.[146] If not all Norman knights in 1066 were men of substance, it is already true that all great men were knights. The young duke William himself was knighted (*arma militaria sumit*) in his adolescence;[147] Ordericus Vitalis could describe

prohibits the fortification of rock sites (*in rupe*) or islands. Cf. de Boüard, *Château-Gaillard*, p. 32.

[143] Many went to Apulia (see p. 17 above) and the Conqueror especially found so much employment for those at home that there is occasional reference to a shortage of knights in Normandy. See Ordericus Vitalis, *Historia Ecclesiastica*, ii, 106; iii, 190, 191; cf. p. 47, below. For ducal control of Norman emigration, or the lack of such control, see F. M. Stenton, *Anglo-Saxon England*, p. 551; de Boüard, 'Le duché de Normandie', loc. cit., p. 14; cf. also the case of Baldric fitz Nicholas, disinherited by the Conqueror for going to Spain *sine mea licencia* (Ordericus Vitalis, *Historia Ecclesiastica*, iii, 248).

[144] For the study of knights, as of castles, vocabulary can be a complicating factor, though in France the word *miles* seems to have completed its significant change of meaning from classical 'soldier' to feudal 'knight' by about the beginning of the eleventh century (See K. J. Hollyman, *Le Développement du Vocabulaire féodal en France pendant le haut moyen âge* (Paris, 1957), pp. 129–34. Cf. p. 97 below).

[145] Navel, *B.S.A.N.*, xlii (1934), pp. 43, 51–2.

[146] The fact that this fusion was already taking place perhaps requires emphasis (cf. Stenton, *Anglo-Saxon England*, p. 628), though for an instance of a young man of humble origin becoming a knight in the time of the Conqueror's father, duke Robert the Magnificent, see the interpolation in William of Jumièges, ed. Marx, pp. 106–9.

[147] William of Poitiers, ed. Foreville, p. 13, who adds, characteristically, that the news alarmed all France. William of Malmesbury *Gesta Regum* (Rolls Series), ii, 286, says, not improbably, that he was knighted by

such eminent men as Ralph de Tosny and Hugh de Grentemesnil simply as *milites* (while calling their vassals, beneath
them in the feudal hierarchy, *barones*);[148] and as early as the
reign of Richard II (996–1026) – who was later said to have
liked to have gentlemen about him[149] – the word *miles* could
be used as a descriptive title of distinction in the attestations
of charters.[150] The chroniclers (and not only Ordericus
Vitalis,[151] whose study in depth of this society carries conviction but comes from a later generation) seem to make it
quite clear that already in pre-Conquest Normandy knighthood was a status and an honour conferred upon a young man
(*tiro*) by a ceremony usually described as the bestowal of
arms, after an apprenticeship as an *armiger*.[152] Of course, not
all the young knights of Normandy were landed, but they
were lordlings if not yet lords, younger sons if not heirs, and
those that had not fiefs hoped to acquire them by their service
– and often enough in this age went off to Italy where oppor-
tunity was greater and fiefs and honours came, with luck,

the king of France. William must have been very young at the time,
since the event is placed before Val-ès-Dunes (1047) at which battle he
was some nineteen years old.

[148] *Historia Ecclesiastica*, ii, 81.

[149] Douglas, *E.H.R.*, lxi (1946), p. 147.

[150] Fauroux, *Recueil des actes des ducs de Normandie (911–1066)*, p. 60.

[151] E.g. the words used by William of Poitiers to describe the knighting
of duke William cited above. Cf. the examples from Ordericus Vitalis,
n. 152 below.

[152] Thus Robert of Grentemesnil (who had studied letters in his youth
before thus turning to a career of arms) was an *armiger* of duke William
for five years and then was knighted by him—'*Deinde ab eodem duce
decenter est armis adornatus, et miles effectus pluribus exeniis nobiliter
honoratus*' (Ordericus Vitalis, *Historia Ecclesiastica*, ii, 40). Cf. William,
son of the banished Arnold d'Echaufour, who took service with the
King of France, '*regisque armiger factus ei servivit donec ab eo arma
militaria accepit*' (ibid., ii, 109). Examples could be multiplied, but cf. the
complaint of William the Conqueror against Robert 'Curthose' that he
had seduced his young knights from his service—'*tirones meos, quos
alui et militaribus armis decoravit*' (ibid., ii, 389). The knighting of the
future Henry I in 1087 is described by Ordericus in some detail (iii, 267)
and there are other occasional references to the belting of knights (e.g.
ibid., ii, 391). According to William of Malmesbury, the Norman knight
who cut up the fallen Harold at Hastings was degraded ('*militia pulsus
est*', *Gesta Regum*, ii, 303).

more quickly. In the meantime the landless knights lived off their lord's maintenance, or pay, or both. Modern analytical historians are too prone to distinguish sharply between enfeoffed knights and stipendiary knights. Contemporaries did not: the former were more elevated than the latter, but both were members of the upper, knightly class, itself extremely fluid.[153] Sometimes we are given a glimpse of the court and military household of a great lord wherein his knights, enfeoffed or landless, served their time, undertaking a variety of gentlemanly employments[154] but above all practising and exercising their military skills. The most valuable and prolonged such glimpse is afforded by the account by Gilbert Crispin of Herluin as a knight in the service of count Gilbert of Brionne in c. 1030.[155] Duke Robert sent a force from his household (*ex ducis domo plurimi*) against the sons of William de Bellême in c. 1028;[156] Mabel de Bellême vented her spite against the abbey of St. Evroul by staying there with large numbers of her knights.[157] The wounded Richard de Heudicourt, as we have seen, decided to become a monk at St. Evroul with the counsel of Hugh de Grentemesnil, his lord, *in cujus familia servierat in armis*,[158] and Ordericus Vitalis also tells the story, from pre-Conquest Normandy, of the accidental death of Hugh fitz Giroie, mortally wounded in a training exercise by a lance thrown carelessly by his esquire (*armiger*).[159]

[153] For references to stipendiary knights in pre-Conquest Normandy, see e.g. William of Poitiers, ed. Foreville, p. 36; William of Jumièges, ed. Marx, p. 118. N.B. again St. Anselm's parable of the courts of princes, cited p. 39 above. For stipendiary knights and mercenaries in post-Conquest England, see below, pp. 231–3.

[154] The final breach between Herluin and count Gilbert's court came when he refused a quasi-judicial assignment (J. Armitage Robinson, *Gilbert Crispin*, pp. 89–90). We may see on the Bayeux Tapestry the knights of Guy count of Ponthieu capturing Harold and at court, or the knights of duke William serving as envoys or as an escort as well as in expeditions and warfare. *The Bayeux Tapestry*, ed. F. M. Stenton, Pls. 9, 11, 12, 13, 16.)

[155] J. Armitage Robinson, ut supra, pp. 87–90.

[156] William of Jumièges, ed. Marx, p. 102.

[157] Ordericus Vitalis, *Historia Ecclesiastica*, ii, 52–3. For the court of her husband, Roger de Montgomery, at Bellême, see ibid., ii, 430–1.

[158] Ibid., ii, 114; cf. p. 42 above.

[159] Ibid., ii, 29. Hugh rather nobly advised him to fly at once before his, Hugh's, brothers heard of the deed and killed him.

The unfortunate incident and its context of military training, are timeless even if the arms employed are not. As soldiers, the Norman knights of 1066 were as professional as the age could make them.[160]

'The Normans are good conquerors; there is no race like them.'[161] The Normans of the eleventh century excelled in the art of war, and carried their victorious arms from the Atlantic to the eastern shores of the Mediterranean. Warfare at this time was increasingly dominated by heavy cavalry and castles, and in the employment and exploitation of both it is evident that the Normans were in the van of contemporary developments. The programme of fortification with which the Conquest of England was consolidated must be among the most concentrated and extensive in the whole history of the West, and the castles then raised were models of their kind, whether the quick, cheap but effective strongholds of earth-work and timber (the perfect instrument of military occupation) or the palatial stone towers at Colchester and London.[162] Though the techniques were scarcely to be required in England, the Norman armies of duke William's day were equally well-versed in siegecraft, and before 1066 the Conqueror had never failed to take a fortress, as also he had never lost a battle. The Norman cavalry, mainly composed of bellicose knights, was a devastating weapon, polished and tempered by continual training and application. It also seems clear that the Norman knights by 1066 were already adopting the new techniques of the couched lance whereby, in classic medieval fashion unknown to antiquity, the momentum of horse and rider were combined in one near-irresistible shock force.[163] But if castles were the bases and

[160] The unhappy remark of Eric John that 'the amateur gentleman-knight was not good enough for eleventh-century warfare' must be amongst the most misinformed ever made even in the subject of medieval warfare where ignorance is customarily rampant (see *Land Tenure in Early England*, Leicester, 1960, p. 159).

[161] Jordan Fantosme, Metricle Chronicle, Rolls Series, *Chronicles of the reigns of Stephen, Henry II, and Richard I*, ed. R. Howlett, iii (1886), p. 217.

[162] For the castles of the Conquest, see below p. 234.

[163] See D. J. A. Ross, 'L'originalité de "Turoldus": le maniement de

heavy cavalry the *force de frappe* of Norman armies in the mid-eleventh century, the Normans with duke William at their head were perfectly well aware of the value and the role of infantry and archers who, like knights, could be hired by the ample ducal resources or otherwise obtained through the ancient ducal right of the *arrière-ban*, and who, combined with cavalry, can be seen in action alike in pre-Conquest Normandy and at Hastings.[164] Norman tactics also, as practised by the Conqueror, give the lie to any lingering concepts there may be, derived from Delbrück and Oman, of medieval warfare as disorganised. Reconnaissance was as frequent as it was neces-

lance', *Cahiers de Civilisation Médiévale*, vi (1963). The suggestion may be added that the Norman knights at Hastings on the Bayeux Tapestry who appear to be brandishing their lances above their heads are not preparing to throw them but to strike overarm in the manner most likely against infantry. Ordericus Vitalis' account of the accidental wounding of Hugh fitz Giroie (*Historia Ecclesiastica*, ii, 29, cited p. 48 above) provides us with one certain instance of lances being thrown in the period c. 1040–60. (For another possible instance dated c. 1061–6, cf. ibid., ii, 114, where Richard de Heudicourt is struck in the back by the lance of a pursuing knight as he attempts to ford the river Epte.) On the other hand, two of the exploits of duke William related by William of Poitiers in illustration of his knightly prowess involve the unhorsing of an opponent which implies the use of the lance couched, as does the same writer's description of the duke at the end of the day at Hastings holding only the stump of his broken lance (ed. Foreville, pp., 24, 36, 203). The couched lance led to the heightening of the saddle bows (as illustrated on the Bayeux Tapestry: see Ross, op. cit.), and in this connection it is worth noting that, according to William of Malmesbury (*Gesta Regum*, Rolls Series, ii, 336–7), the Conqueror's fatal injury at Mantes in 1087 was caused by his saddle bow which must therefore have been high. For the whole subject of the medieval use of the lance, see also François Buttin, 'La lance et l'arrêt de cuirasse' (*Archaeologia*, xcix, 1965), who, writing independently of Ross, seems not to accept the evidence of the Bayeux Tapestry or the Song of Roland for the adoption of the couched lance as early as the mid-eleventh century (e.g. pp. 80–2).

[164] For the *arriére-ban*, see p. 22 and n. 10 above. For infantry at the siege of Mayenne in 1063, see William of Poitiers, ed. Foreville, pp. 96–8; for archers at Varaville, 1057, see Wace, ed. Andresen, ii, 239, 1.5226; for infantry and archers at Hastings, see William of Poitiers, p. 184, Ordericus Vitalis, *Historia Ecclesiastica*, ii, 147, the Bayeux Tapestry, and pp. 168–73 below.

sary;[165] winter campaigns were common;[166] the feigned flight, according to William of Jumièges, was used against the French at St. Aubin-le-Cauf near Arques in the autumn of 1053, thirteen years before Hastings.[167] Above all one may note the discipline of the Conqueror's Norman armies, as exemplified, for example, in the 'wait and see' tactics employed in the campaigns leading up to Mortemer (1054) and Varaville (1057),[168] in Brittany in 1064,[169] or, the most striking instance, during the long wait for favourable winds for the English expedition, first at Dives-sur-Mer and then at St. Valery-sur-Somme, for six weeks in the late summer and autumn of 1066.[170]

Norman achievement in the eleventh century owes much to the solid facts of economic prosperity and an expanding population. While economic revival is a general feature of Western Europe at this time, it appears that here Normandy achieved a flying start and, like Flanders, a development more rapid than that of her other Continental neighbours, by virtue of her continuing close connections with the Scandinavian world throughout the tenth century.[171] For commercial activity across the Channel there is evidence that the men of Rouen were trading in London as early as the reign of Ethelred II (979–1016) and had their own wharf there, at

---

[165] For reconnaissance by the duke himself, see William de Poitiers, ed. Foreville, pp. 36–8, 168. Cf. p. 180.
[166] E.g. Domfront, 1051–2 (Douglas, op. cit., p. 59 and n.), Arques and Mortemer (ibid., p. 67), Exeter, 1068, and the campaigns of 1069–70 (below pp. 191, 195–7 and Ordericus Vitalis, *Historia Ecclesiastica*, ii, 179 et seq., 194 ff.).
[167] William of Jumièges, ed. Marx, p. 120. For the date, see Douglas, *William the Conqueror*, p. 66 and n. For a brief appreciation of Norman military tactics under the Conqueror, see de Boüard, *Guillaume le Conquérant*, pp. 79–80, and for the tactic of the feigned flight, see p. 171 below.
[168] De Boüard, op. cit., pp. 46–7, 49.
[169] William of Poitiers, ed. Foreville, p. 112.
[170] Ibid., pp. 150–2, and below p. 152.
[171] De Boüard, 'Le duché de Normandie', loc. cit., pp. 5, 8–9, 16 and in *Bulletin Institute Historical Research*, xxviii, 8–9, 13. For a brief survey of Norman economic development in duke William's day, see the same author's *Guillaume le Conquérant*, p. 61.

Dowgate, by the time of Edward the Confessor.[172] Agrarian development and wealth similarly lies behind the Norman impact upon the eleventh-century world.[173] Evidence of a money economy meets us at every turn, whether in taxes, in the profitable rights of coinage monopolised by the dukes, the 'farms' or assessed rents of the *vicomtés*, the money rents of burgesses, the employment of paid troops, or in the ducal *camera* which appears in Richard II's reign.[174] Norman economic expansion and commercial activity is also reflected at this time in the precocious development of towns, encouraged and founded by dukes and magnates alike, and given special status and legal 'customs' which, as in the case of the customs of Breteuil, were often to be introduced into England and Wales after 1066.[175] Caen stands to this day as the most eminent example of a ducal new town of the eleventh century, in effect founded by the Conqueror's will and favour from the already expanding hamlets which preceded it, provided with ramparts, a castle and the two great abbeys of St. Stephen's and the Trinity, and serving from *c*. 1050 as the chief base of ducal power in Lower Normandy.[176] And, as one instance of a new seigneurial town in Normandy, one may cite Ordericus Vitalis' history of the lords of Auffai, who, rising through ducal service and the good marriages which resulted, built the town of Auffai and gave to it the customs of Cormeilles.[177] As for the expanding population of eleventh-century Normandy, this, of course, is one immediate explanation of the great Norman emigration of the period and is reflected in page after

[172] Haskins, *Norman Institutions*, p. 48. Cf. S. Deck, *Annales de Normandie*, vi (1956), pp. 245–54.

[173] H. R. Loyn, *The Norman Conquest* (London, 1965), p. 29. Cf. de Boüard, *Guillaume le Conquérant*, p. 61.

[174] For taxation, and the ducal *camera*, see below pp. 54–5. For burgage tenure, see de Boüard, op. cit., p. 61, and 'Le duché de Normandie', p. 12. For stipendiaries see p. 48 above.

[175] Cf. Loyn, op. cit., p. 177; Haskins, op. cit., p. 49. For the fortification of Breteuil see Ordericus Vitalis, interpolation in William of Jumièges, ed. Marx, p. 180.

[176] For Caen, see de Boüard, *Guillaume le Conquérant*, pp. 58–60; *Bulletin Institute Historical Research*, xxviii, 11–12; and *Le Château de Caen* (Caen, Syndicat d'Initiative). Cf. p. 22 above.

[177] *Historia Ecclesiastica*, iii, 42.

page of Ordericus Vitalis in the prodigious families of the new Norman aristocracy. If, as we are told, some of them prayed for sons,[178] their prayers were certainly answered. The classic instance is provided by the twelve sons (by two wives) of Tancred of Hauteville,[179] but Ordericus also tells us of, amongst others, the seven sons (and four daughters) of Giroie, who were 'a race of knights',[180] of the five sons and four daughters of Roger de Montgomery and Mabel de Bellême,[181] and also of the forty knight-nephews of Robert de Witot.[182]

One vital feature of pre-Conquest Normandy which remains to be considered in its own right is the great and growing power of the duke, who by 1066, sovereign in all but name, ruled without question over a united duchy and effectively controlled, as we have seen, the potential rivals of church and aristocracy within it. Economic prosperity combined with the duke's own vast demesne contributed largely to this power,[183] as did the uncommon definition of the duchy's frontiers,[184] the Carolingian inheritance,[185] and, no less, the development of feudalism.[186] While detailed evidence from the tenth century is sparse, the important fact is clear that an hereditary right to rule – coloured but not qualified by the Scandinavian toleration of bastards[187] – was established in the ducal house by the usual device of having the heir recognised and accepted in his father's life-time.[188] As documentary evidence increases

[178] Prentout, *Guillaume le Conquérant*, p. 87 and n.
[179] Ordericus Vitalis, *Historia Ecclesiastica*, ii, 54–5, 88.
[180] Interpolation in William of Jumièges, p. 163.
[181] Ibid., p. 169.
[182] *Historia Ecclesiastica*, ii, 105.
[183] De Boüard, 'Le duché de Normandie', pp. 8–9, 16. For the demesne, see pp. 22–3 above.
[184] Above, p. 21.
[185] Above p. 22.
[186] Above p. 39.
[187] De Boüard, op. cit., p. 5.
[188] The occasion is noted each time by William of Jumièges (ed. Marx, pp. 31, 40, 71–2, 96–7). The first prince to succeed without this preceding recognition was evidently Robert the Magnificent in 1028 in unexpected circumstances (ibid., p. 100). He, however, was careful to have the infant William the Bastard accepted as his successor before departing on his fateful pilgrimage (ibid., p. 111; cf. William of Malmesbury, *Gesta Regum*, Rolls Series, ii, 285).

at the century's end and from the reign of Richard II (996–1026) onwards, we begin to see something of the institutions developing to make the duke's government effective and give expression to his will.[189] The duke's *curia* or court now appears like that of other contemporary feudal princes, varying in size from the minimum itinerant household to the full councils and assemblies of magnates, ecclesiastical and lay, summoned to discuss and assent to important matters such as the succession, an alliance, or the invasion of England in 1066,[190] fluid in composition but normally containing those closest to the duke and the usual great officers, seneschal or steward, constable, chamberlain and butler.[191] Directly reflecting the wealth of the duchy, and still more of the duke, Norman fiscal organisation by the mid-eleventh century was very advanced by the standards of its Continental neighbours. There is evidence of direct taxation, notably the *gravaria*, to swell the ample ducal revenues derived from the demesne, tolls and customs upon trade, the monopoly of coinage, the profits of justice, feudal dues and the other perquisites of regality and lordship.[192] At the centre the duke's *camera* or chamber is referred to as early as Richard II's time, and in the provinces the duke's local officers, the *vicomtes*, farmed, i.e. rendered an agreed fixed sum of money for, his revenues accruing in their *vicomtés* or administrative districts. Later evidence from the twelfth century makes it clear that from the Conqueror's reign, if not before, some written record must have been kept of the

---

[189] For Norman administration in the eleventh century and before 1066 —though here again it is difficult, if not impossible, to draw a firm line at that date—see especially Haskins, *Norman Institutions*, Chapter I, and de Boüard, 'Le duché de Normandie'.

[190] See n. 188 above and e.g. William of Jumièges, ed. Marx, pp. 77–8; Ordericus Vitalis, *Historia Ecclesiastica*, ii, 120–1. For Richard II holding a *placitum generale* in the tower at Rouen, see William of Jumièges p. 89.

[191] De Boüard, op. cit., pp. 5–6, 17; M. Fauroux, *Receuil des Actes des Ducs de Normandie, 911–1066*, pp. 58–63.

[192] See L. Musset, 'A-t-il existé en Normandie au xie siècle une aristocratie d'argent?', *Annales de Normandie*, ix (1959), and the same author in *Revue d'histoire du droit français et étranger* (1960), pp. 433–4. Cf. Douglas, *William the Conqueror*, p. 135; D. J. A. Matthew, *Norman Conquest*, pp. 52–3; Haskins, *Norman Institutions*, pp. 39–40.

duke's charitable grants and alms to be charged against these farms, and it is at least interesting that the most recent Norman historian of the duchy supports Haskin's view that specifically Norman fiscal administration may have made its own contribution to the later organisation of the Anglo-Norman Exchequer.[193] Nor from Richard II's time onwards was Normandy noticeably backward by contemporary standards in the use of written instruments for secretarial purposes, notably the recording of grants of property and rights, and Douglas has pointed out with justice that the 135 extant charters issued or subscribed by duke William from 1035 to 1066 compare very well with the total number of surviving writs and charters issued by Edward the Confessor (1042–66) for the far larger kingdom of England.[194] From the varying styles of these charters it is clear that they were normally written by the beneficiary and that no organised Chancery or secretariat as yet existed in the duke's household to draw up and issue them, just as it is certain that they were not normally authenticated with a seal. Nevertheless, in view of the emphasis nowadays placed upon the superiority of the administrative organisation of pre-Conquest England and the continuity of Anglo-Saxon institutions after 1066, it should be noted more often than it is that evidence exists to suggest that the ducal abbey of Fécamp may at times have served as a ducal Chancery, and that there is also reference to a chancellor in Richard II's reign, and at least some evidence pointing to the occasional use of a seal by that duke and by the Conqueror.[195]

[193] Haskins, op. cit., pp. 39–45; de Boüard, op. cit., pp. 10, 18. Cf., Richard fitz Nigel, *Dialogus de Scaccario*, ed. C. Johnson (London, 1950), p. 14.

[194] D. C. Douglas, *William the Conqueror*, p. 11. See M. Fauroux, op. cit.

[195] Fauroux, op. cit., pp. 41–7. Nos. 18 and 34 are subscribed by *Dudo cancellarius* and *Hugo cancellarius* respectively, and in the latter case Hugh specifically *scripsit et subscripsit* the charter, which, however, only survives in a very early (eleventh-century) copy. Similarly No. 9 is *per Widonem notarium meo rogatu conscriptum*. A pendant seal was recorded for No. 18 in the eighteenth century though it has now vanished. Two charters of Robert the Magnificent (1028–35) refer in their texts to authentication by the duke's signet (*anuli nostri impressione roboramus*, Nos. 61, 90). Two references to the use of a seal by William the Con-

In the eyes of contemporaries the fundamental duties of a ruler were the maintenance of peace and the dispensation of good justice, and in both respects in the mid-eleventh century the duchy was well served. Like the king's peace in England, the duke's own peace in Normandy was not yet technically comprehensive, but it was extensive and it was also reinforced by the Truce of God, introduced by William the Conqueror at Caen in 1047 and thereafter backed by his authority as well as the authority of the church.[196] The right of private war in Normandy, invariably mentioned disapprovingly by English historians, is very severely limited in the *Consuetudines et Justicie* of 1091[197] and there is little evidence for its practice in duke William's reign after the end of his minority and his victory at Val-ès-Dunes in 1047, which victory, says William of Poitiers, resulted in the demolition of many castles and the end of internal wars for a long time (*bella domestica apud nos in longum sopivit*).[198] The dispensation of justice was shared in this age, in Normandy as elsewhere, with magnates and the church, but ducal justice was expanding rapidly in the eleventh century, and though the duke had no monopoly of *haute justice* and the more serious criminal offences, the principle was growing that such jurisdiction in private hands was the delegation of his authority and was finally enunciated in 1080 at Lillebonne.[199] The duke's justice also was dispensed at a distance from his itinerant court by the *vicomtes* in the provinces and by the sending out of special judicial commissions in whose personnel a tendency towards specialisation of function is already apparent.[200] Such commissions connected the

queror before 1066 are not strictly contemporary nor found in the charters themselves. Marie Fauroux also argues that the change made to the English royal, pendant, two-faced seal after the Norman Conquest, whereby the king-duke appears on one side armed and mounted, implies the existence of a ducal, equestrian seal in Normandy before 1066. Cf. however, P. Chaplais in *L'Abbaye bénédictine de Fécamp* (Fécamp, 1959–60), i, 101. See also p. 247 below.

[196] See p. 34 and n. 74 above.
[197] Printed in Haskins, op. cit., pp. 281 et seq.; cf. p. 45 above.
[198] Ed. Foreville, p. 18.
[199] De Boüard, op. cit., pp. 5, 9, 15, 17–18, 20. For the duke's intervention in ecclesiastical jurisdiction see p. 33 above.
[200] De Boüard, op. cit., p. 18.

itinerant ducal household with the provinces as did the *vicomtes* who were frequently at court,[201] and with the *vicomtes*, ducal officials each with judicial, financial, military and general administrative duties in his *vicomté*, the problem of local government, the most difficult governmental problem of the age, had been solved in eleventh-century Normandy more effectively than by any of its neighbours, England included.[202]

Yet, when all is said and done, the early Middle Ages were a period of personal government *par excellence*, and politics, with such immense power concentrated in the hands of so few people, were largely a matter of personal relations. Institutional studies miss half the point and all the fun of history, which is why 'Administrative History', the characteristic product of our century, is generally so dull. Certainly no survey of the mid-eleventh-century Norman duchy, focused on the explanation of how the Norman Conquest of England came to pass, can be anything like complete without reference to the personalities who achieved it and, above all, the personal qualities of duke William. Some kind of group portrait of the new Norman aristocracy has been attempted in this chapter, and their close relations with the duke have been emphasised. William had all the qualities required to gain the support of these warlike, restless and dynamic men, and his ascendancy over them was at least as much the result of his abilities and prestige as of his domestic policies which removed all opposition. Scion of the house of Rollo, born at Falaise in 1127/8 the illegitimate son of duke Robert and Arlette the tanner's daughter,[203] and succeeding to the duchy at the age of seven or eight on his father's untimely death in 1035, his character thereafter was largely moulded by the events of his demanding reign before 1066, which made of him the perfect instrument

[201] See especially Fauroux, op. cit., pp. 60–1.
[202] For the *vicomtes*, who still await their historian, see de Boüard, op. cit., pp. 18–19. The counts enjoyed administrative franchises in their *comtés*, but in duke William's day they were few, loyal and closely bound to him: see ibid., p. 18, Douglas, *E.H.R.*, lxi, and cf. p. 35 above. For some comparison of the Norman *vicomte* and the English shire-reeve or sheriff, see p. 74 below.
[203] Douglas, *William the Conqueror*, p. 15 and Appendix A.

for the task ahead as surely as they produced a situation which made possible his success.[204] The 'anarchy' attendant on his minority – i.e. public disorder, private war and personal vendetta, the inevitable result in early medieval society, feudal or not, of the absence of adult strong rule[205] – all this brought him his 'precocious maturity',[206] and the rising against him personally in 1046–7 brought him his first great victory on the field of Val-ès-Dunes at the age of some nineteen years. From this battle, and the long but successful siege of Brionne which followed, his personal rule and mounting personal ascendancy may be dated. Thereafter the danger shifts from internal strife and insecurity to external threat, posed by the French king, Henry I, who had aided the duke his vassal at Val-ès-Dunes but aided the revolting count of Arques against him in 1052–3, and by Geoffrey Martel, count of Anjou, pursuing an expansionist policy into Maine and the lordship of Bellême on the south and south-west borders of the duchy. In 1060 both king Henry and Geoffrey were dead, but before that they had been severally defeated at the battles of Mortemer and Varaville and the sieges of Domfront, Alençon and Arques, while the house and lordship of Bellême had been brought into the feudal dependency of the duke of Normandy. Then in 1063 the Conqueror invaded Maine in vindication of his right to its succession granted by the deceased count Herbert, and solved the problem of that buffer state by conquest.

Thus when in 1066 king Edward died in England, duke William was free to concentrate upon his English rights, the

[204] The fullest and most recent account of William's reign in Normandy, with particular attention to chronology, will be found in Douglas, op. cit. Other accounts are in de Boüard, *Guillaume le Conquérant*; H. Prentout, *Histoire de Guillaume le Conquérant*; and F. M. Stenton, *William the Conqueror*. There is also, of course, the detailed narrative of Freeman's *Norman Conquest*.

[205] It is a mistake to regard the anarchy, whose degree in any case has probably been exaggerated, as a movement against ducal authority, and even the plot and revolt led by Guy of Burgundy in 1046–7 was directed against William and not his office. See e.g. Prentout, op. cit., pp. 7, 10; de Boüard, op. cit., p. 11, 12–14, 20–1; Douglas, op. cit., pp. 39–42. Some of the more lurid incidents are recounted by Ordericus Vitalis, *Historia Ecclesiastica*, i, 180; ii, 369–70; iii, 229.

[206] De Boüard, op. cit., p. 17.

French kingdom friendly under the regency of his own father-in-law, Baldwin count of Flanders, and the energies of Anjou consumed in a succession struggle. Normandy itself was stronger and more united than ever before under the duke's good peace and by the constant tonic of military success. The ancient breach between East and West had been sealed by Val-ès-Dunes and the new ducal town of Caen to such good effect that in the event more men followed William to Hastings and to England from Lower than from Upper Normandy,[207] and a further indispensable condition of true political cohesion was provided in the Conqueror's reign by the rapid development of a uniform law and custom within frontiers which were now rounded off to the further advantage of the duchy.[208] In the dying speech attributed to the Conqueror by Ordericus Vitalis, the king and duke is made to say that from his accession at the age of eight until the end he had continuously borne the weight of arms.[209] The words are true even if never uttered. In the process he became a knight of knights, fit lord and leader of a martial race, and a consummate general whose youthful, hot-headed recklessness was later controlled by an iron will to enable him to mix cool caution with bold decision.[210] From the point of view of the aristocrats and other warriors who followed him to England, military ability was a prime necessity in a prince, but in his hard school the Conqueror had also become a statesman and a pious churchman of reformist views. He was almost all the age and place could ask for. He even had, this Fortune's favourite, a near-perfect wife, to whom he was devoted, and whom, characteristically, he had

[207] See de Boüard, op. cit., pp. 23–5, and *Bulletin Institute Historical Research*, xxviii, 10–12. Cf. pp. 21–2, 52 above.

[208] Cf. de Boüard, 'Le duché de Normandie', loc. cit., p. 16, and, Lemarignier, *L'hommage en marche*, pp. 19 et seq. The latter remarks at p. 33, '*L'unité de la coutume normande, c'est une unité de puissance qui correspond à une unité territoriale.*'

[209] *Historia Ecclesiastica*, iii, 229, '*ex quo tempore usque nunc semper subii pondus armorum.*'

[210] For examples of his early recklessness, for which he is said to have been reprimanded by the French king Henry I, see William of Poitiers, ed. Foreville, pp. 22–6, 36, 54–8. The change evidently occurs as from the campaigns culminating at Mortemer in 1054 (de Boüard, *Guillaume le Conquérant*, p. 47).

acquired in the teeth of papal censure.[211] Under this man's leadership the power of Normandy would take a lot of stopping, and, as we shall see, the English kingdom led by Harold was unequal to the task.

[211] Douglas, op. cit., pp. 76–80 and Appendix C. Though the marriage probably took place between 1050 and 1052, negotiations with the church occupied the decade 1049–59 and resulted in the foundation of the great churches of St. Stephen's and the Trinity at Caen as a penance.

CHAPTER III

England

Every kingdom divided against itself is brought
to desolation.

Luke, xi, 17

Nowadays, at least upon this side of the Channel, England in
the mid-eleventh century is represented as an ancient kingdom, united, strong and administered by a system of government remarkably developed by the standards of the age.
Certainly, antiquity is in many ways the key to the under-
standing of the Old English state on the eve of its defeat by
the Normans. In the history of Western Europe and Latin
Christendom, kingship is older than feudalism, and by beginning thus we are brought at once to the fundamental and
crucial paradox of Anglo-Saxon history[2] – that whereas in
Frankish and Carolingian Gaul the onslaughts of the Vikings
in the ninth century brought about the collapse of central,
monarchical authority, and the consequent development of
feudal society,[3] in England the case was otherwise. Alfred,
king of Wessex (871–99), as every schoolboy knows, held
out triumphantly against the Danes. It is true that more than
half of England – the north and the east beyond Watling
Street, and beyond a line drawn roughly from Chester to the
mouth of the Thames (See p. xvi) – was occupied and settled

[2] For the history of Anglo-Saxon England, see especially F. M. Stenton,
Anglo-Saxon England (Oxford, 1943; second ed. 1947); P. H. Blair, *An
Introduction to Anglo-Saxon England* (Cambridge, 1959); and H. R.
Loyn, *Anglo-Saxon England and the Norman Conquest* (London, 1962).
An admirable survey and analysis of Old English society will be found
in D. Whitelock, *The Beginnings of English Society* (London, second
ed. 1965).
[3] See p. 10 above.

by the Vikings to form the future Danelaw;[4] but this was to be subjugated by Alfred's great successors, notably by Edward the Elder (899–925) and by Athelstan (925–39), and the result, from the mid-tenth century, was one united English kingdom, ruled over by the royal house of Wessex, in place of the 'Heptarchy' of miscellaneous minor kingdoms into which England had been divided in the centuries before the Danes. This kingdom, in turn, was conquered by Swein Forkbeard of Denmark and Cnut his son in the dark days of king Ethelred 'Unraed' and between 1013 and 1016, but defeat when it came was nation-wide, Cnut succeeded to the throne of his Wessex predecessors, and the united monarchy was maintained and strengthened by his forceful presence, to be taken over in due course by William the Bastard, duke of Normandy. In England therefore, the achievement of political unity, at least in the form of a single monarchy for the whole land, was the paradoxical result of the Viking onslaught in the ninth century, and it is this one fact which more than anything else explains the manifold differences between this country and neighbouring France in the mid-eleventh century, and also much of the subsequent course of English history.

The kingship which had thus survived and waxed in England – while it had waned in France, at least in practice, and in Germany, too, was soon to be diminished – was a potent force, in which the ancient Germanic traditions of the king as a war-leader, descended from the pagan gods, had long since been sanctified by the church and converted into the Carolingian concept of Christian kingship.[5] Anointed with holy oil in the sacrament of his coronation,[6] the king was *rex*

---

[4] For the Danelaw, see also pp. 74–7 below. While most of it was an area of Danish settlement and predominance, the north-west was settled in the early tenth century by Norwegians from Ireland, the Isle of Man and the isles to the north-west of Britain (Loyn, op. cit., pp. 51, 56–8).
[5] For the whole subject of early medieval kingship, see especially F. Kern, *Kingship and Law in the Middle Ages*, trans. S. B. Chrimes (London, 1939).
[6] Thus St. Peter Damiani (d. 1072): 'The fifth sacrament is the unction of a king. Exalted is this anointing because it creates exalted power. . . . He [the king] is then divested, and asperged with the oil of sanctification so that, drenched with allegorical dew, he may glory in the fulness of

et sacerdos, ruling by the grace of God as his vicar and Christ's deputy. Thus Ethelred declared that 'a Christian king is Christ's deputy in a Christian people',[7] and Edward the Confessor was held to be 'appointed by God as ruler over men'.[8] King Edward's seal, which was probably copied from the seal of Cnut, shows him enthroned 'in majesty',[9] and in him both the secular and ecclesiastical hierarchies reached their apex.[10] The royal government of the Old English state, in short, was theocratic,[11] and in their legislation the later Old English kings show themselves to have been in practice what they were in theory – responsible not only for their kingdom but also for their church within it, and concerned no less for the spiritual health of their subjects than for their material well-being.[12]

The Old English kings, as sacramental monarchs, drew much of their prestige and strength from religion, and from the church, which cooperated with them at every level of government, and which, by virtue of their position in this pre-Gregorian world, they still controlled. There were also, of

the heavenly unguent.' *Sermo* lxix, *Patrologia Latina,* ed. J. P. Migne, cxliv, coll. 899–900; quoted by F. Barlow, *The English Church 1000–1066* (London, 1963), p. 33. For the coronation of king Edgar in 973, which in England set the pattern for the future, see F. M. Stenton, op. cit., p. 363. Cf. P. E. Schramm, *A History of the English Coronation* (Oxford, 1937).

[7] viii Ethelred, 2. 1. (A. J. Robertson, *Laws of the Kings of England from Edmund to Henry I,* Cambridge, 1925, p. 119; *English Historical Documents,* i, 411). The fact that the influence, and possibly the hand, of Wulfstan, archbishop of York, is thought to lie behind these and other laws of the period serves only to emphasise the complete integration of church and state implicit in the concept of Christian kingship (see Barlow, op. cit., p. 70, and the authorities there cited).

[8] J. M. Kemble, *Codex diplomaticus Aevi Saxonici* (London, 1839–48), No. 791 (A.D. 1050).

[9] Cf. p. 97 below.

[10] F. Barlow, *The English Church 1000–1066,* p. 140.

[11] Ibid., p. 141.

[12] Ibid., pp. 138 et seq. See, for example, the 'code' of laws issued by Cnut (who enthusiastically adopted the concept of Christian kingship), from which long extracts are printed in translation in *English Historical Documents,* i, 419, et seq. Cf. the same king's charter of *c.* 1020, ibid., p. 415 ('that I should everywhere exalt God's praise and suppress wrong, and establish full security by that power which it has pleased God to give me').

course, other sinews of their power, and important rights and functions in the more purely secular sphere. Amongst the most ancient of royal rights was the king's *feorm* or food rent, due from all the land of England unless he had released it, originally intended to maintain him, his court, companions and officials as they moved about the kingdom, and by the mid-eleventh century often, but not always, commuted to a money payment. Then there was the so-called *trimoda necessitas*, the threefold common obligation of work upon bridges and borough-defences and of military service by land or sea in the royal *fyrd*, which public burdens legally lay upon all free-men and upon all land and were rarely, if ever, lifted.[13] Most impressive of all amongst royal rights in England was the ability of the kings from the late tenth century onwards to raise, and raise regularly, what is in fact the earliest example of a national tax in Western Europe in the Middle Ages. This was the geld or Danegeld, first raised by Ethelred in 991 to buy off the Danes and thereafter maintained – the classic instance in English history of a war tax never cancelled.[14] The geld was a land tax assessed, again, upon all the land of England unless specifically exempted, and paid by all who were liable simply as free subjects of the king. The Old English monarchs had also other valuable rights and revenues, from their own extensive lands, from tolls upon trade, from their monopoly of the mint and coinage, from the sale of privileges and from the profits of justice. As for the last, though the king stood somewhat above the actual working of the law which was chiefly administered in the local and public courts of shire and

[13] For the origin of these common obligations, see Stenton, *Anglo-Saxon England*, pp. 286–8, and, more recently, Eric John, *Land Tenure in Early England* (Leicester, 1960), pp. 64–79. Cf. W. H. Stevenson, 'Trinoda Necessitas', *E.H.R.*, xxix (1914). The fullest and most recent discussion of the fyrd and Anglo-Saxon military service will be found in C. W. Hollister, *Anglo-Saxon Military Institutions* (Oxford, 1962). See also pp. 91–4 below.

[14] In 1051 Edward the Confessor abolished the 'heregeld', taken for the maintenance of a standing fleet and army, but not the principle of the geld, which continued to be taken by William the Conqueror after 1066. See Stenton, *Anglo-Saxon England*, pp. 425, 636–40; H. R. Loyn, *Anglo-Saxon England and the Norman Conquest*, p. 312, and *Norman Conquest*, pp. 71, 78.

hundred,[15] and pleas were but rarely heard before the king himself,[16] he was by his position its ultimate guarantor, and in the dispensation of justice he was coming to play a more positive role at least, as it were, by proxy. The more serious criminal offences were, by the eleventh century, regarded not only as offences against the injured party, as in early Germanic law, but also as offences against the king,[17] and the 'pleas of the Crown' which thus begin to make their appearance in the law codes[18] were expanded by the expanding concept of 'the king's peace' (not yet by any means universal but lying upon individuals and places) to break which was manifestly an offence against the king. So too, through the agency of the king's officials, his earls, his bishops and his reeves, who presided over them, the local, public courts had begun that evolution which was to make of them in due course local royal courts in the provinces. Lastly, the kings of pre-Conquest England were law-givers, or at least law-declarers, and had retained something of the sovereign right of legislation, upon

[15] Thus Cnut, re-enacting a clause of Edgar, 'And let no one apply to the king unless he may not be entitled to any justice within his hundred' (Stubbs, *Select Charters*, pp. 83, 86). It is possible that this enactment indicates a tendency to do what is prohibited, but it certainly does not reflect any active desire for the expansion of royal justice. For the shire and hundred, see below p. 69.

[16] H. G. Richardson and G. O. Sayles, *The Governance of Mediæval England* (Edinburgh, 1963), p. 173; R. C. Van Caenegem, *Royal Writs in England from the Conquest to Glanville* (Selden Society, lxxvii, 1958–9), pp. 16–17; Barlow, op. cit., pp. 121, 129. For a contrary assumption, and examples of the occasional intervention by the king in the dispensation of justice, see D. M. Stenton, *English Justice between the Norman Conquest and the Great Charter* (London, 1965), pp. 8–10. The use of the sealed writ on such occasions is, however, far from certain, see below p. 73.

[17] Hence the splendid remark of T. F. T. Plucknet in *Edward I and the Criminal Law* (Cambridge, 1960), p. 52, 'The law of *wer* and *bot* yielded to the law of *wite*', where *wer* and *bot* are compensatory payments respectively to a slain man's kin and to the injured party himself, and *wite* is the penalty payment to the king.

[18] Some of them are listed for the first time in Cnut's code (Stubbs, *Select Charters*, p. 86, 'These are the rights which the king has over all men in Wessex. . . . And in the Danelaw . . .'). For the interpretation of these clauses, see especially Naomi D. Hurnard, 'Anglo-Norman Franchises', *E.H.R.*, lxiv (1949).

the Carolingian model.[19] From the far-off days of Ethelbert of Kent (560–616) most of the kings of Anglo-Saxon England issued 'codes' of laws, the series ending evidently with the great codes of the alien Cnut (1016–35), since no code is extant for Edward the Confessor, even though after the Conquest and beyond, reference was repeatedly made to the good old laws of the good old days of King Edward.[20]

To assist him in some at least of the major decisions and tasks of government the king had his *witan* or *witenagemot*,[21] his court and council which was the Old English equivalent of the *curia regis* of pre-Conquest Normandy and post-Conquest England,[22] a fluid, expandable and mainly aristocratic assembly of bishops and abbots, earls and thegns.[23] The larger assemblies of the *witan* were summoned to give counsel on big issues like peace and war, taxation, the issuing of laws, the appointments of earls and prelates, or the making of important grants of lands or privileges, and sometimes, no doubt, acted as a very elevated law court to hear and adjudge the great

[19] It is no coincidence that the first extant written 'code' of laws in England came from Ethelbert's Kent and coincides in time with the advent of St. Augustine and the Roman Church (below). Some qualification of the sovereign right of legislation must be made, however, for at least the early Middle Ages, since by tradition law was customary and immutable, and men were, perhaps wisely, diffident about making it. Thus Alfred, in a famous passage in the Preamble to his Laws, describes how he had collected together the laws of his predecessors and of other kings in England, keeping what seemed good and rejecting what seemed bad, 'For I dared not write much of my own; for it was unknown to me how that would please those that should come after us' (Stubbs, *Select Charters*, p. 70). The laws issued by the Old English kings are not 'codes' in the strict sense.
[20] Thus William the Conqueror, *Hoc quoque praecipio et volo, ut omnes habeant et teneant legem Edwardi regis.* (Stubbs, *Select Charters*, 9th. edition, p. 99; translation, *English Historical Documents*, ii, 400.) By the early thirteenth century the law of King Edward had become a kind of shibboleth, like Magna Carta today.
[21] Lit., *gemot* = an assembly or court; *witena* (gen. plur.) = of the wise men. For this subject, see T. J. Oleson, *The Witenagemot in the Reign of Edward the Confessor* (London, 1955).
[22] Cf. p. 54 above and p. 245 below.
[23] See H. R. Loyn, 'Gesiths and Thegns from the seventh to the tenth century', *E.H.R.*, lxx (1955).

pleas of great men – as when, perhaps, earl Godwin defended himself against the charge of responsibility for the brutal murder of the aethling Alfred.[24] Since also, at this time and for long after, in the absence of any strict rule of primogeniture, there was an 'elective' element in the kingship, the *witan*, or those great men who composed it, had an important part to play in the succession of kings.[25]

Though the larger meetings of the *witan* were, no doubt, the major political events of the times and represented the ultimate in authority within the kingdom, as the king, the deputy of God, was seen to rule over both secular and ecclesiastical hierarchies, in their presence, by their counsel and in association with them, it is not these assemblies which in the last half century have increasingly attracted the attention of historians, but, rather, the less spectacular activity of the king's normal, unexpanded, itinerant household, the more or less permanent nucleus of royal clerks, officials and companions, through whom inevitably the normal business of day-to-day royal government was carried out. As T. F. Tout correctly taught us in the 1920's,[26] in an age of personal monarchy, throughout the Middle Ages and beyond, the centre of royal government and the source of executive power lay in the peripatetic household, the king's court (*curia regis*) as it moved

[24] Florence of Worcester, *Chronicon ex Chronicis*, ed. B. Thorpe (2 vols., London, 1848–9), i, 194–5. Cf. F. M. Stenton, *Anglo-Saxon England*, pp. 416–17. Godwin exonerated himself by oath-helpers and also by the gift of a splendid warship to the king (i.e. Harthacnut, 1040–2) which latter move may perhaps bear some relation to the Scandinavian procedure of 'buying' law (ibid., p. 504). Alfred, son of Ethelred and Emma, the younger brother to the future Edward the Confessor, had been murdered, on a visit to England from his exile in Normandy, in 1036 in the reign of Harold Harefoot (1035–40).

[25] See especially T. J. Oleson, op. cit., Chapter 10; see also p. 133 below.

[26] See his great work, *Chapters in Medieval Administrative History* (6 vols., Manchester, 1920–33). S. B. Chrimes, *An Introduction to the Administrative History of Medieval England* (Oxford, second ed. 1959) serves as an invaluable summary and gloss, with qualifications and corrections where necessary. Tout himself was rather less interested in the pre-Conquest that the post-Conquest era. See also L. M. Larson, *The King's Household in England before the Norman Conquest* (Madison, 1904).

about the realm. The origins of English central government are thus to be found in the royal household, and its subsequent development is largely a matter of an ever-increasing specialisation of function, producing specialist 'departments of state', for secretarial business, finance and the dispensation of justice, each an offshoot of the parent stem, i.e. Tout's 'undifferentiated *curia regis*'. Part and parcel of the development of government, also, is an ever-increasing reliance upon written record – putting things down in writing, instead of a primitive reliance upon oral tradition and the spoken word – as king Ethelbert was driven, in Plucknet's phrase, to the 'desperate device'[27] of writing down his laws in Kent, at the very beginning of this process in the early seventh century. The study of government and administration in this sense, 'Administrative History', has been the peculiar contribution of the twentieth century to historical studies, and there is little doubt that this interest, which, pursued with a due sense of proportion, can add a new dimension to the past, has been a principal cause of that up-grading of the Anglo-Saxons in our time, which was noted in the introduction to this book.[28] Emphasis has come to be placed upon an exceptional development of government both central and local in pre-Conquest England,[29] upon the evolution of sophisticated techniques of administration well in advance of other contemporary states in Latin Christendom, and the implications drawn are of a precocious people,[30] a strong, centralised monarchy, and a politically united realm. In this view, there are already, long before the Norman Conquest, clear indications of a specialisation of function at the centre, in the royal household, for both secretarial and fiscal business, if not judicial.[31] The mere

[27] T. F. T. Plucknet, *Edward I and the Criminal Law*, p. 8. For the increasing habit of writing and the slow change from an oral to a literate society, see V. H. Galbraith, *Studies in the Public Records* (London, 1948), Chapter II.
[28] Above p. 3.
[29] See especially Galbraith, op. cit., where the case is strongly and entertainingly made. Cf. R. R. Darlington, 'The last Phase of Anglo-Saxon History', *History*, xxii (1937–8), and the same writer's *Norman Conquest* (Creighton Lecture 1962, London, 1963).
[30] Galbraith, op. cit., p. 36.
[31] Above pp. 64–5 and n. 16.

existence of the geld, a national land tax with its complicated collection and assessment (including 'beneficial hidation' or tax relief) is held to presuppose some specialist organisation in the household, based upon the king's Chamber, as well as a stationary 'well-organised and well-staffed Treasury at Winchester', and written records.[32] So, too, it is thought, the existence within the household, based upon the king's Chapel, of a royal secretariat, writing-office or 'Chancery', is presupposed to some extent by the production of the great charters, diplomas or land-books wherein the king caused his grants of lands and privileges to be recorded, and much more by the vernacular sealed writs, used not only for the same purpose, as title deeds, but also as the written instruments whereby the king's administrative orders could be conveyed throughout his realm.[33] The writ, together with the itinerary of the king, thus linked the localities with the mobile household, and the problem of local government was further solved by the division of almost all the kingdom into shires,[34] and the subdivision of the shires into hundreds (in 'English England') or wapentakes (in the Danelaw). Shire, hundred and wapentake each had its court for the transaction of judicial and public business, but the shire court was the normal point of contact between the royal government and the provinces, and was presided over by the royal officials who administered the shire, namely the bishop and the earl or his deputy the sheriff.[35]

[32] Galbraith, op. cit., p. 45.
[33] Thus Galbraith, op. cit., p. 36: 'The whole structure [of late Anglo-Saxon government] was articulated by the royal writ addressed to the shire court which conveyed the royal orders.' For the vernacular sealed writ, see F. E. Harmer, *Anglo-Saxon Writs* (Manchester, 1952); T. A. M. Bishop and P. Chaplais, *Facsimiles of English Royal Writs to A.D. 1100* (Oxford, 1957). For the diploma, F. M. Stenton, *The Latin Charters of the Anglo-Saxon Period* (Oxford, 1955).
[34] The exceptions are in the north; see F. M. Stenton, *Anglo-Saxon England*, pp. 495–6, 498. South of the Humber the modern counties, save Rutland, were in existence well before 1066. The uniform division of most of the kingdom into shires, with their sub-divisions of hundreds and wapentakes, is evidently part and parcel of the expansion of the Wessex monarchy in the tenth century.
[35] For bishop, earl and sheriff, see also below p. 74.

It is, however, as easy to exaggerate the degree of development of Anglo-Saxon government along these lines as it is important not to. In the first place, the evidence for any considerable specialisation of function, and thus for embryonic 'departments of state', at the centre, in the household, is tenuous and indirect.[36] There is no evidence to show that pleas were often heard centrally before the king.[37] There is – and the point remains worth making – no reference in England before the Conquest to a 'Treasury' and a 'Treasurer', or to a 'Chancery' and a 'Chancellor'. The geld was a national tax very impressive by the standards of the age,[38] though (the comment is not intended as derogatory) characteristic of a surviving Carolingian monarchy. In Galbraith's immortal words, 'the Anglo-Saxon financial system, which collected the Danegeld, was not run from a box under the bed', but nevertheless such sparse and inferential evidence as there is points to some fixed, local organisation rather than to much specialisation in the household.[39] On the secretarial side of government, the case for a royal *scriptorium* or writing office in the pre-Conquest period depends almost entirely upon the diplomatic evidence (shape, form and phraseology) of the two principal types of contemporary documents running in the king's name, i.e. the

[36] For what follows, see also G. Barraclough, 'The Anglo-Saxon Writ', *History*, xxxix (1954), and F. Barlow, *The English Church*, pp. 120 et seq.

[37] See p. 65, and n. 16 above.

[38] There is, however, some evidence of direct taxation in pre-Conquest Normandy (see p. 54 above).

[39] Galbraith, op. cit., p. 45; cf. Barlow, op. cit., p. 123 and note 3. For the story, derived from Ailred of Rievaulx writing in the twelfth century, of the scullion who stole from a box under Edward the Confessor's bed in that monarch's chamber, both treasure chest and chamber evidently being the responsibility of Hugelin the chamberlain, see Barlow, op. cit., p. 123. In general it may be suggested that Tout's concept of all later specialist departments of state developing from the original undifferentiated *curia regis* fits the facts of secretarial organisation better than judicial or financial. The dispensation of justice after all, so far as we know, begins in local courts. In the financial sphere the situation is complicated by the fact that money requires a fixed repository, and kings even less than most men can take all their wealth with them. The financial function of the king and his household was primarily spending rather than collecting, storing or accounting.

diploma and the writ. But, for the former, though it can be argued that in Athelstan's reign (923–39) and for some time afterwards[40] royal diplomas show a degree of uniformity consistent with official production in some permanent office (generally assumed to be within the household[41]), the diplomatic evidence for all other periods of the Old English kingdom points in the reverse direction, and it seems clear that both before and after the tenth century, including the years immediately before the Conquest, royal diplomas were commonly drawn up by the beneficiary.[42] It has been suggested that in the latter period this is because the function of the old-fashioned and inefficient diploma was then being taken over by the more efficient writ,[43] whose diplomatic uniformity and business-like, bureaucratic characteristics argue strongly for a common origin and an established official source, presumably the royal court. But when, in fact, it appears that not only the diploma but also the writ could be written by the beneficiary,[44] it becomes apparent that the evidence for the existence of an established secretariat within the household of pre-Conquest kings is less than satisfactory.[45] This being so, perhaps more attention than is commonly the case should be given to the tradition preserved at Ely in the twelfth century[46] that king Ethelred had given the office of chancellor in the king's court (*in regis curia cancellarii . . . dignitatem*) jointly to the abbots of Ely, Glastonbury and St. Augustine's, Canterbury.

[40] Stenton, *Anglo-Saxon England*, pp. 349, 389; Harmer, op. cit., pp. 38–41; Barraclough, op. cit., p. 205.
[41] But cf. Galbraith, who has his doubts on this (op. cit., p. 32).
[42] Ibid., p. 35; Harmer, op. cit., pp. 38–41; Barraclough, op. cit., p. 212.
[43] Galbraith, op. cit., p. 35.
[44] Bishop and Chaplais, op. cit., pp. xii–xiii (two examples *temp.* Edward the Confessor); Harmer, op. cit., p. 20 (a possible further example *temp.* Edward the Confessor); Chaplais, 'Une charte originale de Guillaume le Conquérant', in *L'abbaye bénédictine de Fécamp* (2 vols., Fécamp, 1959–60) i, 96 (an example *temp.* William Rufus). For some objections to some of these examples, see Darlington, *Norman Conquest*, p. 4, n. 1.
[45] Cf. Barlow, op. cit., p. 128.
[46] *Liber Eliensis*, ed. E. O. Blake (Camden 3rd Series, xcii, 1962) pp. 146–7 (No. 78) and cf. p. 153 (No. 85). The former passage is translated by Galbraith, op. cit., pp. 39–40. See also Barlow, op. cit., pp. 125, 126.

'The abbots of these houses were for the future to divide the year among them, together with the administration of the sanctuaries and other ornaments of the altar. The abbot of Ely used to enter upon his period of ministration on the day of the Purification, at the beginning of February; and so the abbot himself, or whichever of the brothers he named, reverently and diligently acted in that office for four months, that is the third of the year; after which the others, mentioned above, in turn acted for the rest of the year.'

The use of the title 'chancellor' carries no significance in a twelfth-century source, but there is no need to doubt the general truth of the tradition. Such an arrangement (which, we are further told, lasted until the Norman Conquest[47]), whether we interpret it to mean that the three abbots or their deputies resided at court during their terms of office, or that the king's secretarial business was put out in turn to the three conveniently situated abbeys, is a substantial diminution of the generally accepted notion of a highly developed *scriptorium* within the household, staffed by royal clerks. Either interpretation would seem to fit the required conditions both of an early and simple stage in the development of royal bureaucracy and of the production of consistently uniform writs, and may also invite comparison with contemporary arrangements in Normandy where there is some indication that the abbey of Fécamp served at times as a ducal chancery.[48]

It is the vernacular sealed writ above all which has excited historians of Anglo-Saxon England in this present century and has led to an over-emphasis upon the developed efficiency of Old English government on the eve of the Norman Conquest. There is, of course, no doubt of the writ's importance, though one may hesitate to see it and its pendant seal as 'contributions to the civilisation of Western Europe scarcely less important than the Era of the Incarnation which was the discovery of

---

[47] '*donec Anglia sub Normannorum iugo misere depressa ex omni pristino spoliatur honore.*'
[48] Fauroux, *Recueil des Actes des Ducs de Normandie*, p. 43. Cf. p. 55 above. It may be added that Miss Harmer duly noted a 'family resemblance' among Anglo-Saxon writs in favour of the same house, op. cit., p. 57.

Englishmen of Bede's age'.[49] Immediately, it stands as an ingenious – though not entirely original[50] – Anglo-Saxon invention, and, more futuristically, as the *fons et origo* of all later and post-Conquest royal deeds and administrative instruments – charters, letters patent, letters close, and, later still, letters under the privy seal and signet. It was also to be exported to the Continent, though not, significantly, until after 1066 except to Scandinavia.[51] Short, sharp and to the point, relatively quick and easy to produce and easy also to carry, it was above all authenticated by the royal seal which, certainly in Edward the Confessor's reign and probably in Cnut's, was a two-faced pendant seal, and as such unique in Western Europe at that time.[52] But the earliest authentic writ (or rather, text of a writ, since the original document in this case does not survive) dates only from the reign of Ethelred II, and the earliest extant two-faced pendant seal is that of Edward the Confessor. Before those dates all is conjecture, and since it is not permissible to assume that earlier literary references to the king's *gewrit* and *insegel* imply his sealed writ, the sealed writ itself may well be only the invention of the early eleventh century.[53] Nor are we entitled to suppose that it was widely and commonly employed before 1066. It was used by the late Old English kings as a title deed, i.e. to announce the conveyance of land or privilege, though in this function it had by no means yet replaced the ancient diploma. It is difficult to find positive evidence of its use for general administrative purposes to convey the king's will to his officials,[54] though it can be argued that such writs, being

[49] Darlington, *History*, xxii (1937–8), p. 9; R. L. Poole, *Chronicles and Annals* (Oxford, 1926), p. 26.
[50] Cf. the Frankish mandate, sometimes sealed (though *en placard*); Harmer, op. cit., pp. 30–4. For the fundamental distinction between sealing to close and sealing open in the manner of the writ, see Barraclough, op. cit., p. 207.
[51] Ibid., pp. 194–5.
[52] For the seal, see the authorities cited in n. 33, p. 69 above for the writ.
[53] Barlow, op. cit., p. 128. Cf. Barraclough, op. cit., pp. 199 et seq.
[54] Amongst writs whose text has survived, it is possible to speak of some dealing with geld as 'administrative' writs, but in fact they are concerned with assessment and so really fall into the category of grants

ephemeral, have not survived. It is not safe, therefore, to make the Anglo-Saxon writ bear the great weight of government which is sometimes placed upon it; it is unlikely to have been the normal written link between the king and the provinces in the day-to-day business of administration. It is equally unlikely, therefore, to have done much to solve in England the great contemporary problem of remote control and local government, and nor was that problem especially well solved before the Conquest by the effective use of royal officials. The bishop had other things to attend to than secular administration; the great earls of pre-Conquest England had ceased to be, if indeed they ever were, mere royal officials; and the sheriff, the shire-reeve, was only partly the king's representative since he was also the deputy of the earl.[55]

Nearly sixty years ago F. M. Stenton wrote that the apparent unity of Anglo-Saxon England was 'very deceptive',[56] and it does not seem that the more recent concentration upon 'Administrative History' has greatly altered that conclusion. Furthermore, this concentration has tended to obscure the political facts of life in pre-Conquest England, which by themselves would seem to point unmistakably to a lack of unity which was to be disastrous. The Danelaw is the foremost amongst these facts. More than half of England to the north and east[57] had been settled to a greater or lesser extent by the

or privileges, for which reason they were kept by the grantee (see Harmer, op. cit., pp. 19, 32 and Nos. 15, 29, 66, 107). References in other sources to the king's *gewrit* and *insegel* cannot safely be translated as 'writ and seal' and may mean no more than 'message' and 'signet ring/token' (Barraclough, op. cit., pp. 199 et seq. and 207–8). A reference as late as *s.a.* 1051 to the king's *gewrit* and *insegel* for the election of a bishop may be acceptable, but such a writ would be more a kind of title deed to an office—on the analogy of thirteenth-century letters patent—than an administrative writ in the sense of a mandate to an official to do something (see Harmer, op. cit., Appendix IV, No. 6, pp. 542–3). Cf. Bishop and Chaplais' insistence on the primary function of the sealed writ as a title deed, op. cit., p. xi.

[55] W. A. Morris, *The Medieval English Sheriff* (Manchester, 1927), pp. 37–9. Cf. p. 248 below. For a striking reference to the bishop as 'Christ's sheriff' (by Wulfstan in his *Institutes of Polity*, pp. 144–5) see Barlow, op. cit., p. 97.

[56] *William the Conqueror* (1908), p. 9.

[57] See above p. 61 and the map at p. xv.

Danes of Alfred's day, and while the high density of Danish settlement in this great area has of late been questioned (though not disproved) there is no doubt of Scandinavian domination within it.[58] In consequence there remained deep differences, not eradicated by the reconquest of the Scandinavianised provinces by Alfred's successors,[59] between the resultant Danelaw and 'English England'[60], and not least at the fundamental level of law and custom, since Edgar had granted legal autonomy to the Danes.[61] In Normandy in the mid-eleventh century a unified law and custom was at least in the process of formation:[62] in England dichotomy remained. Nor does it seem possible net to see grave political implications in this social cleavage, especially in the context of renewed Scandinavian assaults as from 980, fulfilled by the Danish monarchy established in the person of Cnut and his two sons between 1016 and 1042, and lasting as a menace up to and beyond 1066. Especially, also, are the implications visible in the north, beyond the Humber.[63] Here, in ancient Northumbria, was the centre of Danish influence.[64] Here outright political independence was retained in the form of the Norse

[58] Thus P. H. Sawyer, 'The Density of the Danish Settlement in England', *Univ. of Birm. Hist. Journal*, vi (1957), pp. 16–17 – an article which attempts to challenge Stenton's views on the numbers and nature of the settlement (for which see F. M. Stenton, 'The Danes in England', *Proceedings British Academy*, xiii (1927), and 'The Scandinavian Colonies in England and Normandy', *Transactions Royal Historical Society*, (4), xxvii, 1945. See also Sawyer, *The Age of the Vikings* (London, 1962).
[59] Cf. H. R. Loyn, *Anglo-Saxon England and the Norman Conquest*, p. 51, 'For in spite of their proud military triumphs these English kings did not so much reconquer Scandinavianised England as absorb it.'
[60] 'The line of regional distinction which was all-important in eleventh-century England was that which separated Wessex and English Mercia, jointly, from the Danelaw' (Stenton, *Anglo-Saxon England*, p. 499).
[61] F. M. Stenton, *Anglo-Saxon England*, pp. 366, 498 et seq.; cf. *Proceedings British Academy*, xiii, 44–6.
[62] Above p. 59.
[63] See Dorothy Whitelock. 'The Dealings of the Kings of England with Northumbria in the Tenth and Eleventh Centuries', in *The Anglo-Saxons*, ed. P. Clemoes (London, 1959).
[64] 'The centre of Danish influence lay in the northern Danelaw', F. M. Stenton, *Anglo-Saxon England*, p. 512.

kingdom of York until 954 and the death of its last king, Eric Bloodaxe. Here, in an area larger than all Normandy,[65] the shire system of the rest of England faded out,[66] and much of it was regarded as outside the region covered even by the divided customary law of England.[67] Here there was little royal demesne, the kings of England seldom came, and the northern nobles, for their part, seldom attended the meetings of the *witan* in the south.[68] But if legitimate rulers seldom came, Swein Forkbeard of Denmark came and sailed up the Humber in 1013 to be at once accepted as king there and throughout the Danelaw, and Harold Hardrada of Norway endeavoured to follow his example in 1066,[69] as did Swein Estrithson thereafter.[70] In 1066, also, the Northumbrians at first refused to accept Harold Godwinson as king,[71] and in the previous year, the last year of the Old English state, they had rebelled against Tostig, their southern earl, and forced a reluctant king to banish him, his favourite.[72] In the general writing-up of Anglo-Saxon England which has taken place in recent years, 'Northumbrian separatism' has sometimes been questioned or denied,[73] but it seems at least that William the Conqueror was aware of it, and that it underlies the serious rebellions against his authority in Northumbria, his answering

---

[65] Stenton, *Proceedings British Academy*, xiii, 13.

[66] Above p. 69 and n. 34.

[67] Stenton, *Anglo-Saxon England*, p. 498.

[68] Ibid., p. 543; *Proceedings*, pp. 43–4.

[69] Stenton, *Anglo-Saxon England*, pp. 379–80, 580; below p. 155.

[70] Stenton, op. cit., p. 597; below p. 194.

[71] Stenton, op. cit., p. 573, and n. 1.

[72] Ibid., pp. 570–1 (where, it is argued, the rebellion shows 'the combination of strong provincial feeling with respect for the unity of England'). It is possible that among other offences Tostig had sought to alter the law of Northumbria and thus breach the autonomy granted by Edgar to the Danelaw. Florence of Worcester says the Northumbrians outlawed him 'and all who had prompted him to enact the oppressive law' (ed. Thorpe, i, 223). The *Anglo-Saxon Chronicle* (C) speaks of his 'lawless deeds', and says (D, E) that Harold in making peace with them 'renewed . . . the law of King Cnut' (ed. Whitelock, Douglas and Tucker, p. 138).

[73] See especially B. Wilkinson, 'Northumbrian Separatism in 1065 and 1066', *Bulletin John Rylands Library*, xxiii (1939).

devastation of the north, and also the imposition of the primacy of the See of Canterbury over that of York.[74]

The second phase of Scandinavian attacks, which culminated in the victory of Swein Forkbeard and the accession of Cnut his son as king in 1016, did not bring any new wave of settlement or migration comparable to the first, but it was the outright conquest of the whole country, it established a new Danish aristocracy which, combined with the settlements of the first phase, makes 'Anglo-Danish' rather than 'Anglo-Saxon' the appropriate description for the mixed society resulting, and it set up tensions and divisions scarcely allayed before the final catastrophe of 1066. No one reading the account, however inadequate,[75] of the political history of the Old English kingdom in the last century of its existence can fail to be aware that there was something very rotten in the state of England, and that the times were out of joint. In the first place it is worth emphasising how brief had been the tenth-century hegemony of the Wessex monarchy and the Golden Age of Edgar the Peaceable (959–79). National unity was finally achieved only in 954 with the death of Eric Bloodaxe, and in 980 the Vikings came again. After Edgar's day there was scarcely a succession to the throne which was not disputed,[76] the series only reaching its climax in the great con-

[74] For a positive near-contemporary statement to this effect, see *Hugh the Chantor, The History of the Church of York, 1066–1127*, ed. C. Johnson (London, 1961), p. 3. Cf. p. 254 below.

[75] The chronicle sources, especially, for this period of English history are not very good, and the common assumption that England is better served in this respect than Normandy will not bear close examination (cf. p. 24 nn. above). For the *Anglo-Saxon Chronicle*, see D. Whitelock in *English Historical Documents*, i, 109–16; Douglas, ibid, ii, 107–10; G. N. Garmonsway, the *Anglo-Saxon Chronicle* (London, 1953), pp. xv–xlviii; also the Introduction to *The Anglo-Saxon Chronicle*, ed. Whitelock, Douglas and Tucker (London, 1961). Cf. S. Körner, *The Battle of Hastings, England, and Europe 1035–1066* (Lund, 1964), pp. 1–46, one of whose conclusions is that the various versions of the Chronicle for the eleventh century are not independent of each other (p. 24).

[76] Not even that of Edward the Confessor in 1042 if we accept the story that his mother Emma supported the claim of Magnus of Norway. See Stenton, *Anglo-Saxon England*, p. 420 and A. Campbell's edition of the *Encomium Emmae Reginae* (Camden, 3rd Series, lxxii, 1949), pp. xxii,

flict of 1066. The unhappy reign of Ethelred 'Unraed' began with the dreadful murder at Corfe of his brother Edward the Martyr,[77] and thereafter is chiefly remarkable not only for unrelieved defeat, but also for the dark and spreading stain of treachery and *malaise* of which the turncoat careers of Eadric Streona, Wulfnoth and Thorkell the Tall are representative.[78] Total confusion followed the death of the triumphant Swein Forkbeard in 1014, with the exiled Ethelred received back into his former kingdom upon terms,[79] and his son, Edmund 'Ironside', established as lord of the northern Danelaw against his father's will, and ravaging the English shires of Cheshire, Staffordshire and Shropshire.[80] Edmund's subsequent heroic activity after Ethelred's death in 1016, though it bolstered the national pride of the anachronistic Freeman[81], achieved nothing except the division of the kingdom with Cnut,[82] a division rendered nugatory by his death which followed (30 November 1016). After all this it seems almost fitting that Emma of Normandy, Ethelred's widowed queen, then married Cnut, the conqueror of her husband, and disinherited her children by him, Edward, Alfred and Godgifu.[83] The strong-arm methods of the alien Cnut[84] brought political quiescence, but faction is very evident again in the disputed succession and brief reigns of his two immediate successors,

xlix, n. 4. For the *Encomium Emmae Reginae*, see Campbell's introduction to his edition, and Körner, *Battle of Hastings*, pp. 47–74.

[77] Stenton, op. cit., p. 368.

[78] See e.g. the references in Stenton, op. cit., pp. 376, 377, 378–9, 380, 382–3, 383–4, 387, 391, 392.

[79] An occasion 'of great constitutional interest as the first recorded pact between an English king and his subjects'. See Stenton, op. cit., pp. 380–1.

[80] Ibid., pp. 381–2, 384.

[81] E. A. Freeman, *The Norman Conquest*, i (1870), pp. 378 et seq.

[82] Wessex to Edmund and the whole country beyond the Thames to Cnut. See Stenton, op. cit., p. 387 and n. 2.

[83] Edward, the elder son, was the future Edward the Confessor; for his younger brother, Alfred, see below. Godgifu married Drogo of Mantes, and one of her sons was Ralph, the Norman earl of Hereford in the Confessor's reign. For Emma, see especially A. Campbell's Introduction to the *Encomium Emmae Reginae*, ut supra.

[84] For his executions and his earldoms see Stenton, op. cit., pp. 391, 392.

Harold 'Harefoot' (1035–37), his bastard by Aelgifu of Northampton, and Harthacnut (1037–42), his legitimate son by Emma, while the reign of the former is darkened by the murder of Alfred, son of Ethelred and Emma, which casts its shadow forward towards the Norman Conquest.[85] Nor did quiet times come in again with the restoration of the ancient line of Wessex kings in the person of Edward the Confessor in 1042. A weak king whatever else, and married to a queen he did not love, Edward allowed himself and his kingdom to be dominated first by earl Godwin and then by earl Harold, Godwin's son, and stands as the very antithesis of duke William in Normandy across the Channel, who dominated his new aristocracy by his excelling personality and achievements.[86] Godwin and his sons brought the kingdom to the very brink of civil war in 1051–2,[87] while in subsequent years, as tension again mounted and the question of the succession loomed larger in men's minds, Stenton has drawn attention to the dark sayings of the chroniclers which reflect the political uncertainty of the times.[88] 'We do not know for what reason it was brought about that he was not allowed to see [the face of?] his kinsman, king Edward', is the comment of the 'D' version of the Anglo-Saxon Chronicle on the mysterious but timely death of the aethling Edward, the long-exiled son of Edmund Ironside, brought to England from Hungary as the possible successor in 1057 – and one is left to guess.[89] In his account of the Northumbrian revolt of 1065 another contemporary writer, the author of the Life of King Edward, seems almost to employ a technique of the modern press in denying what is to be made known:[90] 'It was also said, if it be worthy of credence, that they had undertaken this madness against their earl [Tostig] at the artful persuasion of his brother, earl Harold (which heaven forbid!). But I dare not and would not

[85] For what little is known of Harold Harefoot and Harthacnut, see ibid., pp. 413–17 and Campbell's Introduction to the *Encomium Emmae*.
[86] See p. 57 above. For Edward see p. 106 below.
[87] Below. p. 119.
[88] Op. cit., p. 563.
[89] *Ibid.*, and *Anglo-Saxon Chronicle*, p. 133. Cf. p. 126 below.
[90] *Vita Edwardi, i.e. The Life of King Edward who rests at Westminster*, ed. F. Barlow (London, 1962), pp. 52–3.

believe that such a prince was guilty of this detestable wicked-
ness against his brother.'

It is impossible to discuss the political history of Edward
the Confessor's reign except in terms of the great earls who
occupy the centre of the stage or lurk within the wings. The
earldoms of pre-Conquest England,[91] though their origins may
be traced to the expanded ealdormanries of the expanded
Wessex monarchy of the tenth century, were essentially the
legacy of Cnut.[92] As king also of Denmark (and sometimes
Norway), and therefore of necessity a periodic absentee ruler
as well as an alien conqueror, he first divided his English kingdom into the four provinces of Wessex, East Anglia, Mercia
and Northumbria. By the time of his death in 1035 the political pattern of the next thirty years was set, with Siward, earl
of Northumbria, Leofric, earl of Mercia, and Godwin, earl of
Wessex. It is often rightly stressed that these great earldoms
were not near-autonomous constitutional units like the 'counties' of Normandy or Anjou or Maine into which the contemporary French kingdom was divided.[93] But in this, as in all
other matters, the meaningful comparison is not between the
kingdom of England and the vastly larger, and politically
fragmented, kingdom of France, but between England and the
feudal principalities into which France was divided – more
especially Normandy. This accepted, the contrast between
the closely controlled, closely related, counts of William the
Conqueror's duchy and the earls of king Edward's England is
very evident. Whatever the constitutional position of the
Anglo-Scandinavian earls – and by 1066 they were much
closer to hereditary magnates than royal officials[94] – there is

---

[91] See Stenton, op. cit., pp. 392–3, 408–10, 539–40; H. R. Loyn, *The
Norman Conquest* (London, 1962), pp. 67–70; P. H. Blair, *An Introduction
to Anglo-Saxon England* (Cambridge, 1959), p. 228.

[92] The word *iarl*/earl, which replaces the Anglo-Saxon *ealdorman*, is
itself Scandinavian.

[93] E.g. Loyn, op. cit., p. 68.

[94] Thus Leofric as earl of Mercia was succeeded by Aelfgar his son and by
Edwin his grandson. Harold (the second son because of Swein's exile and
death, see below) succeeded his father Godwin as earl of Wessex. Tostig's
appointment as earl of Northumbria (below) was made possible by the
youth of Waltheof, son and heir of the deceased Siward.

no doubt that politically they dominate the Confessor's reign, Nor can it be denied that the theme of the political history of the period is that of the continuous ascendancy of the house of Godwin to the point of swallowing the kingdom in 1066, and the rivalries and tensions thus engendered.

Godwin himself was a *parvenu*[95] who by some means won the favour of Cnut, who gave him his sister-in-law as wife, the earldom of Wessex, and made him one of his most intimate counsellors. There is little doubt of Godwin's responsibility, in the service of Harold Harefoot, for the brutal murder of the aethling Alfred in 1047,[96] and unscrupulous aggrandisement seems the most prominent characteristic of Freeman's most unlikely patriotic hero. By 1051, though king Edward did not like him,[97] he was the most prominent magnate in the realm and had established his house in a paramount position. His daughter, Edith, was married to the king. His own earldom of Wessex covered southern England from Cornwall to Kent. He had recently achieved the restoration of his eldest son, Swein, after the latter's double disgrace of first seducing an abbess and subsequently murdering earl Beorn his cousin,[98] to an earldom comprising Oxfordshire, Herefordshire, Gloucestershire, Somerset and Berkshire. His second son, Harold,

[95] Little is known of his origins, but he was probably the son of the Sussex thegn Wulfnoth who had betrayed king Ethelred (above, p. 78; Stenton, op. cit., p. 411).
[96] See Stenton, op. cit., p. 414–15 and cf. 416–17; C. Plummer, *Two of the Saxon Chronicles Parallel* (2 vols, Oxford, 1892, 1899), ii, 211–15; Campbell, *Encomium Emmae*, pp. lxiv–lxvii.
[97] Stenton, op. cit., pp. 419, 553; F. Barlow, 'Edward the Confessor's Early Life, Character and Attitudes', *E.H.R.*, lxxx, 238–9. The murder of Alfred and Edward's dislike of Scandinavians, especially Danes, are the chief reasons given. Barlow remarks that 'Essentially Godwin represented the Anglo-Danish, parvenu element in the nobility', He owed his position to Cnut, his wife was a Dane, most of his children were given Danish names, and he was uncle to Swein, King of Denmark. For the situation in 1051, see Stenton, op. cit., p. 553.
[98] Stenton, op. cit., pp. 423, 553. The 'C' version of the *Anglo-Saxon Chronicle s.a.* 1046 (ed. Whitelock, Douglas and Tucker, p. 109) relates, 'when he was on his way home [from Wales], he ordered the abbess of Leominster to be brought to him and kept her as long as it suited him, and then he let her go home'. For his murder of earl Beorn, see ibid., pp. 112–14, *s.a.* 1049.

was earl of East Anglia to which were added the shires of
Essex, Cambridge and Huntingdon. It occasions no surprise
to find that in the crisis of 1051, when Godwin and his sons
defied the king, the earls Leofric of Mercia and Siward of
Northumbria took Edward's side.[99] The crisis itself, 'the
English revolution of 1051',[100] evidently arising from the
political friction caused by Edward's Norman 'favourites' and,
already, the question of Norman succession to the throne,
began with Godwin's outright refusal to obey a royal command.[101] Though both sides raised armies, civil war was
averted, and Godwin and his family banished. The next year
they came back again by force of arms, and king Edward had
to make what terms he could. They included the banishment
of his friends, the restoration of the house of Godwin (except
for Swein),[102] and the recall of his queen, Edith, whom in 1051
he had packed off to the nunnery of Wherwell.

The death of earl Godwin which occurred in 1053 seems to
have reduced the political temperature, for Edward evidently
found the new generation of Tostig (whom he liked) and
Harold easier to work with, and, for a time, the house of
Godwin had no more than the single great earldom of Wessex
to which Harold had succeeded (Swein being dead in exile).[103]
Nevertheless, the subsequent rise of the earl of Wessex to
supremacy, albeit slow at first, is 'the most important fact in
the political history of England between 1053 and 1066'.[104] In
1055, on the death of earl Siward, Harold's younger brother

[99] For the events of 1051–2, see Stenton, op. cit., pp. 553 et seq.; F.
Barlow, *The English Church*, pp. 47–51, and *E.H.R.*, lxxx; below,
pp. 119 et seq.
[100] Stenton, op. cit., p. 553.
[101] Godwin was ordered, and refused, to harry Dover (within his earldom) as punishment for an affray between the men of that town and
count Eustace of Boulogne who was on a visit to the king.
[102] Swein was outlawed in 1051 when the rest of the family were
banished, and died, somewhat improbably, on a pilgrimage to Jerusalem.
[103] Of the shires formerly comprising Swein's earldom, Somerset and
Berkshire were added to Harold's Wessex: Oxfordshire and Herefordshire made an earldom for Ralph, king Edward's nephew and son of
Godgifu, Edward's sister, and Drogo of Mantes (cf. n. 83 p. 78 above).
[104] Stenton, op. cit., p. 564.

Tostig was appointed to the earldom of Northumbria.[105] In 1057, after the death of Leofric of Mercia and of the Norman earl Ralph of Hereford, king Edward's nephew,[106] Mercia passed to Aelfgar, Leofric's son, whose former earldom of East Anglia, together with Oxfordshire, formerly held by Ralph, were bestowed upon Gyrth, the fourth son of earl Godwin and Harold's brother. Not only this, but also a new earldom was created for another brother, Leofwine, out of the shires of Essex and Hertford, Middlesex and Buckingham, formerly held by Aelfgar, while Herefordshire, formerly held by Ralph, was added to Harold's own Wessex earldom. In circumstances such as these, though we know so few details of the politics of the time, earl Aelfgar must have felt himself increasingly isolated, surrounded and threatened. Banished once for treason in 1055,[107] he was banished again for an unknown cause in 1058. On both occasions he fought his way back again in arms and in alliance with the kingdom's enemies – with Gruffydd of Wales in 1055 and with Gruffydd and perhaps a great Norwegian fleet in 1058.[108] The historian narrating and assessing these events may have a certain exasperated sympathy with the contemporary chronicler who wrote, under the year 1058, 'It is tedious to relate fully how things went'.[109] Sir Frank Stenton's comment on the death of earl Aelfgar in 1062 is that it was 'one of the determining events of eleventh-century history', for he would never have agreed to Harold's succession to the throne on the death of the Confessor in

[105] Ibid., p. 562.

[106] For these arrangements, see ibid., p. 566.

[107] Florence of Worcester, i, 212, observes under the year 1055 that earl Aelfgar was *sine cul̦a*. Oleson suggests that both exiles were engineered by Harold to rid himself of rivals ('Edward the Confessor's Promise of the Throne to Duke William of Normandy', *E.H.R.*, lxxii (1957), p. 225).

[108] Stenton, op. cit., pp. 564–5, 566–7; J. E. Lloyd, *A History of Wales* (London, 1912), ii, 364–5, 369. The association of Aelfgar's restoration in 1058 with the visit of a Norwegian fleet to English waters in that year depends largely (though not entirely) upon Florence of Worcester (i, 217) who combines two separate notices of *Anglo-Saxon Chronicle* 'D' (p. 134), and is rejected by Körner, *The Battle of Hastings*, pp. 152–3.

[109] *Anglo-Saxon Chronicle*, 'D', p. 134.

1066.[110] As it was, Aelfgar was succeeded in Mercia by his young son Edwin, and when in 1065 the Northumbrians revolted against Tostig Godwinson it was to the rival house of Leofric that they turned in choosing Morcar, Edwin's brother, as their earl.[111] Tostig,[112] exiled, joined Harold Hardrada's invasion of England in 1066, and died with him at Stamford Bridge, slain by his brother Harold, newly crowned. As for the earls Edwin and Morcar, one may have for them a puzzled sympathy in their subsequent short careers. Small wonder that their actions in 1066 and after can scarcely be satisfactorily explained. They had no reason to support any of the three contenders for the English throne, and so, without policy or cause, they were ground down.

Had such political conditions and events prevailed and taken place in Normandy or in some other feudal state in France, it is difficult not to think that historians with anti-feudal tendencies would have dubbed them 'feudal anarchy' to mark their disapproval. The truth is that if ever there were 'over-mighty subjects' in England it was before the Norman Conquest and not after it. English, or Anglo-Scandinavian, society on the eve of 1066 was not feudal, and therefore lacked the centralising discipline which feudalism can provide. The fundamental explanation is that here ancient monarchy had survived, its powers unimpaired.[113] In consequence, whereas the post-Conquest Anglo-Norman kings of England had two sources of their strength, monarchical and feudal,[114] their Anglo-Scandinavian predecessors could draw only on the former. The modern obsession with continuity at and over 1066 has occasioned a revival of the case for Anglo-Saxon feudalism as against the established position, set out by F. M. Stenton and J. H. Round, that feudalism in England owes its origins to the Normans.[115] The best short answer to the former

[110] Op. cit., p. 567.
[111] For the Northumbrian revolt, see ibid., pp. 570–1; Wilkinson, *Bulletin John Rylands Library*, xxiii (1939). Cf. pp. 75–6 above.
[112] For what follows, see also pp. 142–3 below.
[113] Above p. 161.
[114] Below p. 241.
[115] For the established view, see especially F. M. Stenton, *The First Century of English Feudalism* (Oxford, 1932), Chapter 4, and J. H.

case is the magisterial comment of R. R. Darlington: 'the arguments are the old ones which we had thought dead, and resurrection does not make them more convincing'.[116] To it should be added F. M. Stenton's summarising statement: 'It is turning a useful term into a mere abstraction to apply the adjective 'feudal' to a society which had never adopted the private fortress nor developed the art of fighting on horseback, which had no real conception of the speciali-sation of service, and allowed innumerable landowners of position to go with their land to whatever lords they would'.[117]

'Feudalism' is a word difficult to define because, having been invented by writers of a later age to describe a state of affairs already past, it tends to mean different things to different people.[118] Sometimes, and in France perhaps especi-ally, the word is used so widely as to be almost a synonym for 'medieval'.[119] In France, of course, they have no doubts that they were feudal in the mid-eleventh century, and before and after, but in less certain and less happy lands like England some closer definition is desirable before we can decide whether or not society was feudal. The most recent historian of English feudalism has offered the following formula as being generally acceptable, namely that feudalism is an organisation of society 'based on the holding of a fief, usually a unit of land, in return for a stipulated honourable service, normally military, with a relationship of homage and fealty

Round, 'The Introduction of Knight Service into England', reprinted in *Feudal England* (London, 1909). For Anglo-Saxon feudalism see especially Eric John, *Land Tenure in Early England* (Leicester, 1960), Chapter 8, and Marjory Hollings, 'The Survival of the Five Hide Unit in the Western Midlands', *E.H.R.*, lxiii (1948). The former draws upon the latter, and both upon F. W. Maitland, *Domesday Book and Beyond* (Cambridge, 1897).

[116] *The Norman Conquest* (Creighton Lecture, London 1963), p. 24.
[117] Stenton, op. cit., p. 215.
[118] In the English language, according to the *New English Dictionary*, the word 'feudal' first appears in 1639 in the works of Spelman, 'feudal system' appears in 1776 in the works of Adam Smith, and for 'feudalism' we have to wait until 1839.
[119] This is the case, for example, in Marc Bloch's classic work *Feudal Society* (London, 1961).

existing between the grantee and the grantor'.[120] Academically this definition will suffice, and it has the merit of placing the emphasis where it is needed most, that is, upon the upper levels of society. The condition of the peasantry is strictly irrelevant to any argument about the existence of feudalism, and so also is the fact that manorialisation was proceeding apace in pre-Conquest England. Feudal society no doubt rested largely upon the broad backs of the peasantry, but it also prospered with other kinds of economic activity, including trade and industry, and in neither respect does it thus differ from other forms of society, earlier and later. What matters is the *ethos* and the *mores* of the ruling classes, their legal and customary relations with each other, the way they held their lands, the services, especially the military services, which they rendered, and to whom they rendered them. Feudalism is about lords and lordship,[121] more especially about military and tenurial lordship, and the characteristic signs and products of feudal society are knights and castles. Hence the controversy about the origins of English feudalism is conducted, quite properly, chiefly in terms of land-holding and military service.

There was, of course, lordship in Anglo-Saxon England. It appears clearly in the laws and its aristocratic concepts permeate the literature of the times.[122] But this is ancient, Germanic, personal lordship, derived ultimately from the *comitatus* or war-band mentioned as early as Tacitus,[123] and the relationship of a military retainer to his war-leader. Such lordship, common to all Germanic peoples, is one of the basic elements from which feudal lordship developed on the Continent.[124] But in England it evidently had not so developed. The full feudal commendation whereby a man became the vassal of the lord consisted of three parts, the oath of fealty, the act of homage – i.e. the *immixtio manuum* whereby the

[120] C. Warren Hollister, *The Military Organisation of Norman England,* (Oxford, 1965), p. 11, n. 3.
[121] Cf. p. 43 above.
[122] See especially D. Whitelock, *The Beginnings of English Society,* (London, 1952) Chapter II.
[123] *De Situ, Moribus et Populis Germaniae,* c. 13 (extract in Stubbs, *Select Charters,* 9th. edition, p. 62).
[124] F. L. Ganshof, *Feudalism* (London, 1952), p. 4.

would-be vassal, placing his hands between those of the lord-to-be, became his man – and, finally, investiture of the vassal with his fief by the lord.[125] Combined, they made the strongest bond which contemporary society could invent. Few undertakings are more desirable than a thorough study of Old English commendation, but meanwhile most historians are agreed that the bond was fragile, in law if not in aristocratic sentiment.[126] The Old English 'hold-oath' was the rough equivalent of the feudal oath of fealty,[127] and there was a ceremony of 'bowing' which may have been the equivalent of homage, and may have included the *immixtio manuum*.[128] But the tie thus created was personal, not tenurial, and the ceremony of commendation seems never to have been combined with a formal act of investiture to root it in the soil. There were many landless knights in Normandy who were thus as yet bound only personally to their lords, but the fiefs of their aspirations and expectations were unknown in England before 1066, and there can have been few men of substance left in Normandy on the eve of the Conquest who, like their innumerable Anglo-Scandinavian counterparts, were free, in the phraseology of Domesday Book, to go with their land to whatever lords they would.[129] Few facts are more revealing of the Norman introduction of feudalism into England than the formation after the Conquest of feudal 'honours', whereby men who had formerly been only personally commended to the predecessors [*antecessores*] of the new Norman and French lords became, with their lands and their descendants, permanently locked in the tenurial, territorial and jurisdictional unit of the lord's honour.[130]

---

[125] Ibid., pp. 64 ff., 110–12.
[126] Stenton, *Anglo-Saxon England*, p. 484; J. E. A. Jolliffe, *Constitutional History of Medieval England*, p. 153; B. Dodwell, 'East Anglian Commendation', *E.H.R.*, lxiii, 305, 306.
[127] The seeming absence of any Anglo-Saxon noun as the equivalent of the Latin, feudal *fidelis* is worth noting (see Harmer, *Anglo-Saxon Writs*, p. 54).
[128] Dodwell, op. cit., p. 305, but cf. Jolliffe, op. cit., pp. 79–80.
[129] Stenton, op. cit., pp. 482–4. For feudal society in pre-Conquest Normandy, see pp. 39–49 above.
[130] Cf. Jolliffe, op. cit., pp. 140–3, and see also p. 240 below.

Three kinds of land-holding are known in pre-Conquest England, folk-land, book-land and *laen* or leasehold. Whatever the precise implications of the first two, no one could call them feudal.[131] The third, however, is at least a form of dependent tenure, and hence the attention which it receives from historians of Old English society. About the Anglo-Saxon lease there is no mystery, for like a modern lease it conveyed property for a specific period (usually for a term of lives, usually three) in return for specified services or rents. Both lease and fief could be called *beneficium*,[132] and they have this in common, that they enabled a landowner both to eat his cake and keep it, to grant out land without ultimate loss of right and lordship. With this, however, the similarity ceases. In the beginning the fief was not hereditary,[133] and may not have become fully so in Normandy by 1066, but the Anglo-Saxon compromise of a term of lives is seldom found in connection with it. The lease, unlike the fief, does not necessarily involve the homage and fealty of the tenant to the lord,[134] nor jurisdiction by the latter over the former. Above all, the lease does not involve military service by the lessee to the lessor, still less knight-service which is the *raison d'être* of the *fief de haubert* in Normandy and elsewhere in France. In all the modern controversy over the condition of Old English society on the eve of the Norman Conquest perhaps the most telling point is the aphorism of J. E. A. Jolliffe, 'because the English had not the fee, they also had not feudalism'.[135]

In recent years the argument for the existence of both the fief and feudalism in the pre-Conquest bishopric of Worcester, and more particularly in the bishop's liberty or franchise of Oswaldslow, has been revived.[136] Even if the case were proved, it would be reckless to generalise from the particular and con-

---

[131] A convenient summary of Anglo-Saxon land tenure will be found in H. R. Loyn, *Anglo-Saxon England and the Norman Conquest*, pp. 170 et seq.
[132] Cf. Ganshof, op. cit., p. 96.
[133] Ibid., p. 119.
[134] Dodwell, op. cit., pp. 293–4.
[135] Jolliffe, op. cit., p. 78.
[136] For the works of Eric John and Marjory Hollings, and of Maitland which lies behind them, see n. 115 p. 84 above.

clude that Old English society as a whole was feudal before the Norman Conquest, but in fact the case presented carries no conviction. At the outset it is worth remarking that the Western Midlands, including Oswaldslow, were and remained one of the most conservative parts of England,[137] and are thus unlikely to have been in the van of English social development. The triple hundred of Oswaldslow, granted by king Edgar to St. Oswald bishop of Worcester in 964, formed a great ecclesiastical liberty, comprising three hundreds assessed at three hundred hides.[138] Over it the bishops thereafter exercised delegated royal rights and acted on the king's behalf in military matters as in others. The public burdens and common obligations of free subjects to the king, including the *trimoda necessitas* of bridge-building, fortress-work and military service in the fyrd, lay upon Oswaldslow as they lay upon all land of England,[139] but here the difference was that the bishop was responsible as the king's representative for their exaction and organisation, and in consequence could be called the *archiductor* of the military force raised from his liberty.[140] Within Oswaldslow and without, bishop Oswald, with his predecessors and successors,[141] granted out land by leasehold tenure, but these *laen*-lands were no more fiefs than their holders were knights, and the Domesday commissioners who inquired into the tenures of Oswaldslow in 1086 after the Conquest, state in their return that they are not fiefs and cannot be made into fiefs without the bishop's permission – 'nor may

[137] Cf. J. O. Prestwich, 'Anglo-Norman Feudalism and the Problem of Continuity', *Past and Present*, No. 26, 1963, p. 44.

[138] For the hundred, a sub-division of the shire, see p. 69 above. For the hide, at this date the unit of assessment for public burdens and the geld, see below p. 91. It appears to have been originally the amount of land reckoned to support a peasant household.

[139] Cf. p. 64 above; for fyrd-service, see below p. 91.

[140] W. de G. Birch, *Cartularium Saxonicum* (3 vols., London, 1885–93), 1136; printed in Heming's *Chartularium Ecclesiae Wigornensis* (ed. T. Hearne, 2 vols., Oxford, 1723), i, 292, and cited by Hollings, op. cit., p. 470.

[141] Oswald's leases are only part of a series extending from the ninth to the eleventh centuries; see N. R. Ker, 'Hemming's Cartulary: a description of the two Worcester cartularies in Cotton Tiberias A. xiii', in *Studies in Medieval History presented to F. M. Powicke* (Oxford, 1948), p. 69.

he [the tenant] retain the land by usurping hereditary right, nor claim it as his fee except according to the will of the bishop and according to the agreement he made with the bishop'.[142] The surviving leases themselves are not in fact very informative, but if they are read in conjunction with Oswald's memorandum to king Edgar on the subject, and the Domesday *cartula* already cited, it is evident that service is involved at two levels: there are those miscellaneous services, non-military in kind, which the tenants owe to the bishop as landlord in return for the land held of him and as a condition of their tenure, and there are those royal services, the common obligations of bridge-work, borough-work and fyrd service, assessed upon their land as upon all land, and owed only to the bishop as the deputy of the king.[143] The essential feature of the feudal *fief de haubert*, the military service of a knight owed personally to the lord of the fee by the tenant who is his

[142] Hemming's *Chartularium*, i, 287; translated and cited by Eric John, op. cit., p. 143.

[143] Leases, memorandum and *cartula* will all be found in Hemming's *Chartularium*, the memorandum of St. Oswald (Birch, *Cart. Sax.*, 1136) at p. 292. Thus the memorandum states that 'either royal or episcopal service is to be done always at the will and command of the *archiductor* who rules the see, on account of the benefice which has been loaned to them. Let them do this with all humility and submission according to the bishop's will and the amount of land which each possesses' (Hemming's *Chartularium*, i, 294; trans. John, op. cit., p. 146), and the Domesday *cartula* of 1086 states that the bishop has within Oswaldslow *et regis servitium, et suum* (Hemming, i, 287). For the miscellaneous services owed by the tenants to the bishop as landlord and listed in the memorandum, see Stenton, *First Century . . .*, pp. 122 ff. As for military service, in the lease for three lives granted by bishop Ealdred (1044–62) to Wulfgeat, for example (printed and translated by A. J. Robertson, *Anglo-Saxon Charters*, Cambridge, 1939, No. cxi; cited by John, op. cit., p. 147, and by Hollings, op. cit., p. 467), it is 'at the king's summons' that 'the holder shall discharge the obligations on these 1½ hides at the rate of one [hide]' – such obligations presumably including fyrd service, though this is not specifically mentioned (cf. ibid., No. cxii, where the obligations are the *trimoda necessitas* plus church dues). Similarly the military service by land and sea (*expeditio terra marique*) which the Danish thegn Simund was to perform for the church of Worcester in return for the land which his lord earl Leofric compelled prior Aethelwine (c. 1040–c. 1055) to grant him for life, was clearly fyrd service. (Hemming, *Chartularium*, i, 264–5.)

military vassal, is absent. Furthermore, a totally unfeudal note is struck with the realisation that this royal military service is infantry service if the fyrd went by land and naval service in the bishop's ship if it went by sea.[144] With the 'shipful' of Oswaldslow and others like it we are a far cry indeed from those feudal contingents of heavily armed, carefully mounted and thoroughly trained knights who formed the *corps d'élite* of contemporary French armies, and who, launched devastatingly from the duchy of Normandy, were to play the leading role in the Norman conquests of England, southern Italy, Sicily and Antioch, and whose exploits filled the known world.

While many of the details of its organisation remain obscure,[145] the truth is that the military system of Anglo-Scandinavian England was not feudal but national, and, as such, like the Old English kingdom itself, pre-feudal and surviving from an earlier age. Its basis was the ancient, Germanic obligation upon all free men for military service to the king,[146] though in process of time, since early law finds it difficult to deal with the individual, this obligation came to lie upon the land and was assessed from above downwards upon the hide – the hide being originally, as Bede tells us, the amount of land reckoned sufficient to support a peasant household, but by the eleventh century the normal unit of assessment for public burdens and taxation. In this way military service in the fyrd or national levy had become one of the three royal rights and

---

[144] For Oswaldslow as a 'shipful', see John, op. cit., pp. 119 ff., and for the sea-fyrd see p. 192 below.

[145] 'No matter with which we have to deal is darker than the constitution of the English army on the eve of its defeat.' Thus Maitland (*Domesday Book and Beyond*, Cambridge, 1897, p. 156), whose sentiment is echoed by the latest historian of the subject, C. Warren Hollister – 'the reader should be warned that the whole subject of Anglo-Saxon military organisation is notoriously difficult and obscure, and that few if any conclusions can be reached that are much more than tentative' (*The Military Organisation of Norman England*, p. 14).

[146] Thus Ine's Laws, c. 51, 'If a "gesithcund" man owning land neglect the "fyrd", let him pay cxx, shillings and forfeit his land; one not owning land, lx shillings; a ceorlish man, xxx shillings, as "fyrdwite" ' (Stubbs, *Select Charters*, 9th edition, p. 68). Cf. Ethelred, c. 28, and Cnut, cc. 12, 15 (ibid., p. 86).

common obligations – of borough-work and bridge-work and fyrd service – which lay upon all the land of England, no matter whoever held it or of whomsoever held, and assessed upon a uniform pattern. Though both were reinforced by mercenaries, a national system such as this differed as chalk from cheese from the feudal military system of Normandy and post-Conquest England, wherein military service was owed by a vassal to his lord, who might or might not be the ruler, and was assessed by a heterogeneous series of arbitrary personal bargains between lord and tenant upon the fief and honour.[147] By comparison with this essential difference, the details of the Old English military organisation scarcely matter for our present purposes.[148] It seems clear that at some period, to produce better troops, the universal obligation had been reduced from one man for every hide to one man from a group of hides, and also that in certain districts fyrd service by land could take an alternative form of service by sea, hundreds being grouped together into a 'ship-soke' to provide a ship and its complement, like the triple hundred of Oswaldslow assessed at 300 hides.[149] Differences of opinion exist whether the so-called 'Select Fyrd' obtained from the reduced assessment replaced, or was an alternative to, the older, unselective 'Great Fyrd', and whether a reduced assessment of one man for every five hides (the so-called 'five-hide system')

[147] Cf. pp. 39–43 above and pp. 216–33 below.
[148] For what follows see F. M. Stenton, *Anglo-Saxon England*, pp. 286–8, 575, and *First Century of English Feudalism*, especially Chapter IV; C. W. Hollister, *The Military Organisation of Norman England*, pp. 14–16, where the conclusions of his detailed study of the subject (*Anglo-Saxon Military Institutions*) are usefully summarised. Cf. Marjory Hollings, 'The Survival of the Five Hide Unit in the Western Midlands', *E.H.R.*, lxiii (1948); Eric John, *Land Tenure in Early England*, especially Chapter 8; and J. O. Prestwich, 'Anglo-Norman Feudalism and the Problem of Continuity', *Past and Present*, No. 26 (1963).
[149] Cf. p. 91 above. For naval service in pre-Conquest England, see Stenton, *Anglo-Saxon England*, pp. 424–6; and Hollister, *Anglo-Saxon Military Obligations*, Chapter VI. In addition to the force provided by fyrd service, there was from 1012 a permanent nucleus of royal ships manned by paid professionals, until these were disbanded by Edward the Confessor in 1049–50 and a number of ships provided by specific arrangement with certain ports (the probable origin of the later Cinque Port organisation).

such as prevailed in Berkshire[150] was or was not universal throughout hidated England.[151] There is disagreement also whether the Old English thegn served under the common obligation of fyrd service, or whether this fell only upon the free peasant or ceorl, leaving the thegn to serve in response to a personal summons and as an honourable duty arising from his rank and status. In any case, the ancient, Germanic, national system of military service evidently survived in full working-order in pre-Conquest England, whereas in Normandy and elsewhere in France it had been reduced to the subsidiary and shadowy role of the *arrière-ban*,[152] and there the main weight of military duty was borne upon the willing backs of enfeoffed knights, stipendiary knights and mercenaries. There were mercenaries in the Old English kingdom also, and the fyrd was supplemented, stiffened and doubtless led by the hearth-troops, the thegns and housecarls of the king and other magnates, of whom the housecarls at least were semi-professional and well-trained warriors.[153] But the analogy with feudal society can be pressed no further. Neither thegns nor housecarls held fiefs requiring military service, nor served their lords in any real sense in return for land or as a condition

[150] The well-known entry in the Berkshire Domesday runs as follows: 'If the king sent an army anywhere, only one soldier [*miles*] went from five hides, and four shillings were given him from each hide as subsistence and wages for two months' (*Domesday Book*, i, 56 b).

[151] The five-hide system cannot possibly have applied to all England in the eleventh century since the hide itself was not then universal. In the northern Danelaw the ploughland or carucate took the place of the hide and it has been suggested that here a rate of one warrior from six carucates prevailed. In East Anglia there was no uniform type of peasant holding (see Stenton, *Anglo-Saxon England*, p. 575; Hollister, *Military Organisation of Norman England*, p. 15).

[152] Cf. p. 22 above. For the survival of armies of free peasants in Germany as in pre-Conquest England, see P. Guilhiermoz, *Essai sur l'origine de la noblesse en France au Moyen Age* (Paris, 1902), p. 457.

[153] For housecarls and hearth-troops see especially Hollister, *Anglo-Saxon Military Institutions*, Chapter I and p. 25; Stenton, *Anglo-Saxon England*, pp. 406, 424, 574, and *First Century*, pp. 119–21; H. R. Loyn, *The Norman Conquest*, p. 77. It is worth noting that there seem to be no references to any hearth-troop of Edward the Confessor (Loyn, loc. cit.), who abolished the 'heregeld' for their maintenance in 1051 (Stenton, op. cit., p. 425; cf. above p. 64, n. 14).

of their tenure, and, above all, when they fought they fought on foot, after the ancient manner.

In the beginning the Teutonic races, including the Angles, Saxons and Jutes in England, and the Franks in Gaul, fought on foot, and it is agreed that on the continent of Europe the fundamental factor in the origin and development of feudal society was the adoption of heavy cavalry by the Franks from the mid-eighth century, and the consequent demand for mounted retainers, expensively equipped and elaborately trained to fight on horseback.[154] Hence the appearance and the increasing specialisation of knights as heavy cavalrymen, their growing dominance in warfare and society, and hence the fiefs granted to these retainers by their lords for their maintenance and support. It is not surprising, therefore, that in recent years, when the arguments for pre-Conquest English feudalism have been revived, that the attempt has been made to prove that the Anglo-Saxons also used cavalry in the eleventh century, and that Anglo-Saxon thegns, or Scandinavian housecarls, were indistinguishable from knights.[155] The point is an important one, for J. E. A. Jolliffe's dictum could well be adapted to read that 'because the English had not the knight, they also had not feudalism'.[156] Evidence for Anglo-Saxon or Anglo-Scandinavian cavalry is either null or void. That the former, or at least the thegns among them, used horses on the march, and in this were copied

[154] See especially F. Lot, *L'art militaire et les armées au moyen âge en Europe et dans le proche Orient* (2 vols., Paris, 1946), i, 92 et seq.; P. Guilhiermoz, *Essai sur l'origine de la noblesse en France au moyen âge* (Paris, 1902), pp. 450 et seq.; Lynn White, Jr., *Medieval Technology and Social Change* (Oxford, 1962), Chapter I; D. J. A. Ross, 'L'originalité de "Turoldus": le maniement de lance', *Cahiers de Civilisation Médiévale*, vi (1963).

[155] Richard Glover's argument that the pre-Conquest English army could use cavalry when it wished, and that it was at least as good as, or rather, no worse than the Norman army ('English Warfare in 1066', *E.H.R.*, lxvii, 1952) will not stand up to detailed examination. A recent, though somewhat indecisive, discussion of the whole question of pre-Conquest English cavalry will be found in Hollister, *Anglo-Saxon Military Institutions*, pp. 134 et seq. Both writers see the housecarls as the most likely candidates.

[156] Cf. p. 88 above.

by the Danes in the ninth century, was shown by Clapham many years ago, and there is little doubt that this, and only this, is the interpretation of literary references in the eleventh century and earlier to horsed armies (*equestres exercitus*).[157] There is abundant evidence to show that Harold's forces dismounted to fight at Hastings, where no English cavalry took part, nor is this instance to be explained away by special pleading,[158] nor does it stand alone. At the battle of Maldon in 991, ealdorman Brithnoth did as evidently Harold did at Hastings in 1066[159] – 'Then he bade each warrior leave his horse, drive it afar and go forth on foot, and trust to his hands and to his good intent.' Brithnoth himself rode up and down the ranks to counsel and array his men, and then 'he alighted among the people where it pleased him best, where he knew his bodyguard to be most loyal'. Both sides, English and Dane, then fought it out on foot, the East Saxons forming a shield wall as their successors did at Hastings. The Anglo-Saxons had no cause to change their time-honoured infantry habits in the Danish wars because their adversaries also fought on foot. The *Encomium Emmae Reginae*, for example, describes Swein's army landing in England in 1013 and preparing to fight on foot, makes it clear that Cnut's army for his invasion

[157] J. H. Clapham, 'The Horsing of the Danes', *E.H.R.*, xxv (1910). For references to *equester exercitus* and the like, see e.g. Florence of Worcester, i, 212 (1054), 221 and 222 (1063), 225 (1066). The well-known passage in the *Anglo-Saxon Chronicle* (p. 96) under the year 1016 (C, D, E), 'And the Danish army fled before him [king Edmund] with their horses into Sheppey. The king killed as many of them as he could overtake', used by Glover as evidence of Anglo-Saxon cavalry, seems a remarkably cumbersome way to describe cavalry in action. No one has yet seriously argued for English cavalry in king Alfred's day, but Florence of Worcester relates (i, 93) how in 876 the Danes broke the treaty which Alfred had made with them and *omnes equites quos rex habebat occidit*. The significance of this sort of thing is nicely brought out by the same author's description of an action by Danes from England against the Franks in Gaul, *finitoque proelio, Pagani, equis inventis, equites facti sunt* (i, 97–8).
[158] Glover, op. cit. For Hastings, see below, pp. 163–74.
[159] For what follows see 'The Song of Maldon'. The translation used here will be found in D. Whitelock, *English Historical Documents*, i, 293. A superb representation of Harold armed and mounted before Hastings appears on the Bayeux Tapestry (Phaidon Press, ed. F. M. Stenton, Pl. 58).

in 1015 was an infantry force, and specifically calls Ashingdon
in 1016 a severe infantry battle.[160] The only positive evidence
for the accustomed use of pre-Conquest English cavalry comes
from the description of Stamford Bridge (1066) in the un-
acceptable saga source of Snorre Sturlason,[161] which was compiled only in the thirteenth century, commits the stark an-
achronism of referring to barded horses, and leaves the alarm-
ing impression that its author is giving a garbled version of
Hastings with the English in the role of the Normans and
Harold Hardrada of Norway playing the part of Harold of
England.[162] At Hastings on the Bayeux Tapestry none of the
English wear spurs in action, many, including the best armed
thegns and housecarls, bear the round shield of infantrymen,
and many, including Harold himself, wield the infantry
weapon of the axe, long since and necessarily abandoned by
the habitually mounted Frankish and Norman knights.[163]
William of Malmesbury, writing in about 1125, thought that
duke William had taken earl Harold on the Breton expedition
of 1064 to show off Norman armament and 'that he might
perceive how far preferable was the Norman sword to the
English battle-axe'.[164] And if, as seems most likely, the well-
known scene on the Bayeux Tapestry, wherein duke William
confers arms on Harold after the same Breton expedition, re-

[160] Ed. A. Campbell (Camden Third Series, lxxii, Royal Historical
Society, London, 1949), pp. 13, 21, 27.
[161] Snorre Sturlason, *The Heimskringla or the Sagas of the Norse Kings*,
ed. R. B. Anderson, iv (London, 1889), 41 ff. The armoured horses
appear at p. 44. For Stamford Bridge, see p. 157 below.
[162] A point noticed by both Freeman (*Norman Conquest,* iii, 720) and
Oman (*Art of War in the Middle Ages*, London, 1924, i, 150–1).
[163] For round shields borne by English soldiers who are evidently among
the élite, see *The Bayeux Tapestry* (ed. Stenton) Pls. 64–5 and 71, cf. 70,
72. For battle-axes wielded by the English, see Pls. 62–3, 64, 65, 66, 67,
70, 71–2. The scene in which Harold, on foot with an axe, is cut down by
a mounted Norman with a sword (Pl. 72) may remind us of William of
Malmesbury's comment on the Breton expedition of 1064 (below).
Glover's implication that the axe was used by the Normans (op. cit.,
p. 4) is unwarranted; the only 'Norman' axe on the Tapestry is borne
ceremoniously by count Guy of Ponthieu, who was not in any case a
Norman. (Pl. 12.)
[164] *Gesta Regum* (Rolls Series, ed. W. Stubbs, London 1889), ii, 293. For
the occasion, see p. 128 below.

presents the ceremony of knighting,[165] there is deep significance for the condition of Old English society in the implication
that the great earl, the leading subject in the English realm,
was not a knight before. We do not meet in English sources
any pre-Conquest cult of knighthood, such as there was in
Normandy,[166] because there were no English knights, and in
England the very word '*miles*' does not harden into the technical meaning of 'knight' until the early twelfth century, a
hundred years later than in Normandy and France.[167] One
small change, also, brought in by the Norman Conquest may
be anticipated at this point: whereas before 1066 the royal seal
shows on both sides the king enthroned in majesty, after 1066,
and for the rest of the Middle Ages and beyond, one side
shows the king armed and mounted as a knight.[168] There is a
ring of truth in the account, found in Florence of Worcester
and the Anglo-Saxon Chronicle, of an English discomfiture by
the Welsh in 1055 because the Norman earl Ralph of Hereford,
king Edward's nephew, had ordered his native forces 'to fight
on horses contrary to their custom'.[169] It has been argued[170]
that this incident has no general significance because it relates
to the Welsh Marches, naturally unsuitable for cavalry. But in
fact Florence states that the engagement took place near Leominster, which nowadays looks like excellent cavalry country,
and in any case the Normans after 1066 were to ride triumphantly through the Marches. In the mid-twentieth century
to put untrained infantry into tanks would be to invite not

---

[165] Pl. 27. Wace, it should be noted, thus interpreted the incident
(*Roman de Rou*, ed. Andresen, ii, 372, 11. 8619–20). Cf. Freeman,
Norman Conquest, iii (1869), p. 228; Round, *Feudal England*, p. 385.
Cf. Glover's contrary interpretation of Harold's exploits on the Breton
expedition, op. cit., p.8

[166] See p. 46 above.

[167] See Hollister, *Military Organisation of Norman England*, pp. 115–16;
K. J. Hollyman, *Le Développement du Vocabulaire féodal en France
pendant le haut moyen âge* (Paris, 1957), pp. 129–34; Lynn White,
Medieval Technology and Social Change, p. 30 and n. 5.

[168] A. Wyon, *The Great Seals of England* (London, 1887), pp. 3–7 and
Pls. I and II.

[169] *Anglos contra morem in equis pugnare jussit* (i, 213). Cf. *Anglo-Saxon
Chronicle* ('C', *s.a.* 1055), 'before any spear had been thrown the English
army fled because they were on horseback'.

[170] Glover, op. cit., pp. 7–8.

victory but chaos, and the alleged modern habit of the English race of continuing to fight the last war well into the next was much in evidence at Hastings in 1066.

If, as they are, knights and castles are the characteristic manifestations of feudalism, then it is of further significance for the true nature of Old English society that there were no native castles in pre-Conquest England as there were no native knights. Castles, whatever reservations of sovereignty may have been kept by strong rulers like the dukes of Normandy and Norman kings of England, were the private and residential fortresses of lords, the symbol and substance of feudal lordship.[171] The only castles known to have existed in England before 1066 are Hereford, Ewyas Harold and Richard's Castle, all in Herefordshire, and probably Clavering in Essex, each of which was raised by a Norman or French lord already here in king Edward's day.[172] Old English fortification, like the rest of Old English military organisation, was national not feudal, a national system of defence, organised from the top downwards, consisting of royal boroughs, which were communal not private and residential fortresses – a system begun and carried through by Alfred and his successors against the Danes and for the reconquest of the Danelaw, and probably neglected as a system by 1066.[173] Ordericus Vitalis gives the lack of castles in England as one reason for the success of the Norman Conquest,[174] and without doubt the Conquest in the

[171] Cf. pp. 43–5, above. For homage rendered in eighteenth-century France 'à cause de la motte', and for the motte of the early castle as 'le symbole de la seigneurie', see Ph. Siguret in Château-Gaillard, Etudes de Castellologie européenne, I, 1964, p. 135, n. 4. Cf. R. Ritter, Châteaux, Donjons et Places Fortes. . . . (Paris, 1953), p. 25.

[172] See p. 116 below.

[173] Pending research, both archaeological and other, into the origins of English castles, should throw light backwards upon the pre-Conquest borough as well as forwards upon the Anglo-Norman castles.

[174] Ed. Le Prévost, ii, 184. 'Munitiones enim (quas castella Galli nuncupant) Anglicis provinciis paucissimae fuerant; et ob hoc Angli, licet bellicosi fuerint et audaces, ad resistendum tamen inimicis extiterant debiliores – For the fortresses (which the Gauls call castles) had been very few in the English provinces; and on this account the English, although warlike and courageous, had nevertheless shown themselves too weak to withstand their enemies.'

event was achieved and made permanent by a castle-building programme the like of which can seldom if ever have been seen.[175] Since warfare in feudal Europe in the eleventh century was dominated by knights and castles, it would seem that the military capacity of pre-Conquest England has been as over-estimated in recent years as other aspects of Old English achievement.

There was much that was good in pre-Conquest England, and much likely to be particularly attractive to the minds of modern Englishmen – antiquity, a certain proud insularity and, by the standards of the age, the existence of a national monarchy and state. The kingdom also was rich, its wealth, indeed, being part of its attraction to invaders whether Scandinavian or Norman.[176] England, benefiting no doubt in this respect from the impact of the Vikings upon her, shared to the full the expansion of commerce common to Western Europe at this time, trading especially with Scandinavia, the Low Countries and Germany, but also with Normandy and France and with Italy and the Mediterranean lands via the Alpine passes.[177] Two of the principal trade routes of the Western world converged upon her, from Italy via the Rhineland to the Low Country ports, and from Russia via the Baltic to the North Sea. English commerce, both internal and external, was supported by an admirable coinage, carefully and elaborately organised under royal control,[178] and the tenth and early

[175] Cf. p. 45 above and p. 234 below.
[176] See especially, P. H. Sawyer, 'The Wealth of England in the Eleventh Century', *Transactions Royal Historical Society* (5th Series), xv (1965).
[177] For the economy and trade of England on the eve of the Norman Conquest, see F. M. Stenton, *Anglo-Saxon England*, pp. 518 et seq.; H. R. Loyn, *Anglo-Saxon England and the Norman Conquest* (London, 1962), pp. 82 et seq.; and P. H. Sawyer, op. cit.
[178] The standard work on the Old English coinage remains G. C. Brooke, *English Coins* (3rd edition, London, 1950). Amongst an extensive and expanding literature, see also Stenton, *Anglo-Saxon England*, pp. 527–30; H. R. Loyn, *Anglo-Saxon England and the Norman Conquest*, pp. 116 et seq.; *Anglo-Saxon Coins*, ed. R. H. M. Dolley (London, 1961); and P. H. Sawyer, *Transactions Royal Historical Society* (5th Series), xv, ut supra. Well merited praise is generally given both to the elaborate organisation of English pre-Conquest mints and to the standard of the

eleventh centuries witnessed both the emergence of a merchant class and a revival and expansion of towns and urban life.[179] But in pre-Conquest England there were also many weaknesses, in military organisation, in uncertain frontiers,[180] in racial divisions and political instability, in the absence of a unified law and custom, and, not least, in the absence also of the feudal bond. An ancient and self-satisfied society had received in the ninth, tenth and eleventh centuries an infusion of new, alien, Scandinavian blood. The result – viewed comfortably from this great distance of time – was no doubt stimulating, but it was also divisive, and it did nothing to eradicate a certain built-in obsolescence. The centre and power-house of the medieval civilisation of Latin Christendom was, and was to be, northern France, and while no one now argues for total Old English insularity on the eve of the Norman Conquest, the foreign connections of the kingdom were predominantly with Scandinavia, on the periphery of the Brave New World and culturally receiving rather than giving

coins produced, superior to those of contemporary Gaul, including Normandy from which few pre-Conquest coins survive. For the political historian, however, the essential fact remains that the closely controlled royal monopoly of the coinage in pre-Conquest England finds its equivalent in the ducal monopoly of the coinage in pre-Conquest Normandy (above p. 22).

[179] For town planning at this time, see also H. M. Colvin in *Medieval England*, ed. A. L. Poole (Oxford) 1958, pp. 52 et seq. Current excavations at Winchester are revealing a flourishing tenth-century Anglo-Saxon borough. It was symptomatic of Old English society that there was no convention against a thegn's taking part in trade (Stenton, op. cit., p. 520), though no Norman knight would have dreamt of such a thing. Cf. *Of People's Ranks and Law*, 'And if a merchant throve, so that he fared thrice over the wide sea by his own means, then was he thenceforth of thegn-right worthy' (Stubbs, *Select Charters*, 9th edition, p. 89). It is probable that the aristocratic preference for country life stems in this country only from the Norman Conquest, for the Old English nobility frequently had town houses (H. M. Colvin, loc. cit., pp. 70 et seq.).

[180] For the Scottish frontier see especially G. W. S. Barrow, *The Border* (Inaugural Lecture, Durham, 1962). If at any given point in time the line was precisely defined, it was also contested and subject to variation. For the menace of Gruffydd ap Llewelyn in the Confessor's reign until earl Harold's great victories of 1062–3, see J. E. Lloyd, *History of Wales*, ii, 357–71.

in her relationship with this country, and with Germany and the Rhineland, still lingering, like England, in the Carolingian past.

That obsolescence characteristic of the Old English kingdom is very evident in its culture which, like so many aspects of late Anglo-Saxon society, has sometimes tended to be over-praised of late. It is probable that the effect of the tenth-century monastic revival can be exaggerated in stimulating a general intellectual revival,[181] and certain that the intellectual influence of the monasteries was very slight in the reign of Edward the Confessor.[182] There was no Bec in mid-eleventh-century England and, even more important, there were no secular cathedral schools like those in France which were the centres of the new learning and the seed-beds of the renais-sance of the eleventh and twelfth centuries.[183] Old English intellectual activity was essentially old-fashioned, drawing its inspiration from the past, and English scholars, including Aelfric, Wulfstan and Byrtferth, were, by the standards of their contemporaries in France, amateur and second-rate, content to popularise and repeat existing knowledge, either in vernacular literature of admitted distinction or in bad Latin.[184] In artistic achievement, it is now generally agreed that the Anglo-Saxons of the earlier eleventh century excelled in the minor arts, notably in manuscript illumination (e.g. the 'Winchester school') and book production, needle-work, metal-

[181] R. W. Southern, *St. Anselm and His Biographer* (Cambridge, 1963), p. 244.
[182] D. Knowles, *Monastic Order in England*, p. 94.
[183] R. W. Southern, 'The Place of England in the Twelfth-Century Renaissance', *History*, xlv (1960), pp. 202–3.
[184] For the works of Aelfric, Wulfstan and Byrtferth see Stenton, *Anglo-Saxon England* pp. 451–5; R. R. Darlington, 'The Last Phase of Anglo-Saxon History', *History*, xxii (1937–8), pp. 9–11; F. Barlow, *The English Church 1000–1066*, pp. 280 et seq. Cf. Southern, *St. Anselm and His Biographer*, pp. 244–5, 'The literary and intellectual revival associated with the names of Aelfric, Wulfstan and Byrtferth was a brief episode of the early eleventh century, and even these writers were content to popularise learning with which Bede would have been familiar. There was no continuous development: the intellectual interests of 1060 seem little removed from those of 960.' See also Knowles, op. cit., p. 94.

work and ivories,[185] though the assumed superiority of their sculpture has recently been called into question.[186] In the major art of architecture it cannot be denied that Anglo-Saxon work fell far short of the new standards then being set in Normandy and by the other Romanesque schools of France,[187] and belonged, indeed, to a different and an older world. Architectural achievement is to be measured by the more ambitious buildings, and while the greater Anglo-Saxon churches have for the most part been swept away with little trace as the direct result of the Norman Conquest, what physical and documentary evidence of them survives, combined with evidence from lesser churches,[188] points to the conclusion that Old English architecture was obsolete in style and inferior in concept, scale and execution. Carolingian rather than Romanesque, expressing itself in the outworn conventions of debased Roman forms, its affinities were with the Rhineland and the past rather than with France and the

[185] For a convenient and illustrated summary of these matters, see D. Talbot Rice, *English Art 871–1100* (Oxford), 1952.

[186] By Professor George Zarnecki in *Proceedings of the British Academy*, lii (1966).

[187] The best general survey of Romanesque architecture remains that of A. W. Clapham, *Romanesque Architecture in Western Europe* (Oxford, 1936). Clapham's well-known passage in defence of Anglo-Saxon architecture and suggesting what might have happened if the Norman Conquest had never taken place rests necessarily upon supposition and hypothesis (*English Romanesque Architecture before the Norman Conquest*, Oxford, 1930, pp. 77–8), and reads uneasily beside his subsequent passages in praise of Norman Romanesque, which led after 1066 to a 'renaissance of architecture in England which forms one of the great epochs of architectural history', (*English Romanesque Architecture after the Norman Conquest*, pp. 1, 4, 19).

[188] The most recent, ambitious and comprehensive survey of surviving Anglo-Saxon architectural remains will be found in the two majestic volumes of H. M. and Joan Taylor, *Anglo-Saxon Architecture* (Cambridge, 1965). It may be added that current excavations of two major tenth-century Anglo-Saxon churches, the New Minster (c. 903) and the Old Minster (c. 971–94) at Winchester, do not appear to alter the general statements made above; see the interim reports on the Winchester excavations by Martin Biddle in *Archaeological Journal*, cxix (1962) and *Antiquaries Journal*, xliv (1964), xlv (1965), and xlvi (1966). Cf. R. Quirk, 'Winchester Cathedral in the Tenth Century', *Archaeological Journal*, cxiv (1957).

future. Certainly the Normans had no doubt that they could do better, and after 1066 proceeded to do so.[189] The only major churches not rebuilt after the Conquest were earl Harold's Waltham and Edward the Confessor's Westminster, and the latter at least was spared because it was already a 'Norman' church as the Confessor built it, copied from Norman exemplars, most notably Jumièges.[190]

The English church on the eve of the Norman Conquest, while it contributed both in theory and in practice to the strength of the monarchy which controlled it,[191] and was a unifying factor in the kingdom not least by virtue of the complete intermingling of church and state which then prevailed,[192] yet did not provide that positive force towards cohesion and high endeavour which was the peculiar contribution of the Norman Church to Norman achievement in this age.[193] The Old English church, like most Old English institutions, has been marked up in recent years,[194] and no one is now disposed to dismiss it as completely without merit. The key to its assessment, and to any comparison between the church in England in the mid-eleventh century and the contemporary church in Normandy, is that in the English kingdom a great

[189] See pp. 260–2 below.
[190] See p. 107 below. For Westminster Abbey see *The History of the King's Works*, ed. H. M. Colvin, i, 14–17; *The Bayeux Tapestry*, ed. Stenton, pp. 76–8, and the authorities there cited; *Vita Edwardi*, ed. Barlow, pp. 44–6. The perspicacious William of Malmesbury (writing in the early twelfth century) observed of the church that it was the first to be built in England 'in that style which now almost all imitate at vast expense' (*Gesta Regum*, ed. W. Stubbs, Rolls Series, 1887, i, 280 – '*ecclesia . . . quam ipse illo compositionis genere primus in Anglia aedificaverat quod nunc pene cuncti sumptuosis aemulanter expensis*'). Little is known of Harold's church at Waltham, but see *History of the King's Works*, i, 88–9.
[191] Above p. 62. Cf. Barlow, *The English Church 1000–1066*, p. 137, 'The king was more than the patron of the English Church: he was its lord and master.'
[192] Above p. 63. Cf. Barlow, op. cit., p. 152, 'In the Old English kingdom the alliance between church and state was probably more intimate than anywhere else in Europe.'
[193] Above pp. 32.
[194] See, e.g., the then still somewhat defensive praise of R. R. Darlington, 'Ecclesiastical Reform in the late Old English period', *E.H.R.*, li (1936).

ecclesiastical revival had taken place in the tenth century, whereas in the Norman duchy a great ecclesiastical revival was taking place at that very point in time. One fundamental lesson of religious history is that no movement retains its original impetus for long, and it cannot be denied that the tide of the English tenth-century reformation was running out by Edward the Confessor's day.[195] Furthermore, it follows that the church in England looked to the past for inspiration and was in most respects as old-fashioned as the kingdom of which it formed a part. The period 1000–66 in English ecclesiastical affairs has been seen by its latest and most comprehensive historian as 'the slack water between two tides of reform'[196] – and we must certainly note for future reference that the second tide of reform was that which flowed in with the Norman Conquest.[197] While the generalised condemnations of post-Conquest monastic writers are not to be taken at their face value,[198] there was inevitably an overall decline from the standards of tenth-century monasticism,[199] and the absence of any high-level intellectual achievement within the monasteries has already been noted.[200] The great period of monastic foundations and refoundations was over, and so also was the period of direct stimulus from the Continent.[201] In the church as a whole there was, in complete contrast with Normandy, a lack of leadership or direction from the lay ruler and a lack of interest among the earls and great magnates.[202] The standard of the episcopate as a whole can be seen as one of 'general mediocrity',[203] in spite of the 'foreign' element introduced by Edward the Confessor with his Norman and Lotharingian

[195] Barlow, op. cit., p. 39.
[196] Ibid., p. 27.
[197] Cf. pp. 251–62 below.
[198] Thus William of Malmesbury, 'monachi Cantuarienses, sicut omnes tunc temporis in Anglia, seculares haud assimiles erant' (Gesta Pontificum, Rolls Series, 1870, ed. N. E. S. A. Hamilton, p. 70). Cf. Darlington, op cit., p. 403.
[199] Knowles, Monastic Order in England, pp. 58, 73, 78; Barlow, op. cit., p. 52.
[200] Above p. 101.
[201] Knowles, op. cit., p. 69.
[202] Barlow, op. cit., pp. 55 ff., 95.
[203] Ibid., p. 94.

appointments,[204] and against the individual excellence of Wulfstan of Worcester there must be set the outright scandal of Stigand which was of sufficient importance to be counted amongst the causes of the Norman Conquest and of its success.[205] Amongst the prelates, pluralism was common, though there is little evidence of simony and the disregard of celibacy was no worse in England than elsewhere.[206] The organisation of the English church down to 1066 remained little influenced and even less altered by the latest ideas of Continental reformers which were already being put into practice in contemporary Normandy. There were no separate and distinct national councils or synods of the church, ecclesiastical affairs at this level being dealt with in the witan,[207] and no provincial synods save at York, where they were more of the nature of diocesan synods which, apart from York, were held only in the bishopric of Worcester.[208] There is very little evidence of any ecclesiastical jurisdiction in the sense of separate ecclesiastical courts, spiritual pleas being dealt with in the local courts of shire and hundred along with secular pleas,[209] and canon law, the essential instrument both of ecclesiastical jurisdiction and of the Gregorian reform movement as a whole, seems in consequence to have been little developed in England.[210] There is also little evidence for any organisation of cathedral chapters upon the Norman model except at London where it was doubtless undertaken by the pre-Conquest Norman bishops Robert of Jumièges (1044–51) and William (1051–75),[211] and this, together with the rarity of archdeacons (found only at York and Worcester),[212] is symptomatic of a general neglect of ecclesiastical and diocesan organisation which left an old-fashioned and also dangerous gap between

---

[204] See Barlow, op. cit., pp. 81 ff., and below p. 118.
[205] For both Wulfstan and Stigand, see Barlow, pp. 77–81, 90–93.
[206] Ibid., pp. 78, 113, 142.
[207] Above p. 66.
[208] Barlow, pp. 137 ff., 237, 245–6.
[209] Ibid., pp. 255 ff.
[210] Ibid., pp. 285–6.
[211] Ibid., pp. 219–20, 239–42.
[212] Ibid., pp. 247–9.

the bishops and parish priests.[213] It may well be that the wind of change blowing from the Papacy, with whom English relations were traditionally close, would in due course have brought to this country the new reforming spirit and organisation from the Continent, but in the event, as a matter of historical fact, reform was to come as the direct result of the Norman Conquest.[214]

In this period personalities are of supreme importance, and the contrast between Normandy under duke William the Bastard and England under king Edward the Confessor is complete. Whatever kind of man Edward was, he was evidently not a strong ruler. His character to us is enigmatic,[215] and stripped of the later accretions of hagiography[216] there is little left of which we can be certain. He seems to have been more passionate, warlike and active than his subsequent reputation as a saint would allow, yet he allowed himself, as king, to be married to a woman for whom he can have had little affection and by whom he had no heirs, he achieved no reputation as a warrior, and his activity was largely confined to his passion for hunting.[217] Born in c. 1002, the son of Ethelred and Emma,

[213] Ibid., p. 245.

[214] Below, pp. 251–62. The influence of the reformed Papacy began to be felt in England as from 1049, and is manifest in such occasions as the attendance of English prelates at papal councils, or intervention from Rome in the attempted appointment of Spearhavoc to London in 1051 and the translation of Ealdred from Worcester to York in 1061. Such direct relations, however, were largely broken by the irregular position of Stigand after 1052. See Darlington, *E.H.R.*, li (1936), p. 419; Barlow, op. cit., p. 302.

[215] Stenton, *Anglo-Saxon England*, p. 418. For the most recent assessment of Edward's character and kingship, see F. Barlow, *The English Church 1000–1066*, pp. 41 et seq., and the same author's 'Edward the Confessor's Early Life, Character and Attitudes', *E.H.R.* lxxx (1965).

[216] For the cult of Edward the Confessor, which may have begun even before his death, see especially Barlow (ed.) *The Life of Edward the Confessor*, Appendix D, pp. 112 et seq.

[217] Cf. Barlow, ibid., pp. lxvii–lxix. The author of the *Vita Edwardi* says of the king that 'he was of passionate temper and a man of prompt and vigorous action' (ibid., p. 27). Edward married Edith, the daughter of earl Godwin, whom he had good reason to dislike (Stenton, op. cit., p. 419), in 1045. His attitude to her is surely revealed by his actions in 1051–2, repudiating her when he had banished Godwin and his sons and

and over twenty years in exile principally in Normandy, he was about forty years of age when he came to the English throne in 1042, a stranger, ill-prepared, in a half-alien land dominated by an entrenched Anglo-Danish nobility of whom he disapproved.[218] Small wonder, then, that he retained a preference for the Normans and Normandy of his youth and earlier manhood,[219] or that his principal motivation as king seems to have been to avoid going on his travels again.[220] He yielded to events and situations as appeared necessary, not least to the dominance of the house of Godwin save only in his abortive bid for political and domestic freedom in 1051, and from him the affairs of England received little interference, let alone leadership, throughout his reign. His one known positive achievement was the building of the great church of St. Peter at Westminster, modelled upon the new churches of Normandy which it excelled in scale, and there he was buried, probably before its completion, on 5 January 1066.[221] The same day the same church witnessed the hasty coronation of Harold, half-Danish son of the *parvenu* Godwin, though himself a noble and an earl of the second generation. Of his character, as opposed to his career and achievements, even less is known. Though he made a pilgrimage to Rome in *c.* 1056 and refounded the collegiate church of Waltham in Essex, he seems to have been, in sharp contrast to his rival William of Normandy, no great patron of the church and little interested in religious affairs, and he has recently been described as 'secular in outlook and pagan in morals'.[222] The contemporary author

only taking her back again when they were reinstated upon their own terms (above p. 82; Stenton, op. cit., pp. 553 et seq. For a different interpretation of Edward's treatment of Edith at this time, see Barlow, *E.H.R.*, lxxx, 236).

[218] Stenton, op. cit., pp. 418–19; Barlow, *E.H.R.*, lxxx, 238–9. After the death of Godwin in 1053, Edward got on rather better with the younger generation of Godwin's sons, Harold and also his brother Tostig whom the king seems positively to have liked (Barlow, *The English Church*, p. 51).

[219] For Edward's Norman 'favourites', see pp. 114–19 below.

[220] For this and the next sentence see especially Barlow, *E.H.R.*, lxxx, 235, 237.

[221] *The Bayeux Tapestry*, ed. Stenton (1965), pp. 76–8, and Pl. 32; cf. p. 103 and n. 190 above.

[222] Barlow, *The English Church 1000–1066*, pp. 58–60.

of the *Vita Edwardi*, to whom Harold was a hero, permitted himself to say that he was 'rather too generous with oaths', and it is clear that his word was not always his bond.[223] His political education at least well suited him for the crown,[224] and he must have known England and English affairs better on his accession than any king since Ethelred. He also proved himself, within the context of English and Scandinavian warfare, a warrior of renown, defeating Gruffydd and ending the Welsh menace in 1062–3[225] in addition to achieving a great victory at Stamford Bridge in 1066 on the eve of Hastings,[226] though his own defeat on that field owed something to overconfidence as well as to obsolete tactics and the consummate generalship of duke William.[227] How successful a king he might have been we can only guess, for in the words of the Anglo-Saxon Chronicle 'he met little quiet in it as long as he ruled the realm'.[228]

[223] *Vita Edwardi*, p. 53, being possibly a reference not only to Harold's part in the Northumbrian revolt against his brother Tostig – which charge he swore off – but also to his fatal oath to duke William in 1064 about the English succession, for which see pp. 127–32 below.
[224] Barlow, *The English Church*, p. 38.
[225] See J. E. Lloyd, *History of Wales*, ii, 369–71.
[226] Below, p. 157.
[227] Below, pp. 158–74.
[228] *Anglo-Saxon Chronicle*, 'C', 'D', ed. Whitelock, p. 140.

CHAPTER IV

England, Normandy and Scandinavia

Were it farther off, I'll pluck it down

SHAKESPEARE

The Norman Conquest of England in 1066 was not a mere act of war, a straightforward military invasion by an enemy such as the invasions of Swein and Cnut of Denmark in 1013 and 1015, or such as might have been launched in 1804 by Napoleon or in 1940 by Adolf Hitler. William the Conqueror, by contrast, claimed to be the legitimate heir of Edward the Confessor; his claim resulted from a complicated series of events stretching back over more than half a century, during which the affairs of England and Normandy had become increasingly interlocked; and his vindication of his claim is set in the context of a dramatically disputed succession. The interrelationship of England and Normandy, indeed, begins with the very foundation of the latter, for the Normans were Vikings in origin, the establishment of the future duchy of Normandy in Gaul is analagous to the establishment of the Danelaw in England, and there is place-name evidence for the subsequent migration of peasants from the Danelaw to Scandinavian Normandy.[1] Just as the connection between Normandy and its parent Scandinavia was long maintained after 911,[2] so the Viking raiders of Ethelred's English kingdom in the late tenth century found shelter in Norman ports, and the resultant hostility between the two countries led to a formal treaty, negotiated by a papal envoy, in 991, whereby neither was to aid the enemies of the other.[3] The effects of the treaty were

---

[1] Loyn, *Norman Conquest*, p. 49.
[2] Above, p. 23.
[3] Stenton, *Anglo-Saxon England*, pp. 370–1.

evidently not long-lasting, for the great Viking force, sent to England in 997, wintered in Normandy in 1000–1 preparatory to renewing its assaults,[4] and it seems clear that this repeated Norman offence was the reason not only for Ethelred's unsuccessful raid upon the Cotentin about this time, but also for his marriage to Emma of Normandy in 1002, which is probably to be seen as a more diplomatic attempt to close the Norman ports to Scandinavian raiders and a move to gain the alliance of·the new, Norman power in European politics.[5]

Of the importance of the fateful marriage of king Ethelred II and Emma of Normandy, daughter of duke Richard I and sister of Richard II, in the history of the Norman Conquest there can be no doubt. From it there followed the kinship of William the Conqueror, grandson of Richard II, with Edward the Confessor, which was a vital element in his claim to the English succession.[6] As a result of it also, Ethelred and his family were able to find political asylum at the Norman court after Swein's conquest of England in 1013, and from this there followed Edward the Confessor's long exile in Normandy, the Norman claim upon his gratitude for help in time of need, and his own Norman sympathies as king of England from 1042–66. The marriage also brought the remarkable personage of Emma herself into England, and into English politics, which she was largely to dominate for over forty years.[7] After Ethelred's death she was married by Cnut, and was therefore the queen of two English kings and the mother of two more,

[4] Ibid., p. 373; *Anglo-Saxon Chronicle*, 'C', 'D', 'E', ed. Whitelock, p. 85.
[5] William of Jumièges (ed. Marx, pp. 76–7), who is the sole authority for Ethelred's expedition to the Cotentin, is notoriously vague in his chronology. While, therefore, there is no good reason to disbelieve his account, the expedition makes more sense before rather than after the marriage. See A. Campbell, *Encomium Emmae Reginae*, pp. xli–xlii; Loyn, op. cit., pp. 49–50; Douglas, *William the Conqueror*, p. 160. Cf. Stenton, op. cit., p. 374.
[6] See p. 133 below.
[7] For Emma, see especially A. Campbell's 'Introduction' to the *Encomium Emmae Reginae*, and Loyn, op. cit., pp. 50–3. She was in exile in Flanders during the reign of Harold I (Cnut's illegitimate son) from 1037–40. Her political influence presumably ended after Edward the Confessor's confiscation of her lands and property in 1043 (Campbell, op. cit., p. xlix; Stenton, op. cit., pp. 420–1).

Harthacnut[8] and Edward the Confessor.[9] She thus provided an element of personal continuity in a changing English world, and she also provided during these years a continuous and important link with Normandy. There were, inevitably, Normans in her household and in her train, and some of them became established in the country,[10] the precursors of Norman emigration to England which reaches its culmination in and after 1066. It may well be also that she strengthened the commercial ties between England and Normandy which were certainly in existence in Ethelred's day.[11] It is difficult entirely to disagree with Freeman's view that the marriage of Emma and Ethelred 'led directly to the Norman Conquest of England', and that it was 'the first act of the drama'.[12]

Cnut's marriage to Emma in his turn in 1017, was evidently politically inspired to prevent any intervention by Normandy on behalf of Edward and Alfred, the exiled sons of Ethelred by Emma, and it achieved its object to the extent that relations between the two countries remained friendly during the reign of duke Richard II (996–1026) even though the aethlings continued to find shelter at the Norman court.[13] Relations deteriorated, however, in the time of duke Robert the Magnificent (1027–35), who is said to have been particularly devoted to the cause of the two young princes, treating them like brothers,[14] and who in any case had good reason to be alarmed

---

[8] Emma's son by Cnut, and 'in all things obedient to the counsels of his mother' (*Encomium Emmae Reginae*, ed. A. Campbell, p. 6).

[9] Her son by Ethelred. Other children by this marriage were Edward's younger brother Alfred, murdered in 1036, and his sister, Godgifu, who married (1) Drogo count of the Vexin, and (2) Eustace count of Boulogne.

[10] Loyn, op. cit., p. 50; cf. Ordericus Vitalis, *Historia Ecclesiastica*, iv, 297; R. L. G. Ritchie, *The Normans in England before the Norman Conquest* (Inaugural Lecture, Exeter, 1948), pp. 14–15. The best-known is Emma's reeve, Hugh, said by the *Anglo-Saxon Chronicle* ('C', 'D', 'E', p. 86) to have betrayed Exeter to the Danes in 1003. While the Chronicle calls Hugh 'French', Florence of Worcester (ed. Thorpe, i, 156), calls him 'Norman'.

[11] Loyn, op. cit., p. 50. Cf. p. 51 above.

[12] *Norman Conquest*, i (1870), 301, 302.

[13] Stenton, op. cit., pp. 391, 393, 402; Douglas, op. cit., p. 162.

[14] William of Jumièges, ed. Marx, p. 109.

at the growing power of Cnut, king of England and Denmark and for a time lord of Norway, in the world of northern Europe.[15] According to William of Jumièges, having unsuccessfully appealed to Cnut to have the princes back, he launched an expedition which was only prevented by storms and contrary winds from crossing to England to assert their claims by force.[16] The same chronicler also says that subsequently Cnut, then being very ill, sent envoys to Normandy offering half the English kingdom to the aethlings, though the offer was not followed up owing to Robert's departure on his pilgrimage to Jerusalem (and, no doubt, owing to the death of Cnut).[17] Both William of Jumièges and William of Poitiers report that when news of Cnut's death reached Normandy, the future Edward the Confessor himself invaded England, fought an action at Southampton, but then withdrew back to Normandy since his forces were insufficient to win the kingdom.[18] In the event, Cnut was succeeded in England first by

[15] Subscriptions of the aethlings appear on some of duke Robert's charters, and it was at this time that Godgifu, the sister of Edward and Alfred, was married to Drogo, count of the Vexin and Robert's friend and ally. There is a later story that relations between Cnut and Robert the Magnificent were exacerbated by the latter's repudiation of Cnut's sister Estrith, whom Cnut had given him in marriage to maintain the Norman alliance. See Stenton, op. cit., pp. 402–3; Douglas, op. cit., pp. 162–3 and in *E.H.R.*, lxv (1950), 292–5.

[16] Ed. Marx, pp. 109–10. William of Malmesbury (*Gesta Regum*, ii, 300) also makes an interesting reference to this abortive expedition: see n. 56, p. 153 below.

[17] Ibid., p. 111. William of Jumièges is thus the sole authority for Cnut's offer of half the kingdom to the aethlings, if not for Robert the Magnificent's intended invasion of England. Neither incident should be lightly dismissed, for William of Jumièges, though anxious to make the most of Norman support for Edward and Alfred, is an original source for this period of Norman history. Cnut's offer is perhaps less improbable than at first appears: he had, after all, begun his rule in England by dividing the kingdom with Edmund Ironside, and on his death in 1035 his heir, Harthacnut, was in fact too preoccupied in Scandinavia to come to England.

[18] Ibid., pp. 120–1; William of Poitiers, ed. Foreville, pp. 4–6. Cf. F. Barlow, 'Edward the Confessor's Early Life, Character and Attitudes', *E.H.R.*, lxxx (1965), p. 234. No English source refers to this event, though Florence of Worcester (ed. Thorpe, i, 191) says that Edward accompanied Alfred on the latter's fatal visit to England in 1036 (below, p. 113) while all other sources say Alfred came alone.

his illegitimate son, Harold Harefoot (1035–40), and then by Harthacnut (1040–42), his son by Emma of Normandy. Both reigns produced events which were to become strands in the complicated web of the Norman Conquest. Under Harold, by his order and with the complicity of earl Godwin of Wessex, Alfred was murdered on a visit to England in 1036.[19] It is unlikely that Edward the Confessor, in his future relations with Godwin, ever forgot the earl's part in the crime,[20] and it is certain that the Normans did not, but regarded it as avenged upon Godwin's son Harold at Hastings.[21] Meanwhile, Harthacnut in 1041 invited his half-brother Edward to come from Normandy to England 'and hold the kingdom, together with himself',[22] and thus ensured that Edward would succeed him on his death in 1042.

The reign of Edward the Confessor, which began in 1042,[23] ended in 1066 on the eve of the Norman Conquest and with the impending climax of the events which produced it. In king Edward's time the ties between England and Normandy became closer, and those elements other than kinship in duke William's claim to the English succession were forged. Freeman saw the reign as the true beginning of the Conquest itself,

[19] According to the *Anglo-Saxon Chronicle*, p. 103 ('C', *s.a.* 1036) he came 'wishing to go to his mother who was in Winchester', but the visit can scarcely have been without political significance, and both Norman chroniclers say he was accompanied by a strong military force (William of Poitiers, p. 6; William of Jumièges, p. 121). See also *The Life of King Edward the Confessor*, ed. Barlow, p. 20, where it is stated (a) that Alfred 'entered Britain inadvisedly with a few armed Frenchmen', and (b) that he then 'acted rashly about getting possession of the paternal kingdom'. The best discussion of the affair is by Campbell, *Encomium Emmae Reginae*, pp. lxiv–lxvii, and cf. C. Plummer, *Two of the Saxon Chronicles Parallel*, ii, 211–15.
[20] Stenton, op. cit., pp. 415, 419, 553; Douglas, *William the Conqueror*, pp. 164, 166.
[21] William of Poitiers, pp. 10–12.
[22] *Encomium Emmae Reginae*, p. 53. Körner argues, not unreasonably, that this was an act of political necessity rather than affection (*The Battle of Hastings, England and Europe*, pp. 67–71).
[23] Edward succeeded Harthacnut (with Norman assistance according to William of Poitiers, ed. Foreville, pp. 28–30) on the latter's death in 1042, and was crowned at Winchester on Easter Day 1043 (*Anglo-Saxon Chronicle*, p. 107).

and its theme as a political struggle for the control of both the present and future of the realm between a Norman party patronised by the king and a 'patriot' party led first by Godwin and then by Harold.[24] However justified the revulsion from Freeman's absurdly anachronistic national approach, and the reaction against his exaggerations, one may yet feel that his broad interpretation of the overall pattern of events was basically sound, and it is certain that any attempt to explain the Norman Conquest must take into account the Norman sympathies of Edward the Confessor, and also those Norman 'favourites' of the king who were introduced into the realm as a result of his life in exile in Normandy from 1014 until his return to England in 1041.[25] It is not without significance that the dearest achievement of his later years, his great church of St. Peter at Westminster, was modelled upon the new churches then rising in the Norman duchy (its affinities closest with Jumièges, rebuilt at this time by abbot Robert of Jumièges, Edward's friend whom he made first bishop of London and then archbishop of Canterbury),[26] nor that in the account of his death, movingly and convincingly written by the author of the *Vita Edwardi*,[27] it was two Norman monks, the friends of his youth in Normandy, who, in his dying vision, prophesied the doom of the kingdom. As for his Norman 'favourites', it was both inevitable and understandable that Edward, his habits and friendships already formed, returning at the age of about forty as almost a stranger to a land dominated by a largely alien, Anglo-Danish aristocracy,[28] should have brought with him in his household, and later encouraged to follow him, Normans and other Frenchmen[29] to whom he gave

[24] E.g. *Norman Conquest*, i (1870), 526; ii (1870), pp. v, 4 etc. In this struggle Godwin stands out as 'the greatest of living Englishmen' (ibid., p. 30), and Harold as 'the hero and the martyr of our native freedom' (ibid., p. 37).

[25] For the most recent discussion of Edward's earlier years, see F. Barlow, 'Edward the Confessor's Early Life, Character and Attitudes', *E.H.R.*, lxxx (1965).

[26] For Westminster see p. 103 and n. 190 above; for Robert of Jumièges, see p. 118 below.

[27] Ed. Barlow, p. 75.

[28] Cf. Stenton, *Anglo-Saxon England*, pp. 418–19.

[29] It is generally pointed out that not all Edward's Continental friends

his patronage and whom, as king, he established in his kingdom and his counsels. The author of the *Vita Edwardi* states the case reasonably enough: 'when King Edward of holy memory returned from Francia, quite a number of men of that nation, and they not base born, accompanied him. And these, since he was master of the whole kingdom, he kept with him, enriched them with many honours, and made them his privy counsellors and administrators of the royal palace.'[30] Individuals are not easy to identify, but those established amongst the lords of the land in Edward the Confessor's England evidently included Ralph the Staller, who was probably a Breton,[31] and Robert fitz Wimarc, who may perhaps have been a Breton on his mother's side but was also related to Edward the Confessor and William the Conqueror.[32] The lands of these two lay principally in East Anglia,[33] but in the far west of the kingdom a notable Norman colony was planted on the borders of Wales, chiefly in Herefordshire. The most distinguished member of this group was Ralph, king Edward's nephew,[34] who obtained wide estates in Herefordshire, Worcestershire and Gloucestershire and was an earl before 1051.[35]

in England were in fact Normans (e.g. Stenton, op. cit., p. 419), though it may be noted that where the Anglo-Saxon Chronicle vaguely speaks of 'Frenchmen' Florence of Worcester specifically writes 'Normans' (e.g. ed. Thorpe, i, 156, 207, 210: cf. n. 10 p. 111 above).

[30] Ed. Barlow, p. 17. The reference to 'administrators of the royal palace' may possibly relate to Robert fitz Wimarc (below) whom the same author describes as 'steward of the royal palace' at the time of Edward's death (ibid., p. 76).

[31] Stenton, op. cit., p. 420; *Complete Peerage*, 'G.E.C.', ix, 568–71.

[32] Stenton, op. cit., p. 419; Round, *Feudal England* (London, 1909), p. 331. But cf. Barlow, *Vita Edwardi*, p. 76, n. 4, and the authorities there cited.

[33] Robert fitz Wimarc's lands came to form the basis of the post-Conquest honour of Rayleigh, and Ralph the Staller was made earl of East Anglia by William the Conqueror.

[34] He was the son of Drogo, count of the Vexin, who had married Godgifu sister of Edward the Confessor.

[35] *Anglo-Saxon Chronicle*, 'D' (ed. Whitelock, p. 118); Stenton, op. cit. pp. 556, 561; Douglas, *William the Conqueror*, p. 167; *Complete Peerage* 'G.E.C.', vi (1926), pp. 446–7. Ralph seems certainly to have been made earl of Hereford in 1053, but may have been so earlier during Swein's disgrace and banishment.

Also in Herefordshire, at Burghill and Hope-under-Dinmore, was the Norman Osbern surnamed Pentecost,[36] and with him there was associated a certain Hugh,[37] while the Norman Richard son of Scrob, made famous by Freeman's vituperation, was established at Richard's Castle before 1052.[38]

It is also of the greatest interest that these Norman and Breton lords were responsible for the introduction into England of the castles to which they were accustomed in France. Speaking of the flight of 'the Frenchmen' from London in 1052,[39] the compiler of the 'E' version of the Anglo-Saxon Chronicle wrote that 'they took horses and departed, some west to Pentecost's castle, and some north to Robert's castle'.[40] Round identified Pentecost's castle as Ewyas Harold in Herefordshire, i.e. the castle of Osbern Pentecost, and Robert's castle as very probably Clavering in Essex, i.e. the castle of Robert fitz Wimarc.[41] In Herefordshire, it seems certain that there was more than one castle already pertaining to the Norman colony at this time, and there may well have been three or four.[42] Florence of Worcester, writing of the banishment of the Normans in 1052, says that Osbern surnamed Pentecost and his associate (*socius*) Hugh, surrendered their castles (i.e. in the plural) and went to Scotland.[43] In addition, Richard's Castle has a good claim to a foundation as early as this since its lord, Richard the son of Scrob, is known to have been established there by 1052.[44] Earl Ralph himself, who became earl of Hereford in 1053 if not before,[45] almost certainly had a castle at Hereford, though the date of its foundation is not known. The entry in the 'E' version of the Anglo-Saxon

---

[36] Stenton, op. cit., p. 554.
[37] Florence of Worcester, ed. Thorpe, i, 210 (cited below).
[38] Ibid.; cf. Round, *Feudal England*, pp. 317–31.
[39] See below p. 120.
[40] Ed. Whitelock, p. 125.
[41] *Feudal England*, p. 324; *V.C.H.*, *Essex*, i, 345.
[42] I.e. Ewyas Harold, the unidentified castle of Hugh the *socius* of Osbern Pentecost (below), Richard's Castle, and Hereford.
[43] Ed. Thorpe, i, 210: *Osbernus vero, cognomento Pentecost, et socius ejus Hugo sua reddiderunt castella.*
[44] Ibid., but cf. Stenton, op. cit., n. 1 to p. 554.
[45] Cf. n. 35 above.

Chronicle under the year 1051, however – 'the foreigners then had built a castle in Herefordshire in earl Swein's province, and had inflicted every possible injury and insult upon the king's men in those parts'[46] – may well refer to it rather than to Ewyas Harold, just as the reference, in the 'D' version for 1052, to Gruffydd's raid near Leominster being resisted by 'both natives and the Frenchmen from the castle'[47] seems more likely to refer to (a) Richard's Castle or (b) Hereford than to Ewyas Harold which is further from Leominster than either.[48]

---

[46] Ed. Whitelock, p. 119.

[47] Ibid., p. 122.

[48] It should be added that there is also reference to a 'castle' at Dover in 1051. The 'D' version of the Chronicle (ed. Whitelock, pp. 117–18) says that in that year earl Godwin and his sons threatened the king with war 'unless Eustace [count of Boulogne] were surrendered and his men handed over to them, as well as the Frenchmen who were in the castle'. The whole context of this entry suggests Dover rather than any Herefordshire castle (cf. Stenton, op. cit., p. 555) and it is specifically said to be Dover by Florence of Worcester (i, 205–6, *insuper et Nortmannos et Bononienses, qui castellum in Doruverniae clivo tenuerunt*). Later William of Poitiers (ed. Foreville, p. 104) says that Harold, as part of his oath in 1064 (p. 130 below) promised to hand over to duke William Dover castle (*castrum Doveram, studio atque sumptu suo communitum*), and Eadmer in his *Historia Novorum in Anglia* (ed. M. Rule, R.S., London, 1884, p. 7) says that in the same oath Harold promised to make a castle, with a well, at Dover for William's use (*insuper castellum Dofris cum puteo aquae ad opus meum te facturum*), and subsequently, in 1066, makes Harold claim to have done this (ibid., p. 8, *Castellum Dofris et in eo puteum aquae, licet nesciam cui, ut nobis convenit, explevi*). William of Poitiers (p. 210). Ordericus Vitalis (ed. Le Prévost, ii, 153, closely following Poitiers) and Guy of Amiens (*Carmen de Hastingae Proelio*, ed. J. A. Giles, *Scriptores Rerum Gestarum Willelmi Conquestoris*, London, 1845, p. 44) all refer to a castle (*castellum: castrum*) at Dover when duke William and his forces came there after Hastings in 1066, William of Poitiers stating also that the Conqueror spent eight days in adding to its fortifications (*Recepto castro, quae minus erant per dies octo addidit firmamenta* – p. 212. See also p. 177 and n. 174 below. For Guy of Amiens, see n. 12 p. 143 below). At this time, however, feudal terminology, including the words *castrum* and *castellum*, had not yet hardened into the later technical meanings, least of all in England, and it is most likely that the fortress which William took in 1066 was in fact the Anglo-Saxon borough (as Mrs. E. S. Armitage thought long ago – *Early Norman Castles of the British Isles*, pp. 138–143) occupying the pre-existing Iron Age earthwork upon the cliff (see H. M. Colvin,

Edward the Confessor as king of England had the power to control the English church and appointments to high office within it,[49] and the years between 1042 and 1051 saw the appointment of three Norman clerics to English bishoprics.[50] In 1044 the king's particular friend, Robert, abbot of Jumièges, was given the see of London. In 1049 Edward gave the bishopric of Dorchester to Ulf, a Norman priest of his household. Finally, in mid-Lent 1051, Robert of Jumièges was translated to the archiepiscopal see of Canterbury, and later in the same year another Norman priest, William, was appointed to London. The Norman element thus formed in the episcopate was not dominant,[51] can scarcely be conceived as amounting to an attempt to Normanise the Old English church, and was matched by the other 'foreign' element of Lotharingian bishops within it in this period.[52] But it surely reflects again the Norman sympathies and contacts of Edward the Confessor, and it was important. It embraced Canterbury, with its prescriptive rights to the coronation of kings, and London, the chief city of the kingdom.[53] It also caused resentment and trouble, not least through the agency of Robert of Jumièges,

Antiquity, xxxiii, 1959), and that within this larger enclosure the Normans placed their castle, on the analogy of Pevensey and elsewhere (pp. 236–7 below). This hypothesis seems to be confirmed by such architectural and archaeological evidence as we have. The church of St. Mary-in-Castro, of late tenth- or early eleventh-century date, and the cemetery now known from recent excavations to have been associated with it, prove pre-Conquest occupation of the site, while the same recent excavations, though showing the so-called 'Harold's Earthwork' now surrounding the church to date from the twelfth and thirteenth centuries, also showed traces of an earlier bank and ditch cut through the cemetery and very close indeed to the pre-existing church. This latter work, evidently of eleventh-century date, strongly suggests the irreverent urgency of war, and is likely to represent, not any work of Harold before 1066, but the first castle at Dover, raised by the Conqueror after his victory at Hastings.

[49] Above p. 103, n. 191.
[50] See e.g. Stenton, op. cit., p. 458.
[51] Of the ten vacancies in the episcopate between 1043 and 1050 six were filled by Englishmen and a seventh by an Englishman trained in Lorraine (Loyn, *Norman Conquest*, p. 55).
[52] Stenton, op. cit., p. 458.
[53] Ibid., p. 459.

who stood close in the counsels of the king and was a principal opponent of Godwin, earl of Wessex.[54]

That Edward's Norman sympathies and preferments lead into the crisis of 1051, both through the resentment which they caused in themselves and through the recognition of William of Normandy as heir to the English throne, in which they culminated in the same year, is as clear as anything can be in the haze which inadequate English sources draw over the politics of the reign.[55] Certainly the fracas at Dover which is given as the immediate cause of the affair in the Chronicle[56] seems a very inadequate occasion for a rebellion which brought the kingdom to the verge of civil war. Count Eustace II of Boulogne, on a visit to king Edward his brother-in-law, was involved with his followers in an affray with the men of Dover while high-handedly seeking accommodation in the town.

[54] *Vita Edwardi*, ed. Barlow, pp. 17–23. Cf. Loyn, op. cit., p. 55, and below.

[55] One may often sympathise with Round's petulant reference to the Anglo-Saxon Chronicle as 'the arid entries in our jejune native chronicle' (*Feudal England*, pp. 317–18). Other sources for the years 1051–2, which admittedly the Chronicle treats in more detail than usual, are Florence of Worcester and the *Vita Edwardi* (pp. 17–28). It is worth noting that these matters were already both mysterious and controversial when William of Malmesbury wrote in the 1120's (see e.g. *Gesta Regum*, R.S., i, 239, 279). It has even been suggested that Edward's dismissal of his permanent fleet in 1049–50 (n. 149, p. 92 above) was in some way connected with the crisis, either as a preliminary move by Edward himself to facilitate duke William's recognition as his heir (Loyn *Norman Conquest*, p. 64), or as a move engineered by earl Godwin to weaken the king still further (T. J. Oleson, *The Witenagemot in the Reign of Edward the Confessor*, London, 1955, pp. 3, 4.)

[56] 'D' and 'E', ed. Whitelock, p. 117. The former implies that the affair at Dover happened when count Eustace landed in England, and 'E' states that he was on his way back after his meeting with the king. 'E', written at Canterbury, is better informed about affairs in the south-east, gives a longer version of the events of 1051–2, and is pro-Godwin. 'D' was probably compiled in the north and its author is politically more detached. The 'C' version tends to be hostile to the house of Godwin. Florence of Worcester for these years follows 'D' but gives additional and independent information. The affair at Dover is not mentioned in the *Vita Edwardi*. See Douglas, *English Historical Documents*, ii, 107–8; Whitelock, *The Anglo-Saxon Chronicle*, p. xviii; Körner, *The Battle of Hastings, England and Europe*, pp. 31–43.

Eustace complained to the king, who ordered earl Godwin to harry Kent and Dover as punishment, and Godwin refused.[57] But even in the sources at our disposal there are more than hints of more important matters. The return of Godwin and his sons in 1052 was followed by the flight and/or banishment of many (though not all) of Edward's Norman friends, including Robert of Jumièges, Ulf, bishop of Dorchester, and Osbern Pentecost and his associate Hugh.[58] The author of the *Vita Edwardi*[59] reveals that the king's appointment, early in 1051, of Robert to Canterbury was opposed by Godwin in favour of a rival candidate, the monk Aelric, who was a kinsman of his own. He says that the elevation of Robert caused much resentment,[60] and that thereafter the new archbishop 'began to provoke and oppose the earl with all his strength and might',[61] accused him, probably justly, of invading the lands of Canterbury, and turned Edward's mind against Godwin by the accusation that he intended to attack the king as he had formerly attacked and betrayed his brother Alfred [i.e. in 1036].[62] Something of this appears in the 'E' version of the Chronicle, which also touches upon the grievance to Godwin and his sons of the Norman plantation and castles in Herefordshire in their territory.[63] 'The foreigners then', we are told, 'had built a castle in Herefordshire in Earl Swein's province, and had inflicted every possible injury and insult upon the king's men in those parts.' Earl Godwin and his sons, earls Harold and Swein, intended to complain of this to the king and his council at Gloucester, but were forestalled by 'the foreigners'

[57] Thus 'E' (p. 119), adding in explanation that he was 'reluctant to injure his own province'. 'D' (p. 117) says simply that 'Earl Godwine was indignant that such things should happen in his earldom', and forthwith began with his sons to raise an army.

[58] 'C' and 'D' (p. 124); 'E' (pp. 125–7); Florence of Worcester, ed. Thorpe, i, 210. Cf. below p. 125.

[59] Ed. Barlow, pp. 18 et seq.

[60] Ibid., p. 19, 'all the clergy protested with all their might against the wrong'.

[61] Ibid.

[62] Ibid., p. 20. Cf. above p. 113, n. 19. For possible further provocation of Godwin by Robert on his journey to Rome for his pallium, see Barlow, *The English Church 1000–1066*, pp. 48–9.

[63] Ed. Whitelock, p. 119. Cf. Stenton, op. cit., p. 554.

who got in first and persuaded Edward that the earls meant to betray him. The same 'E' version, speaking of the expulsion of the king's friends after Godwin's return in arms in 1052, says that 'Archbishop Robert was declared utterly an outlaw, and all the Frenchmen too, because they were most responsible for the disagreement between Earl Godwin and the king'.[64] Finally, the statement in both the 'D' version of the Chronicle and Florence of Worcester[65] that duke William of Normandy visited king Edward after the banishment of Godwin and his family (i.e. in the autumn of 1051 or the winter of 1051–2), whether true or false,[66] is the only hint in contemporary or near-contemporary English sources that the Great Matter of the succession to the throne was an issue in this eventful year.

The authoritative[67] Norman chroniclers, William of Jumièges and William of Poitiers, both state that Edward the Confessor promised the succession to duke William and nominated him as his heir, and that this promise and nomination was subsequently confirmed by Harold, sent to Normandy for this purpose by Edward shortly before the latter's

---

[64] Ed. Whitelock, pp. 126–7.

[65] Ibid., pp. 120–1; Florence of Worcester, i, 207. The 'Count William (who) came from overseas with a great force of Frenchmen' of the Chronicle is specifically *Nortmannicus comes Willelmus cum multitudine Nortmannorum* in Florence.

[66] See below p. 123.

[67] If they give the Norman version of events, it is also the official version, and has yet to be disproved. William of Poitiers, as a former knight and chaplain to duke William, very much knew what he was talking about, and his chronicle has been described by its most recent editor as *'l'écho direct de la cour anglo-normande'* (*Histoire de Guillaume le Conquérant*, ed. R. Foreville, p. xxi; cf. the same author in *Le Moyen Age*, lviii (1952), p. 44). William of Jumièges also, a monk of the great ducal foundation of Jumièges (at one time presided over by Robert of Jumièges, king Edward's friend and protégé), had access to the best people. Both chroniclers wrote in duke William's reign, after the Conquest of England, and their relationship to each other is close but independent. Cf. n. 26 p. 25 above. In his examination of these and other Norman sources and their interrelationship, Körner (*Battle of Hastings*, pp. 76 et seq.) discusses most of the problems relating to the English succession dealt with in this present chapter, though his arguments and conclusions, based almost exclusively upon textual criticism, seem often unnecessarily negative.

death.[68] It is impossible not to accept the reiterated Norman assertion of the original promise made to William,[69] which is confirmed rather than denied by the significant silence of the pre-Conquest English sources.[70] Furthermore, both William of Poitiers and William of Jumièges say that the formal notification of his nomination was brought to the Norman duke by Robert archbishop of Canterbury,[71] which gives us the date of early in 1051 for the promise itself, since the only time when the new archbishop, appointed in mid-Lent 1051,[72] could have visited the duke for this purpose is during his journey to and from Rome for his pallium between mid-Lent and late June, 1051.[73] Since Godwin's rebellion took place after these events, it is surely very probable indeed that in them we have the real reason for it, and it may also be suggested that the visit of Eustace count of Boulogne to king Edward in the summer,[74]

[68]William of Jumièges, ed. Marx, p. 132; William of Poitiers, ed. Foreville, pp. 30, 109, 174–6. See also Ordericus Vitalis, interpolation in William of Jumièges (ed. Marx) p. 191; *Historia Ecclesiastica* (ed. Le Prévost), ii, 116–17.

[69] Even Freeman accepted it (*Norman Conquest*, ii, 300). F. Barlow, however, has recently attempted to dilute its significance by arguing that Edward pragmatically used the promise of the succession for immediate diplomatic ends (rather as queen Elizabeth I used the prospect of her marriage), citing the possible recognition of the aethling Edward as heir in 1054–7 (below) and the allegation of Adam of Bremen (for which see Körner, op. cit., pp. 138–45, and below n. 153, p. 138), that Edward also promised the succession to Swein of Denmark (*E.H.R.*, lxxx, especially pp. 238, 239–40, 248–9). The force of this argument in weakening the Norman claim is considerably reduced by the subsequent confirmation of the promise to William by Harold in 1064 (below p. 127).

[70] It is accepted by post-Conquest Anglo-Norman chroniclers in one form or another: e.g. Eadmer (*Historia Novorum in Anglia*, R.S., 1884, ed. M. Rule, p. 7, by Edward as a young man in Normandy before his accession), and William of Malmesbury (*Gesta Regum*, i, 278, after the death of the aethling Edward in 1057).

[71] Op. cit., pp. 30 and 132 respectively.

[72] Above p. 118.

[73] *Anglo-Saxon Chronicle* 'E', ed. Whitelock, pp. 116–17; Barlow, *English Church 1000–1066*, pp. 47–9 and n.; Douglas, *William the Conqueror*, p. 169. Robert, of course, must have had access to the duke after his banishment from England in 1052, but was scarcely in any position then to carry out such a mission.

[74] 'Soon after the bishop', i.e. soon after archbishop Robert's return

which sparked off the rebellion, was in the nature of an embassy bringing duke William's acceptance. It is even possible that at this date as well as in 1064 Dover was to be a pledge of Edward's good faith, and that it was Eustace's attempt to occupy it on the duke's behalf that began the trouble.[75] Certainly state visits by reigning princes are rare in this period without good reason; some formal acknowledgement by William was obviously called for; and Eustace was Edward's brother-in-law and William's friend and ally.[76] If duke William himself came to England and to the king in the autumn or winter after Godwin's banishment, as Florence and the 'D' version of the Chronicle say,[77] it must similarly have been for such a formal acknowledgement and confirmation,[78] though some of the most recent work upon Norman history throws doubt upon the visit because of William's preoccupation with the affairs of his duchy at this time.[79] That the original promise and nomination were made early in 1051 and were the fundamental cause of Godwin's rebellion is further confirmed by the more detailed statements of the Norman case given in various parts of his chronicle by William of Poitiers. The promise, he says, was originally made in duke William's absence and with the assent of the English magnates, specifically of Stigand, and earls Godwin, Leofric and Siward, and the son and grandson of Godwin were taken as hostages and sent to

from Rome two days before the Feast of St. Peter (*Anglo-Saxon Chronicle*, 'E', pp. 116, 117).

[75] This would help to explain the prominence given to Dover in Harold's oath of 1064 (below p. 130). The Chronicle ('E', p. 117), enigmatic as ever, says that Eustace 'went to the king and told him what he wished, and then went homewards'.

[76] Stenton, op. cit., p. 552. He had married Edward's sister Godgifu.

[77] Above p. 121 and n. 65.

[78] Thus T. J. Oleson ('Edward the Confessor's Promise of the Throne to Duke William of Normandy', *E.H.R.*, lxxii, pp. 222–3), who, however, does not consider the practical objections to a visit by duke William at this time (below and n. 79).

[79] Douglas, *E.H.R.*, lxviii (1953), pp. 526–34, and *William the Conqueror*, pp. 58–9, 169 and Appendix B. Cf. de Boüard, *Guillaume le Conquérant*, p. 70. Körner, however, accepts William's visit and thinks Douglas too pessimistic about the duke's political preoccupations in Normandy at this date (*Battle of Hastings*, pp. 158–63).

Normandy, evidently at the same time as the mission of Robert of Jumièges to announce the decision.[80] That hostages, namely Wulfnoth his son and Hakon his grandson, were taken from Godwin and sent to Normandy seems certain from the reiterated references to them by Norman and Anglo-Norman chroniclers and from other independent evidence,[81] and the most obvious implication is that earl Godwin was opposed to the nomination of duke William as heir and had to give them as surety for his adherence to it.

In 1051, though earl Godwin and his sons raised a great army and threatened force against the king,[82] Edward with the support of his nephew, earl Ralph, and of earls Leofric of Mercia and Siward of Northumbria, outmanœuvred them politically and was able to banish them in the autumn.[83] On their departure he despatched Edith his queen, earl Godwin's

---

[80] Ed. Foreville, pp. 30, 100, 174–6. Körner (op. cit., pp. 125–31) rejects both the assent of the magnates and the hostages, the former evidently as the result of misunderstanding William of Poitier's chronology. In the first of the chronicler's passages it seems that the assent of the magnates, the sending of the hostages and the mission of Robert of Jumièges all take place at the same time (i.e. 1051), and in the third Harold is said to have sworn, [in 1064] in the duke's presence, what his father and the other magnates had [previously] sworn in the duke's absence [i.e. to support William's succession to the English throne]. Oleson (*E.H.R.*, lxxii, 224), however, would have hostages given in 1052 as part of the returned earl Godwin's settlement with king Edward, which seems unlikely in view of William of Poitiers' statement, though the suggestion agrees with Eadmer's version of these events, unnoticed by Oleson (*Historia Novorum in Anglia*, pp. 5–6). The third passage of William of Poitiers is written as a full and formal statement of his claim made by William the Conqueror in his message to Harold in 1066 before Hastings. The fact, therefore, that at that date and on that occasion Stigand is referred to as archbishop of Canterbury (which he did not become until 1052 after the flight of Robert of Jumièges) is natural and of no significance in dating the original promise itself.

[81] Oleson, op. cit., p. 224, points out that Wulfnoth, alone of Godwin's sons, never held an earldom nor does he appear in Domesday Book as having been a holder of land.

[82] *Anglo-Saxon Chronicle*, 'D', p. 117; Stenton, op. cit., p. 555.

[83] For the events of 1051–2, see Stenton, op. cit., pp. 554–60; B. Wilkinson, 'Freeman and the Crisis of 1051', *Bulletin John Rylands Library*, xxii (1938). Cf. p. 120 above.

daughter, to the abbey of Wherwell,[84] and strengthened the Norman element in his kingdom by appointments which included that of the Norman priest, William, to the vacant see of London.[85] But in the following autumn of 1052 Godwin and his sons came back again in arms, at the head of a large force of ships and men, harrying the English coast in the process, and thereby secured their readmission to the king's peace, and to their lands and dignities. Their return was followed by the reinstatement of queen Edith at court and by the banishment of many of Edward's Norman and French protégés. It was also followed by the irregular and uncanonical appointment of Stigand, a close associate of earl Godwin's, to the banished Robert's deserted archiepiscopal see of Canterbury, which Stigand continued to hold, in plurality with Winchester and, in spite of the anathema of successive popes, until after the Norman Conquest.[86] His position caused grave scandal in reformist circles in contemporary Latin Christendom, and more than any other single factor enabled William the Conqueror to present his invasion to the world as, amongst other things, the means to the end of a necessary reformation of the English church.[87] Meanwhile it is difficult not to interpret the outcome of the English revolution in 1052 as the triumph of earl Godwin's party and a setback to the pro-Norman policies of the king,[88] though some of his Normans were allowed to stay, including earl Ralph[89] and Richard son of Scrob in Here-

---

[84] That Edward repudiated her seems clear from the wording of the 'E' version of the Chronicle where he 'deprived her of all that she owned, land and gold and silver and everything' (p. 121). The *Vita Edwardi*, written in honour of Edith, naturally softens this to a version whereby Edward sent her away (to Wilton, in error for Wherwell) until the political troubles had blown over (ed. Barlow, p. 23).

[85] Stenton, op. cit., p. 557; above p. 118.

[86] Stenton, op. cit., p. 459. He was recognised only by Benedict X (April 1058–January 1059), but since Benedict's own position was irregular this recognition did him more harm than good. See also Barlow, *English Church 1000–1066*, pp. 302–7.

[87] See above p. 105 below p. 252.

[88] Stenton, op. cit., p. 560; Douglas, *William the Conqueror*, pp. 170–1.

[89] Who certainly became earl of Hereford in 1053 in the reshuffle of earldoms after Godwin's death (Stenton, op. cit., p. 561; cf. Loyn, *Norman Conquest*, p. 54).

fordshire, and William, bishop of London.[90] Our estimate of
the extent of Godwin's triumph in 1052 must affect our interpretation of the next event in the unfolding drama of the
English succession, for though the great earl died in 1053 he
was succeeded in the earldom of Wessex and in the headship of
his house by his son Harold,[91] whose rise to pre-eminence in
the kingdom is the dominant theme of English political
history in the decade before the Conquest. In 1054 a mission
under bishop Ealdred of Worcester was sent to negotiate for
the return to England of the aethling Edward, son of Edmund
Ironside, from Hungary, where he had been in exile ever since
the triumph of Cnut in 1016. He arrived at length in 1057, to
die almost at once and before he had met the king,[92] and the
'D' version of the Anglo-Saxon Chronicle adds an element of
mystery by an enigmatic suggestion of foul play – 'We do not
know for what reason it was brought about that he was not
allowed to see [the face?] of his kinsman king Edward.' We
cannot know either, but it seems obvious that he was
brought back to England to be made heir to the throne, as
Florence of Worcester specifically says[93] though the Chronicle
does not. It is scarcely conceivable that he could have come
without the king's acquiescence,[94] and we are left to explain
this inconsistency on Edward the Confessor's part either by
assuming (as seems best) that the aethling was earl Harold's
candidate imposed upon the king to bend the succession away
from Normandy and thus secure his own position as the real

[90] *The Anglo-Saxon Chronicle*, 'D' (p. 124), says as many were allowed to
stay 'as the king should wish to have with him, who were loyal to him
and to all the people'. Florence of Worcester (ed. Thorpe, i, 210) gives
the names of some of them. Oleson (*E.H.R.*, lxxii, 223–4, 227) thinks
that 1052 was far less of a triumph for Godwin than is generally believed,
and that he was compelled at this stage to give his consent to duke
William's succession. This suggestion, however, is based chiefly on the
supposition that the hostages were taken from Godwin in 1052 whereas,
as we have seen above, 1051 is the more likely date for them.
[91] Swein, the eldest son, having died in exile and on pilgrimage to
Jerusalem (Stenton, op. cit., p. 561).
[92] Stenton, op. cit., p. 563.
[93] Ed. Thorpe, i, 215. Cf. *Anglo-Saxon Chronicle*, p. 133.
[94] Though Oleson (op. cit., pp. 225–6) comes close to suggesting this in
the interests of Edward's consistency.

power behind the throne,[95] or by assuming that the king himself more actively sought the aethling's return as an insurance policy against the possible failure of his Norman desire.[96] In either case the move became abortive by the aethling's death,[97] and in 1064 king Edward sent earl Harold to Normandy to confirm the designation of duke William as his heir.

That Edward the Confessor sent Harold to Normandy to confirm the earlier promise of the succession to duke William (at a date not given but generally agreed to have been *c.* 1064), and that Harold there bound himself to the agreement by oath, is, again, asserted by the Norman chroniclers, William of Jumièges and William of Poitiers[98] – to whom we can now add the witness of the Bayeux Tapestry[99] – and, again, is con-

---

[95] Oleson, op. cit., p. 225. It is thought that a possible visit by earl Harold to Flanders in 1056 may have been connected in some way with the negotiations for the aethling's return: see P. Grierson, 'A Visit of Earl Harold to Flanders in 1056', *E.H.R.*, li (1936). The visit is rejected by Körner, op. cit., pp. 205–6, 213–15.

[96] Cf. Loyn, *Norman Conquest*, p. 57. In William of Malmesbury, a twelfth-century writer opposed to Godwin and his sons, the invitation to the aethling is represented as a move by the king against them – Edward, growing old, without an heir, and seeing the sons of Godwin growing in power, sent for the aethling (*Gesta Regum*, i, 278).

[97] For his young son Edgar as a possible claimant to the throne, see p. 138 below.

[98] Respectively pp. 132–3 and pp. 100–14.

[99] The best edition is that of the Phaidon Press, ed. F. M. Stenton (2nd edition, 1965). It is now agreed that the Tapestry was commissioned by Odo, bishop of Bayeux and half-brother to the Conqueror, for the dedication of his new cathedral at Bayeux in 1077, and worked in England between 1066 and that date. Being thus made for public display soon after the events it portrays and during the lifetime of most of the participants, it is most unlikely to contain palpable falsehoods, and its story confirms that of William of Jumièges and William of Poiters (Körner's argument that the Tapestry is not independent and cannot be used to confirm the other Norman sources fails to carry conviction – op. cit., pp. 100–5). Its theme is that of the tragic fate of a man, Harold, who breaks his oath taken upon the relics of Bayeux (ibid., pp. 9, 11, 33–4). Harold's oath thus occupies a central position in the design (Plate 29). Harold's despatch to Normandy by Edward the Confessor, his mission, including his capture by the count of Ponthieu and the Breton expedition as duke William's guest, and his return to England occupy Plates 1–31.

firmed, as it were, by the significant silence of contemporary English sources.[100] The visit began with Harold's unfortunate capture by Guy, count of neighbouring Ponthieu, from which he was released by duke William's powerful intervention, and included an expedition into Brittany on which the duke took his distinguished guest with him, and at its conclusion knighted him by the conferment of arms.[101] There is disagreement about the place at which Harold's famous oath was taken, the

[100] There is no reference to Harold's visit to Normandy in the various versions of the Anglo-Saxon Chronicle, nor in Florence of Worcester who wrote in the earlier twelfth century but largely based himself upon the Chronicle, nor specifically in the *Vita Edwardi*, where, however, references to Harold's being 'rather too generous with oaths' (ed. Barlow, p. 53), and to his having visited the princes of Gaul on his way to Rome (ibid., p. 33), are sometimes taken to relate to it (e.g. Körner, op. cit., pp. 113, 213 et seq.). It occurs in one form or another in later writers. William of Malmesbury's account (*Gesta Regum*, i, 279–80) is chiefly of interest as showing the matter was already controversial in his day. To the idea of some that Edward sent Harold to Normandy to confirm the promise of the succession, he prefers an improbable tale whereby the visit was accidental. On a fishing expedition Harold was blown by storm to Ponthieu; captured by count Guy of Ponthieu, he sent a message to William the Conqueror saying that he had come to confirm the succession in order that the duke would get him released; duly released and in Normandy, he then took his oath about the succession in order to ingratiate himself still further with the duke. In Eadmer's account (*Historia Novorum*, pp. 6–8), Harold went to Normandy with Edward's permission to visit his brother and nephew, i.e. the hostages given by Godwin; there the duke told him of Edward's earlier promise of the succession and he was constrained to swear his support. The embellishment of the employment of trickery, i.e. that Harold took his oath on relics concealed and unknown to him, first appears in Wace, *Roman du Rou* (ed. Andresen), ii, 258.
[101] The Breton expedition is not mentioned in the very brief account of William of Jumièges. In William of Poitiers it comes after, and on the Bayeux Tapestry before, Harold's oath. The conferment of arms by William upon Harold at the conclusion of the campaign, shown on the Tapestry (Plate 27), must surely represent the ceremony of knighting according to the Norman custom of the time (see p. 97 above). This may have carried vaguely vassalic overtones but was in no way the equivalent of the ceremony of commendation whereby a man became the vassal of a lord, which ceremony Harold performed with William on the occasion of his oath in William of Poitier's account (below p. 130).

Bayeux Tapestry, which is unlikely to err in this particular, giving it as Bayeux (and upon the relics of Bayeux),[102] William of Poitiers as Bonneville-sur-Touques,[103] and Ordericus Vitalis (writing in the twelfth century) as Rouen.[104] The only detailed statement of what happened on this occasion is that given by William of Poitiers.[105] He goes out of his way to assure us of the authenticity of his account – 'as men perfectly sincere and trustworthy, who were witnesses of it, have related it'[106] – and we should be unwise to ignore it, for contrary evidence there is none. The earl took an oath of fealty to the duke 'by the sacred right of Christian men',[107] and in the last article of the set form of the oath he pronounced distinctly and of his own free will these words:[108]

[i] 'that he would be the representative [*vicarius*][109] of duke William at the court of his [Harold's] lord, king Edward, as long as he [Edward] should live'.

[102] Plate 29. Cf. n. 99 above.

[103] Ed. Foreville, p. 102.

[104] Ed. Le Prévost, ii, 117.

[105] Ed. Foreville, pp. 102–4. William of Jumièges' brief account agrees in substance with the detailed account of William of Poitiers. He says that Edward the Confessor, having formerly made duke William his heir, sent Harold to Normandy to confirm this (*ut ei de sua corona fidelitatem faceret, ac christiano more sacramentis firmaret*). Harold was released from his captivity in Ponthieu by William's intervention, stayed with the duke for some time, and 'having sworn fealty about the kingdom with many oaths' (*facta fidelitate de regno plurimis sacramentis*) was sent back to king Edward with many gifts.

[106] Foreville, p. 104, '*sicut veracissimi multaque honestate praeclarissimi homines recitavere, qui tunc affuere testes*'.

[107] Ibid., '*Heraldus ei fidelitatem sancto ritu christianorum juravit*'.

[108] Ibid., '*se in curia domini sui Edwardi regis, quamdiu superesset, ducis Guillelmi vicarium fore; enisurum quanto consilio valeret, aut opibus, ut Anglica monarchia post Edwardi decessum in ejus manu confirmaretur; traditurum interim ipsius militum custodiae castrum Doveram, studio atque sumptu suo communitum; item per diversa loca illius terrae alia castra, ubi voluntas ducis ea firmari juberet, abunde quoque alimonias daturum custodibus*'.

[109] The word used, *vicarius*, in classical Latin 'deputy', 'substitute' or 'proxy', can bear also the technical meaning of an executor under Roman law, Harold thus pledging himself to look after William's interests. See Mlle. R. Foreville, 'Aux Origines de la Renaissance Juridique', *Le Moyen Age*, lviii (1952) ,p. 70; Loyn, *Norman Conquest*, pp. 58–9.

[ii] 'that he would employ all his influence and resources to assure him [William] the possession of the English kingdom after the death of Edward'.

[iii] 'that he would meanwhile hand over to the custody of his [William's] knights the castle of Dover, fortified at his [Harold's] own effort and cost'.

[iv] 'also he would similarly hand over, amply provided with supplies, other castles in various parts of the land where the duke should order them to be fortified'.

In addition, Harold did homage to the duke by the *immixtio manuum*,[110] and the duke, evidently before the oath of fealty with its crucial additions, and at Harold's request, gave him, i.e. invested him with, his lands and powers in England.[111] The careful wording of William of Poitiers is very much to be noted, for he is clearly describing the full ceremony of feudal commendation, comprising fealty, homage and investiture, whereby Harold became the vassal of duke William, and what is loosely described by historians as 'Harold's oath', binding himself to support William's succession to the English throne, is incorporated in this solemn occasion as an appendix, or as special articles added, to the normal oath of fealty. Though he alludes to it later,[112] William of Poitiers does not refer at this point in his narrative to the betrothal by duke William of his daughter to Harold, which is asserted by later writers.[113] In his account the Breton expedition, which on the Bayeux Tapestry precedes the oath, now follows it, and he is careful to state that the duke treated his guest as his companion in order to bind him the more closely to him.[114] After this William

[110] Ed. Foreville, p. 104, '*satelliti suo accepto per manus*'. See also ibid., p. 176, '*Se mihi per manus suas dedit*'. Cf. p. 87 above.

[111] Ed. Foreville, p. 104, '*Dux ei, jam satelliti suo accepto per manus, ante jusjurandum terras ejus cunctumque potentatum dedit petenti*'.

[112] Ibid., p. 230.

[113] Ordericus Vitalis, interpolation in William of Jumièges (ed. Marx), p. 191, and in his *Historia Ecclesiastica* (ed. Le Prévost), ii, 118 (where it is denied), 391; Robert of Torigny, interpolation in William of Jumièges (ed. Marx), p. 318; William of Malmesbury, *Gesta Regum*, i, 280, ii, 297, 298, 333; Eadmer, *Historia Novorum*, pp. 7, 8. See Douglas, *William the Conqueror*, Appendix C, pp. 393-5.

[114] Ed. Foreville, pp. 104-6, and n. 3 to p. 105. The word used for 'companion' is *contubernalis*, which in classical Latin signified a young nobleman attached to a commander to be initiated into the military art.

kept Harold with him a little longer, and then sent him back to England loaded with gifts—and with his nephew, Hakon, one of the two hostages of Godwin taken in 1051, specially released in his honour.[115]

In the teeth of the Norman court's constant accusation of Harold's perjury in later taking the throne of England, made before the public opinion of contemporary Europe and made the theme also of the Bayeux Tapestry, and in default of any contrary evidence, it is not possible to reject the substance of the account of 1064 as it is given in the Norman sources.[116] There is a basic unanimity, while the details of Harold's oath and commendation given by William of Poitiers carry conviction. Nor does it seem difficult to explain the actions, and even the motives, of the principal participants. That king Edward should have sent Harold to confirm the earlier promise of the succession to duke William is entirely consistent with what is known of his Norman sympathies and wishes, nor are these seriously questioned by the mysterious affair of the aethling Edward,[117] still less by the alleged grant of his kingdom to Harold on his death-bed.[118] As for Harold, if the mission was unwelcome to him it would have been none the less difficult to refuse, and he may have been motivated also by the thought that if he did not undertake it his brother Tostig would.[119] But it is obvious from William of Poitiers' account that in Normandy he took care to safeguard his own existing position as the pre-eminent magnate in the English realm, his agreement with William being in the nature of a compact

[115] William of Poitiers, ed. Foreville, p. 115. Cf. p. 124 above. See also Ordericus Vitalis, interpolation in William of Jumièges (ed. Marx), p. 191; Eadmer, *Historia Novorum*, pp. 7, 8.

[116] Even Freeman, for whom it was 'one page which I would gladly blot out in the history of Harold', was forced, with whatever agonised discussion and qualification, to admit there was something in it (*Norman Conquest*, iii, 1869, pp. 74, 215 et seq.). Körner (op. cit., pp. 109–21) accepts Harold's visit to Normandy (as part of a diplomatic tour of Europe undertaken at that time – cf. n. 100 p. 128 above), and accepts that the visit had a political motive, though that motive remains unknown.

[117] Above, p. 126.

[118] Below, p. 134.

[119] Oleson, *E.H.R.*, lxxii, 226 n. 3.

which, with or without a betrothal to the duke's daughter, confirmed his own possessions and dignities, and it may be that even as late as this he had not yet dared to plan the unprecedented step of taking the crown for himself, a noble in no way a member of the royal kin. Duke William's own motives and interest are clear enough, and in 1066, on the eve of Hastings, William of Poitiers puts into his mouth a formal statement of his claim against Harold and to the English kingdom, which runs as follows:[120] that king Edward his kinsman had made him his heir, on Harold's admission, in gratitude for the benefits which he and his brother Alfred had received from William and his ancestors, and because Edward thought him the most worthy and the most capable member of the English royal stock. This had been done by the king with the assent of his magnates, and with the counsel specifically of Stigand and earls Godwin, Leofric and Siward, who had sworn to receive William as their lord after Edward's death, and to do nothing against his succession during Edward's lifetime. For this the king had given to the duke the son and grandson of Godwin as hostages, and had finally sent Harold to Normandy 'that he should swear to me there in my presence what his father and the others above named had sworn in my absence'. The duke had obtained Harold's release from captivity in Ponthieu, and Harold had done him homage and given him surety in respect of the English kingdom.[121] On these grounds duke William was prepared to plead his case by the law of Normandy or England, and if Harold refused he was prepared to wage single combat with him – i.e. the Norman judicial combat which put the matter to the judgment of God.

In the event it was Harold who first took the throne in 1066, and thus broke his oath to duke William, on Friday, January 6, on the day after the old king's death and on the very day of his funeral,[122] the great newly consecrated church of St. Peter

---

[120] Ed. Foreville, pp. 174, et seq.

[121] Ibid., p. 176, '*Se mihi per manus suas dedit, sua manu securitatem mihi de regno Anglico firmavit*'.

[122] 'With indecent haste', Oleson, *E.H.R.*, lxxii, 227, and so also Douglas, *William the Conqueror*, p. 182. 'With a haste which shows the

at Westminster witnessing both ceremonies one after the other. At this point it is important to analyse the elements which made a king in this period of the earlier Middle Ages.[123] First came kinship, 'kin-right', a necessary membership of the royal stock, and this is important even though there was no absolute right of primogeniture or strict order of succession to the throne. In their absence the so-called 'elective' element in kingship is in practice the selection of the most suitable member of the royal family – normally the eldest son if worthy and adult – and 'recognition' or acceptance by the magnates of the realm, individually, is to be understood, rather than formal election by a formal assembly summoned for the purpose, the candidate chosen, or self-chosen, seeking as best he could to gain the assent and support, the 'recognition', of those who mattered most. In such circumstances the will of the preceding king was paramount, and can be thought of as part of the process of choice or 'election'. It was common practice for the reigning king to nominate and secure the recognition of his successor, normally his eldest son, in his own lifetime, to ensure continuity and avoid the perils of a disputed succession, and it is in this context that Edward the Confessor's nomination of William the Conqueror as his heir (together with the stress laid by William of Poitiers upon recognition by the magnates),[124] the summons of the aethling Edward from Hungary, and the alleged dying bequest of the kingdom to Harold, are all to be seen – though to leave so important a matter until the last moment is uncommon because unwise, and could be argued as irresponsible in 1066 in view of Edward's earlier commitment. Last in the elements of kingship comes the ceremony and sacrament of coronation and anointing,[125] of crucial importance in itself since alone it made a man king, yet, so far as claimants to the throne are concerned, of its nature *de facto* rather than *de jure*.

urgency of the times', Stenton, *Anglo-Saxon England*, p. 572. The reader must decide for himself.

[123] For what follows, see especially Oleson, *Witenagemot in the Reign of Edward the Confessor*, pp. 82–9; F. Kern, *Kingship and Law* (London, 1939), especially pp. 12–27.

[124] Ed. Foreville, pp. 30, 174–6, 223.

[125] Cf. p. 62 above.

We cannot know when Harold first thought of taking the crown for himself. It is generally supposed that it is unlikely to have been until after the death of the aethling Edward in 1057;[126] it can be argued that his supremacy within the kingdom by 1063–5 must have led him to think of it then,[127] though his commendation and oath to duke William may suggest that he had not dared so far even as late as 1064.[128] But when he did seize the throne in January 1066, there is no doubt at least that he was crowned and anointed king, and this mattered even though it may well be that he was crowned by Stigand, the excommunicated and uncanonical archbishop of Canterbury, which gave the Normans grounds to question the validity of the ceremony.[129] The truth or validity of Edward the Confessor's dying bequest of the kingdom to Harold is a matter about which, in the nature of things, we can never be certain.[130] It is stated as a matter of fact by the 'E' version of the Anglo Saxon Chronicle[131] (favourable to the

[126] Stenton, *William the Conqueror*, p. 148; Douglas, *William the Conqueror*, p. 172; Oleson, *E.H.R.*, ixxii, 227; Freeman, *Norman Conquest*, ii (1870), 420, 429.
[127] Stenton, *Anglo-Saxon England*, p. 568.
[128] Above, p. 132.
[129] William of Poitiers, p. 146, supported, it seems, by the Bayeux Tapestry (Pl. 34) and Ordericus Vitalis, *Historia Ecclesiastica*, ii, 119, iv, 432, states that Stigand crowned Harold. The only authority for the common denial by modern English historians of this assertion is Florence of Worcester (i, 224, quoted n. 133 p. 135, below) who says archbishop Ealdred of York performed the ceremony. But it has been pointed out that Florence, when unsupported, as in this case, by the Anglo-Saxon Chronicle, 'is only a twelfth-century authority, and a late Worcester-York tradition – especially when primatial rights are concerned – inspires little confidence'. The silence of the Chronicle on the matter is, once again, probably significant and 'seems definitely to tip the balance in favour of Stigand'. See Barlow, *English Church 1000–1066*, n. 4, p. 60. Cf. Douglas op. cit., n. 2, p. 182; Körner, op. cit., pp. 131–5.
[130] Generally accepted by modern historians, it is, however, rejected by Oleson (*Witenagemot*, p. 85 and nn.; *E.H.R.*, lxxii, 227, n. 2), chiefly on the grounds of Edward's consistency.
[131] Ed. Whitelock, p. 140, 'And Earl Harold succeeded to the realm of England, just as the king had granted it to him, and as he had been chosen to the position.'

house of Godwin), less explicitly in the 'C' and 'D' versions,[132] and supported by Florence of Worcester,[133] though his contemporary William of Malmesbury is among the first to throw doubt upon it.[134] On the Norman side, it finds no mention in the brief narrative of William of Jumièges,[135] nor in William of Poitiers' account of Edward's death and Harold's succession,[136] though later he evidently accepts it.[137] The one detailed near-contemporary description of the old king's last moments which we have in the *Vita Edwardi* certainly refers to the matter, though the form and manner of Edward's dying speech at this point seem somewhat inappropriate to so momentous an occasion as a grant of the succession, and may be thought to fit much better the context of putting the kingdom into the protection of Harold as the *vicarius*, executor or representative of duke William, the previously nominated and recognised heir.[138] Edward's main concern is evidently for Edith, his wife and queen.[139] 'Then he addressed his last words

[132] Verses, s.a. 1065 (p. 139) –
      'Yet the wise ruler entrusted the realm
        To a man of high rank, to Harold himself'.

[133] Ed. Thorpe, i, 224. '*Quo tumulato* [i.e. Edward], *subregulus Haroldus, Godwini ducis filius, quem rex ante suam decessionem regni successorem elegerat, a totius Angliae primatibus ad regale culmen electus, die eodem ab Aldredo Eboracensi archiepiscopo in regem est honorifice consecratus.*'

[134] Rolls Series, i, 280. Harold seizes the crown and extorts from the magnates their consent. The English say that the king had granted it to him, but William of Malmesbury thinks it improbable that Edward would have transferred his inheritance to a man of whose power he had always been jealous (cf. ibid., p. 278).

[135] Ed. Marx, p. 133.

[136] Ed. Foreville, p. 146.

[137] Ibid., pp. 172, 206–8. In the first instance, Harold in his defiance of William in 1066 admits the earlier promise of the succession to the duke, but asserts the kingdom is now his by right of Edward's dying bequest. In the second, William of Poitiers, denouncing Harold after his death at Hastings, says that his fate proves the lack of validity in the bequest. (Cf. Foreville, *Le Moyen Age*, lviii, pp. 65 et seq.)

[138] Cf. Foreville, op. cit., pp. 68–9.

[139] *Vita Edwardi*, ed. Barlow, pp. 79–80. The Bayeux Tapestry, (Pl. 33) shows the scene of the dying king in his chamber at Westminster, the group about his bed evidently consisting of queen Edith at his feet, Harold, Stigand and Robert the Staller (for whom, see above, p. 115). Cf. *Vita Edwardi*, p. 76.

to the queen who was sitting at his feet, in this wise, "May God be gracious to this my wife for the zealous solicitude of her service. For she has served me devotedly and has always stood close by my side like a beloved daughter. And so from the forgiving God may she obtain the reward of eternal happiness." And, stretching forth his hand to his governor, her brother, Harold, he said, "I commend this woman and all the kingdom to your protection".' Continuing, the king in his next words speaks only of the lady – ' "Serve and honour her with faithful obedience as your lady and sister, which she is, and do not despoil her, as long as she lives, of any due honour got from me" ' – and he ends by commending also to Harold's protection his foreign friends, 'who have left their native land for love of me', and by requesting that his burial should be in his church of Westminster and his death not be kept secret. We are bound to wonder also whether any bequest made was extracted from the dying king rather than freely given, and whether he was in any condition to know what he was doing.[140] As for Harold's 'election' or recognition which followed, it may pass as very probably typical of what contemporaries meant by the election of a king.[141] There must have been many magnates, lay and ecclesiastical, in London and Westminster for the Christmas feast, the consecration of the church of Westminster on December 28 (which Edward was too ill to attend), and, no doubt, because of the old king's impending death. Their assent may well have been unanimous,[142] though recognition throughout the kingdom as a whole was another matter, and Harold was forced to ride north (apparently for the first time in his life)[143] to win over the recalcitrant Northumbrians with the help of bishop Wulfstan of Worcester,[144] as he also felt it necessary to put aside

---

[140] Cf. Douglas, op. cit., p. 182 and n. 3. The author of the *Vita Edwardi* several times states that Edward was not in full possession of his faculties, not only on his deathbed but as from Tostig's banishment in 1065 (ed. Barlow, pp. 53, 75, 76–7).

[141] Oleson, *Witenagemot*, p. 87.

[142] But cf. William of Poitiers, p. 146.

[143] Freeman, *Norman Conquest*, iii, 61.

[144] William of Malmesbury, *Vita Wulfstani*, ed. R. R. Darlington (Royal Historical Society, 1928), pp. 22–3; Stenton, *Anglo-Saxon England*, p. 573.

Edith Swan's Neck and marry another Edith, the sister of earls Edwin of Mercia and Morcar of Northumbria, in an attempt to ensure their support.[145] But the weakest point in Harold's succession to the throne, over and above the perjury and sharp practice of which he stands condemned, is his total lack of 'kin-right', his lack of any drop of royal blood.[146] The peaceful succession, without even a right of conquest which could be regarded as the judgment of God, of a non-royal noble was unprecedented, revolutionary, and politically dangerous even in the tangled state to which the English succession had been brought during the last half-century, and neither national sentiment nor the balm of an anointed king should be allowed to gloss over the fact.

In 1066 Harold, earl of Wessex, and William, duke of Normandy, were not the only contenders and possible rivals for the English throne. The kings of both Norway and Denmark had claims, and in the event the former, as well as duke William, invaded England after Edward the Confessor's death. The claim of Harold Hardrada of Norway, 'the last heroic figure of the Viking age',[147] stemmed ultimately from Cnut's English kingship but more immediately from a treaty of 1038–9 which his father, Magnus, had made with Harthacnut, Cnut's son and successor. Cnut himself, as king of Denmark and of England, had sought without lasting success to impose his rule on Norway, and after his death in 1035 Magnus had made himself master of that country and in his turn waged war upon Denmark. In the course of these wars a treaty between Magnus and Harthacnut made in 1038–9 agreed that in the event of the death of either without heirs, his dominions should pass to the other.[148] In 1042 Harthacnut

---

[145] Ibid.

[146] His mother, Gytha, was the sister of Cnut's brother-in-law, which is scarcely worth mentioning. Körner's conclusion that Harold's succession was 'in accordance with the procedure generally accepted in England during the eleventh century' ignores this essential factor (*Battle of Hastings*, pp. 122–4, 135).

[147] Stenton, op. cit., p. 421.

[148] Ibid., p. 415. Körner, however, points out that the evidence for this treaty comes only from twelfth-century sources (op. cit., pp. 146–54).

did so die, and thereafter Magnus endeavoured to assert his claim to both Denmark and England. When he died in 1047, on the verge of final success in Denmark and ready to turn against England,[149] his claims and ambitions were inherited by his successor, Harold Hardrada. He too spent most of his time and energies during the first nineteen years of his reign in wars against Denmark, now ruled by his contemporary Swein Estrithson, and had it not been for the endemic feud between these Scandinavian kings and claimants to the English throne, it is very probable that England would have once again received an infusion of Viking blood and rule before 1066.[150] In that year Harold Hardrada launched his invasion in pursuance of his claim, to be defeated and slain by the English Harold at Stamford Bridge,[151] while his rival of Denmark, probably from fear of him, gave his support to William of Normandy[152] and made no move. But though Swein Estrithson stood aside in 1066, his claim, by inheritance as the son of Cnut's sister Estrith and as the grandson of Swein 'Forkbeard' (king of England from 1013 to 1014), was to be asserted after the Norman Conquest and taken up and reasserted by his son.[153]

The claims of both Swein Estrithson of Denmark and Harold Hardrada of Norway stemmed from Cnut, but there was, waiting in the wings of the English stage in 1066, another possible claimant in the young person of Edgar aethling, a prince of the royal house of Wessex, the son of Edward aethling who had died on his arrival in England from Hungary in

[149] Stenton, op. cit., pp. 418, 421; Douglas, *William the Conqueror*, p. 165.
[150] As it was, a great raid was launched against England in 1058 under the command of Harold Hardrada's son, and joined in the tumult of that year in which earl Aelfgar fought his way back from exile in alliance with Gruffydd of Wales (Stenton, op. cit., pp. 566–7, and cf. p. 83 above). Cf. Körner (op. cit., pp. 151–4) who thinks the Norwegian threat to England during Edward the Confessor's reign has been exaggerated.
[151] Below, pp. 154–8.
[152] William of Poitiers, ed. Foreville, p. 154, below p. 149.
[153] Below p. 194. According to Adam of Bremen, also, Swein Estrithson had been promised the succession by Edward the Confessor, but this is probably a fabrication (see Körner, op. cit., pp. 138–45, 154–7. Cf. n. 69, p. 122 above).

1057,[154] and thus the grandson of Edmund Ironside and a direct descendant in the male line from Ethelred. His kinright to succeed Edward the Confessor was therefore stronger than that of all the adult contenders for the English throne, and to modern eyes his claim seems better by virtue of heredity.[155] In fact, his rights were passed over by contemporaries,[156] presumably because of his extreme youth,[157] nor does he seem to have asserted them himself, and it was not until the dark days after Hastings and the death of Harold that the men of London, under the leadership of Ealdred, archbishop of York, and with the support of earls Edwin and Morcar, 'elected' him as king.[158] But by then it was too late, and, as the victorious duke William advanced upon London,

[154] Above, p. 126.

[155] There is, however, a possible bar. Edmund Ironside was the son of Ethelred by his first wife, Aelgifu, and it has been suggested that Emma of Normandy, Ethelred's second wife, secured the limitation of the succession to her sons by him on the occasion of her marriage, as she limited it to her sons by Cnut on the occasion of her subsequent marriage to that king. See Barlow, *English Church 1000–1066*, p. 42, and *E.H.R.*, lxxx, pp. 226–7. Cf. Campbell, *Encomium Emma Reginae*, pp. xlv, 32.

[156] William of Malmesbury, however (*Gesta Regum*, ii, 297), states that Edward the Confessor had commended Edgar to the magnates as heir, 'dissimulating his better judgment' – '*Rex Edwardus fato functus fuerat: Anglia dubio favore nutabat, cui se rectori committeret incerta, an Haroldo, an Willelmo, an Edgaro: nam et illum, pro genere proximum regno, proceribus rex commendaverat, tacito scilicet mentis judicio, sed prono in clementiam animo.*' Contemporaries were, of course, aware of the close ties of Edgar by blood with the reigning house of Wessex. The Anglo-Saxon Chronicle, 'D', speaking of Edgar's abortive election as king after Hastings (below, p. 178), adds 'as was his proper due'. Ordericus Vitalis inserts in his history a letter from the monk Guitmond to William the Conqueror refusing preferment in England after the Conquest, wherein Guitmond states baldly that William obtained his crown not by inheritance 'but by the free gift of almighty God, and the friendship of Edward your kinsman. Edgar Aethling and many other scions of the royal stock, are, according to the laws of the Hebrews and other nations, nearer in degree than yourself as heirs to the crown of England' (*Historia Ecclesiastica*, ed. Le Prévost, ii, 231. Cf. ibid., iii, 239).

[157] He cannot have been more than about fifteen years of age in 1066, and therefore only about six on the death of his father in 1057 (Loyn, *Norman Conquest*, p. 99).

[158] *Anglo-Saxon Chronicle*, 'D' (ed. Whitelock, p. 143). Oleson, *Witenagemot*, pp. 88–9. See p. 178, below.

Edgar and his supporters came in to submit to him at Berkhampstead. 'And they submitted out of necessity after most damage had been done – and it was a great piece of folly that they had not done it earlier, since God would not make things better, because of our sins.'[159] Harold Hardrada was slain at Stamford Bridge, Harold of England was slain at Hastings, William of Normandy was crowned and anointed king of England at Westminster, in the Confessor's church, on Christmas Day 1066; the aethling Edgar survived these events, and long after, when William of Malmesbury wrote his chronicle in the 1120's, was living quietly in the English countryside, a remote figure from an earlier age.[160]

'When beggars die there are no comets seen.' The death of Edward the Confessor and the succession of Harold in 1066 were attended by a comet,[161] and set in motion forces, long maturing, whose effects at first no man could foresee, though the eventual outcome of the Norman Conquest was to change the course of English history. The reader, like those living at the time, is not free to choose the best candidate with the best claim to rule. Like them, he must have the decision forced upon him, yet he may also feel that the claim of William the Conqueror combined the most formidable array of rights, judged by the standards of the age.

---

[159] *Anglo-Saxon Chronicle*, 'D' (ed. Whitelock, p. 144); Stenton, op. cit., pp. 588–9.
[160] *Gesta Regum*, i, 278.
[161] Shown on the Bayeux Tapestry (ed. Stenton, Pl. 35. Cf. ibid., p. 181, and William of Jumièges, ed. Marx, p. 133).

CHAPTER V

The Norman Conquest of England

Cry 'Havoc!' and let slip the dogs of war.
SHAKESPEARE

The dramatic events of 1066 began, as we have seen, with Edward the Confessor's death on Thursday, 5 January, followed by Harold's coronation the next day, 'while the grief of the king's death was still fresh'.[1] This *coup d'état* was, in turn, followed of necessity by Harold's hasty visit to the north to overcome the opposition of the Northumbrians, and by his political marriage to Edith, the sister of earls Edwin and Morcar to gain their support, together with the putting aside of Edith Swan's Neck, his mistress or wife *more Danico*.[2] In the event king Harold's reign lasted for nine months and as many days,[3] and, in the words of the Chronicle, 'he met little quiet in it as long as he ruled the realm'.[4] The storm clouds gathered from the start, and as winter gave way to spring and early summer, the comet blazed across the heavens, foretelling doom, or so men thought – 'the long-haired star; and it first appeared on the eve of the Greater Litany, that is 24 April, and so shone all the week'.[5] The historian notes for Harold's

---

[1] Above, p. 132. Cf. William of Malmesbury, *Gesta Regum*, i, 280.

[2] Above, p. 136. The Norman disinclination to submit to Christian marriage in the earlier eleventh century is often held against them and as evidence of their long-continuing Scandinavian habits (cf. Stenton, *Anglo-Saxon England*, p. 547). This instance of 'marriage' *more Danico* is no less interesting as evidence of the Scandinavianisation of the aristocracy in the last decades of the Old English state.

[3] Cf. Florence of Worcester, ed. Thorpe, i, 227–8.

[4] *Anglo-Saxon Chronicle*. ed. Whitelock, p. 140.

[5] Ibid. See also *The Bayeux Tapestry*, ed. F. M. Stenton, Pl. 35 and p. 181; William of Poitiers (ed. Foreville), p. 208; Freeman, *Norman Conquest*, iii (1869), Appendix M.

reign the survival of a single writ and of a voluminous currency,[6] as evidence of continuing government amidst the threat and actuality of war, but in the popular consciousness it is his death on the battlefield of Hastings, on 14 October, that assures his lasting fame. Perhaps, now that the tumult and the torment have long since been over, he is fortunate that it should be so.

First of Harold's enemies off the mark was Tostig, his own brother, former earl of the Northumbrians and banished in 1065.[7] He had spent the winter of his discontent in Flanders, at this time the centre of diplomatic intrigue, and also the emporium of mercenary forces.[8] Tostig's wife, Judith, was the half-sister of Baldwin V, count of Flanders, and was thus a close relative of Mathilda, duke William of Normandy's duchess, who was count Baldwin's daughter. Tostig himself, from Flanders, may well have negotiated with, and sought the help of, both the Norman[9] and Scandinavian claimants to the English throne, and certainly later in the year he was to throw in his lot with Harold Hardrada, king of Norway. Nevertheless, with mainly Flemish forces, he first took unilateral and, as it seems, quite irresponsible action, appearing off the Isle of Wight with a fleet in early May, just as the comet was fading from the sky. There he took money and provisions, and thence ravaged the coast as far as Sandwich, which he occupied, taking both men and ships into his service, until he put to sea again at the news of king Harold of England's advance against him from London. In Thanet, Tostig was joined by his old comrade-in-arms and fellow-exile from the north, Copsi, who now came to him with seventeen ships from the Orkneys, then under Norwegian domination.[10] Together the pair of them

[6] Stenton, *Anglo-Saxon England*, p. 573.
[7] For Tostig's activities in 1066, see especially Stenton, op. cit., pp. 578–9; H. R. Loyn, *The Norman Conquest*, pp. 88–90. Cf. p. 84, above.
[8] For Flanders, see also P. Grierson, 'The relations between England and Flanders before the Norman Conquest', *Transactions Royal Historical Society* (4), xxiii (1941).
[9] Ordericus Vitalis, interpolation to William of Jumièges (ed. Marx), p. 192, and *Historia Ecclesiastica*, ed. Le Prévost, ii, 119–20, 123–4.
[10] A fact which may indicate that Tostig was already in some degree in league with Harold Hardrada (Stenton, op. cit., p. 579).

sailed north up the east coast of England, ravaging as they went, to be beaten off from the Parts of Lindsey and Northumbria by earls Edwin and Morcar. Deserted by many of his ships and men, Tostig went on to take refuge with Malcolm Canmore, king of Scots, and remained in Scotland all the summer, preparing for further action. It was probably at this time that he made his formal alliance with Harold Hardrada of Norway, whom he joined in the Tyne when the latter launched his invasion of England in the autumn.[11] Tostig fell by Harold Hardrada's side at Stamford Bridge in September, slain by his brother, Harold of England – an unpleasant tragedy by the standards of any age, and one which enabled the Normans to add fratricide to the list of Harold's crimes.[12]

According to the Anglo-Saxon Chronicle, it was Tostig's appearance in May and his occupation of Sandwich that first led Harold to mobilise his forces by land and sea, 'larger than any king had assembled before in this country', though the Chronicle states specifically that these defence measures were directed against the threat of invasion from Normandy – 'because he had been told as a fact that count William from Normandy, king Edward's kinsman, meant to come here and subdue this country'.[13] We are told that it was a long time before the fleet could be assembled (Harold meanwhile waiting at Sandwich),[14] and, by another version, that Harold at some

[11] Below, p. 155.
[12] E.g. William of Poitiers (ed. Foreville), pp. 166, 206; *Carmen de Hastingae Proelio* (ed. Giles, *Scriptores . . . Willelmi Conquestoris,* London 1845), p. 31. The texts of the *Carmen* and of William of Poitiers are obviously related each to each. The previously held view that the former is the earlier, the work of Guy, bishop of Amiens, and completed before 1068 (see Ordericus Vitalis, *Historia Ecclesiastica,* ii, 158, 181), was challenged by G. H. White (*Complete Peerage,* xii, Part I, Appendix L, pp. 36–7) but the challenge has recently been rebutted by S. Körner (*Battle of Hastings,* pp. 91–100). The view of Foreville, that William of Poitiers, who wrote his biography in *c.* 1073–4, used the *Carmen* but added material of his own (*Guillaume de Poitiers,* pp. xix–xx, xxxv–xxxviii) seems the most reasonable, and it follows that both sources merit respect. Cf. Douglas, *William the Conqueror,* p. 200, n. 2.
[13] Ed. Whitelock, p. 141, 'C' and cf. 'D'.
[14] Ibid., p. 142, 'C'. For Edward the Confessor's dismissal of the permanent fleet, from which this may result, see n. 149, p. 92 above.

stage in the summer 'went out with a naval force against William'.[15] It seems inconceivable that Harold was entirely unaware of Norwegian intentions and preparations, yet it also seems that the Norwegian invasion of the north in September took him by surprise,[16] and it is certain that all summer long the English defences were concentrated in the south against the threat from France and the known preparations of duke William – presumably because Harold thought that his Norman adversary would be ready first, and possibly because he was concerned to defend his own lands and interests in the south.[17] Contingents of the fyrd were stationed 'everywhere along by the sea',[18] and the fleet, when assembled, lay off the Isle of Wight with the king himself in command. But, says the Chronicle, 'in the end it was no use'. In marked contrast to the triumphant solution of the same problem of logistics by duke William of Normandy,[19] the strain of the long wait proved too much for the English defensive system and Harold's general-ship. About 8 September, Harold was obliged to dismiss his forces. 'The provisions of the people were gone, and nobody could keep them there any longer. Then the men were allowed to go home, and the king rode inland, and the ships were brought up to London, and many perished before they reached there.'[20] The way was thus left open to the Norman

[15] Ibid., p. 140, 'E'.

[16] Ibid., p. 142, 'C'. Cf. Stenton, op. cit., p. 380. William of Malmesbury, however, writing in the early twelfth century, has things the other way about, stating that at first Harold did not take the Norman threat seriously and would not have mobilised had it not been for fear of Norway (*Gesta Regum*, ii, 297–8).

[17] Cf. Douglas, *William the Conqueror*, p. 191; de Boüard, *Guillaume le Conquérant*, p. 83. The latter suggestion, in itself reasonable enough in the very local world of the eleventh century, comes from Douglas. The thought, however, that Harold may have been less concerned about the defence of the north than the south, the basis of the Old English kingdom, cannot be pressed too far in view of his immediate and dramatic reaction to the news of Harold Hardrada's invasion.

[18] *Anglo-Saxon Chronicle*, p. 142, 'C'.

[19] Below, p. 152.

[20] *Anglo-Saxon Chronicle*, p. 142, 'C'. Duke William's fleet appears to have had losses, presumably by storm, in its move from Dives to St. Valery-sur-Somme at about the same time (William of Poitiers, ed. Foreville, pp. 158–60, and below p. 152). Körner's suggestion (*Battle of*

fleet, now in readiness across the Channel and waiting only for a favourable wind to carry them to England. Meanwhile, it was at this moment of confusion that Harold learnt of the Norwegian invasion in the north and that Harold Hardrada of Norway and earl Tostig had sailed with a great fleet up the Humber and were approaching York.[21]

In Normandy, preparations to vindicate by force of arms duke William's right to England had been going forward urgently since mid-winter. We may be sure that intelligence of Edward the Confessor's death and Harold's coronation had swiftly reached the duchy – the Bayeux Tapestry shows a ship bearing the news to Normandy,[22] and Wace has William informed of it while hunting near Rouen[23] – and we may surmise that William must have thought of his Grand Design even before the events which rendered it necessary. For so vast and hazardous an enterprise a first priority was obviously the counsel and consent of the Norman magnates, both ecclesiastical and lay. A series of great councils was held, of which there is evidence of one at Lillebonne,[24] another, which may be represented on the Bayeux Tapestry, at Bonneville-sur-Touques,[25] and a third at Caen in June.[26] According to William of Poitiers, many barons at first sought to dissuade the duke from an undertaking at once perilous and beyond

---

Hastings, pp. 264–5), that at this point Harold did not dismiss his forces through a failure in logistics but regrouped them while he himself went north against Harold Hardrada seems to be (a) sheer hypothesis, uncharacteristic of this scholar, and (b) contrary to the specific statement of the Chronicle quoted above. Cf. also Hollister, *Anglo-Saxon Military Institutions*, pp. 86–7.

[21] *Anglo-Saxon Chronicle*, p. 143, 'C', see p. 156, below.
[22] Ed. F. M. Stenton, Pl. 36.
[23] *Roman de Rou*, ed. H. Andresen (Heilbronn, 1877–9), ii, 264.
[24] William of Malmesbury, *Gesta Regum*, ii, 299, according to whom it took place after the receipt of papal support and the papal banner (below, p. 148).
[25] Ordericus Vitalis, *Historia Ecclesiastica*, ii, 125. Douglas (*William the Conqueror*, p. 184), suggests that William was concerned with the construction of his fleet on this occasion, in which case cf. *The Bayeux Tapestry*, ut supra, Pl. 37.
[26] Douglas, op. cit., pp. 184–5; Fauroux, *Recueil des Actes des Ducs de Normandie*, No. 231.

the resources of the duchy,[27] and Wace, elaborating the passage, has the doubters won over by William fitz Osbern, the duke's seneschal and closest friend.[28] It has been suggested that William of Poitiers may have invented the episode in order to emphasise the heroism of his hero,[29] and it is unlikely that many of the Norman aristocracy of this age could have long resisted a martial adventure promising such rich rewards as this. Certainly in the event duke William had the full support of all his vassals, and only less impressive than the conquest of England which they jointly brought about are the peace and order which prevailed in Normandy during the prolonged absence of the great majority of its lords. At one or other of these great councils, also, the necessary arrangements were made for the government of the duchy in the absence of the duke. His duchess Mathilda was established as regent in association with their eldest son, Robert, who, now aged about fourteen, was probably at this time formally recognised as his father's heir in Normandy. To assist them, certain elder statesmen and prominent members of the aristocracy were to remain behind, notably Roger of Montgomery, and Hugh son of Richard, *vicomte* of Avranches.[30] And amidst all the military preparations of these months, and regarded as an essential part of them, that muscular Christianity characteristic of mid-eleventh-century Normandy and the age ensured that those bound for England should first make their offerings to their God of Battles. The duke, as always, led the way. In June, he and Mathilda presided over the solemn dedication of her great church of Holy Trinity at Caen, and together they gave, amongst other things on that occasion, their daughter Cecilia to religion in that place. Again,[31] a well-known donation of duke William at this time is of the land of Steyning in Sussex to the ducal abbey of Fécamp in Normandy, the grant to take effect 'if God should give him victory in England'.[32] Other Norman

[27] Ed. Foreville, p. 148.
[28] *Roman de Rou*, ii, 270–5.
[29] F. M. Stenton, *William the Conqueror*, p. 165.
[30] Douglas, op. cit., pp. 185–6.
[31] Fauroux, op. cit., No. 231, p. 446.
[32] *Regesta Regum Anglo-Normannorum*, i (1913), ed. H. W. C. Davis, No. 1. For the grant of Steyning to Fécamp by Edward the Confessor

lords followed the duke's example, and few things are more evocative than the echo of their voices across the centuries from the eve of their great adventure. One Roger, son of Turold, 'being about to put to sea with count William', gave land to Holy Trinity at Rouen, and another grant was made to the same house by 'a certain knight' called Osmund de Bodes as duke William's fleet and army waited to invade England. Both donors, in the event, were to die on the expedition.[33]

Scarcely less important than these domestic preparations were the diplomatic preparations which preceded the Norman conquest of England.[34] It has often been pointed out how favourable was the position of Normandy *vis-à-vis* her neighbours in 1066, and indeed, though this scarcely detracts from the magnitude of the achievement, it is unlikely that duke William could have attempted the conquest at any date much earlier in his reign. His two chief enemies were both dead by 1066 and the powers they had wielded at least neutralised.[35] King Henry I of France had been succeeded on his death in 1060 by Philip I, who was not only a minor but also under the guardianship of count Baldwin of Flanders, duke William's father-in-law. In Anjou, the death of count Geoffrey, also in

and its seizure by Harold, see D. Matthew, *The Norman Monasteries and their English Possessions* (O.U.P., 1962), pp. 20–2.

[33] *Cartulaire de l'abbaye de la Sainte-Trinité du Mont de Rouen*, ed. A. Deville, printed in *Cartulaire de l'abbaye de Saint-Bertin*, ed. M. Guérard (*Documents Inédits sur l'Histoire de France*, Paris, 1841), pp. 451, 453, Nos. lvii, lxiii. Cf. Douglas, 'Companions of the Conqueror', *History*, xxviii (1943), pp. 141–2; and *William the Conqueror*, pp. 186–7; G. H. White, 'Companions of the Conqueror', *Genealogists' Magazine*, ix, (1944). See also Körner, *Battle of Hastings*, pp. 243–50, who in asserting that No. lxiii cannot be safely dated to 1066 misses the point that the grant by Roger, son of Turold, was originally made when 'about to put to sea with *count* William' and subsequently confirmed by 'William *king of the English*' (ibid. p. 248–9).

[34] For what follows, see Stenton, op. cit., pp. 577–8; Douglas, op. cit., pp. 187 et seq.; de Boüard, op. cit., p. 80. The long discussion by Körner (op. cit., pp. 217 et seq.), does not seem to invalidate this statement, nor the belief generally held by historians in the considerable support received by duke William for his venture from Latin Christendom, both officially and in the form of individual volunteers for his army.

[35] Above, p. 58.

1060, had been followed by civil war about the succession in the country. The buffer state of Maine, whose control had been in dispute between Normandy and Anjou, had been conquered by William in 1063. Of the duke's other near neighbours, the rich and powerful count of Flanders was his ally; so, at this time, was count Eustace of Boulogne; the county of Ponthieu had been under William's feudal suzerainty since 1054; and in Brittany, partly as the result of his expedition there in 1064, there was a pro-Norman faction which helped to assure that the Bretons were the most numerous of those contingents of non-Norman volunteers who followed the duke to England in 1066. One vital result of this favourable situation was that all the ports and harbours facing England from the Scheldt to Finisterre were under the direct or indirect control of Normandy.[36] Yet all this was not enough, and in the early months of 1066 a diplomatic offensive was successfully conducted to gain the moral approbation and political acquiescence of Western Europe for the Norman cause. Formal protest was evidently sent to England,[37] and soon after that, unlike Harold, who, for whatever reason, made no such move,[38] duke William laid his case before the Papacy. The outcome was the papal blessing for the enterprise and the gift of a papal banner to march under.[39] The duke's right to the English succession

---

[36] Cf. William of Malmesbury, cited n. 38, below.

[37] Thus William of Jumièges, ed. Marx, p. 133; William of Malmesbury, *Gesta Regum*, ii, 298; Wace, *Roman de Rou*, ii, 266. Other exchanges between William and Harold are reported at various times before the battle of Hastings: see William of Poitiers, ed. Foreville, pp. 156, 170, 172–8; *Carmen de Hastingae Proelio* (ed. J. A. Giles, *Scriptores Rerum Gestarum Willelmi Conquestoris*. London, 1845), pp. 33–6; William of Malmesbury, ut supra, pp. 300–1. Cf. Körner, op. cit., p. 261.

[38] William of Malmesbury suggested that Harold omitted to do this 'either because he was proud by nature, or because he distrusted his cause, or because he feared that his envoys would be obstructed by William and his supporters who beset every port' (*Gesta Regum*, ii, 299).

[39] For the banner, or 'gonfanon', which is shown on the Bayeux Tapestry at Hastings, see e.g. William of Poitiers, p. 154; Ordericus Vitalis, *Historia Ecclesiastica*, ii, 123; William of Malmesbury, *Gesta Regum*, ii, 299; *The Bayeux Tapestry*, ed. Stenton, Pl. 69. According to Wace, Pope Alexander II also sent a relic, a hair of St. Peter set in a precious ring, which William wore about his neck at Hastings (*Roman de Rou*, ii, 281).

was thus recognised by the highest international court in Christendom, any taint of a merely aggressive war was removed by the judgment of the mid-eleventh-century equivalent of the modern United Nations, and the Norman expedition against England was given something of the colouring of Holy War in the interest of the reformation of the English church by the Norman champion of reform.[40] In addition, the Norman envoys at this time obtained some form of alliance with the young emperor, Henry IV of Germany, or those who governed in his name,[41] and, more remarkably, even with one of the two Scandinavian claimants to the English throne, Swein Estrithson of Denmark, who, no doubt, was chiefly moved by fear and jealousy of his more potent rival, Harold Hardrada, king of Norway.[42]

In the event, however, the success or failure of the undertaking would depend upon the raising of a sufficient fleet and army. Neither was immediately available even in the military and militant Norman duchy, and the manner of their provision, equipment and maintenance in the few months between January and September 1066 is one of the most remarkable chapters in the history of the Norman Conquest. The fleet had to be built for the purpose. According to William of Malmesbury, it was at the council of Lillebonne that William obtained promises of ships from his magnates, each according to his means,[43] and a quasi-authentic list of these contributions survives, beginning with the sixty vessels of William fitz Osbern, and ending with the noble ship which the duchess Mathilda provided for her husband. This was called the *Mora*, and had as a figurehead at the prow a boy wrought in gold, pointing to England with his right hand and holding to his lips an ivory horn in his left.[44] The Bayeux Tapestry energetically portrays

[40] For William as the champion of reform, and the Normans as the exponents of the new concept of Holy War, see above, pp. 18, 34.
[41] William of Poitiers, p. 154; Stenton, op. cit., p. 578.
[42] William of Poitiers, p. 154; Loyn, *Norman Conquest*, p. 87. William of Poitiers goes on to say that Swein later broke his word, and later states that he sent abundant help (*copiosa . . . auxilia*) to Harold at Hastings (ibid., p. 186). Cf. Körner, op. cit., p. 220, and below, n. 123, p. 166.
[43] *Gesta Regum*, ii, 299.
[44] The list is printed by Giles, *Scriptores . . . Willelmi Conquestoris*, pp.

the construction of the fleet, with duke William giving orders for the work, possibly at Bonneville-sur-Touques.[45] The ships, as completed, were assembled in the estuary of the Dives, and were all ready, perhaps to the number of some six or seven hundred, by early August.[46] By that time the army had also been assembled in the same place, a total force of perhaps 7,000 men, including probably 2,000 or 3,000 knights and mounted esquires with their horses, and with their arms, equipment and supplies.[47] While the hard core, and the heart

21–2. *The Bayeux Tapestry* (ed. Stenton, Pl. 43 and enlargement) shows the *Mora* with an animal's head carved at the prow, and on the stern a figure with a blown horn in the right hand and a lance with gonfanon in the left.

[45] Ibid., Pls. 37–9.

[46] See William of Poitiers, p. 151, and Foreville's note, ibid., for the eleventh-century geography of the area. For the dates, see Douglas, op. cit., p. 398. For the size of the fleet, see n. 47 below.

[47] The figures are in no way accurate but are intended to give some indication of the size of the force involved. While modern commentators on the Hastings campaign tend to put the numbers on either side at the battle in the region of 7,000 men, their calculations are more or less rational guesswork, proceeding from the principle of reducing the conventional and picturesque exaggerations of medieval chroniclers to a consideration of such factors as the number of ships in William's fleet and their capacity, the time taken by the Normans to embark and disembark, and the position and disposition of Harold's army at Hastings. Unfortunately these factors cannot be known with any accuracy either. The number of ships in the Norman fleet varies in the eleventh-and twelfth-century writers from 696 of Wace allegedly on his father's information (*Roman de Rou*, ed. Andresen, ii, 285) to the 3,000 of William of Jumièges (ed. Marx, p. 134) and beyond (e.g. 11,000 in Gaimar, cited by Freeman, iii (1869), p. 381, n. 1), and their (varying?) capacity is unknown. Even if the exact extent of Harold's position at Battle were certain, we still should not know its depth in terms of the number of ranks of men which composed it, while to proceed from a calculation of the numerical strength of the English army based on this factor to an estimate of the numerical strength of the Norman army which opposed it is to further increase the element of guess-work. Chronicle references to the numbers of the Norman force will be found in William of Poitiers (ed. Foreville, pp. 150, 170: 50/60,000) and Ordericus Vitalis (*Historia Ecclesiastica*, ii, 144: 50,000 knights plus a force of infantry). For modern estimates of the numbers of both armies, see H. Delbrück, *Geschichte der Kriegskunst im Rahmen des Politische Geschichte*, iii (Berlin, 1923), p. 156; W. Spatz, *Die Schlacht von Hastings*

and soul, of this great army was Norman, made up of the
duke's vassals and their contingents, its numbers were necessarily augmented by the volunteers who flocked into Normandy, as the news of the expedition spread, 'from all parts
of the horizon',[48] far and near – from Brittany and Flanders,
from Picardy, Ponthieu and Maine, from the Ile de France and
Aquitaine, and from the ebullient Norman colonies now established beyond the Alps in southern Italy.[49] Some were magnates, but many more, like many of the Normans from Normandy, were landless knights, the characteristic product of
the age,[50] attracted by the lure of adventure, by William's
well-known and lordly generosity, above all by the prospect of
fiefs in England, and (so William of Poitiers insists) by the
justice of the ducal cause. As with the First Crusade a few
years later, so with the Norman Conquest of England: if some
went to do good, most who went, and survived, did well. The
achievement of welding this polyglot force into an effective
and an offensive weapon, and its sustained control, with dis-

(Berlin, 1896), pp. 30, 33–4; F. Lot, *L'Art militaire et les armées au
moyen âge*, i, 284–5; Stenton, *Anglo-Saxon England*, p. 584; D. C.
Douglas, *William the Conqueror*, pp. 198, 199. The estimates of F. H.
Baring (*Domesday Tables* . . ., London, 1909, p. 219) go rather above the
c. 7,000 figure, and those of W. J. Corbett (in *Cambridge Medieval
History*, v, 498), and J. F. C. Fuller (*Decisive Battles of the Western World*,
London, 1954, pp. 372, 373–4), rather below. Modern estimates of the
number of ships in the Norman fleet range from Fuller's 450 (op. cit., p.
372), through Corbett's 700 (loc. cit., p. 498) to Spatz 1,500 (op. cit.,
p. 28). The Bayeux Tapestry shows the loading of arms, equipment and
supplies (ed. Stenton, Pls. 40–1). The Normans took their war-horses
with them (ibid., Pls. 42–5), and Guy of Amiens refers to the difficulties
of embarking them – '*Plurima cogit equos equitum pars scandere naves*'
(*Scriptores* . . ., ed. Giles, p. 29). For earlier instances of the transport by
sea of horses, and of 'combined operations' by the Normans in southern
Italy, and their probable influence upon the invasion of England in
1066, see D. P. Waley, 'Combined Operations in Sicily, 1060–78',
Papers of the British School at Rome, xxii (1954).
[48] De Boüard, *Guillaume le Conquérant*, p. 81. For Körner's view that
the number of non-Norman volunteers in the Conqueror's army has
been exaggerated, see his *Battle of Hastings*, pp. 237–55, and cf. n. 34,
p. 147, above.
[49] William of Poitiers, p. 151; Stenton, op. cit., p. 577; Douglas, op. cit.,
p. 191.
[50] Above, p. 17.

cipline and morale unimpaired, throughout the long weeks of waiting for a favourable wind, first at Dives-sur-Mer from the 12th of August to the 12th of September, and then at St. Valery-sur-Somme for a further fortnight,[51] must come very high on any list of claims of William the Conqueror to be ranked among the consummate generals of his age, and gives the lie to any lingering notions, derived from Oman[52] or others, of medieval warfare as undisciplined, unplanned and undirected chaos. William of Poitiers, in a famous passage, describes with justified wonder the discipline at Dives, as the duke forbade all plunder and maintained his knights and soldiers at his own expense:

> 'He made generous provision both for his own knights and those from other parts, and did not permit any of them to take their sustenance by force. The neighbouring peasantry could pasture their cattle and sheep in peace either in the meadows or in the open countryside; the crops awaited untouched the sickle of the harvester without being ridden down by the arrogant passage of knights or cut by forragers. Weak or un-armed, any man might move about the district at his will, singing on his horse, without trembling at the sight of soldiers.'[53]

Then on 12 September, a few days after Harold on the opposite shore in England had been obliged to dismiss his forces because he could not keep them together any longer,[54] duke William took advantage of a westerly wind to move his fleet and army to St. Valery-sur-Somme in the county of Ponthieu – possibly to keep them occupied, possibly to ease the problem of sup-plies, possibly to gain a shorter passage, and perhaps to line them up upon the previously selected targets of Pevensey and Hastings.[55] Still for two more tedious weeks the wind stayed

[51] For the dates, see especially Douglas, op. cit., Appendix D and p. 398.
[52] Sir Charles Oman, *A History of the Art of War in the Middle Ages* (London, 1924. Reissued and revised by J. H. Beeler, Ithaca, New York, 1953).
[53] William of Poitiers, ed. Foreville, p. 152. The passage is repeated, by accident or design, ibid., p. 262.
[54] Above, p. 144.
[55] William of Poitiers, pp. 158–60 (implying losses by storm on the way. Cf. p. 144, n. 20, above). See also Freeman, *Norman Conquest*, iii,

contrary to the duke's desires. The Norman chroniclers and poets describe how William watched the weather-cock on the church of St. Valery, and prayed, and also kept up the morale of his men.[56] At length the body of St. Valery himself was brought out of the church for solemn veneration in procession – and the wind changed. At once, on the 27th of September, the hasty and joyful embarkation took place, urged on vigorously by the duke. 'The eagerness was such that even while one was calling for his esquire and another for his companion, most of them, forgetful alike of followers, companions or provisions, were anxious only in their haste not to be left behind.'[57] So on the evening tide[58] of that memorable Wednesday, the Norman ships cleared the mouth of the Somme for a rendezvous on the high seas, ordered by the duke both so that they might form up again into a fleet and so that they should not reach the English coast before daylight.[59] Then, in the dark, at the signal of a horn blown from the *Mora* and a lantern at her masthead, they sailed for England. The speed of duke William's ship, his duchess's gift, we are told was such that she outstripped the rest, and at dawn he and his company found themselves alone in the middle of the Channel – whereat the

(1869) 390 et seq.; Douglas, op. cit., pp. 192–3; Stenton, op. cit., p. 580; de Boüard, op. cit., p. 85. William the Conqueror's invasion was the result of long and careful preparation, and there seems no reason to doubt that the place of disembarkation would be chosen with care. It is worth noting that Ordericus Vitalis specifically names Hastings and Pevensey among the ports Harold had guarded during the summer (*Historia Ecclesiastica*, ed. Le Prévost, ii, 143).

[56] William of Poitiers, p. 160; Guy of Amiens, *Carmen* (ed. Giles, *Scriptores* . . .), pp. 28–9. William of Malmesbury (*Gesta Regum*, ii, 300) says that murmurings against the whole expedition took place especially among the lower ranks (*vulgus militum, ut fieri solet*), some saying that God must be against it since He prevented the wind they wanted, and others (most interestingly – cf. p. 112, above) that the duke's father, Robert the Magnificent, had attempted the same expedition only to be forced to give it up.

[57] William of Poitiers, ut supra. A very detailed account of events at St. Valery, with full reference to the sources, is given, as always, by Freeman iii (1869), pp. 391 et seq.

[58] Cf. J. Beeler, *English Warfare 1066–1189* (Ithaca, N.Y., 1966), p. 12, who gives all possible information about tides and times.

[59] William of Poitiers, p. 162.

intrepid duke showed what military Selection Boards in the last war called 'Man Management' and 'Officer-like Qualities', calmly calling for and consuming his breakfast, washed down with wine, 'as if in his chamber at home'.[60] In due course the rest of the fleet came up, and without further incident an unopposed landing was made at Pevensey on 28 September.[61] There a castle was constructed, where it still is, but then only with ditch and bank and palisade, within the Roman fortress of Anderida, and soon afterwards, leaving a garrison behind, the army and the fleet moved on to the better base of Hastings. There, too, a castle was constructed,[62] and the duke waited upon the event which he desired and planned, that Harold should be drawn as soon as possible to the arbitrament of battle.[63]

Meanwhile, the northerly wind which had held duke William land-locked so long at St. Valery-sur-Somme had carried king Harold Hardrada of Norway to England. His preparations, of which we know little,[64] must have been impressive also, and he is said to have arrived off the north coast with a fleet variously estimated at 300 ships and 'more than 500', to be met in

[60] Ibid., p. 164, *acsi in coenaculo domestico.*
[61] Ibid., William of Jumièges, ed. Marx, p. 134; *Carmen* (ut supra), pp. 30–1; *Anglo-Saxon Chronicle* (ed. Whitelock), 'D', p. 142. The time of landfall is given as 9 a.m. by Guy of Amiens. For the date see Douglas, *William the Conqueror*, p. 397. The story that the duke himself fell upon landing, and that the incident was turned into a good omen by a knight near him (*'Tenes'*, inquit, *'Angliam, comes rex futurus'*) begins with William of Malmesbury (*Gesta Regum*, ii, 300), and is taken up by Wace (*Roman de Rou*, ed. Andresen, ii, 291).
[62] William of Poitiers, pp. 164, 168; William of Jumièges, p. 134; *Anglo-Saxon Chronicle* (ed. Whitelock), 'D', pp. 142–3. It is thought that William moved from Pevensey to Hastings on the 29th (Douglas, op. cit., p. 397). It is not unlikely that at Hastings, as at Pevensey and Dover (p. 177, below), the Norman castle (for which see *Bayeux Tapestry*, ed. Stenton, Pl. 51) was constructed within existing fortifications. Cf. *Carmen* (ed. Giles), p. 31:

> '*Littora custodiens, metuens amittere naves,*
> *Moenibus et munis, castraque ponis ibi:*
> *Diruta quae fuerant dudum castella reformas.*'

[63] See p. 162, below.
[64] See Freeman, iii (1869), 340.

the Tyne by Tostig from Scotland with a further force.[65] Thence the Norwegian king and Tostig sailed down the east coast, ravaging as they went, entered the Humber and proceeded up the Ouse to Riccall, some ten miles by road from York, where they disembarked and made their base.[66] From Riccall they marched upon York, to find their way blocked at Gate Fulford, now a suburb of York, two miles from the city, by earls Edwin and Morcar with an army raised from their earldoms. At the battle of Fulford, on Wednesday 20 September,[67] the Norwegians, under their banner, the 'Landravager',[68] won the day, but only after a prolonged and bloody conflict whose importance has been rightly stressed, for Harold Hardrada's losses, combined with the confidence of victory, may well have effected the outcome at Stamford Bridge, and the far heavier losses of the earls may well provide

[65] *Anglo-Saxon Chronicle* (ed. Whitelock), 'C', pp. 141–2; Florence of Worcester, ed. Thorpe, i, 225–6; Stenton, *Anglo-Saxon England*, p. 580. According to the sagas of Snorre Sturlason (*Heimskringla or the Sagas of the Norse Kings*, ed. R. B. Anderson, iv, 1889, p. 36), Harold Hardrada voyaged via the Orkneys and Shetlands, where he picked up reinforcements, and according to the 'D' and 'E' versions of the *Anglo-Saxon Chronicle* (p. 141) he joined Tostig in Scotland. The best modern accounts of the campaign of Harold Hardrada and Stamford Bridge will be found in Stenton, op. cit., pp. 580–2, drawing heavily on Freeman, *Norman Conquest*, iii, 339 et seq., and in F. W. Brook's pamphlet, *The Battle of Stamford Bridge* (East Yorks. Local History Society, 1963).
[66] There is no evidence in support of Stenton's suggestion (op. cit., pp. 580, 581, 586, n. 1) that English shipping in Northumbrian waters withdrew before the Norwegian fleet, up the Humber, the Ouse and the Wharfe, to Tadcaster, there to be met by Harold of England on his arrival on 24 September (see also F. W. Brooks, op. cit., p. 9). The theory is derived from Freeman and evidently depends upon a misinterpretation of the Anglo-Saxon Chronicle, 'C', where Harold reviews his 'lithsmen' at Tadcaster (*and thaer his lith fylcade*). But *lithsmen* are not necessarily sailors, and therefore do not imply a fleet, and the passage should properly be rendered 'and there marshalled his troops'. See Freeman, op. cit., iii, 347 and n. 3, 348, 362 and n. 3; C. W. Hollister, *Anglo-Saxon Military Institutions* (Oxford, 1962), p. 17; *Anglo-Saxon Chronicle*, ed. Whitelock, p. 144; C. Plummer, *Two of the Saxon Chronicles Parallel* (Oxford, 1892–9, 1952), i, 197.
[67] *Anglo-Saxon Chronicle* (ed. Whitelock), 'C', 'D', pp. 141, 143.
[68] Snorre, *Heimskringla*, ut supra, p. 38.

at least one reason for their absence from the field of Hastings.[69]
After this, Harold Hardrada triumphantly entered York,
whose leading citizens not only surrendered to him but entered
into an alliance to march south with him against the rest of
England[70] – a startling confirmation of Northumbrian separatism at this time, and a no less startling indication that the
degree of political unity achieved in the Old English state on
the eve of the Norman Conquest, and in the brief reign of
Harold,[71] should not be overstressed.[72]

While Harold Hardrada, king of Norway, was at York
Harold, king of England, was advancing north towards the
city, with all the speed and all the men that he could muster –
'day and night as quickly as he could assemble his force'[73] –
on a rapid and decisive march which never fails to impress
historians whether primarily interested in military affairs or
not. Unfortunately we do not know the precise dates and
times involved before he reached Tadcaster on Sunday 24
September.[74] It is likely that the Norwegian fleet appeared in
the Tyne and began ravaging the coast between Tyne and
Humber in the first week of September; the most detailed
version of the Anglo-Saxon Chronicle states that Harold
received news of the invasion soon after he had dismissed his
forces in the south on 8 September; and we should probably
allow three days for any messenger to reach him in the south
from Yorkshire.[75] It seems, therefore, that he can have had
only two weeks at the most to make his decision, organise his

[69] Stenton, op. cit., p. 582.
[70] Anglo-Saxon Chronicle, 'C', p. 144, 'arranging that they should all go
with him southwards and subdue this country'.
[71] Stenton (op. cit., p. 581), 'terms which show that the recent northern
progress of Harold Godwinson had failed to conciliate them'.
[72] Above, p. 76.
[73] Anglo-Saxon Chronicle, 'C', p. 143.
[74] Ibid., p. 144.
[75] For a discussion of the dates, see F. W. Brooks, op. cit., p. 12, and for
Harold's dismissal of his forces in the south followed by news of the
Norwegian invasion, see Anglo-Saxon Chronicle, 'C', pp. 142–3. The
statement or implication in the 'D' and 'E' versions of the Chronicle (p.
141) that Harold's first knowledge of the invasion included the battle of
Fulford, fought on September 20, is plainly irreconcilable with his
arrival at Tadcaster on the 24th.

force, and march to Tadcaster, nine miles from York. The nature and the number of that force must be even more con-jectural – presumably Harold's own housecarls and retainers, who would be mounted for the march, and such levies as time allowed him to muster on the way[76] – but it is difficult to see how large numbers can have been involved, and Freeman's contention that 'the whole strength of southern and central England'[77] was brought to bear must surely be an exaggeration. Arrived at Tadcaster on the 24th, Harold rested his troops for the night, and then, on Monday morning, 25 September, 'went right on through York'[78] (whose citizens must have looked upon him with mixed feelings) to Stamford Bridge, seven miles out on the other side, where Harold Hardrada, Tostig and the Norwegians, unprepared and knowing nothing of his approach until too late, were awaiting hostages from the sur-rounding countryside. Of the battle that ensued we know very little save its elegiac decisiveness, for the only detailed medieval description of it, in the Norse sagas of Snorre Sturlason, is thoroughly unreliable, anachronistic and in error, and has done more to confound than to inform the student of military history.[79] Stamford Bridge was a battle fought by both sides on foot, in the ancient Teutonic and Viking manner, for the last time on English soil, hand to hand and axe to axe.[80] Harold's force was evidently held up at first on the bridge, at one stage by a single Norse Horatio,[81] but then were able to cross over to assault the main body of the enemy, hastily

[76] Stenton, op. cit., p. 581; F. W. Brooks, op. cit., p. 12.
[77] *Norman Conquest*, iii, 361.
[78] *Anglo-Saxon Chronicle*, 'C', p. 144.
[79] *Heimskringla*, ed. Anderson, iv, 40–50. Cf. p. 96 above; Brooks, op. cit., pp. 10, 14–15; Freeman, op. cit., pp. 363–7 and Appendix CC. A recent defence of Snorre by Richard Glover, in order to prove that the pre-Conquest English used cavalry, does not inspire confidence ('English Warfare in 1066', *E.H.R.*, lxvii, 1952).
[80] In the manner beloved of Freeman (op. cit., ii, 1870, pp. 126–7).
[81] The story first appears in a later addition to the 'C' version of the *Anglo-Saxon Chronicle* (ed. Whitelock, pp. 144–5). Cf. William of Malmesbury, *Gesta Regum*, i, 281; Henry of Huntingdon, ed. T. Arnold (Rolls Series, 1879), p. 200. For the local tradition surviving until recent times, see Brooks, op. cit., p. 16.

drawn up, the king and the Land-ravager in the centre,[82] on the higher ground of the present Battle Flats beyond. At the end of the long and crude engagement, which is said to have lasted until late in the day[83] with great losses on both sides, both king Harold Hardrada and earl Tostig had been slain, and the Norwegian army shattered. Its remnants, and Olaf the king's son, having given hostages and oaths not to attack England again, were allowed to sail home, and according to one source 24 ships, and according to another 20, were enough to take them.[84]

Of Gate Fulford and Stamford Bridge the compiler of the 'D' version of the Anglo-Saxon Chronicle observed that 'These two pitched battles were fought within five nights'.[85] They were; but more, and worse, was yet to come. On or very soon after 1 October, still in the north, probably at York, and by tradition at a feast to celebrate his recent victory, Harold received the news of duke William's landing at Pevensey.[86] From that moment onwards dynamic speed, or, more probably, reckless and impulsive haste, is the theme of his campaign against the Normans. Within the space of thirteen days at most, he, with such of his force and following as could keep up with him, had ridden the 190 miles from York to London, assembled an army in the latter city,[87] and accom-

[82] Snorre, *Heimskringla*, iv, 42, 48.
[83] *Anglo-Saxon Chronicle*, 'C', p. 144.
[84] Ibid., 'D', p. 142; Florence of Worcester, ed. Thorpe, i, 227.
[85] Ed. Whitelock, p. 142.
[86] That Harold was still in the north when he received the news of William's landing is stated or implied by William of Poitiers, p. 166; Florence of Worcester, ed. Thorpe, i, 227; and the (twelfth-century) *Brevis Relatio de Origine Willelmi Conquestoris* (ed. Giles, *Scriptores . . .*), p. 6. Cf., however, Ordericus Vitalis, Interpolation in William of Jumièges (ed. Marx), p. 195, and *Historia Ecclesiastica* (ed. Le Prévost), ii, 145. The tradition that Harold was at a feast in York seems to begin with Henry of Huntingdon (ed. T. Arnold), p. 200; cf. Wace, *Roman de Rou*, ii, 293–5. For the chronology of Harold's movements before Hastings, see Stenton, *Anglo-Saxon England*, pp. 583–4; Douglas, *William the Conqueror*, pp. 398–400. See also Freeman, iii (1869), Appendix FF and p. 733.
[87] Ordericus Vitalis states that he spent 6 days in London assembling an army (Interpolation in William of Jumièges, ed. Marx, p. 196; *Historia Ecclesiastica*, ii, 146) and Gaimar says 5 days (*Lestoire des Engles*, Rolls

plished a forced march of between 50 and 60 miles from London to the place of battle, where he evidently arrived on the evening (or later) of Friday 13 October.[88] By the evening of the next day he was dead, together with his brothers, Gyrth and Leofwine, and 'the greater part of the nobles of England'.[89] The object of all this rapidity of movement, when, in truth, time was on Harold's side and ran against duke William, was evidently what the Norman chroniclers say, to come upon the Normans unawares and crush them by a surprise or night attack[90] – to repeat, in short, the tactics and the victory of

Series, ed. C. T. Martin, i, 223 and ii, 166). These days are generally reckoned to be c. 5–11 October.

[88] Although William of Jumièges (p. 134) states that Harold rode all night and appeared on the battlefield in the morning [i.e. of 14 October], that he arrived in the vicinity of the battlefield in the evening or night of 13 October may be assumed from the necessity of rest for his troops (who, in the event, were able to fight throughout the whole of the next day), and from the fact that William learnt of his approach during the day-time of the 13th (below p. 160) – and is certainly implicit in the tradition, which begins with William of Malmesbury (*Gesta Regum*, ii, 302) that the English spent the night before the battle in drinking and singing while the Normans spent it in prayer and confession. The irrepressible Wace, of course, elaborates the tale (*Roman de Rou*, ed. Andresen, ii, 320) and his relevant verses should surely be quoted in any history of the English race:

> '*Bublie crient e weisseil*
> *E laticome e drincheheil,*
> *Drinc hindrewart e drintome,*
> *Drinc folf, drinc half e drinc tode.*'

[89] *Brevis Relatio* (ed. Giles, *Scriptores*), p. 8, *maxima pars de nobilitate Anglorum*. Cf. Florence of Worcester, ed. Thorpe, i, 227, *fere nobiliores totius Angliae*.
[90] William of Poitiers, p. 180; William of Jumièges, p. 134; Ordericus Vitalis, *Historia Ecclesiastica*, ii, 146. It is also stated by William of Poitiers (loc. cit.), by the *Carmen* (ed. Giles, *Scriptores*, p. 36) and repeated by Ordericus (loc. cit.) that Harold sent a fleet to cut off any attempted withdrawal of the Normans by sea. For Harold's offensive intentions, see also Spatz, *Die Schlacht von Hastings*, pp. 40–3; Fuller, *Decisive Battles*, pp. 373, 375; Burne, *Battlefields of England*, pp. 20–1; C. H. Lemmon, 'The Campaign of Hastings', in *The Norman Conquest* by D. Whitelock and others (London, 1966), pp. 95, 107; D. C. Douglas, *William the Conqueror*, p. 197. For Freeman, of course (iii, 1869, pp. 438–42) Harold's 'consummate generalship' admitted of no mistakes

Stamford Bridge – and, indeed, only a strong element of surprise could crown with success an offensive action by an infantry force against an enemy strong in cavalry. This time the gamble failed. William the Conqueror was not the man to be caught by surprise in war, and Harold played into his hands by giving him without delay the decisive engagement which he wanted near his base at Hastings.[91] On 13 October the duke's scouts informed him of Harold's approach; that night the Norman army stood to arms; and early in the morning of Saturday, 14 October, William seized the initiative.[92] The Norman army advanced from Hastings against Harold, and imposed upon him a defensive action, hastily prepared, in a position something less than ideal, with an army weaker in numbers than it need have been, and already worn by its own exertions.[93] While it is true that most of our detailed information about Hastings comes from Norman sources, the incommunicative English chroniclers are at least unanimous on the points that in this campaign king Harold sacrificed numbers for speed, and that his tactics failed, nor should we shrug this off as special pleading to excuse a great defeat. The 'D' version of the Anglo-Saxon Chronicle,[94] having stated that Harold 'assembled a large army and came against him [William] at the hoary apple tree', goes on to add, 'And William came

and his intention from the start was a defensive action fought on a site previously chosen by himself.

[91] For William's intentions, see below p. 162.

[92] That William's scouts reported the approach of the English the day before the battle is clear from William of Jumièges' statement that the duke, fearing a night attack, ordered his men to stand to arms from dusk to dawn (ed. Marx, p. 135), and from William of Poitiers' account (pp. 180–2), in which, though it runs straight on to the battle without specific mention of a night, the news is received while most of the army is out foraging. It is also implicit in the tradition, already referred to, of how the two armies spent the night before the battle – a tradition which in so far as it relates to Norman piety, probably finds its origins in William of Poitiers' account (loc. cit.). Further, since William began his march from Hastings to the battlefield on or before first light on Saturday October 14 (below p. 163), there is simply no time for any other events that morning.

[93] For the English position, and the composition of the English army, see below, p. 165. For its numbers, see n. 47, p. 150 above.

[94] Ed. Whitelock, p. 143.

against him by surprise before his army was drawn up in battle array. But the king nevertheless fought hard against him, with the men who were willing to support him,[95] and there were heavy casualties on both sides.' The 'E' version of the same Chronicle [96] says that Harold 'fought with him [William] before all the army had come'. Florence of Worcester is even more emphatic.[97] He says that Harold, on receipt of the news of William's landing, 'at once moved his army to London with great haste; and although he knew very well that some of the bravest men in all England had fallen in the two battles [i.e. of Fulford and Stamford Bridge], and that half his army was not yet assembled, yet he did not hesitate to meet his enemy in Sussex as quickly as he could, and nine miles from Hastings he gave them battle, before a third of his army was drawn up.' As though this were not enough, Florence goes on to say that owing to the confined position in which they were constrained to fight many men deserted (*de acie se multi subtraxere*). The last word may perhaps be left to William of Malmesbury. Having asserted that many deserted Harold on the Hastings campaign and would not serve because he had refused to share the loot of Stamford Bridge with his soldiers,[98] he says that Harold took with him chiefly stipendiary troops and few 'from the provinces',[99] and gives it as his opinion that it is a mistake, and no commendation of the Normans, to exaggerate the numbers of the English at Hastings and underrate their courage – 'they were few in number, and brave in the extreme'.[100]

Duke William in the Hastings campaign exhibited again

[95] This remark should be compared with the statements of Florence of Worcester and William of Malmesbury about desertions, cited below.

[96] Ed. Whitelock, p. 141.

[97] Ed. Thorpe, i, 227.

[98] Freeman, of course (iii, 422–3), leaps to Harold's defence.

[99] *Gesta Regum*, i, 281–2, '*Haroldus, triumphali eventu superbus, nullis partibus praedae commilitones dignatus est: quapropter multi, quo quisque poterat dilapsi, regem ad bellum Hastingense profiscentem destituere; nam, praeter stipendiarios et mercenarios milites, paucos admodum ex provincialibus habuit. Unde . . . astutia Willelmi circumventus, fusus est . . .*' See also ibid., ii, 300.

[100] Ibid., i, 282, '*immo vero pauci et manu promptissimi fuere, qui, caritati corporum renuntiantes, pro patria animas posuere.*'

those qualities of patience, self-control and will-power already shown to so great a degree at Dives and St. Valery, and they brought him again the success which they deserved.[101] The reckless bravery of his youth[102] was tempered now by maturity and endless military experience to produce a generalship too much for Harold's over-confident impetuosity. When his army disembarked at Pevensey on 28 September, the duke cannot have known the outcome of the Norwegian invasion of the north, and according to William of Poitiers he first heard of it from Robert fitz Wimarc, a Norman kinsman established in England in Edward the Confessor's day.[103] Robert's information was of Harold's victory at Stamford Bridge, and of his great preparations to repel the new invaders, against which they would have no chance; his advice was that at least William should stay behind his defences and not seek an engagement. The duke's reply states his intention: far from sheltering within defences, he would engage Harold in battle as soon as possible. To the Norman army, in a hostile foreign land, a quick, decisive action was eminently desirable, but it was also desirable to keep in close touch with their fleet and lifeline,[104] and draw the enemy to them. In achieving this double aim duke William was to be entirely successful. The ravaging of the countryside about Hastings is said by William of Poitiers to have provoked Harold to yet greater haste,[105] and there may have been an element of provocation also in

---

[101] Richard Glover's tendentious remarks ('English Warfare in 1066', *E.H.R.*, lxvii, 1952, pp. 2–4) to the effect that William engaged in 'supine loitering' on the Sussex coast out of fear of the English army form part of a wholly tendentious article which, if stimulating, nevertheless misrepresents the evidence and betrays a misunderstanding both of military matters and of the history of the period.

[102] See p. 59, above.

[103] William of Poitiers, p. 170. Cf. p. 115, above.

[104] Guy of Amiens, *Carmen*, p. 31, *Littora custodiens, metuens amittere naves.*

[105] Ed. Foreville, p. 180. For the ravaging, which left its traces in Domesday Book twenty years later, see also Guy of Amiens, *Carmen*, p. 31, and *Bayeux Tapestry* (ed. Stenton), Pl. 52. Cf. Freeman, iii (1869), pp. 411–12, and Douglas, op. cit., p. 196. The intended provocation is also accepted by Spatz, op. cit., pp. 23, 25, but rejected by Delbrück, *Geschichte der Kriegskunst*, iii (1923), p. 160.

the messages which passed between the duke and his rival in the days before Hastings.[106] It is probable also that William knew his man,[107] and it is certain that he was assiduous in his reconnaissance, which brought him news of Harold's advance when the latter was more than seven miles away.[108] And so, when the eagerly awaited news came on Friday, 13 October, there was ample time to prepare for the offensive action beloved of Norman knights, to seize the initiative, strike, and take Harold by surprise. Before daybreak[109] on Saturday, 14 October, duke William, having heard Mass, partaken of the Sacrament, and hung about his neck the relics upon which Harold had taken his oath two years before,[110] set off along the road from Hastings, with his army and his papal banner, in the known direction of the English host. On Telham Hill his scouts brought him further information of the enemy's position,[111] and as he and his knights put on their hauberks and prepared to deploy for action, the duke swore to found an abbey on the battlefield if God granted him the victory.[112]

Because William the Conqueror had his victory and therefore founded Battle Abbey, with its high altar upon the spot

[106] For the exchange of envoys between William and Harold at various stages before the battle (which may be accepted as a fact though we do not have to accept the details of the exchanges), see e.g. William of Poitiers, pp. 172–80; *Carmen*, pp. 33 et seq.; William of Malmesbury, *Gesta Regum*, ii, 301–2; Wace, *Roman de Rou*, ii, 298–302, 312. Cf., however, Körner, op. cit., p. 261.

[107] Cf. Burne, *Battlefields*, p. 22.

[108] Since William received the intelligence of Harold's approach during the daytime of, and Harold reached the vicinity of the battlefield in the evening of, October 13 (pp. 159–60, above) it follows that the Norman knights on reconnaissance spotted the English army more than seven miles away, seven miles being the distance from Battle to William's base at Hastings.

[109] According to Beeler, *Warfare in England, 1066–1189*, p. 15, sunrise on October 14 1066, was 6.48 a.m. (Local Apparent Time).

[110] William of Poitiers, pp. 180–2.

[111] *Bayeux Tapestry*, Pls. 56–8. By this time also English scouts had observed the Norman approach. For Telham Hill, see Baring, *Domesday Tables*, pp. 225–6.

[112] *Chron. monasterii de Bello* (ed. J. S. Brewer, *Anglia Christiana Soc.*, London, 1846), pp. 3–4.

where Harold fell at the foot of his standard,[113] the site of the Battle of Hastings[114] is known with certainty, while contemporary or near-contemporary sources provide an unusual amount of information about its course even though many details necessarily remain unknown.[115] Harold planted his

[113] The one, or possibly two, standards shown on the Bayeux Tapestry (ed. Stenton, Pl. 71) are in the form of the Dragon of Wessex. The standard described by William of Malmesbury (*Gesta Regum*, ii, 302) is that of the Fighting Man. Freeman (iii, 1869, p. 475) assumes that both were present at the battle.

[114] Freeman's attempt to foist the name of Senlac, derived from Ordericus Vitalis (*Historia Ecclesiastica*, ii, 147), upon the battle deservedly met with no lasting success. See Round, *Feudal England*, pp. 333–40.

[115] The best contemporary accounts of the battle are those of William of Poitiers (ed. Foreville, pp. 180–204; a translation into English is available in *English Historical Documents*, ii, ed. D. C. Douglas, pp. 224–9) followed by Guy of Amiens' *Carmen de Hastingae Proelio* (in *Scriptores . . .* ed. Giles) and the unique record of the Bayeux Tapestry. William of Jumièges allows himself to say little (ed. Marx, pp. 134–5), and the English compilers of the Anglo-Saxon Chronicle (ed. Whitelock, pp. 141–3) evidently could not bring themselves to say much more. Anglo-Norman chroniclers of the next generation, notably Florence of Worcester, William of Malmesbury, Ordericus Vitalis (who follows William of Poitiers too closely to be of much use), and Henry of Huntingdon, add certain facts or comments, but they and their twelfth-century successors obviously need to be used with increasing caution, down to and including the ebullient and ingenious Wace (*Roman de Rou*, ed. Andresen, ii, 320 ff.), whose details are often as irresistible as they are held to be unreliable. In our own day, the definitive history of the Battle of Hastings remains to be written. The account by H. Delbrück (*Geschichte der Kriegskunst*, iii, 2nd edition 1923, pp. 150 et seq.) and the full-scale study of W. Spatz (*Die Schlacht von Hastings*) are alike marred by their adherence to, and propagation of, the theory that medieval warfare was chaos, incompetently waged by individualistic exhibitionists, a heresy subsequently preached in this country by Sir Charles Oman, *A History of the Art of War in the Middle Ages*, and still current. The best short modern account is still that of Stenton, *Anglo-Saxon England*, pp. 585–8. In the commentaries by modern military, writers, what is gained by military insight tends to be offset by inadequate historical knowledge, but see Fuller, *Decisive Battles*, Burne, *Battlefields of England*, and Lemmon, 'The Campaign of 1066' in *The Norman Conquest* by D. Whitelock and others. The latest account of the battle by Professor Beeler in his *Warfare in England, 1066–1189* is largely a précis of Lemmon. Richard Glover's misleading article 'English

standard and thus established his command post, on the highest part of a low hill[116] running east and west, facing south upon the advancing Norman army, and connected by a narrow isthmus behind with the forest of the Weald through which he had come.[117] This narrow neck of land (along which Battle High Street now runs) made any withdrawal difficult,[118] and the whole position, if Florence of Worcester is to be believed,[119] was too constricted even for the numbers at his disposal. It is clear, from the unanimous and reiterated assertions of the Norman, and later Anglo-Norman, chroniclers that the English army was massed together in very close order – William of Poitiers says the dead could scarcely fall and that even those lightly wounded could not withdraw and were thus slain also[120] – and it is certain that all, from the king downwards,[121] were on foot. Those who were mounted left their horses before the fight began, in the ancient Teutonic and Scandinavian manner which by now seemed contemptible

Warfare in 1066' (*E.H.R.*, lxvii) has been referred to in n. 101, p. 162 above. See also F. Lot, *L'art militaire . . . au moyen âge*, i, 282–5; G. H. White, 'The Battle of Hastings and the Death of Harold', *Complete Peerage*, xii, Part I, Appendix L.

[116] *Carmen*, p. 38, *In summo montis vexillum vertice fixit.*

[117] Ibid., p. 37, *Mons silvae vicinus erat vicinaque vallis*; Cf. William of Poitiers, p. 186, *locum editiorem praeoccupavere, montem silvae per quam advenere vicinum.* For the site see also e.g. Freeman, iii (1869), pp. 442–4, and the minutely contoured map appended to Baring's *Domesday Tables*.

[118] In the event, it was also to give trouble to the pursuers, hence the '*Malfosse*' incident, p. 174, below.

[119] According to Florence (i, 227) many deserted Harold because of the confined position, see p. 161 above.

[120] *Obnimiam densitatem eorum labi vix potuerunt interempti* (p. 192); *Leviter sauciatos non permittit evadere, sed comprimendo necat sociorum densitas* (p. 194). Cf. his *densius conglobati* (p. 186) and *maxime conferti* (p. 188). Cf. *Carmen*, pp. 37–8.

> '*Anglis ut mos est, densatim progredientes*
> *Haec loca praeripiunt Martis ad officium.*'

See also William of Malmesbury, *Gesta Regum*, ii, 302, and Henry of Huntingdon, p. 203 (both cited below, n. 129, p. 167),

[121] William of Malmesbury, *Gesta Regum*, ii, 302, *Rex ipse pedes juxta vexillum stabat cum fratribus. . . .*

to the Norman writers and their knightly patrons.[122] Beyond this, the composition and disposition of the English army is largely a matter of reasonable conjecture. Harold's troops are thought to have comprised the semi-professional housecarls of the personal followings of himself and his two brothers, earls Gyrth and Leofwine, well-armed thegns and freemen who, also being mounted, had ridden with the king from York, or joined him in time in London, or come in since, and, together with all these, levies more lightly armed from the neighbouring shires.[123] The total number amounted to perhaps some 7,000 men.[124] The principal weapons were the spear, the sword and, most formidable of all, the great two-handed battle-axe, the weapon *par excellence* of the housecarls and, like them, of Scandinavian extraction.[125] But to a total and fatal absence of

[122] Thus William of Poitiers, p. 186 – *Protinus equorum ope relicta, cuncti pedites constitere densius conglobati*, cf. *Carmen*, p. 38 –

> '*Omnes descendunt et equos post terga relinqunt,*
> *Affixique solo, bella ciere tubis.*'

For a note of contempt, see ibid.,

> '*Nescia gens belli solamina spernit equorum,*
> *Viribus et fidens haeret humo pedibus.*'

and cf. Wace, ii, 372–3,

> '*Engleis ne saueient ioster,*
> *Ne a cheval armes porter,*
> *Haches e gisarmes teneient,*
> *Od tels armes se combateient.*'

For further discussion of Anglo-Saxon infantry tactics see p. 94, above.
[123] See Stenton, op. cit., p. 584. Light-armed English troops are certainly shown in the *Bayeux Tapestry* at Pl. 67, which may be thought to give substance to Stenton's reference to 'half-armed peasants'. Though there seems to be no other mention of it elsewhere, William of Poitiers says that abundant help, presumably armed forces, were sent to the English from Denmark (p. 186, *Copiosa quoque auxilia miserat eis cognata terra Danorum*. Cf. Körner op. cit., p. 220).
[124] Ibid., and above n. 47 p. 150.
[125] For the battle-axe, see William of Malmesbury, *Gesta Regum*, ii, 302 (*pedites omnes cum bipennibus*) and *Bayeux Tapestry* Pls. 62–6, 70, 72. Cf. p. 96 above. William of Poitiers (p. 188) says that the offensive weapons (which he does not name) of the English easily penetrated the shields and armour of the Normans. Wace (ii, 358–9) has a Norse axe (*hache norresche*), wielded by an unnamed Englishman, felling both

cavalry there seems also to have been added a serious deficiency of archers, for to them the sources make little or no reference, in contrast to the emphasis placed upon the archers in the Norman army, and only one English archer is shown upon the Bayeux Tapestry.[126] The whole line, perhaps 10–12 ranks in depth, extended for some 600–800 yards, i.e. 400 yards to the west of Harold's standard and 200–400 yards to the east of it.[127] The *corps d'élite* of housecarls were grouped in the centre about the king and his two brothers, and also, it is reasonable to assume,[128] composed or stiffened the front rank. The formation adopted was that of the traditional 'shield-wall', whereby the solid mass of infantry, shields overlapping to the front, seems an impenetrable barrier to the foe.[129]

---

horse and rider with one blow. William of Malmesbury (*Gesta Regum*, ii, 303) attributes the same feat (though not specifically with an axe) to Harold (who is shown with an axe on the Tapestry, Pl. 72).

[126] Pl. 63.

[127] For a total length of 600 yds., see Stenton, op. cit., p. 586; Fuller, op. cit., p. 376; Baring, *Domesday Tables*, pp. 218–19. For 800 yds, see Burne, op. cit., pp. 23, 38–40; Lemmon, op. cit., pp. 99–100. The difference depends upon whether one places the English left (east) flank in the area of the present junction of the Hastings and Sedlescombe roads or in that of the present school.

[128] Not all agree, but mass their housecarls only in the centre. Thus Freeman, iii (1869), pp. 472–6, and map opp. p. 442; Spatz, op. cit., pp. 40–1; Fuller, op. cit., p. 376.

[129] For the shield-wall at Maldon, see p. 95 above. The best description of it at Hastings is, admittedly, in the later sources, though the *Bayeux Tapestry*, Pl. 63, does its best to depict it. Thus William of Malmesbury (*Gesta Regum*, ii, 302), *pedites omnes cum bipennibus, concerta ante se scutorum testudine, impenetrabilem cuneum faciunt;* and cf. Henry of Huntingdon, p. 203 (*Haraldus totam gentem suam in una acie strictissime locasset, et quasi castellum inde construxisset, impenetrabiles erant Normannis*). An element of poetic licence must be allowed in the descriptive phrase 'shield-wall', for obviously the shields must be parted in order to wield offensive weapons, notably the two-handed axes (cf. Spatz, op. cit., pp. 44–5; Burne, op. cit., pp. 24–5). Wace (ii, 372–3) noted the particular disadvantage of this terrifying weapon, pointing out that if a warrior wanted to deliver a great two-handed blow he left himself dangerously unguarded as he raised the axe. It may be added that it was Henry of Huntingdon's comparison of the English formation and shield-wall to a castle in the passage just cited together with Wace's confused lines at ii, 339–40, that led Freeman into his unhappy

And thus they stood and waited, as if rooted to the soil.[130]
  Against them William deployed his army in three divisions, the Bretons on the left (i.e. west), the French on the right (i.e. east), and the main body of the Normans in the centre.[131] The duke himself rode beneath the papal banner in the midst of his Normans, where he could direct operations by voice and gesture.[132] Each division was drawn up with archers and cross-bow-men in front, heavy infantry next, and the knights and heavy cavalry in the rear.[133] The battle began, we are told, at

error of the English palisade at Hastings – for which see, *inter alia*, Round, *Feudal England*, pp. 340 et seq.

[130] *Carmen*, p. 39, *Anglorum stat fixa solo densissima turba*. Cf. William of Poitiers, p. 194, *velut humo affixa*.

[131] *Carmen*, p. 39 –

> Sed levam Galli, dextram petiere Britanni;
> Dux cum Normannis dimicat in medio.

Cf. William of Poitiers, p. 190, *Britanni, et quotquot auxiliares erant in sinistro cornu.* There were, however, Normans on the right with the French, e.g. Robert de Beaumont and his contingent (ibid., p. 192, and below). For further details, see Freeman, iii (1869), pp. 458–60.

[132] See *Carmen*, p. 39 ut supra, and William of Poitiers, p. 184, *ipse fuit in medio cum firmissimo robore, unde in omnem partem consuleret manu et voce*. Those modern commentators (Spatz, p. 67; Burne, p. 34; Fuller, pp. 378–9; Lemmon, pp. 104, 106) who would have William at some 'Headquarters' in the rear until he came forward to stop the incipient retreat (below) are obviously wrong, and it is difficult to understand how in such circumstances the rumour could have started that the duke had been slain (below). The *Brevis Relatio* (ed. Giles, *Scriptores*, p. 7), which has William lead the first charge and kill the first Englishman, may be wrong but comes closer to the spirit of the period and the man. The papal banner is mentioned by William of Poitiers (p. 184). According to Ordericus Vitalis (*Historia Ecclesiastica*, ii, 147) it was borne by Turstin, son of Rollo. According to Wace (ii, 330–3), the honour had first been refused by Ralph of Tosny (because it would prevent his fighting) and by Walter Giffard (because he was too old).

[133] William of Poitiers, p. 184 – '*Pedites in fronte locavit, sagittis armatos et balistis, item pedites in ordine secundo firmiores et loricatos; ultimo turmas equitum, quorum ipse fuit in medio* . . .' etc. as above. Cf. *Carmen*, p. 37 –

> 'Praemisit pedites committere bella sagittis,
> Et balistantes inserit in medio.'

William of Malmesbury, *Gesta Regum*, ii, 302. On the Bayeux Tapestry, some of the Norman archers have hauberks (*lorice*) and some not (ed. Stenton, Pls. 61–2).

9 a.m. with the terrifying sound of trumpets,[134] to which the war-cries of each side were soon to be added.[135] The archers were sent in first, to harass the English by their fire and if possible to provoke them to break ranks. But they had little effect, and were themselves met with a hail of miscellaneous missiles from the serried ranks above them while the enemy stood firm.[136] Next came the knights, hard-riding up the hill, charging with lance and cutting with the sword.[137] It proved, however, to be heavy work; William of Poitiers says the

[134] William of Poitiers, pp. 186–8. All sources agree that the battle commenced 'at the third hour', i.e. before noon, i.e. prime, i.e. 9 a.m. (ibid., p. 208; William of Jumièges, p. 135; Florence of Worcester, i, 227, etc.), but Freeman's remark (iii, 477, n. 2) is worth noting – 'I cannot help noticing the tendency to make the hours of the battles and of other great events coincide with the hours of the church.'

[135] According to Wace (ii, 350) the Normans cried 'God help us', and the English 'Out! Out!' –

> 'Normant escrient: "Deus aie!"
> La gent englesche "ut, ut!" escrie.'

[136] William of Poitiers, p. 188. And so Carmen, p. 38 – 'Pedites, miscete sagittis'. The story of Taillefer (Incisor-ferri) the minstrel who, having begged of the duke the honour of the first strike, began the battle, riding in alone, singing songs of Roland and Roncesvaux and tossing his sword in the air, appears first in Guy of Amiens (Carmen, p. 38) and is taken up by Henry of Huntingdon (pp. 202–3) and Wace (Roman de Rou, ii, 348–9). William of Malmesbury has songs of Roland but no Taillefer (Gesta Regum, ii, 302). See also Douglas, William the Conqueror, p. 199, n. 5.

[137] William of Poitiers is quite specific that the knights came to the aid of the infantry at this stage, 'and [thus] those who were last became first' (p. 188) – thus making untenable the theory of some modern military writers that the duke held back his cavalry until after the first retreat (Burne, pp. 28–9, 30–1; Fuller, pp. 378–9; Lemmon, pp. 106, 108). For the Norman knights, see, of course, the Bayeux Tapestry, Pls. 60 et seq. Pace Richard Glover (E.H.R., lxvii, 14), there is very little evidence from the Tapestry of Norman knights throwing spears – they strike with their lances over-arm or under-arm, or couch them in what will become the developed medieval fashion (cf. n. 163, p. 49 above). In the literary sources for the battle we hear more of the knight's sword than his lance, but this may be because the lance broke at a first encounter and then the sword was used. Thus duke William, at the end of the battle by the 'Malfosse', was armed only with the stump of a broken lance (William of Poitiers, p. 202).

English were helped by their superior position on higher
ground, by the fact that they stood on the defensive and did
not have to move to the attack, and by the ease with which
their weapons cut through their opponents' shields and mail.[138]
Then on the left the Breton knights and infantry began to
give way.[139] The movement spread, as such movements do, to
the centre and the right, the Normans themselves only giving
way, William of Poitiers assures us, because of a rumour that
the duke himself was dead.[140] Some of the English forces began
to advance down the hill in pursuit.[141] It was a crisis, perhaps
the one crisis of the day from the Norman point of view, and
duke William coped with it. Spurring in front of them he
checked those who would flee, striking and menacing them
with his lance, lifting his helmet so that his face could be
clearly seen, and shouting (according to William of Poitiers),
'Look at me. I am living and with God's help I shall be
victor! What madness leads you to flight?' He also shouted at
them the facts that he is said to have stressed in his speech
before the battle – that there was nowhere to escape to, that
only the sea was behind them, and that there was no choice
save to win or die.[142] The scene is vividly depicted on the
Bayeux Tapestry, where the duke bares his head, count
Eustace of Boulogne points to him, and Odo, bishop of
Bayeux, plays his part by encouraging 'the boys', the young
men, *tirones*, experiencing probably their first battle and un-
nerved by it.[143] The duke himself, sword in hand, led a counter-

---

[138] Ibid., p. 188.
[139] Ibid., pp. 188–90.
[140] Ibid., p. 190. Guy of Amiens offers no excuses – *Normanni fugiunt,
dorsa tegunt clipei.* In his account, however, this real retreat comes after
the feigned flight, not before it – *Et fuga ficta prius fit tunc virtute coacta*
(*Carmen*, p. 40, and see below).
[141] William of Poitiers, p. 190. It is generally assumed that they broke
orders in so doing, though in fact it is only in Wace that Harold is made
to give orders specifically to stand firm, no matter what (*Roman de Rou*,
ii, 338). Fuller (pp. 378–9) thinks that Harold missed a great chance here
to launch a counter-attack and win the victory; Lemmon (pp. 107–8) goes
further and thinks the counter-attack was ordered, but prematurely.
[142] William of Poitiers, p. 190 and cf. ibid., pp. 182–4. So also *Carmen*,
p. 40.
[143] Pls. 68–9 (with the break very awkwardly made in the printed

attack, and those of the English who had come down from their position in pursuit were surrounded and cut down.[144]

After this, the assault against the summit of the hill was renewed, certainly by the knights, with or without the assistance of the infantry.[145] The English strove above all to prevent breaches in their ranks, though not always successfully, and whenever or wherever one was opened, says William of Poitiers, the men of Maine or Aquitaine, the Bretons or the French, above all the Normans, bravely exploited it, young Robert de Beaumont (son of Roger, left behind in Normandy), though this was his first battle, especially distinguishing himself at the head of his contingent on the right wing.[146] At length, however, seeing that the enemy, so massed and so determined, could not be overcome without very heavy losses, the Normans and their associates decided upon the strategem of the feigned flight, remembering with what success the pursuing English had been, in the event, cut down earlier in the battle.[147] It was

edition). Count Eustace is there thought to be holding the papal banner, though by Ordericus Vitalis and Wace this is said to have been borne by Turstin son of Rollo (n. 132, p. 168 above).

[144] William of Poitiers, pp. 190–2. The Tapestry (Pls. 66–7 and cf. p. 187) depicts an incident of light-armed English defending themselves on an isolated hill against Norman cavalry in difficulties at the foot of it, and it is thought that the incident may relate to the slaughter of the English pursuers after the retreat just described, though in the Tapestry it is shown before that retreat, not after it. William of Malmesbury (*Gesta Regum*, ii, 303) describes an incident very like that shown on the Tapestry, but relates it to the feigned flight (below, p. 172), not to the real retreat, which he does not mention. Henry of Huntingdon (p. 203) has the Normans ride into a dug and concealed ditch after the feigned flight, and Wace (ii, 351 and cf. 342) has them ride into a dug fosse during the real retreat. These three later written accounts need not perhaps detain us did they not seem to receive some support from the Tapestry. As matters stand, we cannot know whether there was a fosse incident in the middle of the battle as well as the '*Malfosse*' incident at the end (p. 174 below), or whether the former is a confusion with the latter. None of the sources mentioned in this note, save William of Poitiers, has any reference to *Malfosse*.

[145] William of Poitiers, p. 192, mentions only knights, including young Robert de Beaumont with his contingent on the right wing.

[146] Ibid.

[147] Thus William of Poitiers, p. 194. The feigned flight is very well attested by all the principal sources for the battle, except the Tapestry.

a cavalry manœuvre, twice conducted;[148] each time the English were tempted to break ranks in pursuit, and the knights, wheeling their horses about,[149] surrounded them and slew them to a man. But still the main position held, no decision had been achieved, and evening, by all accounts, was now approaching.[150] The Normans continued to press home their

---

Guy of Amiens has it before, rather than after, the real retreat (*Carmen*, pp. 39, 40), and this sequence is preferred by Körner, op. cit., pp. 98–100. Cf. Ordericus Vitalis, *Historia Ecclesiastica*, ii, 148 (following William of Poitiers); William of Malmesbury, *Gesta Regum*, ii, 302–3; Henry of Huntingdon, p. 203; Wace, ii, 354–7. It has been doubted to the point of rejection by many modern commentators, chiefly because of their adherence to the theory that medieval warfare is chaos and therefore disciplined manœuvres are impossible (e.g. Spatz, pp. 55 ff., 61–2, 67; cf. Delbrück, p. 165; Burne, pp. 31, 42–3; Lemmon, pp. 108–10). The suggestion of Burne and Lemmon that 'feigned flight' is a euphemism invented by the chroniclers to cover up Norman retreats which could not be admitted is at once ruled out by the fact that all three principal Norman sources, William of Poitiers, Guy of Amiens and the Tapestry, admit the real Norman retreat. Those who suggest that the manœuvre was carried out by groups of knights, as distinct from the whole force of cavalry at once, may be getting near the truth of the matter rather than detracting from it (thus Stenton, op. cit., p. 587; cf. Delbrück, p. 165). There is reason to believe that the Norman knights fought in groups or contingents, or '*conrois*', under their lords (hence the *gonfanons*? In general, see J. F. Verbruggen, 'La tactique militaire des armées de chevaliers', *Revue du Nord*, xxix, 1947. Cf. young Robert de Beaumont with his contingent, William of Poitiers, p. 192 and above. The word *conrei* is several times used by Wace, e.g. pp. 343, 367). Such contingents were well-trained and homogeneous groups of knights, as professional as the age could make them, and well-known to each other. There is no reason whatever in probability why such groups, or even groups of such groups, should not employ the tactic of the feigned flight. In fact, there are other references to Norman knights employing the same tactic in this period – at St. Aubin-le-Cauf near Arques in 1052/3 and near Messina in 1060 – and to its employment by Robert le Frison of Flanders at Cassel in 1071. (See William of Jumièges, p. 120 and cf. p. 51 above; D. P. Waley, 'Combined Operations in Sicily A.D. 1060–1078', in *Papers of the British School at Rome*, xxii, 123; A. Fliche *Le Règne de Philippe I, roi de France*, Paris, 1912, pp. 258–9. See also Douglas, *William the Conqueror*, p. 201, n. 2.)

[148] *Bis eo dolo simili eventu usi*, William of Poitiers, p. 194.

[149] Ibid., *regiratis equis*.

[150] It may be worth noting that William of Poitiers (p. 194) says at this

assault, all-out, firing arrows, cutting with their swords, thrusting with their lances.[151] It was, wrote William of Poitiers, a strange engagement, one side with all mobility, attacking in every way, the other standing fast and just resisting.[152] Towards the end the fog of war as well as the dusk of an October evening settles upon the historian's account. King Harold, by the standard, his housecarls still about him but his brothers, Gyrth and Leofwine, long since slain,[153] was killed himself, either by an arrow in his brain, or cut down by a party of Norman knights, or both.[154] Despair as well as exhaustion seized the English host, and at last they broke and fled into the gathering darkness, some upon horses they were able to seize, most upon foot, some along the roads but most across the open and broken countryside.[155] The Norman cavalry, fresh yet with the exhilaration of victory, pursued them, duke

point that the English position still remained difficult to surround. All accounts agree that the battle ended at evening.

[151] Ibid., p. 194. William of Poitiers refers to archers again at this stage, though it may be a literary device to indicate an all-out assault – *Sagittant, feriunt, perfodiunt Normanni.* The tradition that duke William, towards the end of the battle, ordered his archers to fire into the air and use high-trajectory arrows against the English first appears in Henry of Huntingdon, p. 203, and is taken up by Wace (ii, 354).

[152] *'Fit deinde insoliti generis pugna, quam altera pars incursibus et diversis motibus agit, altera velut humo affixa tolerat'* (p. 194).

[153] *The Bayeux Tapestry* (Pls. 64–5) depicts them slain early in the battle.

[154] William of Poitiers (p. 200) gives no information of the manner of Harold's death. Guy of Amiens (*Carmen*, pp. 42–3) describes in gory detail his slaying by a group of four knights. The best interpretation of the famous scene from the *Bayeux Tapestry* (Pls. 71–2) is that Harold is not the figure with an arrow in his eye (Pl. 71) but the figure being cut down by the Norman knight (Pl. 72) – whose sword, as it happens, is shown by Harold's thigh. William of Malmesbury (*Gesta Regum*, ii, 303), who may be following the Tapestry, says that Harold was killed by an arrow in his brain, but thereafter his thigh was slashed by a Norman knight as he lay, for which unworthy act duke William deprived the knight of his knighthood (*militia pulsus est*). Both Henry of Huntingdon (p. 204) and Wace (ii, 354, 381–2) have Harold first wounded by an arrow in his eye and thereafter slain in the final press of knights (Wace, surprisingly without details). The whole question of the manner of Harold's death is very fully discussed by G. H. White, in *Complete Peerage*, xii, Pt. I. Appendix L.

[155] William of Poitiers, pp. 200–2.

William included, though three horses had been killed under him that day,[156] and armed only with the stump of a broken lance.[157] It was at this stage that the incident of the '*Malfosse*' took place, involving both William and count Eustace of Boulogne, and long remembered afterwards, when a body of fleeing English, housecarls perhaps, turned upon their pursuers, and many a Norman horse and rider tumbled blindly and fatally into a ravine.[158] So it ended, and night had fallen when William the Conqueror rode back to the battlefield, now covered far and wide with the slain youth and nobility of England.[159]

The next day, Sunday, 15 October, saw the beginning of the burial of the Norman dead, and of the burial of such among the English dead for whom anyone came in to perform the office.[160] It is now, also, that the history of Harold's life and death begins to dissolve into legend – that his mutilated body could only be identified by Edith Swan's Neck, his former mistress,[161] by marks known only to her; that he was taken for honourable burial to his own recently founded church of Waltham Holy Cross in Essex; that he somehow survived the

[156] Ibid., p. 198. The details of how he lost two of them are given by Guy of Amiens, *Carmen*, pp. 40–2. On these occasions he fought on foot until remounted, to the admiring amazement of his knights.
[157] William of Poitiers, p. 202.
[158] The '*Malfosse*' incident as occurring in the final pursuit depends chiefly on our best source, William of Poitiers, who relates it in great detail (pp. 202–4), followed by Ordericus Vitalis (Interpolation in William of Jumièges, ed. Marx, p. 197; *Historia Ecclesiastica*, ii, 150), and supported by the Battle Abbey Chronicle (ed. J. S. Brewer, p. 5, where the name '*Malfosse*' is given) as the proper receptacle of a long-lasting local tradition. William of Jumièges, p. 135, also has duke William return to the battlefield 'in the middle of the night', evidently after the pursuit of the enemy who had fled 'as night approached'. According to William of Poitiers, the duke, unheeding, was advised to turn back by count Eustace of Boulogne, who immediately afterwards was wounded by a great blow between the shoulder blades. See Baring, op. cit., pp. 229–30. A photograph of the '*Malfosse*' is bravely attempted by Lemmon op. cit., Pl. 6b.
[159] William of Poitiers, p. 204.
[160] William of Poitiers, p. 210. William of Jumièges (p. 135) adds that the loot was also collected from the battlefield.
[161] For whom see p. 141, above.

battle, to live on through many adventures and eventually to die a hermit at Chester.[162] Contemporary Norman chroniclers vouch for Harold's mutilation which made recognition difficult,[163] and they put on good authority the offer by his mother of his weight in gold if she might have the body, an offer which the Conqueror refused.[164] But they also leave no room for doubt that the dead Harold, by the Conqueror's order and by the hand of William Malet, was buried on the shore near Hastings, under a stone whose epitaph Guy of Amiens gives us.[165] Whether the persistent tradition, early beginning[166] and still continuing, that he lies at Waltham allows us to conclude that he was subsequently moved there must remain an open question.[167]

---

[162] The legends are most conveniently surveyed by Freeman, iii (1869), pp. 514 et seq., and Appdx. MM., pp. 754 et seq. See also the note by Foreville to p. 206 of William of Poitiers. They derive mainly from the Waltham sources, *De inventione sanctae crucis Walthamensis* and the *Vita Haroldi*, both edited by F. Michel in *Chroniques anglo-normandes*, vol. ii.

[163] William of Poitiers, p. 204; cf. *Carmen*, p. 43. The body when found was taken to the camp at Hastings wrapped, according to Guy of Amiens, in a purple cloth.

[164] William of Poitiers, p. 204; *Carmen*, p. 44.

[165] William of Poitiers, p. 204; Guy of Amiens (p. 44) writes:

> '*Corpus enim regis cito sustulit et sepelivit*
> *Imponens lapidem, scripsit et in titulo:*
> "*Per mandata ducis, rex, hic, Heralde, quiescis,*
> *Ut custos maneas littoris et pelagi*".'

The same slightly sick joke about guarding the shore is related by William of Poitiers, loc cit.

[166] Thus William of Malmesbury, *Gesta Regum*, ii, 306–7, where Harold's body is given to his mother (though payment is refused) and he is straightway buried at Waltham. Wace (ii, 387) is unusually discreet –

> '*Li reis Heraut en fu portez,*
> *A Watehan fu enterrez;*
> *Mais io ne sai qui l'enporta*
> *Ne io ne sai qui l'enterra.*'

By Wace's time, of course, Waltham had become a royal abbey under the patronage of Henry II, and its feelings had to be respected.

[167] This was Freeman's suggestion (iii, 518, 756) and it seems not unreasonable.

The triumphant William of Poitiers wrote of the Battle of Hastings that by it duke William conquered all England in a single day, 'between the third hour and the evening'.[168] The best modern comment upon Hastings is that of Sir Frank Stenton: 'Events were to show that he [William] had won one of the battles which at rare intervals have decided the fate of nations.'[169] But Stenton adds that its full significance was only slowly to appear, and certainly it was long before the *pax Normannica* prevailed over all England. Although after Saturday, 14 October, 1066, there was to be no more united, still less national, resistance, yet local resistance, piecemeal risings and individual recalcitrance – especially in the north – prevent the historian from writing *Finis* to the Norman Conquest before 1071, and even after that the peace of the Norman establishment could be broken. After the battle, William, still duke of Normandy but now with God's judgement declared for him in the matter of his right to England, moved back to his camp at Hastings. He remained there, we are told, for five days, to rest his troops, and, according to the Anglo-Saxon Chronicle, to await submissions from the surviving English leaders.[170] None came, and the duke with his army set out on the long, formidable task of establishing his rule in England.[171] He made first for Dover[172] – no doubt significantly since there is reason to believe that Edward the Confessor may have promised him Dover in 1051 as Harold had done in 1064.[173] It seems clear from the descriptions of both William of Poitiers and Guy of Amiens that the Anglo-Saxon borough then occupied the heavily fortified position of

---

[168] P. 208.
[169] *Anglo-Saxon England*, p. 588.
[170] *Carmen*, p. 44; *Anglo-Saxon Chronicle*, 'D', p. 144.
[171] *Ibid.*, 'But when he understood that no one meant to come to him, he went inland with all his army that was left to him, and that came to him afterwards from overseas.' Norman casualties at Hastings had been heavy, and that reinforcements arrived after the battle is highly probable. Cf. Baring, *Domesday Tables*, p. 209.
[172] Via Romney, where 'he took what vengeance he would for the slaughter of his men' (William of Poitiers, p. 210). Presumably the men of Romney had cut up a detached party of Normans at some stage.
[173] See above, pp. 123, 130.

the pre-existing Iron Age earthworks high on the cliff,[174] but in spite of its strength the place was surrendered to the duke on his approach, and within it, having ejected some at least of the inhabitants from their houses,[175] he raised a castle, as he had done soon after his landing at Pevensey and Hastings.[176]

At Dover, William of Poitiers says that William spent eight days,[177] and also that dysentery broke out in his army, but the duke would not be further delayed, and, leaving a garrison behind together with the sick, he turned inland towards Canterbury[178] – and also towards London. Canterbury surrendered to him even before his arrival at the city,[179] and here, in Guy of Amiens' words, the men of Kent came in to make their submissions 'like flies settling on a wound'.[180] Near Canterbury also the duke himself fell ill, but still he would not delay.[181] By now, as the order of William of Poitiers' narrative

[174] Cf. n. 48, p. 117 above. Thus William of Poitiers, p. 210 – '*Situm est id castellum in rupe mari contigua, quae naturaliter acuta undique ad hoc ferramentis elaborata incisa . . . .*' Cf. *Carmen.* p. 44 – *Sed castrum Doverae pendens a vertice montis. . . .* Note also Guy of Amiens' statement (n. 175 below) that when the duke entered the fortress the English were turned out of their houses in it. In the fullness of time, the castle planted within the borough by William the Conqueror in October, 1066 (below, p. 235) expanded to occupy the whole area as it does now (see R. Allen Brown, *Dover Castle*, Official Guide, H.M.S.O., 1966).

[175] *Carmen*, p. 44 –

> '*Clavibus acceptis, rex intrans moenia castri,*
> *Praecipit Angligenis evacuare domos.*'

William of Poitiers, pp. 210–12, adds that during the negotiations for the surrender of Dover, some of the young men (*armigeri*) of the Norman army fired it, for which duke William punished them severely and gave compensation to the townsmen.

[176] *Recepto castro, quae minus erant per dies octo addidit firmamenta* (Ibid., p. 212). Cf. p. 154 above.

[177] See n. 176 above.

[178] P. 212.

[179] Ibid.

[180] *Carmen*, p. 45.

[181] William of Poitiers, p. 212. The duke had made his camp at 'the Broken Tower' – a place which, intriguingly, has never been identified. William of Poitiers is explicit that the duke would not delay – *noluit indulgere sibi moras ibi agendo*. The suggestion, based upon Guy of Amiens, that the duke was delayed in the area of Canterbury for a

implies, he may well have heard the news from London, where one or both archbishops, Stigand of Canterbury and Ealdred of York, together with earls Edwin and Morcar, and the leading citizens, had elected the aethling Edgar as king and declared their intention of fighting for him – though the move was shortly to prove abortive and the words of the English chronicler still echo in despair the political confusion and panic prevailing in the city: 'but always the more it ought to have been forward the more it got behind, and the worse it grew from day to day, exactly as everything came to be at the end'.[182] Though a detachment of his army reached London Bridge, defeated a sortie sent against them by the Londoners, and fired Southwark, William did not assault the city directly on

month (*Carmen*, p. 45. *Per spatium mensis cum gente perendinat illic*; cf. Douglas, *William the Conqueror*, p. 205; Stenton, *Anglo-Saxon England*, p. 588) conflicts with William of Poitiers and with the fact that the duke's slow and intimidating encirclement of London involved a march of over 350 miles between Canterbury at the end of October and the entry into London before Christmas (Baring, *Domesday Tables*, p. 208 and n. 3).
[182] *Anglo-Saxon Chronicle*, 'D', pp. 143–4. According to this writer, 'Archbishop Ealdred and the citizens of London wanted to have Edgar *Cild* as king, as was his proper due' (cf. p. 139 above) and he adds that 'Edwin and Morcar promised him that they would fight on his side'. William of Poitiers (p. 214) lists the group as Stigand, Edwin, Morcar and other magnates. There is thus a discrepancy between the Chronicle, which mentions only Ealdred, and William of Poitiers, who mentions only Stigand. Edwin and Morcar had been absent from Hastings, either because of a political disinclination to support Harold, as Freeman thought (iii, 1869, pp. 421–2; cf. above p. 141), or because of their losses at Fulford (Stenton, op. cit., p. 582). Florence of Worcester (ed. Thorpe, i, 228) having said plainly that earls Edwin and Morcar had withdrawn with their armies from the Hastings campaign (*qui se cum suis certamini subtraxere*) glosses the 'D' version of the Chronicle's general statement of political confusion which follows ('but always the more it ought to have been forward the more it got behind . . . ' etc.) into a specific statement that, while the others were prepared to fight, the two earls withdrew with their forces and went home (i.e. to the north? – *comites suum auxilium ab eis retraxere, et cum suo exercitu domum redierunt*). William of Malmesbury (*Gesta Regum*, ii, 307), writing in the next generation, went further. According to him, when Edwin and Morcar heard of Harold's death at Hastings they came to London and tried to get one or other of themselves made king. When this failed they went back to Northumbria, thinking that William the Conqueror would never come there.

his advance from the south-east, but made a slow, threatening circuit about it, his army divided into several corps, through the counties of Surrey, Hampshire and Berkshire (where he crossed the Thames at Wallingford), Oxfordshire, Buckinghamshire, Bedfordshire, Cambridgeshire, Hertfordshire and Middlesex, to enter the city at last from the north.[183] Though the degree of deliberate devastation by his forces on the march can be exaggerated, and probably was exaggerated by English chroniclers,[184] the results of this intimidation were all that could be desired. In the course of the long march from Canterbury, the great city of Winchester submitted itself to him.[185] At Wallingford, where William caused a castle to be raised (again as at Dover within the existing ramparts of an Anglo-Saxon borough), Stigand came in, the first of the main English leaders to submit, doing homage and swearing fealty to the duke, as William of Poitiers is careful to describe, and denying Edgar.[186] The date by now may well have been

[183] The most detailed treatment of the Norman campaign between Hastings and London, based upon the Domesday evidence of the decline in value of the places along the line of march, as well as upon the chronicle evidence, is that of Baring, in his Appdx. 'A' to *Domesday Tables*, pp. 207 et seq. This is largely followed by Beeler, *English Warfare*, pp. 25–31. See also G. H. Fowler, 'The Devastation of Bedfordshire and the Neighbouring Counties in 1065 and 1066', *Archaeologia*, lxxii (1922), and Stenton, op. cit., pp. 588–90. For the affair at London Bridge and Southwark, see William of Poitiers, pp. 214–16; Baring, p. 209; Stenton, p. 588.
[184] Baring, op. cit., pp. 214, 216. Cf. *Anglo-Saxon Chronicle*, 'D', p. 144 (*bis*); Florence of Worcester, i, 228. By contrast, William of Malmesbury in the next generation (perhaps out of necessary tact, though he prided himself on his detachment) says that William proceeded with his army towards London 'not in hostile but in royal manner' (*Gesta Regum*, ii, 307).
[185] *Carmen*, p. 45; Baring, op. cit., p. 209.
[186] William of Poitiers, p. 216 (Stigand *manibus ei sese dedit, fidem sacramento confirmavit, abrogans Athelinum quem leviter elegerat*). For the castle, see William of Jumièges, p. 136. If, as seems just, we accept Baring's argument that the general submission of the party from London was made at Little, not Great, Berkhampstead, then Stigand's submission characteristically antedates that of the others by two or three weeks (Baring, op. cit., p. 214, and see below). Körner, *Battle of Hastings*, p. 279, has doubts about Stigand's submission at Wallingford because it is not mentioned by the *Carmen* or William of Jumièges.

mid-November,[187] and at Berkhampstead some weeks later[188] all, or most, of the remaining English leaders from London came in to submit to the Conqueror – Edgar aethling himself, archbishop Ealdred, Wulfstan bishop of Worcester, Walter bishop of Hereford, and, in some accounts, earls Edwin and Morcar, together with the chief men of London.[189] 'And they gave hostages and swore oaths to him', says the Anglo-Saxon Chronicle, while William of Poitiers adds that they prayed him to take the crown, urging him that they were accustomed to serving a king and wished to have one.[190] In other words, for their part they recognised, and thus elected him, as king.[191] Nevertheless, according to his principal biographer, duke William hesitated before thus seeming to go to meet his fortune and bend fate to his will.[192] He felt that the political situation was still too confused, with many rebels against him; he would prefer peace to be more fully established before being crowned king; he would also prefer to wait until his wife Mathilda could come to England and be crowned with him. But he was, we are told, persuaded by the unanimous desire of his army, and especially by the argument that the remaining rebellious English would more easily submit to him as king. And so the march on London was resumed and the city entered, evidently without any serious opposition.[193] Orders

[187] Beeler, *English Warfare*, p. 29 and n. 101.

[188] Baring's arguments in favour of the submission at Little Berkhampstead rather than Great Berkhampstead (op. cit., pp. 210, 212, 213) seem entirely convincing. According to William of Poitiers (p. 216) the submission took place when London was in sight. The date therefore must be well into December. Cf. Körner, op. cit., pp. 280–1.

[189] Wulfstan of Worcester and Walter of Hereford are added by Florence of Worcester (i, 228) to the list otherwise given by the *Anglo-Saxon Chronicle*, 'D' (p. 144). Both authorities give earls Edwin and Morcar as present at Berkhampstead, but if Florence's assertion (supported by William of Malmesbury) that the earls withdrew from London to the north is correct (n. 182, p. 178 above), then William of Poitiers' statement that they submitted to William at Barking after the coronation (p. 236) may be preferred. Cf. Körner, op. cit., pp. 281–2.

[190] *Anglo-Saxon Chronicle*, 'D', p. 144; William of Poitiers, p. 216.

[191] Cf. Oleson, *Witenagemot*, p. 89; cf. p. 133 above.

[192] William of Poitiers, pp. 216–18.

[193] William of Poitiers says there was so little opposition that the duke could have gone hunting had he wished (pp. 218–20), and the English

were given for the construction of a castle, within the south-east corner of the surviving Roman walls where the great White Tower of London was later to rise, and preparations were put in hand for a new king's coronation.[194]

The coronation of William the Conqueror as king of England took place on Christmas Day, 1066, in the great, new church at Westminster which, at the beginning of that same moment-ous year, had witnessed first the funeral of its founder, Edward the Confessor, and then, immediately, the hurried coronation of king Harold. The ceremony was conducted by Ealdred, archbishop of York, Stigand being debarred by the correct and careful Normans because of his uncanonical tenure of the see of Canterbury,[195] for nothing could be allowed to mar the absolute legitimacy of the occasion. The ancient rites were followed, including the threefold oath administered by Ealdred,[196] and the Norman chroniclers, triumphantly re-counting these events,[197] emphasise in turn the elements which in this period gave sanction to the majesty of kings – royal blood and election, unction and coronation, to which might now be added the right of conquest, seen as the mani-festation of the judgment of God.[198] As the solemn liturgy proceeded, however, there was at least one addition[199] to past precedent, in the presentation, now imported from France, whereby the king-elect was presented to the people, as first archbishop Ealdred, in English, and then Geoffrey de Mow-bray, bishop of Coutances, in French, demanded of those present if they would have William crowned.[200] The tumult of

chroniclers mention no resistance. Guy of Amiens, however, has a long account of a siege prepared and of negotiations between the duke and the city's leaders, while William of Jumièges refers to a skirmish when the city was entered (*Carmen*, pp. 45–8; William of Jumièges, p. 136).
[194] William of Poitiers, pp. 218, 236.
[195] Ibid., p. 220.
[196] *Anglo-Saxon Chronicle*, 'D', p. 145; Florence of Worcester, i, 229.
[197] Guy of Amiens (who ends his poem, as no doubt the Bayeux Tapestry once ended, with the coronation) devotes twenty-six lines to a des-cription of the crown (*Carmen*, p. 49).
[198] Thus Guy of Amiens, pp. 50–1; William of Jumièges, p. 136; William of Poitiers, pp. 220, 222. Cf. p. 133 above.
[199] For this, and others, see Douglas, *William the Conqueror*, pp. 248–9.
[200] William of Poitiers, p. 220; cf. *Carmen*, p. 50.

the acclamation following caused a most unhappy and dramatic incident. The Norman knights and soldiers standing guard
outside the church, mistaking the sound of shouting for a riot,
fired the surrounding houses.[201] Ordericus Vitalis, in a vivid
passage, describes how panic spread within the church as men
and women of all degrees pressed to the doors in flight, and
only a few were left to complete the coronation of king
William, who, he says, was 'violently trembling'.[202] For William
this must indeed have been the one terrifying moment of his
life. He is not known ever to have shown physical fear, but
this was a matter of a quite different order. Exemplifying the
qualities of the Norman lords he led, he had courage and piety
in equal measure. He had served God faithfully all his life in
the Norman church and state. He believed implicitly in his
right to England, and God had seemed to favour that right
and to deliver His judgement on the field of Hastings. And
now, at the supreme moment of anointing and sanctification
at his coronation, when the Grace of God should come upon
him and make him king and priest, there came a great noise,
and the windows of the abbey church lit up with fire, and
people fled all about him. It must have seemed to him then
that in spite of all previous signs and portents he was wrong,
unworthy, that his God had turned against him and rejected
both him and his cause, and it is no wonder that he trembled
until the awful moment passed and the world came right again.

For the months which immediately followed king William's
coronation, and which saw the beginnings of the Norman
establishment in England, there is a sharp and illuminating
contrast between the enthusiastic pages of the Norman pane-
gyrist and biographer, William of Poitiers, and the terse
entries of the dry annals of the Anglo-Saxon Chronicle, which
give us at this period the native and worm's eye view of conquest. For the former all is sweetness and light as he praises
his newly royal master's clemency to the defeated English,
the moderations of his exactions, his love and dispensation of
justice and his maintenance of peace.[203] For the latter, 'people

[201] William of Poitiers, p. 220.
[202] *Historia Ecclesiastica*, ii, 157.
[203] William of Poitiers. pp. 222–38.

paid taxes to him, and gave him hostages and afterwards bought their lands',[204] and again, when the king went to his Norman duchy in the early spring of 1067 ('and took with him hostages and money'),[205] 'Bishop Odo [of Bayeux] and earl William [fitz Osbern] stayed behind and built castles far and wide throughout this country, and distressed the wretched folk, and always after that it grew much worse. May the end be good when God wills.'[206] If the attitudes of conquered and conquerors were in future years, in some persons and some places, to prove irreconcilable, the two views of the initial impact of the Conquest are not, but are two sides of the one coin. Of course the Conqueror took his abundant share of the wealth of England, as William of Poitiers makes clear even as he breathlessly describes it, and of course he distributed it in abundance to those who had followed him to England, and fought for and won his cause, and to the churches in Normandy and elsewhere which had prayed for the success of his great enterprise.[207] This was good lordship; this is what lords were for; loot has ever been one of the principal motivations of war; and the Normans and others who invaded England did not do so only as crusaders for the right. William of Poitiers also admits the taxes,[208] nor need we wonder at them. Of course, too, while the lands of those who fell at Hastings were confiscated to the rightful king against whom they had rebelled,[209]

[204] *Anglo-Saxon Chronicle*, 'E', p. 142.
[205] Ibid., 'E', p. 146.
[206] Ibid., 'D', p. 145.
[207] William of Poitiers, pp. 222–6, 244, 254, 256–8. See also the description of the Easter festivities at Fécamp in 1067, ibid., pp. 260–2, and below p. 188. Amongst the gifts listed are those to Rome, which included Harold's banner, taken at Hastings, bearing the image of a fighting man woven in the purest gold (*vexillum Heraldi, hominis armati imaginem intextam habens ex auro purissimo*. Ibid., p. 224). In a thousand churches of France, Aquitaine, Burgundy and Auvergne, declares William's biographer (ibid., pp. 224–6), his memory and the memory of his munificence were preserved – but, he adds, the richest gifts of all were reserved for Normandy.
[208] Ibid., p. 234.
[209] See Stenton, *Anglo-Saxon England*, p. 591, and the writ of the king to the abbot of Bury St. Edmunds ordering the confiscation of the holdings of those under his jurisdiction 'who stood against me in battle

those who submitted afterwards could expect to buy the victor's favour and pay for the restoration of their lands, nor were all the tributes from English towns and magnates,[210] and the 'gifts' from English churches,[211] exacted by force even if they were not wholly voluntary. The Norman settlement on the land begins now with the distribution by the king of the property of the fallen to his vassals,[212] but historians are disposed to praise the orderliness of it and to accept William of Poitiers' claim that no Frenchmen received anything that had been unjustly taken from an Englishman.[213] We may also accept without much difficulty William of Poitiers' assertion that even among the English many were better off after the Conquest than before.[214] Copsi, who found favour in Norman eyes and was sent to Northumbria as earl, was probably one such,[215] and the young, unfortunate Edgar aethling another, to whom the Conqueror now gave ample lands, and whom he treated especially well and honourably as one of Edward's race.[216] Nor is there any cause to doubt the Conqueror's determined efforts to keep order in his kingdom. His biographer relates his precepts and advice to his great vassals, who were to conduct themselves as Christians in a Christian country, without oppression (which might cause revolt), and as Normans who bore with them the good name of Normandy. Lesser knights and men-at-arms were subject to appropriate regulations: women were not to be molested, brothels were prohibited, together with excessive drinking, brawling and all violence and looting.[217] And here, in the king's strong peace,

and were slain there' (ibid., and D. C. Douglas, *Feudal Documents from the Abbey of Bury St. Edmunds*, London, 1932, p. 47).

[210] William of Poitiers, p. 224.

[211] Ibid., p. 258.

[212] Ibid., p. 238. Cf. below p. 206.

[213] Ibid., p. 238. Cf. Stenton, op. cit., p. 618.

[214] '*Ejusdem liberalitatis dono acceperunt Angli complures, quod a parentibus vel a prioribus dominis non acceperant*', p. 238.

[215] William of Poitiers, pp. 236, 268–70. For Copsi see also p. 142 above.

[216] Ibid., pp. 236–8.

[217] Ibid., p. 232. Discipline of a different sort was imposed by the church upon the Conqueror's army in 1070 when the papal legate, Ermenfrid, bishop of Sitten, in council with the Norman bishops, issued a penitential code for those who took part in the invasion of

the two sides were eventually to meet in praise, for William of Poitiers' statement that he forbade all brigandage and ordered that all the ports and roads of the kingdom were to be safe for merchants and kept from violence,[218] is echoed in due course by the Anglo-Saxon Chronicle, seeking to assess the rule of William the Conqueror after his death in 1087. 'Amongst other things the good security he made in this country is not to be forgotten – so that any honest man could travel over his kingdom without injury with his bosom full of gold; and no one dared strike another, however much wrong he had done him.'[219]

Only a fraction of England as yet, however, was in actual Norman possession. After his coronation and the attendant Christmas festivities, while fortifications were being completed in the city to rivet the king's control upon it,[220] William himself set off upon a politico-military progress, evidently into East Anglia, a crucially important region not least because of its exposure to the continuing threat of Scandinavian invasion.[221] He went first to Barking, where more English not-

England. The main interest of the code, as Stenton says, 'lies in its particularity'. The penances are graded according to the type of warrior, heavier for those who fought for gain (mercenaries?) than for those who fought 'as in a public war' (*in bello publico* – for which concept in the later Middle Ages see M. H. Keen, *The Laws of War in the Late Middle Ages*, London, 1965, pp. 106 et seq.), or than for archers who, in the nature of things, could not know how many they had killed or wounded. Special provisions are made for clerks in arms, and even, monks, and for those who had killed 'apart from the actual battle' (i.e. of Hastings), the penances in that case being heavier for slaying after the king's coronation than before it. The code is printed in translation in *English Historical Documents*, ii, 606–7; cf., Stenton, *Anglo-Saxon England*, p. 653.

[218] Ibid., p. 234.

[219] *Anglo-Saxon Chronicle*, 'E', p. 164.

[220] William of Poitiers, p. 236, '*dum firmamenta quaedem in urbe contra mobilitatem ingentis ac feri populi perficerentur*'. William adds that it was of the first importance to subdue the Londoners. It is likely that the fortifications comprised not only the royal castle in the south-east corner of the city (where later in the reign the Tower of London was to be raised), but also two others, Baynard's Castle and Montfichet Castle, long since vanished, in the south-west. See F. M. Stenton, *Norman London* (Historical Association Leaflet, London, 1934), pp. 7–8 and map.

[221] The suggestion of East Anglia is based upon the facts that, while in

ables came in to submit to him. They included Copsi, Tostig's former associate, probably (as William of Poitiers says) earls Edwin and Morcar,[222] and (according to Ordericus Vitalis) Thurkill of Arden, Siward Barn and Edric the Wild.[223] From Barking William moved on (we are not told where), meeting no resistance but receiving further submissions, and arranging matters to his will.[224] These matters presumably included the planting of castles, for we are told that he appointed valiant Frenchmen to the custody of (unspecified) castles and gave

William of Poitiers' account (pp. 236–42, and the only one we have except for Ordericus Vitalis, *Historia Ecclesiastica*, ii, 165–7, who copies William of Poitiers) it is vaguely stated that William visited 'various parts of the kingdom' (p. 236), the two places specifically mentioned are Barking (p. 236) and 'Guenta' (p. 238). That Freeman (iv, 1871, pp. 67 and n. 3, 72 and n. 5) was right in identifying the latter as Norwich rather than Winchester seems certain from William's description of it, notably that it could quickly receive help from the Danes and was fourteen (Roman) miles from the sea which separates the English from the Danes ('*Danos in auxilium citius recipere potest. A mari, quod Anglos a Danis separat, millia passuum quatuordecim distat*'). To this it may be added that Winchester would be an odd place in which to put William fitz Osbern with the charge of governing the kingdom 'towards the north', which, in William of Poitiers' account, is what was done (cf. Stenton, *Anglo-Saxon England*, p. 591). As to the threat of Danish invasion, which is an undercurrent to much of William the Conqueror's reign, Swein Estrithson, king of Denmark, himself a claimant to the English throne (p. 138 above), had been William's ally immediately before the Norman invasion (p. 149 above) but did not long remain so. He sent a great fleet to join the northern rebels in 1069 (below p. 194), while William of Poitiers says that the English sought Danish help in 1067 (p. 264. Cf. Ordericus Vitalis, *Historia Ecclesiastica*, ii, 172), and even that Harold had Danish help at Hastings (p. 186). The East Anglian coast was, and is, commonly the invasion coast of England, and the threat of Danish invasion is generally seen to lie behind the huge keep soon to be built by William the Conqueror at Colchester, which is larger even than the Tower of London which it otherwise closely resembles (see *History of the King's Works*, ed. H. M. Colvin, London, H.M.S.O., 1963, i, 31–2 and ii, 615). Norwich under the Normans (1094–1096) was to receive the seat of the bishop and thenceforward to become the capital of East Anglia which it has since remained.
[222] William of Poitiers, p. 236; cf. n. 189 p. 180 above.
[223] *Historia Ecclesiastica*, ii, 165–6. For Edric the Wild, whose submission at this stage Freeman doubted (iv, 1871, p. 21), see below p. 190.
[224] William of Poitiers, p. 236.

them large garrisons of horse and foot.[225] Next he came to Norwich, which had access to the sea and was thus dangerously accessible to Danish aid.[226] Here he raised, within the walls of the town, another castle, and placed William fitz Osbern, his closest friend, in charge, with a commission to govern all England towards the north in his absence[227] – for by this time the king was anxious to embark for Normandy. Similarly he therefore put his half-brother, Odo, bishop of Bayeux, in charge of the new castle at Dover, with a commission to guard Kent,[228] and, thus having arranged for the care of his hard-won but as yet less than half-occupied kingdom, he returned in March again to Pevensey,[229] where six short months before he had first landed on English soil.[230]

For William his triumphant return to Normandy, and to his wife, in March, 1067, must have been almost as much the personal consummation of his success as his coronation in December.[231] At Pevensey he lavishly paid off those knights who were returning home, that they might share with him the fruits of victory.[232] There he was met also by a company of English notables who were to go with him – Edgar aethling, Stigand of Canterbury, earls Edwin, Morcar and Waltheof, Aethelnoth abbot of Glastonbury, and many others[233] – partly as hostages for peace in England, partly to denude the country of any possible leaders of revolt, partly as trophies, but treated honourably as companions in his household. The

[225] Ibid., p. 238.
[226] Ibid. See n. 221 above.
[227] Ibid. See n. 221 above.
[228] Ibid., p. 240.
[229] Ibid., p. 242.
[230] Ibid., p. 246.
[231] The fullest description, followed here, of William's visit to Normandy in 1067 is that of William of Poitiers, pp. 242–62, with a long diversion suitably and ingeniously comparing the respective conquests of England by William the Conqueror and Julius Caesar (pp. 246–54).
[232] Ibid., p. 244, '*At milites repatriantes, quorum in tantis negotiis fideli opera usus fuerat, larga manu ad eundem portum donavit ut opimum fructum victoriae secum omnes percepisse gauderent.*'
[233] Ibid., p. 244; cf. *Anglo-Saxon Chronicle*, 'D', p. 145. For Waltheof, the son of Siward, and his earldom, see Stenton, *Anglo-Saxon England*, p. 591.

fleet which weighed anchor in Pevensey Bay was equipped with white sails as symbols of peace and victory, and crossed with calm seas and with a favourable wind.[234] In Normandy when he landed, we are assured, though it was still winter the sun shone as if it were summer-time, and though it was also Lent, in all the churches they celebrated as though it were a major feast.[235] In every place where a glimpse of the duke and king might be obtained great crowds assembled from far and wide, and at Rouen the whole populace, old men, women and children, turned out, so that it seemed as if the entire city were applauding. Sumptuous offerings, gold and silver, ornaments and vestments, were made to churches, including those he could not personally visit, and including his own foundation of St. Stephen's at Caen, which received too many to be listed. Easter was spent and celebrated at the great ducal abbey of Fécamp,[236] where, after the royal duke had set the example of humbly attending the services in the choir, splendid feasts were held, not only for Norman vassals and prelates, but also for visiting lords from France, including Ralph de Mondidier, count of Valois and Crépy, father-in-law of the young French king. These, as they were meant to do, gazed with wonder at the long-haired English nobles,[237] at the rich robes of William and his companions, at the vessels of gold and silver, or of horn tipped and ringed with the same precious metals, from which the entire huge company drank, and afterwards they

[234] William of Poitiers adds that, as one result of this passage, the sea was cleared of pirates for a long time (p. 244).

[235] Ordericus Vitalis (*Historia Ecclesiastica*, ii, 168) glosses this sentence of William of Poitiers (p. 254) to the splendid point of saying that in the Norman churches Easter was brought forward in his honour – '*Dies erant hiberni et quadragesimales; sed in episcopiis et coenobiis, ubi novus veniebat rex, initiabantur Paschalia festa.*'

[236] Above, p. 27.

[237] The long hair of the English upper classes, and their moustaches, contrasted with the clean-shaven appearance of the Norman knights, with their close-cropped hair, as shown on the Bayeux Tapestry. For the story of Harold's scouts returning before Hastings to report that most of the Norman army seemed to be priests because of their shaven heads, see William of Malmesbury, *Gesta Regum*, ii, 300–1 (and Wace, *Roman de Rou*, ii, 310–12). In this, as in so many larger ways, two different worlds, from England and from Normandy, met in 1066.

took home news of the impressive majesty of the duke of Normandy, now king of England.

Almost all the recorded activities of William and his court in this joyful spring and summer of 1067 are ecclesiastical ceremonies, characteristic, we may feel, of Norman faith and piety, and of the theocratic duchy whose duke was now become an anointed king. In early May the duke was present at the dedication of the new church of the abbey at St. Pierre-sur-Dives, where the previous summer he and his fleet and army had waited so long for the wind which never came,[238] and on 1 July there was the even bigger ceremony of the dedication of the church of Jumièges[239] (whose ruins yet remain), begun over twenty years before by that abbot Robert of Jumièges who was king Edward's friend and archbishop of Canterbury, and, it is thought, largely the inspiration of Edward's own Westminster Abbey. On this occasion there were present, amongst many others, John, bishop of Avranches, Geoffrey, bishop of Coutances and already a notable figure in England, Hugh, bishop of Lisieux, Baldwin, bishop of Evreux, and the aged and saintly Maurillius, archbishop of Rouen, who died soon after this, his last known public function. As summer turned slowly into autumn and then winter, we may be sure the duke devoted his attention increasingly to secular affairs on both sides of the Channel, and when at length he returned to England, making a night crossing on 6 December, 1067, he brought with him his friend, Roger of Montgomery, who had formerly stayed in Normandy as a prominent member of Mathilda's council, and left once more his duchess (though all now called her queen)[240] to govern the duchy in his name, as she had so successfully done during his absence on the conquest of England in the previous year.[241]

[238] Ordericus Vitalis, *Historia Ecclesiastica*, ii, 168–9. See above, p. 152.
[239] The fullest description of this occasion is found, not surprisingly, in William of Jumièges, p. 137.
[240] William of Poitiers, p. 260.
[241] Ordericus Vitalis, op. cit., pp. 177–8, who adds that Robert, eldest son and heir of William and Mathilda, now adolescent, was to be associated with his mother in the government of the duchy. Cf. William of Jumièges, p. 139. For Robert 'Curthose', see especially C. W. David,

From the celebration of its triumph king William returned to England to face the hard facts of his conquest, and the up-hill task of the settlement of his new kingdom. Already in his absence, owing, according to William of Poitiers, to the recalcitrance of the English, or, according to the English sources (and the sympathetic Ordericus Vitalis in the next generation), to the arrogant oppression of the Normans,[242] there had been trouble during 1067. In the far west, Edric the Wild, in alliance with Welsh princes and in arms against the garrisons of Hereford and Richard's Castle who had raided his lands, had devastated Herefordshire as far as the river Lugg.[243] In the south-east, in bishop Odo's province, there had been the curious affair of Dover, when count Eustace of Boulogne, at the invitation of the men of Kent, had attempted a surprise assault on the new castle, to be beaten off with ease and ignominy, even though the garrison was under-strength by the absence of the commandants, Odo of Bayeux and Hugh de Montfort, on service beyond the Thames with many of their knights.[244] Whatever motives lay behind these particular events, the unresolved political situation was given a further dimension of seriousness by the hostile activities of English exiles overseas, and especially negotiations between the dissidents and Swein of Denmark[245] – himself a claimant to the

Robert Curthose, Duke of Normandy (Cambridge, U.S.A., 1920) and cf. below, p. 199.

[242] William of Poitiers, pp. 262–4; *Anglo-Saxon Chronicle*, 'D', p. 145; *Historia Ecclesiastica*, ii, 171–2.

[243] Florence of Worcester, ed. Thorpe, ii, 1–2; *Anglo-Saxon Chronicle*, 'D', p. 146. For Edric the Wild, see especially Freeman, iv (1871), Appdx. I, and the rather splendid Note 1 to p. 212 of D. C. Douglas, *William the Conqueror*.

[244] For which see William of Poitiers, pp. 264–8 (after which that invaluable source breaks off and ends); William of Jumièges, p. 138. Count Eustace had been duke William's ally at Hastings (though William of Poitiers says he had given a son as hostage to the duke 'before the war' – p. 264) and was to be again, but at this stage was for some reason estranged. William of Poitiers (p. 266) says that Eustace came with a picked force of knights, but most of them did not bring their horses – a nice point of contrast with the carefully prepared, full-scale Norman invasion of 1066.

[245] For both Danish negotiations and English exiles, see William of

kingdom and increasingly inclined to make a bid for it now that his erstwhile rival, Harold Hardrada of Norway, had failed and fallen at Stamford Bridge.[246] King William, after Christmas spent in London,[247] was forced in 1068 to concentrate first upon the west, where the citizens of Exeter defied him.[248] In a winter campaign, itself an indication of Norman determination, and with English as well as French for the first time in his army,[249] he marched into Devonshire, laid siege to Exeter for eighteen days, and gained entry by undermining the walls.[250] The rebels were treated with clemency and no looting was allowed, but a castle was ordered to be constructed in the northern corner of the city, within the walls, and placed in charge of Baldwin de Meules.[251] Later, after the king had returned to Winchester for Easter, Baldwin led an expedition further west into Cornwall where, not long after these events, first Brian of Brittany, and, subsequently, the king's half-brother Robert, count of Mortain, were to be established in a great feudal honour.[252] By such means Norman control of the south-west was soon made effective; a raid, later in the summer of 1068, by three illegitimate sons of Harold from Ireland was beaten off by the men of Somerset,[253] and when in the next

Poitiers, p. 264; Ordericus Vitalis, *Historia Ecclesiastica*, ii, 172. For the former, see also n. 221 p. 186, above.

[246] Cf. p. 149, above.

[247] Ordericus Vitalis, op. cit., ii, 178–9.

[248] According to Ordericus Vitalis (op. cit., ii, 179–80), they would not swear fealty to the king, nor admit him to their city, and would render only the accustomed dues. William's reported answer is worth noting – '*Non est mihi moris ad hanc conditionem habere subjectos.*'

[249] Ibid., p. 180, '*et primo in ea expeditione Anglos eduxit*'.

[250]Ibid., pp. 179–81; *Anglo-Saxon Chronicle*, 'D', p. 146. Ordericus' reference to mining (*subtus murum suffodere*) may be compared to the statement of William of Malmesbury that the city was entered because part of the walls fell down. The same writer has an unprintable story of an insult offered to the Norman army, greatly to the king's rage, by a defender standing on the walls (*Gesta Regum*, ii, 307).

[251] Ordericus Vitalis, op. cit., ii, 180–1. Cf. *History of the King's Works*, ed. H. M. Colvin, ii, 647. Baldwin de Meules, sometimes 'of Clare', was a son of count Gilbert of Brionne.

[252] Ordericus Vitalis, op. cit., ii, 181; *Complete Peerage*, iii, 427–8; cf. n. 28 p. 209, below.

[253] *Anglo-Saxon Chronicle*, 'D', p. 148.

year the men of Devon and Cornwall rose again and attacked Exeter the citizens were both victorious and loyal, 'for they had not forgotten the sufferings they had formerly endured'.[254]

Henceforward the principal concentration of Norman effort and the expansion of Norman domination were to be of necessity in the untamed north, culminating in the terrible devastation of the winter of 1069–70. But meanwhile, in the spring of 1068, king William thought the situation to be sufficiently stable at last to bring Mathilda from Normandy and make her queen. She came, with a great retinue of lords and ladies, and was solemnly crowned, on Whit Sunday at Westminster by Ealdred of York, in a splendid ceremony attended by English as well as French and Norman magnates.[255] Thereafter the storm-clouds swiftly gathered. Already, as it seems, Edgar aethling, his mother and his sisters, had left the court and fled to Scotland,[256] and soon afterwards earls Edwin and Morcar left also, bent on rebellion, alienated, it is said, because the king had withheld from Edwin (at the instigation of jealous Normans) a promised marriage to his daughter'.[257] They allied with their Welsh nephew, Bleddyn,[258] and they found support especially in Northumbria and at York. 'Then the king was informed that the people in the north were gathered together and meant to make a stand against him if he came.'[259] He undertook, therefore, his first northern expedition. What followed has been called, by a recent Norman historian, 'a mili-

[254] Ordericus Vitalis, op. cit., ii, 193. Cf. below p. 195.
[255] *Anglo-Saxon Chronicle*, 'D', p. 148; Ordericus Vitalis, op. cit., ii, 181–2. Ordericus says that Guy of Amiens was in her train, and he also duly notes the subsequent birth of a son, Henry, to the king and queen, in England early in 1069. For some of those attending, see the witnesses of Nos. 22 and 23 of the *Regesta Regum Anglo-Normannorum*, i (ed. H. W. C. Davis, Oxford, 1913).
[256] The absence of Edgar from the witness lists of the two Whitsun charters of n. 255 above strongly suggests he had already gone. For his going, see *Anglo-Saxon Chronicle*, 'D', p. 146; Florence of Worcester, ii, 2 (after Mathilda's coronation).
[257] Ordericus Vitalis, op. cit., ii, 182.
[258] Ibid., pp. 183–4. Bleddyn was the son of Gruffydd and Edith, i.e. the sister of Edwin and Morcar, who was Gruffydd's widow when she was married by king Harold in 1066 (p. 141 above).
[259] *Anglo-Saxon Chronicle*, 'D', p. 148.

tary promenade',[260] and Ordericus Vitalis describes how William moved about the kingdom planting castles in the most suitable places to hold down his enemies.[261] The foundation of the castle at Warwick was followed by the submission of earls Edwin and Morcar, and that of the castle at Nottingham by the submission of York. The king then went to York and founded the first castle there (on the site of what is now Clifford's Tower), and while he was in the north the bishop of Durham, as his representative, made peace with Malcolm king of Scots who swore fealty. On his march south again, William raised castles at Lincoln, Huntingdon and Cambridge, and at the end of the campaign felt able to pay-off and dismiss his stipendiary knights.[262]

Within a year, however, the king was to be compelled to undertake two further northern campaigns, the one swift and immediately effective against mere native opposition, the other long, bitter and decisive, the result of Danish intervention and a cumulative determination to make an end to the threat of Northumbrian separatism. On 28 January 1069, Robert de Commines, the third or fourth earl of Northumbria since the Conquest and the first Norman as opposed to native magnate to be appointed to that dangerous honour, was slain with most of his force at Durham.[263] Anarchy and confusion spread, and at York the Norman commandant and constable, Robert fitz Richard, was also slain, while Edgar aethling from Scotland, with Cospatric and other Northumbrians, attacked

---

[260] De Boüard, *Guillaume le Conquérant*, p. 103.

[261] Op. cit., ii, 184 – *Rex igitur secessus regni providentius perlustravit, et opportuna loca contra excursiones hostium communivit.* There then follows the well-known passage in which Ordericus attributes the success of the Norman Conquest partly to the absence of castles in England. For the campaign, see ibid., pp. 184–5; *Anglo-Saxon Chronicle*, 'D', p. 148 (the statement in the latter that two castles were raised in York in 1068 is incorrect).

[262] Ordericus Vitalis, op. cit., ii, 187.

[263] *Anglo-Saxon Chronicle*, 'D', 'E', p. 149; Stenton, *Anglo-Saxon England*, p. 593. Copsi (p. 184 above), sent north by William in 1067 was slain five weeks later. Oswulf, son of Eadwulf, head of an ancient local dynasty, then maintained himself as earl until he was slain in the autumn of the same year. His cousin, Cospatric, next bought the earldom from the king, but joined Edgar aethling as a rebel in 1068.

the city and the castle.[264] The new constable, William Malet, sent an urgent message to the king that he could not long hold out without relief. William himself therefore came to York with a rapidity that must have rivalled Harold's much-praised march in September 1066, relieved the city, routed the rebels, drove the aethling back to Scotland, and planted a second castle in York on the right bank of the Ouse.[265] Leaving earl William fitz Osbern in charge, he was back in Winchester to hold the Easter feast, where the earl joined him, and the north seemed quiet. Nevertheless, we are told, in view of so many dangers, he thought it wise to send Mathilda back to Normandy,[266] and in the autumn his fears were realised by the appearance of a great Danish fleet off the east coast, which, having raided at Dover, Sandwich, Ipswich, and Norwich, sailed, as always, up the Humber.[267] Variously estimated at 240 and 300 ships, the Danish force did not include king Swein himself,[268] but numbered amongst its leaders three of his sons together with earl Osbern, his brother. In Northumbria it was met by 'the aethling Edgar and earl Waltheof and Maerleswein and earl Cospatric with the Northumbrians and all the people, riding and marching with an immense army rejoicing exceedingly, and so they all went resolutely to York'.[269] Before they got, there, archbishop Ealdred, a man who had done more than most to reconcile the two worlds of England and Normandy, died at the news of their coming, on 11 September,[270] and on the 19th the Norman garrisons fired the houses adjacent to the two castles (so that their materials might not be used to fill up the ditches) and the fire spread to the rest of the city and to the

[264] For this, and what follows, see Ordericus Vitalis, *Historia Ecclesiastica*, ii, 187–8; Stenton, op. cit., pp. 593–4.

[265] See E. S. Armitage, *Early Norman Castles*, pp. 242 et seq.

[266] Ordericus Vitalis, op. cit., p. 188.

[267] A good modern account of the subsequent events of 1069–70 will be found in Stenton, op. cit., pp. 594–7. The fullest near-contemporary account is that of Ordericus Vitalis, op. cit., ii, 190–9. Cf. Florence of Worcester, ii, 3–4; *Anglo-Saxon Chronicle*, pp. 149–50.

[268] Though according to *The Anglo-Saxon Chronicle*, 'E', p. 151, he joined it in 1070.

[269] *Anglo-Saxon Chronicle*, 'D', p. 150.

[270] Thus Florence of Worcester, ii, 3.

Minster.[271] When the Danes with their English allies did arrive, the Norman garrisons, presumably over-confident, made a sortie against them and were disastrously defeated, only a few, including William Malet and his wife and two children, with difficulty escaping, leaving the city and the castles open to the pillage which they then received. King William, according to Ordericus Vitalis,[272] received news of the Danish fleet while hunting in the Forest of Dean, and, having sent warning ahead to York, himself set off north at once with an army, leaving other spontaneous but unco-ordinated risings in Devon and Cornwall, Dorset and Somerset, and Cheshire, to be dealt with by his lieutenants, William fitz Osbern, Brian of Brittany and Geoffrey, bishop of Coutances.[273] Arrived at York, his enemy fled before him down the Humber in their ships, first to the Isle of Axholme and then recrossing to the Yorkshire side. Leaving his half-brother Robert, count of Mortain, to watch them, the king with the rest of his army crossed the Pennines to deal with the rising in Staffordshire and then, at Nottingham on his way back, hearing that the Danes were preparing to reoccupy York, headed north again. By now mid-winter was approaching and he was held up for three weeks at the crossing of the river Aire by a broken bridge near Pontefract,[274] which possibly gets its name from this incident. At length, a ford having been found by one of his knights, he resumed his march towards York, where the Danes again withdrew before him and soon afterwards

[271] Ibid., p. 4.
[272] Op. cit., ii, 192.
[273] Ibid., pp. 193–4; Stenton, op. cit., p. 595. The rising in Dorset and Somerset was directed against the castle of Montacute and was suppressed by bishop Geoffrey of Coutances. According to Ordericus Vitalis, the two earls, William and Brian, were first sent to the north-west where the men of Chester with the aid of the Welsh and Edric the Wild were attacking Shrewsbury, though the king himself was twice to march into this area during the winter of 1069–70 (below). In Devon and Cornwall the rebels mainly concentrated against Exeter, which remained loyal to the king (cf. p. 192 above). In the south-west a further raid by the illegitimate sons of Harold had been beaten off by Brian of Brittany earlier in the year (Ordericus Vitalis, ii, 189–90).
[274] Details in Ordericus Vitalis, ii, 194–5. Cf. Freeman, *Norman Conquest*, iv (1871), pp. 284–5.

allowed themselves to be bought off, the agreement being that
they should remain in the Humber and obtain what supplies
they could throughout the winter and then withdraw from
England.[275]

The king held his Christmas at York, his regalia being
ordered up from Winchester[276] that nothing might be lacking
in the impress of his majesty, and then set his forces to the
systematic devastation of the north. 'In the fulness of his
wrath he ordered the corn and cattle, with the implements of
husbandry and every sort of provisions, to be collected in
heaps and set on fire until the whole was consumed, and thus
destroyed at once all that could serve for the support of life in
the whole country lying beyond the Humber.'[277] The area
covered comprised not only Yorkshire but also Cheshire,
Shropshire, Staffordshire and Derbyshire.[278] Famine followed,
and seventeen years later Domesday Book still shows large
areas derelict.[279] It was an act of state, of a sort not confined
to any period, and the political reasons at the time no doubt
seemed as compelling as such reasons always do.

Certainly in this terrible northern campaign of the winter
of 1069–70 William the Conqueror spared neither himself nor
his army. Early in the New Year he reached the Tees, after a
march so difficult that he often had to go on foot, and there
Waltheof and Cospatric submitted to him.[280] Ordericus Vitalis
describes in detail the hardships and endurance of the subsequent march back to York, 'in the depth of winter during a
severe frost', by mountainous routes never before attempted
by an army, with the king keeping up the spirits of his men by
his own example.[281] At York the two castles were restored and,
though it was still winter, William then called for one more

---

[275] Florence of Worcester, ii, 4.
[276] Ordericus Vitalis, ii, 196.
[277] Ibid., pp. 195–6.
[278] Stenton, op. cit., pp. 596–7.
[279] The Domesday evidence of waste and depopulation in Yorkshire at
least, however, is not always a direct reflection of the devastation of
1069–70: see T. A. M. Bishop, 'The Norman Settlement of Yorkshire',
in *Studies in Medieval History presented to F. M. Powicke* (Oxford, 1948).
[280] Ordericus Vitalis, ii, 196–7.
[281] Ibid., pp. 197–8.

expedition, westwards to crush the men of Cheshire and the Welsh who were attacking Shrewsbury. At this there was near-mutiny among the mercenary elements in his army, from Anjou, Brittany and Maine (but not, it may be noted, from the Normans). 'They said, for their justification, that they would not serve under a lord who was venturing on enterprises which were unexampled and out of all reason, nor carry into effect impracticable orders.'[282] The Conqueror, however, could manage men, and set off notwithstanding, saying that those who chose could stay behind as cowards. Again we are told of near-impassable mountain routes, 'never before travelled by horses', with William often leading the way on foot, in savage winter weather. The Cheshire plains were duly reached, the province pacified, and castles founded at Chester and at Stafford.[283] Then, at last, the king turned south and at Salisbury paid and dismissed his troops, though retaining the would-be mutineers for a further forty days of service.[284]

Thus by the spring of the year 1070 the Norman Conquest of England, decided in the autumn of 1066, had been completed and confirmed, and the authority of king William established from east to west and south to north. Two postscripts yet remain, however, to be added. The campaigns which, after his coronation, finally established William's rule in England ended as they began in East Anglia. There, in the fastness of the Isle of Ely, part of the Danish forces and the remnants of the English opposition (including earl Morcar, whose brother Edwin was already dead)[285] defied the Norman king once more,

---

[282] Ibid., p. 198.

[283] Ibid., pp. 198–9.

[284] Ibid., p. 199. The latter incident may well be regarded as further evidence for the forty-day period of feudal service.

[285] Edwin and Morcar had not rebelled in 1069–70, but in 1071 they 'fled away and travelled aimlessly in woods and moors until Edwin was killed by his own men and Morcar went to Ely by ship' (*Anglo-Saxon Chronicle*, 'D', p. 154). According to Florence of Worcester they fled the court because William intended to imprison them, and Edwin was on his way to Scotland when he was killed. Morcar was captured when Ely fell and was imprisoned for the rest of the reign (cf. Ordericus Vitalis, op. cit., iii, 245).

to be reduced, between 1070 and 1071, by a characteristically thorough and brilliantly conducted siege whose culmination was a causeway two miles long from Aldreth to the Isle.[286] Then, in 1072, there came the 'natural sequel'[287] to the recent wars in the great expedition by sea and land against Malcolm king of Scots, the ever-willing harbourer of English exiles since 1068, and the husband of Margaret, sister of the aethling Edgar, since 1070. The result was the submission of Malcolm who became William's vassal and gave him his eldest son as hostage, while the aethling was constrained to leave Scotland for Flanders.[288]

It is difficult not to feel a sense of anti-climax about the later years of William the Conqueror's life and reign, though reason indicates that this is largely false. The drama of the conquest of England had to end, the sooner the better for all parties, and the ever-increasing momentum of the Conqueror's career from 1035 to 1070 could not indefinitely be maintained. There were, too, substantial achievements yet to come, not least the maintenance of Norman rule and the ordered and peaceful establishment of the Norman settlement on the land, while the accomplishment of the Domesday survey alone, between 1086 and 1087, would be enough to ensure the lasting fame of any lesser king in English history. Yet also there were troubles, mostly surmounted, and sadnesses, which had to be endured. As time passed, the friends and relatives of William's youth in Normandy were gradually removed by death or circumstance, until at the end his half-brother, Robert count of Mortain, Roger of Montgomery, earl of Shrewsbury, and Lanfranc, archbishop of Canterbury, almost alone remained. His greatest friend, William fitz Osbern, earl of Hereford, 'the bravest of all the Normans', was slain in Flanders in 1071, in a war to maintain his master's influence in that pro-

---

[286] The fullest account of the affair of Ely, and of Hereward the Wake, is that of Freeman, iv (1871), pp. 454 ff. Cf. Stenton, op. cit., p. 597. For the siege of Ely, see *V.C.H. Cambridgeshire and the Isle of Ely*, ii, 381–5, and E. O. Blake, *Liber Eliensis*, pp. liv–lvii.
[287] Stenton, op. cit., p. 598.
[288] For this campaign, its interest and importance, see Douglas, *William the Conqueror*, pp. 226–7.

vince, to which he had gone 'gaily as if to a tournament'.[289] In 1082, the king's other half-brother, Odo, bishop of Bayeux and earl of Kent, was disgraced, and imprisoned in the tower of Rouen for the rest of the reign, for reasons which remain obscure.[290] In November, 1083, Mathilda, his beloved wife, duchess and queen, died and was buried in her church of the Trinity at Caen, where her tomb remains. The Conqueror, we are told, wept for days at her passing,[291] and the wound, we may guess, remained. Hard to bear also, as William and his contemporaries grew old, was the rise of a new generation of young lords, impatient to enter their inheritance and rebelling, often enough in arms, against their fathers' loyalties. Roger of Breteuil, the new earl of Hereford, son and heir of William fitz Osbern, rebelled on a famous occasion in England and met with perpetual imprisonment,[292] and worse still was the more or less sustained rebellion from 1078 of the king's own eldest son, Robert 'Curthose', who attracted many of the young bloods of Normandy into his conspiracy, joined cause with his father's enemy, the king of France, and was the cause of the only known quarrel between the Conqueror and Mathilda.[293]

Political troubles in these later years continued,[294] even in England, where the seemingly purposeless 'rebellion of the

[289] Ordericus Vitalis, op. cit., ii, 234–5. Cf. Stenton, op. cit., pp. 598–9; Douglas, op. cit., pp. 224–5. For William's friendship for fitz Osbern, 'whom of all his intimates he had loved the most since their childhood together', see William of Poitiers, p. 240 and also p. 38 above.

[290] Chroniclers of the next generation state that he aspired to the Papacy and recruited knights and vassals including Hugh, earl of Chester, to serve his cause. Stenton points out that there was war between Pope and Emperor at this time, and Odo may have hoped to earn credit at Rome by intervening on the papal side (see Ordericus Vitalis, op. cit., iii, 189–92; William of Malmesbury, *Gesta Regum*, ii, 334; Stenton, op. cit., p. 608).

[291] William of Malmesbury, op. cit., ii, 331.

[292] For the rebellion of the three earls in 1075, see below.

[293] See Douglas, op. cit., pp. 237–9, 243, and David, *Robert Curthose*.

[294] The political events of the Conqueror's later years in England and in Normandy, which it is no part of the purpose of this book to deal with in any detail, will be found in Stenton, op. cit., pp. 598 et seq., and Douglas, op. cit., Chapter 9. The latter authority stresses the interconnection of the problems and events on both sides of the Channel.

earls' was suppressed in 1075,[295] further trouble in the north was also suppressed in 1080, and the last serious threat of Scandinavian invasion proved abortive in 1085–6.[296] On the Continent, where the king/duke had of necessity to spend much of his time, the situation deteriorated as the exceptionally favourable circumstances of 1066[297] inevitably broke up, and William in his duchy found himself once more, as in his youth, surrounded by a sea of troubles. In Flanders the friendly rule of his father-in-law, count Baldwin, was replaced by that of his future enemy, Robert the Frisian, in 1071. In Anjou the succession disputes which had followed the death of Geoffrey Martel in 1060 were ended in 1066 by the establishment as count of the formidable Fulk 'le Rechin', who, in particular, sought to break the Norman hold on Maine and encouraged the recurrent rebellions which took place there between 1069 and 1084. There was trouble, too, in neighbouring Brittany where at Dol in 1076 the Conqueror sustained a rare defeat at the hands of the king of France. And in the Ile de France a new king, Philip I, had grown to manhood and lost few opportunities of striking at the duke of Normandy, his overmighty neighbour. Prophetically, for the future of the duchy and of the union of Normandy and England which the Conqueror had brought about, it was by war against the king of France that William ultimately met his death. The vital border district of the French Vexin had in recent years come under Philip's domination, and from it, in 1087, raids were be-

---

[295] The three earls were Roger, earl of Hereford (see above), Ralph de Gael, earl of East Anglia, and (somewhat half-heartedly) Waltheof, then earl of Northumbria and of an extensive earldom in the midlands. For their motives, one is inclined to turn to the strong suggestion in William of Malmesbury (*Gesta Regum*, ii, 313) that they were all drunk when they plotted the rebellion at the wedding of Ralph to Roger's sister. Cf. the speeches put into their mouths by Ordericus Vitalis, op. cit., ii, 258–60. Roger was imprisoned, Ralph went into exile in Brittany, and Waltheof, an Englishman, suffered the death penalty of English law for treason – 'So far as is known, he was the only Englishman of high rank whom king William executed' (Stenton, op. cit., p. 604).

[296] The threat was taken very seriously by William's government in England but failed to materialise with the death of Cnut, king of Denmark, who was responsible for it. See Stenton, op. cit., pp. 608–9.

[297] See p. 147, above.

ing made against the duchy. The Conqueror invaded it with fire and sword in the last week of July,[298] and in the burning streets of Mantes received an internal injury which proved lethal.[299]

There are two full accounts of the lingering death of William the Conqueror in the summer of 1087, one by an anonymous monk of Caen, the other, longer and later, by Ordericus Vitalis.[300] He was brought back from Mantes to Rouen, and lay there for six weeks, retaining his faculties to the end. After a time, the noise of the city proving intolerable, he was moved to the priory of St. Gervase, on a hill in the western suburbs. Amongst those about him were his sons, William and Henry (but not Robert, who was still absent and with the French king), his half-brother Robert of Mortain, William de Bonne Ame, his archbishop of Rouen, his friend and physician Gilbert Maminot, bishop of Lisieux, and Guntard, abbot of Jumièges, 'with some others, well-skilled in medicine, [who] carefully watched over him, devoting themselves zealously to their master's welfare both spiritual and temporal'.[301] He made a lavish and carefully recorded distribution of alms, not omitting compensation for the damage he had done to Mantes. He ordered the release of his political prisoners,[302] though Odo of Bayeux was included only with much reluctance and at the instance of the archbishop and Robert of Mortain. Finally he disposed of his dominions, leaving Normandy, again reluctantly, to Robert, his eldest son, but England to his second son, William, who was dispatched at once to take it. He died early

---

[298] Ordericus Vitalis, iii, 225.
[299] In some accounts he was overcome by fatigue and heat, in others his stomach was injured by the pommel of his saddle when his horse stumbled.
[300] *De obitu Willelmi*, printed by J. Marx in his edition of William of Jumièges; Ordericus Vitalis, op. cit., iii, 226–49. Both are translated in *English Historical Documents*, ii (ed. D. C. Douglas), pp. 279–89.
[301] Ordericus Vitalis, iii, 227.
[302] They included earl Morcar and Siward Barn, captured at Ely in 1071, and Wulfnoth, son of earl Godwin and brother of king Harold, a hostage since 1051 (see p. 124 above), who briefly appear again in history 'like ghosts from another world' (Stenton, *William the Conqueror*, p. 372).

in the morning of Thursday, 9 September, with a prayer on his lips:

'. . . the king woke just when the sun was beginning to shed its rays on the earth, and heard the sound of the great bell of the cathedral of Rouen. On his enquiring what it meant, his attendants replied: "My lord, the bell is ringing for Prime in the church of St. Mary." Then the king raised his eyes to heaven with deep devotion and lifting up his hands said: "I commend myself to Mary, the holy mother of God, my heavenly Lady, that by her blessed intercession I may be reconciled to her well-beloved Son, our Lord Jesus Christ." Having said this he died at once.'[303]

Though not without anti-climax of a very real and distasteful kind,[304] he was taken to Caen and buried in his church of St. Stephen on the other side of the town from where Mathilda lay in her church of the Trinity.

[303] Ordericus Vitalis, iii, 248; *English Historical Documents*, ii, 289.

[304] In the confusion immediately attendant on his death (whereat his servants robbed the apartment and then fled) the transport of his body to Caen was only arranged with difficulty and by a simple knight called Herluin. On arrival at Caen the funeral procession to the church was disorganised by a fire in the town (reminiscent of his coronation at Westminster). The funeral service was interrupted by a certain Ascelin, son of Arthur, who claimed compensation for the ground in which he was to be buried, saying that it had been taken from his father without compensation when the church was built. Finally, by the mason's error, the stone coffin was found to be too small for the dead king, who had grown corpulent in his later years, and the body broke when the attendants forced it in. Full details (needless to say) are to be found in Ordericus Vitalis, iii, 249–54.

CHAPTER VI

Norman England

But it sufficeth that the day will end,
And then the end is known.

SHAKESPEARE

In the broadest sense, to set down the results of the Norman Conquest is to write the rest of English history down to the present day, and to add the histories of all those countries who were to feel the impact or the influence of post-Conquest England. In 1066 certain forces of causation were set in motion, and a chain-reaction follows. This, we can only say, is how things happened, and in no other way, and anything else is merely guess-work and hypothesis. We cannot know what would have happened, and what it would have been like, had Hastings not been fought and won by William, duke of Normandy. In this sense, at least, the cry of Carlyle[1] – 'Without them [the Normans] what had it ever been?' – must be accepted and remain unanswered. The Norman Conquest was a turning-point in the history of England, and only less dramatically in the history of Western Europe and of Latin Christendom.

More immediately, in England in the strenuous years which followed on from 1066, we should expect to find elements of continuity, because of sheer practical necessity, because of the known Norman genius for adoption and adaptation shown elsewhere in their history, in Normandy itself, in Italy, in Sicily and in Antioch,[2] and not least because William the Conqueror came as king Edward's heir,[3] the legitimate successor to the

---

[1] See p. 1, above.
[2] Cf. p. 23, above.
[3] 'The cardinal principle of the Conqueror's government was the wish to rule, and to be accepted by Englishmen, as King Edward's legitimate successor' (F. M. Stenton, *Anglo-Saxon England*, p. 614).

rights and powers of English kings and the inheritor of whatever institutions already existed for the government and administration of the English realm. But we should also expect to find drastic, profound and increasingly wide-ranging changes, especially because the Norman Conquest involved, whatever else, a revolution in the upper levels of society, a complete change of personnel at the top, the imposition of a new and alien ruling dynasty and ruling class. It seems very probable that amongst English historians the modern emphasis and over-emphasis upon continuity in and after 1066[4] springs from the modern preoccupation with institutions at the expense of personalities and people. But in England after 1066 the firm was under entirely new management. The dynamic Norman house of Rollo replaced the ancient and somewhat effete Wessex dynasty; a new aristocracy, French and predominantly Norman, was settled upon the land, and looked, like their kings, towards France, rather as settlers in North America once looked towards Europe; and the English church was similarly directed by French and Norman prelates. By the end of William the Conqueror's reign in 1087 there were only two Englishmen left, Thurkill of Arden and Colswein of Lincoln, as persons of any political consequence holding estates of any considerable extent directly of the king,[5] and only three important native prelates in the English church.[6] In an age when not only the kings but also the ruling classes really ruled, and moulded the lands they dominated into the pattern of their wills, so sweeping a change of lordship could not but be important, and after it nothing could ever be the same again. Nor could it be accomplished without a legacy of bitterness which lasted at least into the second generation, when the new order became the *status quo*, when English interests made the Normans Anglo-Normans, when those of the surviving English who wished to rise in the world aped their betters to become Normanized, and when intermarriage had at least begun to heal the ancient wounds.[7] Yet William of

[4] Cf. p. 3, above.
[5] Stenton, op. cit., p. 618; Loyn, *Norman Conquest*, pp. 171–2.
[6] Stenton, op. cit., p. 671; see p. 252, below.
[7] Ordericus Vitalis speaks of the intermarriage as early as *c.* 1070 *Historia Ecclesiastica*, ii, 214). William of Malmesbury refers to inter-

Malmesbury, himself the product of a mixed marriage, could write, about the year 1125, that 'England is become the residence of foreigners and the property of aliens. At the present time there is no English earl (*dux*), nor bishop nor abbot; strangers all, they prey upon the riches and vitals of England.'[8] In the same generation, Ordericus Vitalis, again, it seems, the offspring of a French father and an English mother, born in England soon after the Conquest and regarding himself always, with self-engendered bitterness, as an English exile in the foreign house of St. Evroul, indulged himself with vitriolic passages about the Norman rape of England – 'Possessed of enormous wealth' they 'gave reign to their pride and fury. . . . Ignorant upstarts, driven almost mad by their sudden elevation, wondered how they arrived at such a pitch of power, and thought they might do whatever they liked . . . .'[9]

To begin at the top with kings, it is certainly to be noted that Harold's own usurpation in January 1066 involved a change of dynasty, but we do not know what sort of rulers he or any heirs he might have had would have become. What we do know is that he was replaced by William of Normandy, a prince of proven worth before his accession to the English throne, a master of politics, war and the management of men, a convinced ecclesiastical reformer, and a king whose constructive powers had not been equalled since Charlemagne.[10] His sons and immediate successors, William Rufus and Henry I, were inferior only to him in purposeful rule, creative energy and ambition, and the weak kingship of his nephew Stephen was followed by the dynamic rule of the Angevin kings, which

marriage by the Normans with their subjects (*Gesta Regum*, ii, 306), and by the later twelfth century Richard fitz Nigel could write that 'nowadays, when English and Normans live close together and marry and give in marriage to each other, the nations are so mixed that it can scarcely be decided (I mean in the case of freemen) who is of English birth and who of Norman' (*Dialogus de Scaccario*, ed. C. Johnson, p. 53; *English Historical Documents*, ii, ed. D. C. Douglas, p. 523).
[8] *Gesta Regum*, i, 278.
[9] Op. cit., ii, 224–6. For Orderic, see Le Prévost, ibid., v., xxxiii, et seq.; Darlington, *Anglo-Norman Historians*, pp. 11–12; and H. Wolter, *Ordericus Vitalis* (Weisbaden, 1955), pp. 47–50.
[10] Cf. R. W. Southern, *Saint Anselm and his Biographer* (Cambridge, 1963), p. 4.

itself could never have come about without the Norman Conquest. By that time the realm and society of England were set in a mould to last for the rest of the medieval period and we need follow the new line of kings no further, though it remains to stress one change of incalculable importance as from 1066, which even the mere mention of Anglo-Norman and Angevin kings makes obvious enough. The Norman Conquest, by a change of ruling dynasty, as well as by the importation of a new French aristocracy who were the king's companions, wrested England from Scandinavian domination (mixed with affiliations with the Old World of Germany and the Rhineland, and sheer insularity) and brought the country into direct relationship with the Brave New World of Normandy and France.

The disappearance and decimation of the Anglo-Scandinavian and Old English aristocracy in the first generation of the Norman Conquest was nothing short of catastrophic. That in the beginning king William had intended to establish a genuine Anglo-Norman state is proved by his patronage of and patience with the aethling Edgar, earls Edwin and Morcar, Waltheof and Copsi, and those other members of the pre-Conquest nobility of England who submitted to him and made their peace after Hastings, as by his maintenance in their positions of English sheriffs and other officials.[11] Yet also the resettlement of England, more particularly in the south and east, began almost at once, and of necessity, to meet the claims of those who had supported his invasion on the promise of rich rewards,[12] and out of the wide lands of those of the English lords, from the house of Godwin downwards, who had fought against him and fallen at Hastings, or who had thereafter not submitted. Referring to those submissions, the Anglo-Saxon Chronicle states bleakly that after William's coronation 'people . . . gave him hostages and afterwards bought their lands',[13] while the alternative of confiscation is illustrated by a well-known writ of the Conqueror, dating from 1066–70, commanding abbot Baldwin of Bury St. Edmunds to

[11] Cf. p. 184, above; Stenton, op. cit., pp. 614 et seq.
[12] William of Poitiers, ed Foreville, pp. 158, 182, 218.
[13] Ed. Whitelock, p. 142, 'E'.

surrender to the king the lands of those under his jurisdiction 'who stood in battle against me and were slain there'.[14] But to the survivors there could have seemed little hope of lasting power or influence in the new order of Norman England, and their frustration was no doubt a motive for those rebellions which, between 1067 and 1075, finally destroyed them.[15] By the time of Domesday Book in 1086 the Old English and Anglo-Scandinavian earls, thegns and housecarls have vanished from the top ranks of society. Many, of course, had been slain in the three great battles of 1066, at Fulford, Stamford Bridge and Hastings, or in the rebellions which followed; many must have been squeezed out, no doubt by the rigid application of the new feudal law of succession whereby there was no absolute right of inheritance to the fiefs which their lands had now become;[16] many must have been suppressed in the social hierarchy with new lords placed above them; and very many, without doubt, went into exile, to Scotland, Scandinavia, Flanders, and even in considerable numbers to far-off Byzantium, where they took service in the Eastern Emperor's Varangian Guard and fought again against the Normans, this time from southern Italy.[17] The continent of Europe in the last decades of the eleventh century was full of English exiles who, for a time, were something of a standing menace to the Norman polity.[18]

Those who replaced them in England were French, members of a different race and for the most part already prominent members of a different society with different laws and different customs. Not all of them found England to their liking, and

---

[14] *Regesta Regum Anglo-Normannorum*, i (Oxford, 1913), ed. H. W. C. Davis, p. 119, No. vi; D. C. Douglas, *Feudal Documents from the Abbey of Bury St. Edmunds* (London, 1932), p. 47, No. 1.

[15] See pp. 190–8 et seq., above.

[16] Cf. Loyn, *Norman Conquest*, pp. 117–18, 171–2. Presumably those English lords who 'bought' their lands after Hastings received them back as fiefs. Stigand is said specifically to have done homage at Wallingford (William of Poitiers, p. 216; cf. p. 179, above). For the power of post-Conquest kings as feudal suzerains to make or break families by the manipulation of inheritances, see p. 241, below.

[17] Loyn, op. cit., p. 117; Ordericus Vitalis, op. cit., ii, 172–3 and note.

[18] Cf. p. 190 above, and William of Poitiers, p. 264.

not all those who followed William the Conqueror in 1066 or later[19] subsequently settled. Ordericus Vitalis tells with approval of Gilbert de Heugleville, a kinsman of the king, who fought for him in all the campaigns of the Conquest but thereafter refused the offer of ample English lands and returned to Normandy because he did not wish to possess stolen property (*de rapina quidquam possidere noluit*).[20] Gherbod, advocate of St. Bertin in Flanders, was the Conqueror's first earl of Chester in 1070 but soon gave up his earldom and his English fiefs to return home,[21] as Aubrey de Coucy later withdrew from the earldom of Northumbria and England in *c*. 1081.[22] There could be personal difficulties. The intrepid Mathilda came over to join her royal husband and to be crowned in 1068, and many Norman ladies came with her.[23] But others evidently feared to follow her example and, according to Ordericus Vitalis, demanded the return of their lords on pain of desertion. Under such domestic pressure Humphrey de Tilleul and Hugh de Grentemesnil amongst others returned to Normandy, though the latter at least came back again, and it is satisfactory to find both him and his wife amply enfeoffed with English lands in Domesday Book.[24] Those who stayed, or rather, those who accepted fiefs in England and thereafter had interests on both sides of the Channel like the king himself, formed and perpetuated a new French aristocracy, dominating the land they ruled and reshaping it closer to their heart's desire. About them scarcely less than about the new royal dynasty most of the subsequent history of medieval England has to be written. Amongst them there were notable non-Norman elements. From the lands to the north-east of Normandy, from Picardy, the Boulonais and

---

[19] Roger of Montgomery, for example, together with Hugh d'Avranches and William de Percy, came to England only in December, 1067 (Ordericus Vitalis, ii, 178; cf. Loyn, op. cit., p. 121).

[20] Op. cit., iii, 44. Cf. his story of the monk Guitmond who similarly eschewed the spoils of a conquered land (ii, 226–32, and below, p. 251).

[21] Ordericus Vitalis, op. cit., ii, 219,; *Complete Peerage*, 'G.E.C.', iii (1913), p. 164.

[22] Ibid., ix (1936), p. 705; Stenton, *Anglo-Saxon England*, p. 606.

[23] Ordericus Vitalis, op. cit., ii, 181; above p. 192.

[24] Ibid., ii, 185–6 and note.

Flanders, there came, for example, Arnulf de Hesdin, established at Chipping Norton, count Eustace of Boulogne, whose great honour lay principally in Essex, and Gilbert 'de Gand', enfeoffed in the northern Danelaw and elsewhere.[25] There was also an important Breton contingent,[26] including at its head Alan the Red, established in East Anglia, Lincolnshire and at Richmond in Yorkshire, founder of the line of Breton earls of Richmond,[27] and, in the far west, Judhael of Totnes in Devon, whose honour in the twelfth century owed the service of more than seventy knights.[28] The very numerous Breton element in the post-Conquest settlement of England was reduced after the rebellion of 1075, which resulted in the exile of Ralph 'de Gael', earl of East Anglia, of part-Breton extraction, and many of his supporters,[29] but has been traced in almost every county. To it, as an instance, we owe the agreeable place-name (amongst others) of Helion's Bumpstead in Essex, derived from a certain Tihel de Helléon, near Ploermel in Brittany.[30] But when all due allowance has been made

[25] Stenton, op. cit., p. 621; Douglas, *William the Conqueror*, pp. 266–7. For count Eustace and the 'honour of Boulogne' see especially J. H. Round, *Studies in Peerage and Family History* (London, 1930), pp. 147–80. Gherbod, appointed earl of Chester in 1070, was also from Flanders but early withdrew (above).

[26] See especially F. M. Stenton, *First Century of English Feudalism*, pp. 24–8. In some districts, notably in Lincolnshire and the North Riding of Yorkshire, the Breton settlement seems to have been on the scale of a minor migration rather than the establishment of a rural upper class.

[27] For this family, see C. T. Clay, *Early Yorkshire Charters*, iv, 84 ff., and *Complete Peerage*, 'G.E.C.', x (1945), pp. 779 ff.

[28] Another very important Breton lord of the first generation of the post-Conquest settlement was 'count Brian', brother of Alan the Red of Richmond, who may have been the Conqueror's first earl of Cornwall and was also the lord of extensive lands in Suffolk. By 1086 he had been replaced in both districts by Robert, count of Mortain, and his early disappearance from England may be connected with the rebellion of 1075 (below). See Stenton, *Anglo-Saxon England*, pp. 621–2; Douglas, *William the Conqueror*, pp. 267, 268; *Complete Peerage*, iii, 427; Round, *Genealogist*, N. S., xvii, 1.

[29] Douglas, op. cit., pp. 231–3. Earl Ralph was lord of the great barony of Gael in Brittany and son of Ralph the Staller, for whom see p. 115, above.

[30] Stenton, *First Century*, p. 25; Round, *Transactions Essex Archaeological Society* (New Series), viii (1903).

for other elements, the new lay ruling class established in England increasingly after 1066 was predominantly Norman, just as the Conquest itself was pre-eminently a Norman enterprise. With only a few prominent exceptions, mostly already noted, those whom Domesday Book shows to have been the greatest lords in the Conqueror's England are Normans – Odo, bishop of Bayeux and earl of Kent; Robert, count of Mortain; William fitz Osbern, earl of Hereford; Roger of Montgomery, earl of Shrewsbury; Hugh d'Avranches, earl of Chester; William de Warenne; Richard of Clare, son of count Gilbert of Brionne; Geoffrey de Mandeville; and Geoffrey de Mowbray, bishop of Coutances. To these great names we may add from the second rank of the new nobility others to conjure with – Malet of Eye, Ferrers of Tutbury, Bigod, Giffard, Braiose, Crispin and Taillebois, Peverel and Lacy, Montfort and Tosny, Mortimer, Vere, Beaumont and Beauchamp.[31] There will, of course, be changes as the post-Conquest period unfolds, some of them soon like the fall of Roger de Breteuil, earl of Hereford and son of William fitz Osbern, in 1075,[32] the disgrace of Odo of Bayeux in 1082,[33] or the breaking of the great house of Montgomery-Bellême by Henry I;[34] but the men who subsequently rise into this new nobility will be fundamentally the same type as those they supplant or join, French

[31] Cf. Douglas, op. cit., pp. 268–9. While the details of the Norman settlement form a subject much in need of further prolonged research, most of our present general knowledge of the distribution of English lands among William the Conqueror's followers comes from W. J. Corbett's fundamental work on Domesday Book, summarised in his chapter, 'The Development of the Duchy of Normandy and the Norman Conquest of England' in Volume V of the *Cambridge Medieval History* (1926). His conclusions have been glossed, improved and expanded by R. Lennard, *Rural England 1086–1135* (Oxford, 1959), Chapters II and III. Fundamental work of a scarcely less valuable kind into the Norman origins of the new Norman lords in England will be found in L. C. Loyd, 'The Origins of Some Anglo-Norman Families' (*Harleian Society*, ciii, Leeds, 1951).

[32] Cf. p. 199, above.

[33] Cf. p. 199, above.

[34] See especially J. F. A. Mason, 'Roger of Montgomery and his sons (1067–1102)', *Transactions Royal Historical Society* (5th series), xiii (1963).

or Anglo-Norman, the break and change at this top level of society in and after 1066 is complete, and by 1087 the principal actors of future English history are already in their places or waiting in the wings.[35]

We do not know the number of Normans and other French who settled in England in William the Conqueror's reign, but if we make a reasonable guess at perhaps something like ten thousand in a total population of about one and a half million[36] it will at least serve to emphasise both the small proportion of the invaders and the overall pattern of the Norman Conquest, which is of the imposition of a new landed ruling class in church and state, with far less change of personnel among townsmen and very little among the peasantry. Many other factors also added to and emphasised the natural cohesion of this small group of invaders occupying an alien land, with the result that a degree of political unity was achieved unknown in the last disturbed decades of the Old English state.[37] The remarkable unity of pre-Conquest Normandy[38] was reproduced on a larger scale in England chiefly through the agency of the same ruler and the same aristocracy, with the assistance in due course of a similarly organised church. The most notable feature of the Norman settlement in England, apart from its orderliness and the firm control maintained by king William throughout, was the huge concentration of wealth in the hands of the few which it brought about. The Domesday Survey of 1086 shows that in the course of the Conqueror's reign several thousand English estates had been concentrated into the lord-

---

[35] Which, of course, is what Round, the genealogist, had in mind when he confessed to his, often criticised, 'instinctive feeling that in England our consecutive political history does, in a sense, begin with the Norman Conquest' (*Feudal England*, p. 317).

[36] Thus Domesday Book records about 1,400 tenants-in-chief and a further 8,000 under-tenants, but these figures include an English element and there are other complications which prevent their being used for statistical purposes. Cf. Loyn, *Norman Conquest*, p. 119. The total number of knights owing service to the Conqueror as the result of his enfeoffments is reckoned at some 5,000 (Round, *Feudal England*, p. 292; see p. 221 below).

[37] Cf. pp. 74–84, above.

[38] Cf. pp. 20–60, above.

ships of less than two hundred major lay tenants-in-chief,[39] who between them controlled some fifty-four per cent of Domesday England.[40] Within this again, twenty of the greatest lay lords together with twelve of the richest prelates held some forty per cent of all the land in Domesday Book expressed in terms of value,[41] and almost a quarter of England was settled by the Conqueror upon only eleven of his principal lay vassals[42] – Odo of Bayeux, Robert, count of Mortain, William fitz Osbern, Roger of Montgomery, William de Warenne, Hugh d'Avranches, Eustace, count of Boulogne, count Alan the Red, Richard of Clare, Geoffrey de Mowbray and Geoffrey de Mandeville. Those whom the Conqueror most richly rewarded in England were meant to share the burden of the government of his realm, and they did so not only in their localities but also by attending him in counsel.[43] Most of his greatest vassals in England were not only Normans but also his own kinsmen or closest friends, or both, like his half-brothers Odo of Bayeux and Robert of Mortain, or William fitz Osbern and Roger of Montgomery (or, in the church, Lanfranc, established at Canterbury from 1070). They were also well known to each other, and often closely related each to each. Baldwin de Meules placed by the Conqueror at Exeter in 1068 was brother of Richard 'de Bienfaite' established in his great honours of Tonbridge and of Clare;[44] the first wife of Robert, count of Mortain, was Maud, a daughter of Roger of Montgomery;[45] Ralph de Tosny, established in East Anglia and the southern midlands, married his daughter to Roger Bigod of Norfolk, and was himself the brother of Robert of Stafford, the greatest magnate in Staffordshire, and probably the nephew of Robert de Tosny, founder of Belvoir castle, and the kinsman of Ralph de Limesy, a leading magnate in central

[39] Stenton, *Anglo-Saxon England*, p. 618.
[40] Lennard, *Rural England*, p. 25.
[41] Ibid., pp. 25–6.
[42] Douglas, op. cit., p. 269.
[43] Ibid., p. 286; Stenton, op. cit., pp. 623–4.
[44] Above, p. 191; *Complete Peerage*, 'G.E.C.', iii (1913), pp. 242 et seq.; Round, *Feudal England*, pp. 472–3 (pedigree).
[45] *Complete Peerage*, iii, 428.

England.[46] In Oxfordshire there is an interesting affiliation of a different kind, where two of the most prominent Norman lords, Robert d'Oilly and Roger d'Ivry, had taken part in the great adventure of the Conquest of England as sworn brothers,[47] and held certain of their lands in common, presumably as the result of this confederation. Again, while all those who followed duke William to England and afterwards accepted fiefs there were greatly enriched as a result, most of his chief lords in England were men of substance in Normandy before they came and had previously served him closest in his duchy,[48] while those, comparatively few, whose fortunes stemmed almost entirely from the Conquest, like Bigod, Port and Lacy,[49] were unlikely to be less loyal as a result.

The cohesion of the new ruling class which imposed a new degree of political unity upon England was further augmented by the natural tendency for the pattern of tenurial settlement already established in Normandy to be reproduced in England. Thus modern scholarship increasingly shows the neighbours and presumed tenants of a great lord in Normandy becoming also the tenants and vassals of the same lord in England, having, we may suppose, followed him as members of his contingent to England and to Hastings, as the great lords themselves followed the duke.[50] Also contributing to the unity of the realm was that territorial dispersion of lordships, of honours, fiefs and estates at all levels in the social hierarchy of the upper classes, which is so marked a feature of the Norman settlement.[51] This feature has often been noted by historians of the Conquest, but in the past has often also been misinterpreted. It was absurd ever to suppose that it resulted from a consciously 'anti-baronial' policy on the part of William the Conqueror, designed to weaken the power of those upon whom in reality he depended most to govern and defend his realm

---

[46] Stenton, op. cit., p. 623.
[47] *Fratres jurati et per fidem et sacramentum confederati.* See Lennard, *Rural England*, p. 65.
[48] Cf. Douglas, op. cit., p. 269.
[49] Loyd, *Origin of Some Anglo-Norman Families*, pp. vii–viii.
[50] Douglas, op. cit., pp. 95, 203, 270; cf. Loyd, op. cit., pp. 139–40.
[51] F. M. Stenton, *First Century of English Feudalism*, pp. 63–5; Lennard, op. cit., pp. 28 et seq., 45 et seq.

and maintain the Norman hegemony. In fact those closest to the king and most in his favour are often found to have the most dispersed estates, while the estates of the king himself were as dispersed as those of any other lord.[52] The territorial dispersion of estates is largely the natural result of their accumulation in different places and often at different times. As a feature of English lordship it was not new at the time of the Conquest but was greatly increased by it. The actual process of the Norman settlement was one whereby the confiscated lands, usually *en bloc* and often already scattered, of an English lord were granted to a new Norman beneficiary; the displaced Englishman was the *antecessor* of his Norman supplanter, and the most important Norman lords, most richly rewarded, received the lands of many *antecessores* in many places. Thus it came about that by the time of Domesday Book Robert de Busli had succeeded some eighty *antecessores* in Nottinghamshire and south Yorkshire, the count of Mortain held land of the king in twenty counties, the earl of Chester in nineteen counties in addition to his earldom, some twenty tenants-in-chief had lands in ten or more counties, and in any given county the lands of any given lord are likewise likely to be scattered.[53] If there was any conscious political motive in this process beyond the need and desire of the Conqueror to reward his followers with land as it became available, it was to secure greater control of his realm by giving power to his most trusted vassals where they were most needed – the establishment of William fitz Osbern and Roger of Montgomery both in the Welsh marches and upon the south coast being a case in point.[54] The long-term and unforeseen results, however, were of profound importance in future English history, for the geographical dispersion of most of the great honours and the widespread territorial interests of their lords worked against any possible development of local particularism, and in the long run weakened the honorial courts to the advantage of the

[52] Cf. p. 244, below.
[53] Stenton, *Anglo-Saxon England*, p, 618; Lennard, op. cit., pp. 28–9.
[54] They, his closest friends, alone amongst his great vassals were thus distinguished in responsibility. Cf. Mason, *Transactions Royal Historical Society* (5th Series), xiii (1963), p. 3. See also p. 215, below.

king's courts and the common law, while the kaleidoscopic nature of feudal geography contributed to the development of a self-reliant and competent local gentry who were fit material for the techniques of 'self-government at the king's command' employed by medieval and post-medieval governments.[55]

The characteristic dispersion and intermingling of honours, fiefs and estates did not preclude the concentration of the lands and power of particular lords in particular areas for strategic reasons.[56] While the Norman Conquest and settlement of England destroyed the great sprawling earldoms of Edward the Confessor's day, together with over-mighty subjects who had held them, the Conqueror's realm was ringed on the frontiers by earldoms and other viable military commands. The most obvious instances are the three 'marcher' earldoms against Wales, Chester (Hugh d'Avranches), Shrewsbury (Roger of Montgomery) and Hereford (William fitz Osbern), but with them should be compared the earldoms of Kent (Odo of Bayeux) and Cornwall (Robert, count of Mortain), and the ancient earldoms of East Anglia and Northumbria which it was found necessary to retain. Comparable are the compact *castellarie* or castellanies formed by the rapes of Sussex in the south-east and each organised about the new castle at its centre, Hastings (Robert, count of Eu) and Pevensey (Robert, count of Mortain), Lewes (William de Warenne), Bramber (William de Braose), Chichester[57] and Arundel (Roger of Montgomery). In this area the Isle of Wight is another similar instance of a compact military command, while in the far north there was the *castellaria* or honour of Richmond (count Alan of Brittany), and there are traces of *castellarie* in the interior of the kingdom, centred upon the castles of Pontefract (Lacy), Tutbury (Ferrers) and Dudley (fitz Ansculf). Particular arrangements such as these, like the Norman settlement as a whole, have to be seen and interpreted in the light

[55] Lennard, op. cit., pp. 33 et seq., 61–2. The preference of the new French and Norman aristocracy for living in the countryside tended, of course, in the same direction (cf. p. 100, above).
[56] Stenton, *Anglo-Saxon England*, pp. 619–20, and *First Century of English Feudalism*, pp. 192–4; Lennard, op. cit., pp. 30–2.
[57] For Chichester, see *V.C.H.*, *Sussex*, iv (1953), pp. 1–20; Mason, op. cit., pp. 2–3.

of immediate circumstances as they appeared to king William and his vassals. They did not all endure (there was no earl of Hereford or East Anglia after 1075 nor of Kent after the fall of Odo of Bayeux) but at the time they ensured the permanence of the Conquest, and from their lordships in the west and north the Normans were to penetrate into Wales and, more peacefully, into Scotland, as well as to maintain the defence of their new kingdom.

Also contributing to a new degree of social cohesion, political unity and royal power was the introduction of feudalism into England, which must be listed high among the most important results of the Norman Conquest. The society of pre-Conquest England was a survival from an older world and cannot in any meaningful way be described as 'feudal' in the absence of full, feudal commendation, in the absence of the fief, and in the absence of native knights and castles.[58] All four fundamental characteristics of contemporary feudal society were rapidly established in England from 1066 onwards as the Norman duke William, his companions and his and their knights, brought with them, naturally and inevitably, the habits and laws, social relationships and methods of warfare, to which they were accustomed in their home lands,[59] established their lordship, piecemeal, over all England, and faced and overcame the problems of its defence. The social revolution involved in the imposition of a new ruling class was accompanied by a tenurial revolution in the terms by which the land was held in the upper ranges of society, and the clean sweep of lordship effected by the Conquest provided the occasion for the establishment of a feudal hierarchy, culminating in the king as suzerain, more comprehensive, definite and precise than is easily to be found upon the continent of western Europe. In France in general, and more particularly in the feudal principalities among which France at this date was divided, including Normandy, though the quasi-sovereign power of princes was everywhere becoming dominant, feudalism was and had been a natural growth, developing at least in part from the bottom upwards, with pockets of allodial land untidily surviving here

[58] Cf. pp. 84–99, above.
[59] For feudal society in pre-Conquest Normandy, see pp. 34–49, above.

and there.[60] In England, a country (in Marc Bloch's phrase) of imported feudalism,[61] in the special circumstances of the Conquest, the new tenures, services and attitudes were introduced by comparison suddenly, and the tenurial change proceeded from the top downwards as the new king first enfeoffed his companions and his vassals with their honours, and they subsequently and in turn enfeoffed their own men upon them.[62] By the end of the Conqueror's reign all England save the broad estates of the king himself and the church had been parcelled out to new lords who held the lands granted to them as fiefs, that is to say on conditional tenure from the king in return for military and other knightly services. In the case of church lands there was, of course, the continuity of institutional lordship at and over 1066 (since the English church was not dispossessed but enriched by the Conquest), but military knight-service was likewise imposed by William upon the bishoprics, and upon the religious houses at least in the south and east, so that the prelates concerned were also henceforth tenants-in-chief holding baronies of the king.[63] By 1087, also,

[60] Cf. p. 40, above. Allodial land is land in full ownership as opposed to feudal tenure.

[61] *Feudal Society* (trans. L. A. Manyon, London, 1961), pp. 187–9.

[62] There is no true analogy with the English situation, for even in other countries of 'imported feudalism' by conquest, such as southern Italy and Sicily, or even Antioch, the conquest and settlement was an affair of private enterprise by comparison with the state-directed and centrally controlled conquest and settlement of England.

[63] J. H. Round, *Feudal England*, pp. 249–52; H. M. Chew, *English Ecclesiastical Tenants-in-Chief and Knight Service* (London, 1932), especially Chapter I. It has recently been suggested or implied that, because all the religious houses in England subsequently known to have owed knight-service were ancient foundations in the south and south-east, such service in reality was merely the continuation of a pre-Conquest obligation (thus D. J. A. Matthew, *The Norman Conquest*, London, 1966, p. 120). Setting aside the weight of all other evidence in favour of the introduction of knight-service by William the Conqueror upon lay and ecclesiastical tenants-in-chief alike, it may be more particularly noted that it was the south and east which first came under effective Norman domination, that there was at the time of the Conquest no surviving monasticism north of Trent and Humber (see Knowles, *Monastic Order in England*, pp. 165 et seq., and cf. p. 259, below), and that the episcopal sees owing knight-service are not similarly geographically confined.

the subsequent and secondary process of 'subinfeudation'
had gone far, similarly based upon the fundamental
concept of the fief or fee, as the newly established tenants-
in-chief both lay and ecclesiastical, in order to meet the
obligations of knight-service imposed upon them by the
king, in order to meet the needs of the management and
administration of their own honours, and in response to the
social pressures upon them no less than upon the king to
reward followers and companions with that land which was
the substance of wealth and power and status, enfeoffed upon
similar terms of conditional tenure their own knights and
vassals upon their estates.[64] When Domesday Book was compiled at the end of William the Conqueror's reign the Norman
tenurial revolution in England was more or less complete, and
the two great underlying principles, with their heavy social
and constitutional overtones, are writ large on every page –
the principle of *nulle terre sans seigneur*, and the principle that
all land is held directly or indirectly of the king as suzerain.[65]

   That all this, which, fundamentally, is the introduction of
the fee, the *fief de haubert*,[66] into England, with its essential
concomitants of knight-service to the lord[67] and the close bond

---

[64] Cf. C. W. Hollister, *The Military Organization of Norman England*,
pp. 54–5; Stenton, *First Century of English Feudalism*, p. 136.
[65] Cf. V. H. Galbraith, *The Making of Domesday Book* (Oxford, 1961),
pp. 28–30, 160.
[66] For the *fief de haubert*, see p. 40, above, and for the use of the term in
England see Stenton, op. cit., pp. 14–15.
[67] It is of the essence of the *fief de haubert* or knight's fee that military
service, specifically knight-service, is owed by the tenant to his lord,
who may or (more often) may not be the king or prince (cf. p. 90,
above). It is often said to be a feature of English feudalism after the
Conquest that all knight-service was the king's (e.g. Hollister, op. cit.,
p. 134), i.e. that a lord, at least outside the marches of Wales, could only
call upon his knights for military service on the king's behalf. This
proposition, however, is open to considerable doubt. It may be the
implication of the language of ecclesiastical writers dealing with the
particular case of knight-service imposed upon the lands of prelates, or
of one of the very few surviving charters of enfeoffment of the Conqueror's reign, which relates to the doubly special circumstances of the
king's using his influence to have one of his own knights enfeoffed upon
the lands of the abbey of Bury St. Edmund's ('Peter promises that he
will serve on behalf of the abbot within the kingdom with three or four

of full feudal commendation, comprising fealty, homage and investiture,[68] between the lord and vassal, was new to England in 1066 – or at least was alien to the native Anglo-Scandinavian society of pre-Conquest England[69] – cannot really be denied, though the attempt has too frequently been made in recent years, to the evident confusion of students of English history and to the dismay of their more responsible teachers. The great thesis of John Horace Round, reinforced by Frank Merry Stenton, remains untouched though not unchallenged:[70]

knights at their own expense if he has been previously summoned by the king and the abbot') but it is certainly not implied by the language of the other, and more normal, two charters of the period (see *English Historical Documents*, ii, ed. D. C. Douglas, pp. 895–8, No. 220 and Nos. 219, 221. For further discussion of these charters see p. 228 below), and is positively contradicted by certain later charters, dating admittedly from Stephen's reign, cited by Stenton (op. cit., pp. 183–4), one of which plainly distinguishes between royal service and knight-service (*ab omnibus servitiis terrenis, tam regalibus videlicet quam militaribus*, ibid. p. 184 and n. 2). There is also the consideration of surplus knights, i.e. knights over and above the requirement of their *servitia debita*, enfeoffed by many lords. Even in the late twelfth century Glanville expressed some doubt whether or not a lord might levy an aid from his knights to maintain his [own] war – *utrum vero ad guerram suam manutenendam possint hujusmodi auxilia exigere quaero* (extract from *De Legibus et Consuetudinibus Anglie* in Stubbs, *Select Charters*, 9th edition, p. 193). For the whole question, see also Stenton, op. cit., pp. 5, 183–5.

[68] Cf. pp. 42, 86, above.

[69] For Edward the Confessor's Norman and French 'favourites', and their settlement especially in Herefordshire, see pp. 115–16, above.

[70] J. H. Round, 'The Introduction of Knight Service into England', printed in his *Feudal England*; F. M. Stenton, *First Century of English Feudalism*. The principal modern critics of this established view are Marjory Hollings, 'The Survival of the Five Hide Unit in the Western Midlands', *E.H.R.*, lxiii (1948), and Eric John, *Land Tenure in Early England* (Leicester, 1960), Chapter 8. Richard Glover ('English Warfare in 1066', *E.H.R.*, lxvii, 1952) follows an approach at least refreshingly different from arguments about tenure, seeking, without success, to show that the pre-Conquest English had cavalry, and therefore knights and therefore feudalism. Richardson and Sayles in *The Governance of Mediæval England* (Edinburgh, 1963), e.g. p. 61, adopt without question or examination Richard Glover's argument and thus, having no revolution in the art of war, can have no social revolution either. Latest in the trampled field, D. J. A. Matthew (*The Norman Conquest*, pp. 117 et seq. and n. 54), seems to follow Richardson and Sayles.

at the top level of the feudal hierarchy, the quotas, the *servitia debita*, of knight-service, known from unimpeachable evidence to have been owed by tenants-in-chief to the Crown in the later twelfth century when written records are comparatively plentiful, can be traced back to the reign of William the Conqueror but no further,[71] and in no case, not even in that of the bishopric of Worcester,[72] does the quota of knight-service demanded from a magnate's honour correspond in any way to the previous assessment of the same land for military service in the pre-Conquest fyrd.[73] The quotas consist of rough, round numbers[74] – sixty knights or forty knights, thirty, twenty-five, twenty, fifteen or ten knights – multiples for the most part of five or ten, bearing no exact relationship to the size or value of the honours from which they are due, based very probably on the *constabularia* or *conroi*, the contingent and unit of the feudal host,[75] and evidently the result of individual and arbitrary bargains between William the Conqueror and his tenants-in-chief, made as the Norman settlement of England proceeded. By his enfeoffments king William obtained from

[71] Richardson and Sayles, however (op. cit., pp. 85–91, followed by Matthew, op. cit., p. 117 and n. 54), would have the quotas not fixed suddenly by William the Conqueror but slowly worked out and established in the course of the twelfth century down to 1166, largely as a financial matter to settle obligations at the Exchequer. This novel suggestion runs counter to the positive evidence of the Evesham writ and the chroniclers (see below), and in any case concerns the definition or limitation of knight-service, not the introduction of the service itself. See also Hollister, op. cit., pp. 266–7.

[72] See p. 88 above; J. O. Prestwich, 'Anglo-Norman Feudalism and the Problem of Continuity', *Past and Present*, No. 26, 1963, p. 44; E. John, op. cit., p. 158.

[73] Cf. Hollister, op. cit., p. 41.

[74] Those which are known are listed by Round, op. cit., pp. 249, 251, 253–6; see also *English Historical Documents*, ii, 904–6.

[75] If Round was overhasty in assuming a *constabularia* of ten knights as 'the unit of the feudal host', the Bury *constabularia* upon which he pinned his faith being thus organised for castle-guard duty rather than for service in the field, there is not much doubt that knights of this period fought in groups under their lords. See Round, op. cit., pp. 259–60; Hollister, op. cit., pp. 32–4 and the authorities cited in his n. 6 to p. 32. See also n. 147 p. 171, above.

his vassals the obligation of some five thousand knights,[76] and between this, the so-called feudal host of historians, and the pre-Conquest military system of the fyrd there is no continuity – still less when the necessary corollary facts are added that the pre-Conquest obligation of fyrd service produced infantry and naval forces, and was maintained after 1066, while the quotas of the Conqueror superimposed upon it were designed to produce knights, the heavy cavalry and *corps d'élite* of Norman and feudal armies. The great tenants-in-chief of the king, too, in the subsequent process of their subinfeudations, were concerned above all with the enfeoffment of their own knights and with obtaining knight-service, and the enfeoffments which they made were as arbitrary as those made by the king; their more important tenants[77] might owe them the service of several knights (and subinfeudate in their turn), but again the service owed bore no necessary relationship to the previous assessment of the land which was granted to them, while the fees created for individual knights – fees, that is, owing the service of one knight – were as heterogeneous as the circumstances and arrangements which produced them and varied widely in extent, value and previous assessment.[78] While innumerable instances are not so found, some single knights' fees are found rated at five hides in the post-Conquest period, notably in the bishopric of Worcester,[79] and in such cases the Anglo-Saxon five-hide unit[80] may be said to survive the Conquest as a fee. The fact, however, is literally one of mere antiquarian interest and of no further significance. The process and method of subinfeudation was a matter for the tenant-in-chief or other tenant and of no necessary concern to the king or other superior lord.[81] If it pleased the bishops of

---

[76] Round, op. cit., p. 292.

[77] For the substantial mesne tenants, the 'honorial baronage', see Stenton, op. cit., Chapter III.

[78] Round, op. cit., pp. 293–5; Stenton, op. cit., pp. 157, 163; Hollister, op. cit., pp. 43 et seq.

[79] Marjory Hollings, 'The Survival of the Five Hide Unit in the Western Midlands', *E.H.R.*, lxiii; cf. Hollister, op. cit., pp. 46–9.

[80] See p. 92, above.

[81] It still seems probable, for example, that the Conqueror's own interventions in the process of subinfeudation were exceptional rather than

Worcester and their officials, in the conservative western Midlands,[82] to make their fees up out of parcels of five hides, that was their own affair. It is reasonable to expect the development in detail of feudalism in England to be influenced by pre-existing English custom,[83] especially at the level of subinfeudation which lies, so to speak, at the grass roots of the new military tenures, and more especially upon ecclesiastical estates which were by and large exempt from violent dispossession and change of lordship, and where in consequence some elements of continuity are more likely to survive.

If, as historians, we stand back and survey the introduction of feudalism into England at the time of the Norman Conquest, then from one point of view it represents the imposition of a new and expensive knight-service by tenure upon the land already charged with the common obligations, including military service, owed to the king in the Anglo-Saxon period.[84] Against the exponents of continuity in his own day, Round, seeking to establish his own cataclysmic view of the Conquest in terms of the introduction of this knight-service by the Conqueror, remarked that 'the assumption that the Conqueror cannot have introduced any new principle in the tenure of land lies at the root of the matter',[85] and his most

normal, but cf. D. C. Douglas, *Feudal Documents from the Abbey of Bury St. Edmunds* (London, British Academy, 1932), pp. xcv–c.

[82] J. O. Prestwich, op. cit., p. 44; cf. above, p. 89.

[83] This is the eminently reasonable theme of Professor Hollister's *Military Organisation of Norman England*, though it may be thought that in the event he much exaggerates particular instances, not least the surviving post-Conquest importance of the fyrd and the influence of pre-Conquest English custom and habits upon post-Conquest military tactics, length of service and commutation. See the review by the present writer in *Medieval Archaeology*, x (1966).

[84] Above, p. 64.

[85] Op. cit., p. 247. Round had in mind (as always) Freeman, who had written (*Norman Conquest*, v, 1876, p. 372), 'There is no ground then for thinking that William directly or systematically introduced any new kind of tenure into the holding of English lands. There is nothing to suggest any such belief, either in the Chronicles of his reign, in the Survey which is his greatest monument, in the genuine, or even in the spurious, remains of his legislation' – two sentences which, significantly enough, are quoted with approval by E. John, op. cit., p. 152. For the alleged silence of the sources, see below.

recent critic (to date) returns to the attack armed with a similar general assumption – 'it is altogether incredible that the Conqueror introduced an entirely novel military obligation'.[86] At bottom, as Round saw, it is a matter of approach – 'The tendency to exalt the English and depreciate the Norman element in our constitutional development has led them, I think . . . to seek in Anglo-Saxon institutions an explanation of feudal phenomena'[87] – and without doubt it is the revived emphasis upon continuity by many English historians of our own day which has led to the revival of would-be arguments for Anglo-Saxon feudalism on the one hand[88] or to a depreciation of the effects of the introduction of Norman feudalism upon the other. It is sometimes alleged that had such new tenures and new services been rapidly introduced by the Normans after 1066 more trace would have been left upon historical records, not least in the form of complaints by monastic chroniclers at new secular impositions upon the church.[89] The argument *e silentio* is always dangerous but in this case verges upon the reckless. Setting aside the probability that the surviving importance of fyrd service after 1066 may well have been exaggerated[90] and that the obligation was not therefore in itself much of a burden to be added to, setting aside

[86] D. J. A. Matthew, op. cit., p. 117.
[87] Ut Supra.
[88] Cf. p. 84, above.
[89] Thus Freeman, *Norman Conquest*, v, 372, quoted in n. 85 above; E. John, op. cit., pp. 152–3; Matthew, op. cit., p. 117, n. 54. Cf. Prestwich, op. cit., p. 44; Hollister, op. cit., pp. 25–7.
[90] Prestwich, op. cit., pp. 45–6, 47–8. The right of calling upon all freemen for military service, with which in any case he was familiar in Normandy (see p. 22, above), was not one which the Conqueror or his successors were likely to allow to lapse (nor did they, as witness Henry II's Assize of Arms in 1180, and other later and similar enactments), but one may entertain doubts as to the efficacy of any force thus raised. Even for the pre-Conquest period, modern research tends heavily to emphasise the importance of mercenary and professional troops (see Hollister, *Anglo-Saxon Military Institutions*, especially Chapter I). Further, it does not follow that English troops referred to in the armies of William the Conqueror and his successors were fulfilling the obligation of fyrd-service. The evidence for the survival of the fyrd in the post-Conquest period is fully set out by Hollister in his *Military Organisation of Norman England*, Chapter VIII, and also his Addendum (pp. 261–7).

also the probability that at least in the first generation, before the growth of commutation, knight-service must often have appeared as the personal duty of the new lords rather than as new charge upon the land, and noting as we must that contemporary written sources in the period immediately following the Conquest, apart from Domesday Book, are few and slight, we are still in a situation in which such evidence as we have points all in one direction – to the introduction of feudalism, that is to say full feudal commendation, the feudal tenure of the fief, feudal knight-service, knights and castles, and feudal attitudes and assumptions not met in our sources before 1066.

Domesday Book itself, quite apart from its incidental references to fees and honours, knights and castles, has been very properly described by its latest historian as 'the formal written record of the introduction of feudal tenure, and therefore of feudal law into England',[91] for the commissioners and clerks of the great survey of 1086 laboriously arranged the information they obtained from the ancient administrative and territorial divisions of vills and hundreds into the new-fangled categories of the king's demesne and the fiefs and honours of his tenants-in-chief. A surviving writ of William the Conqueror from as early as 1072, upon which Round rightly placed great reliance as 'the climax of [his] argument',[92] summons Ethelwig abbot of Evesham to come to the king at Clarendon with the five knights owed in respect of his abbey, and it is known from twelfth-century evidence that the quota of Evesham abbey was five knights.[93] Round also drew attention to a passage of the thirteenth-century chronicler Matthew Paris, who (following Roger of Wendover) stated that in the year 1070 the Conqueror imposed military service upon the bishoprics and abbeys holding baronies, enrolling the number of knights due from each according to his will.[94] Much

[91] V. H. Galbraith, *The Making of Domesday Book*, p. 160.
[92] Op. cit., p. 303.
[93] '*Tu etiam illo die ad me venias et illos quinque milites quos de abbatia tua mihi debes tecum paratos adducas*'. The writ (No. 63, p. 17, of *Regesta Regum Anglo-Normannorum*, vol. i, ed. H. W. C. Davis, Oxford, 1913) is printed by Round, op. cit., p. 304, and in Stubbs, *Select Charters* (9th edition), p. 97; translation in *English Historical Documents*, ii, 895.
[94] '*Episcopatus quoque et abbatias omnes quae baronias tenebant, et eatenus

scorn has been poured upon the lack of authority to be attributed to a thirteenth-century writer's version of events two centuries earlier,[95] but the tradition of the well-informed house of St. Albans stands somewhat closer to those events than do twentieth-century historians, the selection of the date 1070 is interesting and suggests the ring of truth, and in any case Matthew Paris' testimony by no means stands alone, as Round indeed went on to demonstrate. The reign of William the Conqueror in England is a period particularly devoid of exactly contemporary chroniclers.[96] The great period of Anglo-Norman chroniclers begins in the early twelfth century with the reign of Henry I; before this, on the Norman side, William of Jumièges ends in 1072 and the text of William of Poitiers as it has come down to us breaks off in 1067,[97] while, on the English side, the Anglo-Saxon Chronicle, ever an over-rated source, becomes after 1066 even less informative, more removed from the centres of power and policy and from the main stream of events, and chiefly valuable in providing a kind of worm's-eye view of the Norman Conquest. Nevertheless, the native Chronicle refers in its own terms to the new Norman settlement in its reference to the submission after 1066 of the English leaders who 'afterwards bought their lands',[98] and in its references to the building of castles which it associates with oppression,[99] while William of Poitiers, even

---

ab omni servitute seculari libertatem habuerant, sub servitute statuit militari, inrotulans episcopatus et abbatias pro voluntate sua quot milites sibi et successoribus suis hostilitatis tempore voluit a singulis exhiberi', Historia Anglorum, ed. F. Madden (3 vols., Rolls Series, 1866–9), i, 13. Cited by Round, op. cit., p. 298. See also Wendover, *Flores Historiarum* (5 vols., ed. H. O. Coxe, London, English Hist. Society, 1841–4), ii, 7.

[95] Thus E. John, op. cit., p. 153; Richardson and Sayles, op. cit., pp. 62 et seq.

[96] Though according to E. John 'an age full of excellent chroniclers' (op. cit., p. 152). See, for a useful summary of the chroniclers of the period, *English Historical Documents*, ii, 97–9. Cf. R. R. Darlington, *Anglo-Norman Historians*.

[97] Though it originally ran to 1070 and is closely followed down to that date by Ordericus Vitalis (see *Historia Ecclesiastica*, ed. Le Prévost, ii 217).

[98] Ed. Whitelock, p. 142, 'E'.

[99] Ibid., p. 145, 'D'; p. 164, 'E'.

in the one year after Hastings for which his text survives, refers to the king placing French castellans in his castles and granting them rich fiefs (*opulenta beneficia*),[100] and specifically refers to the homage and fealty rendered by Stigand on the occasion of his submission at Wallingford,[101] as he had previously carefully described the fealty, homage and investiture of earl Harold in 1064.[102] Monastic chroniclers of the next generation, including the most reliable, are by no means silent, and some of them describe in clear terms both the introduction of knight-service in general and its imposition on the English church in particular. Ordericus Vitalis, having described in detail the settlement and distribution of lands to the Conqueror's companions in *c.* 1071 after the fall of Ely, adds that the king disposed of the lands of England among his followers in such a way that he was able to command the service of 60,000 knights.[103] We do not have to accept literally the figure of 60,000, which simply means a large number,[104] but the general statement is unequivocal. The Abingdon chronicler, again writing in the twelfth century but showing himself well informed of the events of the later eleventh century as they affected his church, states categorically à *propos* of the Norman Conquest that 'after the disturbances had died down, it was noted in the annals by the king's command what knights should be demanded from bishoprics and abbacies for the defence of the realm when need arose',[105] and goes on to

---

[100] Ed. Foreville, p. 238, '*Custodes in castellis strenuos viros collocavit, ex Gallis traductos . . . Ipsis opulenta beneficia distribuit, pro quibus labores ac pericula libentibus animis tolerarent.*'

[101] Ibid., p. 216, *manibus ei sese dedit, fidem sacramento confirmavit.*

[102] Ibid., p. 104; see also p. 130, above.

[103] Ed. Le Prévost, ii, 218 et seq., 224. '*Terras autem militibus ita distribuit, et eorum ordines ita disposuit, ut Angliae regnum lx millia militum indesinentur haberet, ac ad imperium regis, prout ratio poposcerit, celeriter exhiberet.*' It is curious that E. John (op. cit., p. 153) should have called attention in particular to 'the silence of Ordericus Vitalis' as 'an argument of weight'.

[104] Cf. Round, op. cit., pp. 289–93.

[105] '*At his sopitis incursibus, cum jam regis edicto in Annalibus annotaretur quot de episcopiis, quotve de abbatiis ad publicam rem tuendam milites (si forte hinc quid causae propellendae contingeret) exigerentur*', Chronicon Monasterii de Abingdon (ed. J. Stevenson, 2 vols., Rolls Series, 1858)

describe the necessary subinfeudations which abbot Athel-
holm subsequently made (from the land of thegns who had
fallen at Hastings, in each case declaring 'what would be the
obligations involved in its tenure'),[106] having already made it
clear that the peculiarly feudal knight-service of castle-guard
(at Windsor) was imposed upon the abbey by William the
Conqueror at an early date after 1066.[107] The twelfth-century
Book of Ely also, whose recorded traditions of eleventh-century events are by no means to be despised,[108] states that in
1072 for his Scottish campaign[109] the king demanded the
knight-service due from the bishops and abbots of England,
which service was to be henceforth the Crown's perpetual
right,[110] and later says that in the first year of his reign
William Rufus demanded from the churches the due service
(*debitum servitium*) of knights which his father had imposed
upon them.[111] Further, the chronicler leaves us in no doubt
that in the Conqueror's time the complaints of Ely were loud
and long at the new imposition, but a personal visit by abbot
Simeon to the king himself only resulted in the command to
maintain forty knights in the Isle (i.e. the later known *servitium debitum* of the church of Ely),[112] and in due course, as at
Abingdon, the necessary subinfeudations were made.[113]

ii, 3; translation in *English Historical Documents*, ii, 902; cf. Round, op.
cit., p. 299. The curious *in Annalibus annotaretur* should perhaps be
compared with the *inrotulans* of Matthew Paris (n. 94 p. 224, above).
[106] Ibid., ii, 3–5.
[107] Ibid., ii, 3, 7.
[108] Cf. p. 71, above.
[109] Cf. therefore the Evesham writ, cited p. 224, above, which probably
relates also to this occasion.
[110] *Liber Eliensis*, ed. E. O. Blake, p. 216. '*Iusserat enim tam abbatibus
quam episcopis totius Anglie debita militie obsequia transmitti, con-
stituitque ut ex tunc regibus Anglorum iure perpetuo in expeditione
militum ex ipsis presidia impendi . . . .*'
[111] Ibid., p. 218, '*debitum servitium, quod pater suus imposuerat, nunc ab
ecclesiis violenter exigit*'. Both these passages from the *Liber Eliensis*
were cited by Round, op. cit., p. 299.
[112] '*At rex preces eius et munera sprevit, male statuta convelli non desinit,
sed iugum agravare intendens, precipit illi ex nutu regio custodiam xl
militum habere in insulam (Liber Eliensis, p. 217).*'
[113] '*Ex hoc enim abbas, compulsus non ex industria aut favore divitum vel
propinquorum affectu, quasdam terras sancte Aetheldrethe invasoribus in*

There is also other written evidence of a sort even more direct than the statements and allusions of chroniclers and the general tenor of Domesday Book. Charters of enfeoffment are very rare in the first generation of the Norman Conquest when such conveyances at least in the lay world still generally depended for their validity solely upon the visual and oral ceremony of commendation and investiture,[114] but before they become increasingly commonplace in the course of the twelfth century, some survive even from the reign of William the Conqueror, and they speak of a new tenure in a new language which is not heard in England before 1066. Thus a well-known charter from Bury St. Edmunds opens with the announcement that 'Peter, a knight [*miles*] of king William, will become the feudal man [*feodalis homo*] of St. Edmund, by perform-ing the ceremony of homage (*manibus iunctis*)', and goes on to speak of the fief which Peter will hold of the abbot in return for the knight-service which he will render to him.[115] Another by Robert Losinga, bishop of Hereford, dated 1085, records the enfeoffment of Roger de Lacy, knight (*miles*), by the counsel of the bishop's men (*consilio suorum*), with land from the bishop's demesne (*proprio dominio*) at Holme Lacy for the service of two knights (*ut duobus militibus serviet sibi*) as Roger's father had held it before him.[116] A third, by Gilbert

feudum permisit tenere' (ibid.). After the Conqueror's death matters became even worse for the church of Ely, for in the first year of his reign Rufus demanded the service of 40 knights over and above the 40 required for guard duty in the Isle – an interesting and early instance of the uncertainty which evidently prevailed at least until Magna Carta as to whether castle-guard duty was an alternative to service in the field or an additional obligation (ibid., p. 218; cf. Magna Carta, c. 29, printed in Stubbs, *Select Charters*, 9th edition, p. 296).

[114] Cf. Stenton, *First Century of English Feudalism*, p. 152.

[115] Douglas, *Feudal Documents from the Abbey of Bury St. Edmunds*, p. 151, No. 168; translation, *English Historical Documents*, ii, 896, No. 220. For the knights and *feudati homines* of Bury St. Edmunds, see Douglas, op. cit., pp. lxxxii et seq., who writes (p. lxxxv), 'Long before Domesday the *servitium debitum* has clearly been imposed upon the abbey of Bury, and practical steps have been taken on the abbey lands to supply when need be the quota of knights which had been so promptly assigned by the Conqueror.'

[116] Printed with facsimile and commentary by Galbraith, *E.H.R.*, xliv (1929); translation, *English Historical Documents*, ii, 897, No. 221.

Crispin, abbot of Westminster and a friend and pupil of Lanfranc from Bec, records the grant to William Baynard of land
at Westminster, 'to be held by him for the whole of his life
by the service of one knight (*pro servicio unius militis*)';
William is to have in the land all the customs and liberties of
the church of Westminster except tithes and except the aids
which the church receives from its knights (*exceptis auxiliis
nostris que inde . . . de militibus accipiemus*).[117] In other charters
and documents of the Conqueror's reign also, though not themselves directly relating to enfeoffments by knight-service, the
unmistakable vocabulary of feudalism increasingly appears,
as when, in his charter of foundation for his priory of Eye in
Suffolk, Robert Malet both refers to his castle at Eye and
grants to his monks there 'all the other liberties which my
lord William king of England granted to me when he gave me
my honour',[118] or as when in the king's writs the barons and
knights of the shire take the place of the thegns of old.[119] The
development of feudal terminology in this country requires
more attention than it has yet received,[120] but meanwhile the
evidence of vocabulary can certainly be seen as a straw in the

[117] Printed by J. Armitage Robinson, *Gilbert Crispin, Abbot of Westminster* (Cambridge, 1911), p. 38; translation, *English Historical
Documents*, ii, 895–6, No. 219. The aid or *auxilium* was an obligation
upon tenants by knight-service to pay money to the lord, for which see
p. 243 and n. 187, below.
[118] Cartulary of Eye Priory (Essex Record Office, D/DBy, Q19,f.17v.),
'*habeantque omnes alias libertates quas dominus meus Willelmus rex
Anglie mihi concessit quando honorem mihi dedit*'. I owe this reference to
my pupil, Miss V. M. Elsley. Cf. Stenton, op. cit., p. 56 and n. 3. Robert
Malet probably succeeded his father, William Malet, soon after 1071.
For the honour of Eye, see also J. E. A. Jolliffe, *Constitutional History of
Medieval England*, pp. 142–3.
[119] H. W. C. Davis, *Regesta Regum Anglo-Normannorum*, i, e.g. Nos. 43,
122, 175, 185, 202, 215, 221, Appdx., Nos. III, IX, XXIII, XXV, XXX.
For thegns cf. Nos. 84, 87, 100, 108–9, 267–8.
[120] Valuable examples of the importance of such enquiries occur in
Stenton's *First Century of English Feudalism*, e.g. pp. 14 et seq., 54 et
seq., 83 et seq., 132–5, 171 et seq., 192–4, but there is no full-scale study
for England comparable to K. J. Hollyman, *Le Développement du
Vocabulaire Féodal en France pendant le haut moyen âge* (Paris and
Geneva, 1957) – though it may be noted that even that work regrettably
omits *castrum* and *castellum*.

wind of change. It is inconceivable that the kind of vivid feudal imagery employed by St. Anselm at the turn of the eleventh and twelfth centuries[121] could have come from the mouth or pen of a native English prelate before 1066, just as it may be thought inconceivable that the sophisticated system of feudal tenures and services revealed by the records of Angevin England could have developed naturally from the tenures and obligations of Anglo-Saxon England without the cataclysmic intervention of the Norman Conquest.

But there is more to feudalism than knight-service and knights' fees which were themselves at bottom one method of obtaining and maintaining the knights who achieved and perpetuated the Norman Conquest of England and sustained the militant policies of the new Norman royal dynasty. The Norman and French knights whom the Bayeux Tapestry depicts glamorously and forcefully contributing to the victory at Hastings thereafter appear in English sources not only enfeoffed upon the land but also riding in the Conqueror's armies across the length and breadth of England, in Scotland and in Wales, in Normandy and Maine, and riding also in the households of his greater vassals. The military household of the king as the nucleus and headquarters of an army, making all necessary qualifications for the type of warfare waged, is probably the one basic link between the military systems of pre- and post-Conquest England.[122] The pre-Conquest earls had also evidently kept their housecarls and retainers,[123] and the Norman magnates of the new régime after 1066 certainly found it necessary in the circumstances of the time to keep large military households, especially of knights.[124] Clattering and jingling contingents of mounted knights, with gonfanons and shields displayed, must have been a familiar sight in rural England as they rode upon the business of their lords, and lorded it over the countryside, and it is because the knights

[121] See R. W. Southern, *St. Anselm and his Biographer* (Cambridge, 1963), pp. 107–14.
[122] Prestwich, 'Anglo-Norman Feudalism and the Problem of Continuity', *Past and Present*, No. 26, 1963, p. 50.
[123] E.g. Hollister, *Anglo-Saxon Military Institutions*, pp. 12, 18.
[124] For the military households of lords in pre-Conquest Normandy, see pp. 48–9, above.

appeared to the eyes of the native English first and foremost
as the retainers of lords, that they applied to them the Anglo-
Saxon word '*cniht*', meaning servant or retainer, and in this
way and in due course the English word 'knight' has survived
in the English language instead of the French 'chevalier'.[125]
We hear much in the Conqueror's reign of household and
stipendiary knights. Ordericus Vitalis says of Hugh d'Avranches, lord of the marcher earldom of Chester against north
Wales and of much else besides, that he had so many that
he always moved about with an army rather than a household
– *non familiam secum, sed exercitum semper ducebat.*[126] William
fitz Osbern, earl of Hereford and lord of the Isle of Wight, also
kept a multitude of knights and paid them liberally.[127] In the
new Norman society of French chivalry now established in
England,[128] to maintain a retinue of knights was a mark of
status as well as a military necessity, and the habit evidently
spread to the surviving English lords. Even Wulfstan, bishop
of Worcester, that paragon of Old English virtues, adopted,
according to William of Malmesbury, the customs of the
Normans in his household – '*Nam et consuetudines Normannorum non omittebat, pompam militum secum ducens, qui
stipendiis annuis cotidianisque cibis immane quantum popula-
bantur*'.[129] The abbots of Ely and Abingdon also, and no doubt
other prelates, at first kept the knights which the Conqueror
demanded of them in their household, but finding their
presence not conducive to monastic peace and discipline soon
came to enfeof them.[130] But because most of the knights of the

[125] See Stenton, op. cit., pp. 132–5.
[126] *Historia Ecclesiastica*, ed. Le Prévost, ii, 219.
[127] William of Malmesbury, *Gesta Regum*, ii, 314. '*Erat in eo mentis ani-
mositas quam commendabat manus pene prodiga liberalitas: unde factum
est, ut militum multitudine, quibus large stipendia dabat, hostium avidi-
tatem arceret, civium sedulitatem haberet; quare pro effusis sumptibus
asperrimam regis offensam incurrit, quod gazas suas improvide dilapidaret.*'
[128] As later in Scotland – see G. W. S. Barrow, 'The Beginnings of
Feudalism in Scotland', *Bulletin Institute of Historical Research*, xxix
(1956), pp. 6–7.
[129] *De Gestis Pontificum Anglorum* (ed. N.E.S.A. Hamilton, Rolls
Series, 1870), p. 281. Cf. *Vita Wulfstani*, ed. R. R. Darlington (London,
Royal Historical Society, 1928), pp. xxxvii, 46, 55.
[130] *Liber Eliensis*, p. 217, '*habuitque ex consuetudine secundum iussum*

first generation of the Norman Conquest, whether serving
under lay or ecclesiastical lords, were successful in obtaining
the fiefs of their desires, as part and parcel of the great land
transfer which followed the victory of Norman arms, it would
be a mistake to suppose that either the aristocratic military
household or the stipendiary knight is a feature exclusive to
this early period of Norman England. The ethos of the new
feudal military aristocracy did not change, and there would
always be younger sons and surplus knights anxious to take
service with king or lord and hoping for a fief or an heiress as
their eventual reward, and for a young man of good or fair
birth taking up arms, as most did, a career open to talent long
remained a viable prospect – as the remarkable life and achievement of William Marshal illustrates a century and more after
1066.[131] Stipendiary knights also, and mercenary forces of
other ranks as warfare became ever more sophisticated and
complex not least as the result of castles and siegecraft, likewise continued to be a prominent feature of Anglo-Norman
armies, as, indeed, mercenary forces had been a prominent
feature of Anglo-Scandinavian armies before 1066.[132]

In their settlement of England, their enfeoffments and subinfeudations, the Conqueror and his vassals in and after 1066
were coping with an immediate situation, full of peril as well
as promise, in the way they best understood; they were not
to know that thereby they were laying the solid foundations
of a system of feudal tenure and feudal law that would endure
until 1660 and beyond.[133] It is probable that the direct military
value of William's *servitia debita* of some 5,000 knights can be,
and in the past has been, exaggerated, as, after the first genera-

---

*regis pretaxatum militie numerum infra aulam ecclesie, victum cotidie de
manu celerarii capientem atque stipendia, quod intolerabiliter et supra
modum locum vexare potuit'.* Cf. *Chron. Monasterii de Abingdon,* ii, 3;
English Historical Documents, ii, 902.

[131] Sidney Painter, *William Marshal, Knight-Errant, Baron and Regent
of England* (Baltimore, 1933).

[132] Hollister, *Anglo-Saxon Military Institutions,* Chapter I. For the
importance of mercenary forces in the Anglo-Norman period, see J. O.
Prestwich, 'War and Finance in the Anglo-Norman State', *Transactions
Royal Historical Society,* 5th Series, iv (1954).

[133] Cf. Stenton, op. cit., pp. 151–2; *Anglo-Saxon England,* p. 629.

tion, all the weakening complexities inseparable from an increasingly hereditary landed military class – sickness, old-age, heiresses, minors and fractional fees[134] – began to take effect and the Crown, however unwillingly, had perforce to accept financial commutation, i.e. scutage,[135] in place of personal service. Certainly from the beginning the feudal host of knights serving in return for their fiefs was reinforced by stipendiary knights and other ranks serving for pay, and by fyrd service, i.e. the right of English kings to call upon the military service of all free men, which no Norman, Angevin or later monarch was likely to let go. These things happened in the feudal age without incongruity, and (to express oneself with something less than clarity) there is nothing necessarily 'unfeudal' about the 'non-feudal' elements of 'feudal' armies. 'Mercenary' in our own age has become a word loaded with disapproval, but St. Anselm in one of his parables refers in the most natural way to the three sorts of knights to be found at the courts of princes – those who serve in return for their fiefs, those who serve in the hope of regaining lost fiefs, and those who serve for pay.[136] It is as well to treat our eleventh-century mercenaries with respect when we discover that William the Conqueror, recruiting great numbers of stipendiary knights in 1086, even hired Hugh, brother of the king of France, together with his company, regardless of expense.[137] The authentic contemporary note is struck, signifying the difference in status and thus honour, but scarcely class, when the frustrated Robert Curthose, the Conqueror's eldest son, allowed to have no real lordship or responsibility, declared that he would not for ever be his father's mercenary.[138]

---

[134] For the early appearance of fees owing only part of a knight's service, see Stenton, *First Century*, pp. 185–6. In 1166 Alfred of Lincoln stated that 'a certain old woman' held of him the sixteenth of a knight's fee (*Red Book of the Exchequer*, ed. Hubert Hall (Rolls Series, 3 vols., 1896), ii, 215).

[135] The earliest known reference to scutage, i.e. the commutation of knights' service, occurs in 1100. See Stenton, op. cit., p. 177.

[136] *The Life of St. Anselm Archbishop of Canterbury by Eadmer*, ed. R. W. Southern (London, 1962), p. 94. Cf. p. 37, above.

[137] William of Malmesbury, *Gesta Regum*, ii, 320.

[138] Ordericus Vitalis, *Historia Ecclesiastica*, ed. Le Prévost, ii, 378.

Castles, the symbols and much of the substance of feudal lordship,[139] were no less a Norman importation into England than the knights, and, like the knights, were a principal means whereby the Norman Conquest was achieved and perpetuated. And here at least the surviving evidence is not only unanimous but also abundant, whether we put on the stout boots of the archaeologist, look at surviving monuments like the Tower of London,[140] study the Bayeux Tapestry,[141] note the record in Domesday Book of the houses and property destroyed in towns and cities to make way for the new fortifications,[142] or read contemporary histories and hear the complaints of the Anglo-Saxon chronicler,[143] or the curse of archbishop Ealdred upon Urse d'Abbetot the sheriff for raising the castle of Worcester so close to the church that its ditches encroached upon the monks' cemetery – 'Hattest thou Urs, have thou Godes kurs'.[144] Ordericus Vitalis cites the lack of English castles as a reason for the success of the Norman Conquest.[145] The only known castles in England before 1066 are those very

[139] Cf. pp. 98–9 and n. 171 above. The original and seminal work upon early English castles is that of Mrs Ella S. Armitage, *Early Norman Castles of the British Isles* (London, 1912), who over half a century ago established by a brilliant survey of all the evidence, and a commentary upon it, that castles were a Norman importation into England. See also R. Allen Brown, H. M. Colvin and A. J. Taylor, *History of the King's Works* (London, H.M.S.O., 1963), i, 19–32; cf. B. K. Davison, 'The Origins of the Castle in England', *Archaeological Journal*, cxxiv (1967).
[140] See p. 236, below.
[141] *The Bayeux Tapestry*, ed. F. M. Stenton and others (2nd edition, 1965), Pls. 14, 23, 24, 25–6, 28, 51, and pp. 81–3.
[142] E.g. at Lincoln (166 houses), at Norwich (113), at York, Cambridge, Shrewsbury, Stamford, Warwick and Wallingford (*Domesday Book*, 1783 edition, i, 56, 189, 238, 252, 298, 336, 336b; ii, 116).
[143] Ed. Whitelock, p. 145, 'D' (1067), 'Then bishop Odo and earl William stayed behind and built castles far and wide throughout this country, and distressed the wretched folk, and always after that it grew much worse. May the end be good when God wills!' Ibid., p. 164, 'E' (obituary of William the Conqueror) –

'He had castles built
And poor men hard oppressed.'

[144] William of Malmesbury, *Gesta Pontificum*, p. 253.
[145] Ed. Le Prévost, ii, 184, quoted n. 174, p. 98, above.

few – Hereford, Ewyas Harold, Richard's Castle, Clavering – founded by the French and Norman 'favourites' of Edward the Confessor already here.[146] By the end of the Conqueror's reign he and his great vassals had almost literally dug themselves in and planted their castles across the length and breadth of the land to rivet their rule upon it. Amongst duke William's first acts upon English soil is the construction of castles at Pevensey and Hastings.[147] In the course of their advance after the battle of 14 October, 1066, the victorious Normans raised castles at Dover,[148] Wallingford[149] and ultimately London.[150] After the coronation of the new king on Christmas Day, 1066, the subsequent progress of the Norman Conquest and settlement of England is similarly marked and measured by the castles which were raised. The chroniclers both Norman and English, are full of general references to the construction of castles,[151] and we are told specifically, for example, of a castle at Norwich in 1067,[152] at Exeter in 1068[153] and, later in the same year in the course of William's 'military promenade' to the north, of castles planted at Warwick, Nottingham and York, at Lincoln, Huntingdon and Cambridge.[154] By the end of the Conqueror's reign casual references in Domesday Book relate to some fifty castles in England and Wales which are known to be only a proportion of the number then in existence, just as the eighty-four castles proved from documentary sources to have been founded in England alone before the eleventh century ended are certainly only a fraction of the total.[155] An authentic glimpse of the network of

[146] Above, pp. 116–17.
[147] William of Jumièges, p. 134; William of Poitiers, p. 168; *Chron. Monasterii de Bello*, p. 3; *Anglo-Saxon Chronicle*, 'D', p. 143; *Bayeux Tapestry*, ed. Stenton, Pl. 51. Cf. p. 154, above.
[148] William of Poitiers, p. 212. See also p. 177, above.
[149] William of Jumièges, p. 136. Cf. p. 179, above.
[150] William of Poitiers, pp. 218, 236. Cf. p. 181, above.
[151] William of Jumièges, p. 142; William of Poitiers, p. 238; Ordericus Vitalis, ii, 166, 184; *Anglo-Saxon Chronicle*, 'D', p. 145 (quoted n. 143, p. 234, above).
[152] William of Poitiers, p. 238. Cf. p. 187, above.
[153] Ordericus Vitalis, ii, 181.
[154] Ibid., ii, 184–5.
[155] Mrs. Armitage, *Early Norman Castles*, pp. 94–5. A century later, in

castles rapidly established in England after the Conquest as the focal point of Norman military power, and thus of local government and administration, is afforded by the Anglo-Saxon Chronicle referring to the journey undertaken, in the year 1074, by Edgar aethling and his household from Scotland to William in Normandy – 'And the sheriff of York came to meet them at Durham and went all the way with them and had them provided with food and fodder at every castle they came to, until they got overseas to the king.'[156]

After a lull of some fifty years[157] the archaeological and architectural type of these early castles, both in England and in Normandy, is now again under close investigation, but meanwhile it remains possible to make valid generalisations. Stone fortification, such as already existed in some cases in Normandy,[158] is found as early as the reign of William the Conqueror in England, probably, for example, in the early curtain wall and eleventh-century Scolland's hall at earl Alan's castle of Richmond, Yorkshire, in the early gatehouse there which preceded the present keep,[159] and in the similar gatehouse probably raised by Baldwin de Meules at Exeter,[160] in William fitz Osbern's stone hall or keep incorporated in the present keep at Chepstow,[161] and, above all, in the great keeps or *donjons* raised at Colchester and London, closely similar each to each but otherwise unique in their design, probably derived from the earlier model of the long-since-vanished tower of the ducal palace at Rouen, and still standing (one ruined, the other not) four-square as symbols of the Norman Conquest and of the strength of feudal kingship.[162] Yet in the

the much more fully documented period of Angevin England, written references still do not account for all castles known then to have been in existence (see R. Allen Brown, 'A List of Castles, 1154–1216', *E.H.R.*, lxxiv, 1959).

[156] *Anglo-Saxon Chronicle*, 'D', p. 156.
[157] I.e. since the publication of Mrs. Armitage's work.
[158] Above, p. 44.
[159] Sir Charles Peers, *Richmond Castle* (Official Guide, H.M.S.O., 1953); *V.C.H.*, *Yorkshire, North Riding*, i, 12 et seq.
[160] *History of the King's Works*, i, 32.
[161] J. C. Perks, *Chepstow Castle* (Official Guide, H.M.S.O., 1955).
[162] *History of the King's Works*, i, 29–32; *Bayeux Tapestry*, ed. Stenton (2nd edition), p. 81.

immediate circumstances of the Conquest when the rapid military occupation of actually or potentially hostile territory was the prime necessity, it was doubly inevitable that the other type of contemporary fortification in France and Normandy, the comparatively simple but effective castle of earthwork and timber, capable of being rapidly constructed,[163] should at first, and for some time thereafter, predominate in Norman England. It is coming to be established that such castles themselves varied in form more often than used to be supposed, and may be divided into the two sub-types of those with mottes and those without. For the latter, it was certainly not unusual for the Normans to plant their castles within pre-existing fortifications where such were found, as was evidently the case in 1066, in the first campaign of the Conquest, at Pevensey and Dover, Wallingford and London, and possibly at Hastings. In such instances the simplest course, followed at least at Pevensey and London, was to cut off one corner of the existing large enclosure of Saxon borough, or Roman camp, or city, by a ditch and bank and palisade, the smaller enclosure thus resulting forming the castle on a scale more commensurate with feudal practice and resources. But research at the present time is also seeking to establish that the earliest castles planted *de novo* in open country might also often take the form of a simple enclosure of ditch, bank and palisade, containing the necessary domestic and military buildings, the unsatisfactory term 'ring-work' being currently applied by archaeologists to such sites.[164] Meanwhile there is

[163] Eight days is the period allowed to the Conqueror for the construction of Dover Castle in 1066 by William of Poitiers (p. 212) and of the second castle at York in 1069 by Ordericus Vitalis (ii, 188).

[164] Unsatisfactory because it takes no account of size and thus of the type and purpose of the fortification. The difference in concept between the feudal castle, which is essentially the private fortified residence of a lord, and the communal fortifications of other ages and societies is vividly emphasised, for example, by an aerial photograph of Old Sarum in Wiltshire, where the castle originally occupied only the centre of the far larger Iron Age fortress. Both could be covered by the term 'ring-work'. Little has yet been published on the subject of ring-works in this country, but see B. K. Davison, 'The Origins of the Castle in England', *Archaeological Journal*, cxxiv (1967). See also L. Alcock, 'Castle Tower, Penmaen: a Norman ring-work in Glamorgan' (with biblio-

no doubt that the most common and characteristic type of early Norman castle in the first century of English feudalism is that which has long been known as the 'motte-and-bailey' castle, wherein the enclosure of the bailey is further defended and dominated by the motte – a great mound of earth, artificial, natural, or a combination of both, with its own ditch and bank at the base, and its own palisade round the top, serving militarily as the strong-point of the fortress and serving also in some cases at least to carry the residential accommodation of the lord upon its summit.[165] The Bayeux Tapestry depicts graphically enough the mottes existing in the Conqueror's day before 1066, at Dol, Rennes and Dinan in Brittanny and at Bayeux in Normandy,[166] as it also shows the Normans raising the motte at Hastings before the battle,[167] while the countless mottes still standing all over England (and in Wales, in Scotland and in Ireland also), often as the sole remaining indication of an early castle long-since forgotten and no longer recognised as such even by the local population, are to this day the silent but impressive memorials to the Norman Conquest and to the social and military revolutions which it brought about. The castles of England, of whatever archaeological type, which numbered hundreds in the first century of English feudalism,[168] are not confined to the frontier districts marching with Wales, Scotland or the English Channel, but are broadcast throughout the land, and there is no county which cannot produce its examples. Sir Frank Stenton

graphy), *Antiquaries Journal*, xlvi (1966), and, for Normandy, de Boüard, '*Les petites enceintes circulaires d'origine médiévale en Normandie*', in *Château-Gaillard, Etudes de Castellologie européenne*, I.

[165] Cf. the well-known description of Lambert of Ardres of the timber house or tower upon the motte at Ardres, three storeys high, quoted by Mrs. Armitage, op. cit., pp. 89–90. All four mottes in Brittany and Normandy shown on the Bayeux Tapestry carry some form of tower, which at Bayeux is evidently an elaborate structure (*Bayeux Tapestry*, ed. Stenton, 2nd edition, Pls. 23, 24, 25–6, 28). It seems often to have been the case in the Middle Ages that the higher you were in the social hierarchy the higher you lived. For the subject of mottes and motte castles, see ibid., pp. 82–3 and the authorities there cited.

[166] See n. 165, above.

[167] Ibid., Pl. 51.

[168] R. Allen Brown, *English Castles* (London, 1962), pp. 187–8.

wrote of them that they 'are the most authentic memorials remaining of the age of militant feudalism. . . . They show that
the process of castellation was one of the cardinal facts of
Anglo-Norman history, and they raise in a concrete form the
whole question of the relations between the Anglo-Norman
baronage and the king.'[169] The last point is one which would
undoubtedly repay the investigation which it is now hoped it
will shortly receive.[170] Meanwhile we may be sure that the
Conqueror kept a close control of fortification in his new kingdom as he did also in his duchy,[171] for fortification came close
to sovereignty. But we may also surmise that he and his successors looked upon the baronial castles with far less alarm
than some modern historians do,[172] for in this age the defence
of the realm and the maintenance of internal security, no less
than the prosecution of successful government and war,
depended upon the cooperation of king and baronage.

There is, indeed, no heresy more pernicious yet more long-
lasting than that which proclaims an essential dichotomy
between feudalism and monarchy, or between baronage and
king. In the foregoing pages the attempt has been made to
stress, amongst other things, the fact that the introduction
of feudalism into England through the agency of the Norman
Conquest brought about of itself a new and potent degree of
political unity within the kingdom. The great magnates of
the realm, lay and ecclesiacstical, held their lands, however
widespread the accumulation of their honours and estates, by
conditional tenure of the king their feudal suzerain, to whom
they were bound by the solemn ties of fealty, homage and
investiture. The same solemn ties bound each member of the
social hierarchy of the upper classes as lord and vassal each
to each, and, extending lower yet, fused the loose and brittle
affiliations of English pre-Conquest commendation into the

---

[169] *First Century of English Feudalism*, p. 197.
[170] From my pupils, Mrs. Alexandra Samson for the Anglo-Norman
period, and Mr. Charles Coulson for the later Middle Ages. See also,
R. Allen Brown, 'A List of Castles, 1154–1216', *E.H.R.*, lxxiv.
[171] See above, pp. 44–5, and the *Consuetudines et Justicie* of 1091, quoted
in n. 142 p. 45, above.
[172] E.g. Beeler, *Warfare in England 1066–1189*, p. 50, and cf. Hollister,
Military Organisation of Norman England, pp. 277–8.

territorial nexus of the Anglo-Norman honour.[173] The hard training, technical achievements, common attitudes and growing cult of knighthood[174] gave a new degree of cohesion to the largest and most dominant class of lay society,[175] while the basic feudal concept of service in return for land overflowed, as it were, from the military sphere into others, so that ministers and officials might come to hold land in return for their official duties by sergeanty tenure,[176] churches were deemed to hold those of their lands which were not burdened with secular services by the ecclesiastical tenure of frankalmoign in return for the service of prayer,[177] and, at the bottom of the social scale, the Anglo-Saxon free peasant continued his slow decline to the status of unfree villein, bound to the soil. Nor is this all, for the English kingdom, its military potential now realised by the injection of new men and the latest techniques of warfare, its frontiers extended and its local particularisms crushed, was held in the grip of Norman rule and Norman peace by means of the feudal castle. In addition, the power of the monarchy, which is to be the dominant theme of English medieval history at least until the fourteenth century, was greatly augmented by the change. Succeeding to all the prestige and powers, real and potential, of their predecessors as crowned and anointed, sacerdotal kings – which, among other manifestations, enabled them to take oaths of fealty direct from their subjects 'no matter whose vassals they might be', as was done at Salisbury in 1086[178] and upon other sub-

---

[173] Admirably illustrated by Jolliffe in the two examples of the formation of the honours of Mandeville and Eye, in large part from the lands of freemen who before the Conquest had only been personally commended to the *antecessores* of the new Norman lords (*Constitutional History of Medieval England*, pp. 140–3).

[174] For knighthood in pre-Conquest Normandy, see p. 46, above.

[175] Cf. Stenton, *First Century of English Feudalism*, p. 131.

[176] For sergeanty tenure, see E. G. Kimball, *Serjeanty Tenure in Medieval England* (New Haven, 1936), and A. L. Poole, *Obligations of Society in the Twelfth and Thirteenth Centuries* (Oxford, 1946), Chapter IV.

[177] For frankalmoign tenure, see Pollock and Maitland, *History of English Law* (1895), i, 218–30; E. G. Kimball, 'Tenure in Frank Almoign and Secular Services', *E.H.R.*, xliii (1928).

[178] *Anglo-Saxon Chronicle*, p. 162; Florence of Worcester, ed. Thorpe, ii,

sequent occasions – William of Normandy and his successors were also feudal suzerains. Each was not only *rex* but also *dominus Anglorum*, and the accretion of political and financial resources brought about thereby should not be underestimated. Feudal monarchy has justifiably been called the New Leviathan of the age.[179] The French doctrine of *nulle terre sans seigneur* meant that all land was held directly or indirectly of the Crown. The leading subjects of the realm were also the king's tenants and his vassals, holding their lands of him upon conditional tenure. Nor in England could there be any doubt that this was so, since their honours had been bestowed upon the tenants-in-chief by the Conqueror himself, and henceforward those lords who held land *a conquestu Anglie* held also of necessity *de rege*. If the conditions of feudal tenure were broken, notably by rebellion or disloyalty, and even by the greatest lord, the lands could be confiscated, and were so confiscated, as in the instances of Roger, earl of Hereford, and Ralph Guader, earl of East Anglia, in 1075.[180] And what the king and suzerain took away from one he could bestow upon another. In addition to this direct power of making and breaking, less dramatic but scarcely less effective, was the ability of any feudal lord, but the king especially as the greatest feudal lord of all, to control or strongly influence the succession and descent of fiefs. In the beginning the fief was not hereditary, and was scarcely to become so as of right in England

19. In spite of all the necessary qualifications that are nowadays made, pointing out the special political circumstances of 1086 and the relatively small number of those who could have attended the assembly, it is possible that the importance of 'the Salisbury Oath' still tends to be exaggerated. It was not a unique occasion, and its principal interest is to show that the sovereign rights of princes to the allegiance of their subjects, over and above the personal and tenural ties of feudalism, were maintained in England after the Norman Conquest, as indeed we should expect. See H. A. Cronne, 'The Salisbury Oath', *History*, xix (1934); F. M. Stenton, *Anglo-Saxon England*, pp. 610–11, and *First Century of English Feudalism*, pp. 111–13; Loyn, *Norman Conquest*, pp. 127–8; J. E. A. Jolliffe, *Constitutional History of Medieval England*, pp. 162–3.
[179] R. H. C. Davis, *History of Medieval Europe* (London, 1957), p. 295.
[180] Above, p. 200.

before 1154,[181] and though in practice the descent of fiefs by due inheritance rapidly came to be regarded as the desirable norm by tenants, the process could still often be bent by lords through their control of the marriage of minors, heiresses and widows. The huge power of patronage thus accruing to the kings of England in the first century of English feudalism is scarcely to be measured by the standards of any other age, later or earlier, and is the very stuff of politics.[182] To be 'In' was vital, to be 'Out' could be disastrous, and the favour of the feudal king was paramount. The hand-picked quality of the new Norman aristocracy who followed William the Conqueror to England was characteristic of the age,[183] but, in a world so dependent on personal relations, favour, and with it position, might change between one generation and the next. One can see the young men falling away from their fathers' loyalties in the later years of the Conqueror's reign;[184] the competing claims of the Conqueror's sons to England and to Normandy were to cause impossible strains of loyalty amongst their Anglo-Norman baronage; and the catastrophic fall of the house of Montgomery-Bellême in the reign of Henry I is more an instance of what it could mean to lack the favour of a new king than it is the merited result of political crime, whatever may be implied to the contrary by the vitriolic malice of Ordericus Vitalis or by the almost universally bad press which the family has had in England from his day to our own.[185]

If feudalism brought to monarchy in England political power of a sort unknown before 1066, it also brought new and important financial resources. The king, like any other feudal

[181] F. L. Ganshof, *Feudalism* (London, 1952), pp. 43 ff., 119 et seq. Cf. R. H. C. Davis, 'What happened in Stephen's reign?', *History*, xlix (1964).

[182] For the 'patronage' of post-Conquest English kings, a subject which has scarcely received the attention it deserves, see especially R. W. Southern, 'The Place of Henry I in English History', *Proceedings British Academy*, xlviii. Cf. R. H. C. Davis, op. cit.

[183] Above, p. 38.

[184] Above, pp. 38, 199.

[185] Cf. J. F. A. Mason, 'Roger de Montgomery and his sons (1067–1102)', *Transactions Royal Historical Society* (5th series), xiii (1963), pp. 26–7.

lord, but, as always, more so, could demand from his tenants-in-chief not only knight-service (which itself by the turn of the century could be commuted into the money payment of scutage)[186] but also financial 'aid', *auxilium*, i.e. the service of the purse in addition to the service of the body, upon occasions and upon a scale which only slowly came to be defined and limited by the opposition of a hard-pressed baronage as the twelfth century passed into the thirteenth.[187] Also, as a lasting sign of the original precarious nature of the fief, the king, like any lord but again on a greater scale, was entitled to a 'relief' (*relevium*, or entry fine), for long arbitrary in amount, from an heir or incoming tenant by knight-service,[188] as he also had the custody, together with the profits, of fiefs and honours during a minority. Such custodies and wardships could be, and were, farmed out and leased to the highest bidder, and closely related to them was the right of wardship over minors and heiresses and the control of their marriages, which, with the marriage of widows, could be disposed of for money on the marriage market.[189] As late as the sixteenth

---

[186] Above, p. 233.

[187] For aids, see Pollock and Maitland, *History of English Law* (1895), i, 330–2. Glanville (*De Legibus et Consuetudinibus Anglie*) towards the end of the twelfth century says that a lord may take an aid for the knighting of his son and heir, for the marriage of his eldest daughter, and questions whether he may take an aid to maintain his war (cf. n. 67 p. 218, above). Magna Carta, cc. 12, 14, 15, limits the occasions when an aid may be taken as of right to three, *viz.* the ransom of the lord's body, the knighting of his eldest son and the first marriage of his eldest daughter: an aid on any other occasion requires consent. Neither text defines the amount of aids except that they must be 'reasonable' (Stubbs, *Select Charters*, 9th edition, pp. 193, 294–5).

[188] See Ganshof, op. cit., pp. 122–5; Poole, op. cit., pp. 94–6. By Glanville's time, and probably earlier, £5 was regarded as a 'reasonable' relief, 'according to the custom of the kingdom' for the fee of a knight, but he stresses that the amount payable for the chief baronies to the king was arbitrary according to his will – '*de baroniis vero nihil certum statutum est, quia juxta voluntatem et misericordiam domini regis solent baroniae capitales de suis releviis domino regi satisfacere*'. Magna Carta, c. 2, while confirming the rate of £5 ('at most') for a knight's fee, lays down £100 for an earldom or barony (Stubbs, *Select Charters*, pp. 193, 293).

[189] For wardship and marriage, see Poole, op. cit., pp. 96 et seq.

and seventeenth centuries, the surviving feudal rights of the Crown could still be made Big Business for Tudor and early Stuart monarchs through the Court of Wards. In the post-Conquest period and in the course of the twelfth century the kings of England came increasingly to rely upon aids and scutages, and the so-called feudal 'incidents' of relief, wardship and marriage, as the principal source of extraordinary revenue. Taxation, in short, like most other things, came to be feudal, with the result that the geld itself dropped out of use,[190] and Magna Carta in 1215, like Henry I's Charter of Liberties of 1100 before it, consists above all of clauses limiting and defining feudal obligations and promising the redress of the grievance of the excessive exploitation by the king of his feudal rights.[191]

In addition to conferring these extensive rights over the lands, and indeed the persons of others, the Norman Conquest also doubled the direct territorial resources of the monarchy, that is to say, the Crown lands and the revenues therefrom, and though in this respect, statistically, Hastings only confirmed the result of Harold's own succession,[192] as a result of the Conquest and the Norman settlement the lands of the king were much more widely, and therefore better, distributed than had been the case before – a point of some importance in an age when land was the basis of power as well as wealth. In the Domesday Survey the lands of king William himself, together with those of Mathilda, his queen, and those assigned to Edith, the widow of Edward the Confessor, amount to $17\frac{1}{4}$ per cent of all the landed wealth of England there recorded.[193]

[190] Technically, it was taken for the last time in 1162, save for a temporary revival in 1194 as one of many types of levy for Richard's ransom. The 'carucage' which took its place in 1198 was upon a new assessment.

[191] For the Latin texts of Henry I's Charter of Liberties and Magna Carta, see Stubbs, *Select Charters*, pp. 117, 292; translations respectively in *English Historical Documents*, ii, 400, and J. C. Holt, *Magna Carta* (Cambridge, 1965), p. 317.

[192] Earl Harold was so wealthy that his own accession in 1066 almost doubled the land revenues of the Crown (Corbett in *Cambridge Medieval History*, v, 482).

[193] Lennard, *Rural England 1086–1135*, pp. 25, 28; Corbett, op. cit., pp. 505, 508–9.

In terms of land as in all other ways the Conqueror was the greatest lord of all within his realm, and something of the majesty of his kingship, and the kingship of his successors, becomes apparent when it is emphasised again that he was also Edward the Confessor's heir, and as such inherited all the powers and rights and institutions of the ancient Wessex monarchy and pre-Conquest English government.[194] Because king William was, and insisted on being accepted as, king Edward's heir, it is here in the field of government institutions and administrative techniques that we should expect to find and do find continuity linking the Anglo-Norman present with the Anglo-Saxon past. But because the personnel and management at almost all levels are new after the first few years,[195] there are also innovations, and there are also developments so rapid as themselves to amount to changes.

To help him in the decisions and the task of government king William had the assistance and the counsel and advice of those he trusted most. His council, like the council of his old English predecessors[196] (and his own in Normandy before the Conquest),[197] was infinitely fluid, varying in numbers from those who were about him in his household on any given day, his household officials, his companions and visiting magnates, able to help in the normal process of day-to-day administration, to full sessions of his royal court summoned on certain occasions for social purposes and to discuss the more important business of the realm. But whether or not we accept the triannual solemn Crown-wearing of the post-Conquest period (Christmas at Gloucester, Easter at Winchester and Whitsun at Westminster) as a Norman innovation,[198] it is

[194] Above, pp. 62–9.
[195] Above, p. 204.
[196] Above, p. 66.
[197] Above, p. 54.
[198] 'Also he was very dignified: three times every year he wore his crown, as often as he was in England. At Easter he wore it at Winchester, at Whitsuntide at Westminster, and at Christmas at Gloucester, and then were with him all the powerful men over all England, archbishops and bishops, abbots and earls, thegns and knights' (*Anglo-Saxon Chronicle*, 'E', p. 164; Stubbs, *Select Charters*, p. 95). Cf. William of Malmesbury, *Gesta Regum*, ii, 335. Richardson and Sayles (*Governance of Mediœval*

generally agreed amongst historians that the 'great councils' or 'common councils' of Anglo-Norman kings are more formal in their basic composition than the full meetings of the witan of old, for they comprise pre-eminently the king's tenants-in-chief, his vassals. The witan, in short, becomes feudalised, and into these assemblies is introduced the feudal principle that a vassal owes counsel to his lord[199] – a principle of some consequence in constitutional history since the line between the duty to give counsel and the right to be consulted can obviously at times be very thin. Again of considerable importance for the future of royal government, the amalgamation of England and Normandy which the Norman Conquest brought about, and the frequent absence of the king from England which resulted, necessitated the frequent appointment of a viceregent to act for him, and thus the reign of William the Conqueror sees the origins of the greatest of all early medieval officers of state, the chief justiciar, unknown because unnecessary before 1066.[199A] Beneath this highest level of policy and counsel and consent, in the sphere of routine administration, it is also now, after the Norman Conquest, that we can observe, on the secretarial side of central government, and whatever may have been the case before,[200] the development of a Chancery within the king's itinerant household with the appearance of a specific office of chancellor immediately after 1066,[201] with the survival of administrative writs,[202] and

---

England, pp. 405–12) have recently argued that the solemn crown-wearings of the first two Anglo-Norman kings, generally thought to have been an innovation, were a continuation of Anglo-Saxon practice.

[199] Ganshof, *Feudalism*, pp. 83–4.

[199A] See F. J. West, *The Justiciarship in England 1066–1232* (Cambridge, 1966), especially pp. 2–10.

[200] Above, p. 69–74.

[201] Stenton, *Anglo-Saxon England*, p. 634; Bishop and Chaplais, *Facsimiles of English Royal Writs to A.D. 1100*, pp. xiii, xv; *Handbook of British Chronology*, ed. F. M. Powicke and E. B. Fryde (London, Royal Historical Society, 1961), pp. 80–1. It is, however, to be noted that upon occasion the writ might still be drawn up by the beneficiary (see p. 71 n. 44, above).

[202] *Regesta Regum Anglo-Normannorum*, i, ed. H. W. C. Davis, e.g. Nos. 50, 63, 93–4, 151–6, 184, 188, 258. N.B. also Nos. 78–83 by Lanfranc, No. 189 by the queen, and Nos. 190–1 by William the king's son.

with the general increase of the use of the Anglo-Saxon sealed
writ for all purposes to make of it henceforward without
doubt the normal written instrument of government.[203]
There are also two innovations in the sealed writ itself, sym-
bolic of deeper change. After about 1070 the language alters
from Anglo-Saxon to Latin,[204] thus bringing official England,
as it were, into conformity with Continental usage, and king
William's seal, used to authenticate the writs, is different in
one significant respect from that of Edward the Confessor –
whereas the latter shows on both faces the king enthroned in
majesty, the seal of William the Conqueror, and of all his post-
Conquest successors, shows only on one face the king in
majesty and on the other the king fully armed and mounted
as a knight, reflecting, surely, the concepts of feudal society.[205]
Meanwhile on the fiscal side of government it is not until after
the Conquest that we first hear specifically of a treasurer,[206]
and if the Conqueror willingly took over the right and appara-
tus of the geld,[207] it is also a fact that his revenues were greatly
increased over those of his predecessors by the augmented
Crown lands, by his feudal rights and also it may be added,
by the increasing profits of justice.[208] It will not be very long
after the Conquest before the next great development in
English government finance is brought about by the inaugur-

[203] Bishop and Chaplais, op. cit., p. xiii; Barraclough, 'Anglo-Saxon
Writ', *History*, New Series, xxxix, 213, 215; R. C. Van Caenegem,
Royal Writs in England from the Conquest to Glanville (Selden Society,
lxxvii, 1958–9), p. 177; Matthew, *Norman Conquest*, pp. 159–60.
[204] Bishop and Chaplais, op. cit., p. xiii.
[205] For the seals of Edward the Confessor and William the Conqueror,
see Bishop and Chaplais, op. cit., and Wyon, *The Great Seals of England*.
It has been suggested that in breaking with English practice to show
himself armed and mounted on one, 'the Norman', side of his seal (cf.
P. Chaplais, 'Une Charte Originale de Guillaume le Conquérant . . .', in
L'Abbaye bénédictine de Fécamp, ii, 95), the Conqueror was following the
model of his ducal seal in pre-Conquest Normandy (cf. p. 55 n. 195,
above). Subsequent private, baronial seals in the medieval period
followed the equestrian pattern of the royal seal.
[206] Stenton, op. cit., p. 635; Richardson and Sayles, op. cit., pp. 217,
219, 220; cf. Galbraith, *Studies in the Public Records*, pp. 44–5. For pre-
Conquest fiscal organisation, see pp. 69–70, above.
[207] Stenton, op. cit., p. 636.
[208] Below.

ation of the Exchequer,[209] and it should at least be noted that Richard fitz Nigel, the later twelfth-century treasurer, expert in and historian of the Exchequer, thought its origins might be attributed to Norman rather than to English provenance.[210]

In local government after the Conquest the tenth-century organisations of shire and hundred were continued, but the removal of the over-mighty Anglo-Scandinavian earls brought the king into direct contact with the former through the agency of the sheriff, who was now without any qualification an out-and-out royal official, of greater social status and there-fore power in the Conqueror's reign than before, and, in most cases, had as his base the castle of the county town, and mounted knights to carry out as necessary the delegated royal will.[211] The new institution of the honorial court, also, gave a new element of social cohesion to the governing classes in the provinces,[212] while at a lower level the Norman frankpledge system, characteristically the development and amalgamation of the two Anglo-Saxon institutions of the surety group (*friborh*) and tithing (a police group), bound the rural popu-lation in a thorough-going system of social and territorial units for the maintenance of peace and order.[213] It is, however, in the realm of law and justice that the impact of the Normans and the Norman Conquest was to have some of its profoundest

[209] The date of the origin of the Exchequer is unknown. The first reference to it (in a writ, *ante* 1118) and the first records of it (the Pipe Roll of 1130), come from the reign of Henry I, but its origins may be earlier. See A. Hughes, C. G. Crump and C. Johnson, *Dialogus de Scaccario* (Oxford, 1902), pp. 13–43; R. L. Poole, *Exchequer in the Twelfth Century* (Oxford, 1912), pp. 57 et seq.; and for a useful brief survey of the subject, S. B. Chrimes, *Introduction to the Administrative History of Medieval England* (Oxford, 1959), pp. 29–31. Richardson and Sayles (op. cit., e.g. pp. 157 et seq.) differ from most historians in maintaining that the Exchequer was established as a court of general competence (as opposed to a financial bureau) for the office of Chief Justiciar, both dating in effect from 1109.

[210] *Dialogus de Scaccario*, ed. C. Johnson (London, 1950) p. 14; cf. p. 55 and n. 193, above.

[211] See Morris, *Medieval English Sheriff*, Chapter III; cf. p. 74, above.

[212] Stenton, *First Century of English Feudalism*, pp. 41 et seq.

[213] See W. A. Morris, *The Frankpledge System* (New York, 1910). Morris observed 'no more highly centralised and thorough-going scheme of surety-ship to secure order was ever devised on European soil' (p. 1).

repercussions upon the subsequent development of English government and society. Though the Conqueror insisted upon the maintenance of the laws and customs of his predecessors,[214] it is not to be supposed that the Conquest brought no change to English justice beyond the introduction of the forest law,[215] the *murdrum* fine[216] the judicial duel,[217] or beyond the increased use of writs for judicial purposes[218] and the increased use of the jury, whose origins still remain controversial.[219] While in the sphere of criminal law the Conqueror's good peace won praise even from the native Chronicle,[220] in the no less crucial sphere of pleas and litigation about land the innovation of feudalism meant also the innovation of feudal law, and the chief energy of English lawyers for centuries to come was to be devoted to the working out of the rights and obligations of feudal tenures, their protection and their avoidance. Further, if it is true that beneath those many influences which combine to make the English common law there 'lies the basis of the Anglo-Saxon past', it is also true that 'the impact

---

[214] '*Hoc quoque praecipio et volo, ut omnes habeant et teneant legem Eadwardi regis in terris et in omnibus rebus* – This also I command and will, that all shall have and hold the law of king Edward in lands and in all things' (from the 'Laws of William the Conqueror', printed in Stubbs, *Select Charters*, p. 99; translation in *English Historical Documents*, ii, 400).

[215] Stenton, *Anglo-Saxon England*, pp. 674–5; Matthew, *Norman Conquest*, pp. 150–2.

[216] Stenton, op. cit., p. 676; Matthew, op. cit., pp. 143–4.

[217] F. Pollock and F. W. Maitland, *History of English Law* (1895), ii, 630–1.

[218] Matthew, *Norman Conquest*, p. 155.

[219] For recent discussions of the origin of the jury (both the jury of presentment and the more important inquest or jury of recognition) which used to be generally regarded as a Norman innovation in England, see N. D. Hurnard, 'The Jury of Presentment and the Assize of Clarendon', *E.H.R.*, lvi (1941); R. C. Van Caenegem, *Royal Writs in England from the Conquest to Glanville*, pp. 57 et seq.; D. M. Stenton, *English Justice between the Norman Conquest and the Great Charter*, pp. 13 et seq. Lady Stenton, however, though by no means disposed to give the Normans more than their due, accepts that 'The establishment of the jury as an integral part of English civil procedure belongs to the Norman rather than to the Anglo-Saxon age' (ibid., p. 17).

[220] *Anglo-Saxon Chronicle*, 'E', ed. Whitelock, p. 164, quoted p. 185, above.

of Norman energy on Saxon traditionalism [broke] the ground for the foundation of a new legal system'.[221] The development of the common law is coterminous with the expansion of royal justice, and in the dispensation of justice by the king himself or his agents, in the increasing intervention by both in the administration of justice hitherto carried out by local doomsmen in local, popular courts according to traditional methods, the Norman Conquest seems to mark a watershed. There is little evidence of pleas held centrally before the king before 1066[222] but much thereafter, and much also of the sending out of special commissioners, the precursors of the itinerant justices of the twelfth century, to try cases in the king's name. There can be no doubt that the Conquest brought a great stimulus to the development of royal justice, for on the one hand, in accordance with feudal theory and practice, the king's own court, the *curia Regis*, became automatically the proper place for the hearing of pleas between and concerning the tenants-in-chief over whom he had jurisdiction as their feudal lord, and, on the other, the tenurial revolution of the Norman settlement brought a great series of disputes, claims and counter-claims about land and rights for whose solution men turned to the king.[223] William the Conqueror, according to Ordericus Vitalis, sought to learn English in order to do better justice,[224] and the evidence of his surviving writs shows him sitting with his barons and his prelates to hear and adjudge pleas on both sides of the Channel, as he sat all one Sunday (at Laycock in Wiltshire?) 'from morn to eve' to hold a plea concerning William de Braose and the property of the abbey of Fécamp.[225]

---

[221] D. M. Stenton, op. cit., p. 21.

[222] See p. 65 and n. 16, above.

[223] Stenton, *Anglo-Saxon England*, pp. 640–3. Cf. Matthew, op. cit., pp. 153–4.

[224] *Historia Ecclesiastica*, ii, 215. Ordericus (who is probably following the lost portion of William of Poitiers' biography) adds that the king did not progress far in his studies because of his age and preoccupations.

[225] *Regesta Regum Anglo-Normannorum*, i, No. 220. Cf. Nos. 120, 138, 139, 183a. A glimpse of how these things may sometimes have appeared is afforded by a memorandum recording the confirmation by king William of a grant by Humphrey de Bohun to the churches of St.

The impact of the Norman Conquest upon the church in England was scarcely less than upon the state, and, indeed, though in accordance with the new wave of Continental thinking the English church after 1066 became more of a separate order within the state, the two yet remained integral parts of one unified Norman polity. In the ecclesiastical sphere the most obvious results of the Conquest were a reorganisation of the English church to bring it up to date on the Norman and Continental model, and, as in the sphere of lay lordship, a complete, or almost complete, change of personnel at the top, and neither were, or could be, entirely unconnected with political considerations. In terms of personnel, in spite of the embittered calumnies of Ordericus Vitalis,[226] it was inevitable that Norman clerics should look for preferment in the new realm of their master, and no less inevitable that William the Conqueror should look to France and above all to Normandy to find the men to carry out those necessary reforms in England which had been put before the conscience of Latin Christendom as one justification for the Norman Conquest.[227] Yet in the nature of things there could be no dramatic replacement of English prelates, and in the event moderation was the order of the day. It was not until 1070 that the new king could turn his attention to his new church, and then only

Martin de Marmoutier and St. George de Bohun about the year 1081 – 'This was done at Humphrey's request when the king was at Bernouville [in Normandy], sitting on his carpet between the church and the forester's house, after he had returned from England' (ibid., No. 133).

[226] According to whom the Norman clergy were no better than the laity in clamouring for a share of the spoils of England, and behaved like mercenaries demanding pay. He cites with relish the scandal of Thurstan of Caen at Glastonbury (below, p. 258) and then writes at length of the edifying exception of the monk Guitmond of La Croix-St.-Leufroi who refused preferment in conquered England, writing an outspoken letter to the king in the process ('I look upon England as altogether one vast heap of booty, and I am afraid to touch it and its treasures as if it were a burning fire'. For his letter see also p. 139, above). It should be noted, however, that Guitmond subsequently became bishop of Aversa in Norman Italy. See *Historia Ecclesiastica*, ii, 224–32.

[227] Cf. p. 149, above. At an early stage the Conqueror applied to Cluny for a dozen monks, but was refused by abbot Hugh, such undertakings being no part of Cluny's policy (Knowles, *Monastic Order in England*, p. 107).

Stigand and two other bishops were deposed (a third resigned) together with a handful of pre-Conquest abbots,[228] even though the monasteries posed a particularly difficult problem as privileged enclaves of Englishmen with patriotic sympathies which could at times be activated.[229] But as time took its toll there were no further native appointments either to sees or religious houses. By 1087 at the Conqueror's death there survived only one English-born and pre-Conquest bishop, namely Wulfstan of Worcester, and only two English abbots of any importance, namely those of Ramsey and Bath,[230] while of the eighteen bishops appointed between 1070 and the death of Lanfranc in 1089 at least sixteen were of Norman birth or training.[231] In this small group of very powerful men, mostly endowed with considerable abilities, set down in an alien land which often seemed to them barbaric in its outdated habits and modes of thought, its cramped and inadequate churches,

[228] At a council held in April 1070 in the presence of papal legates, Stigand, who held both the archbishopric of Canterbury and bishopric of Winchester, was formally deposed, together with Aethelmaer of East Anglia, his brother. The following Whitsun bishop Aethelric of Selsey was also deposed at a subsequent council at Windsor. Leofwine, the married bishop of Lichfield, resigned before the blow could fall. In all, about six abbots either fled or were deposed (Stenton, *Anglo-Saxon England*, 651–3; Knowles, *Monastic Order*, pp. 103–6, 111). Surprise is sometimes expressed that Stigand should have survived until 1070 in view of the prominence given to his case in pre-Conquest propaganda. The Conqueror, however, scarcely had time for ecclesiastical affairs before 1070, and in view of Stigand's power and influence with the English it was doubtless wise to leave the matter to papal initiative (Stenton, op. cit., p. 651. Cf. William of Poitiers, pp. 214, 234. For an indication of Stigand's immense wealth and power, which put him on a level with the greatest new Norman magnates, see Corbett, *Cambridge Medieval History*, v, 510.)

[229] See especially Knowles, op. cit., pp. 103–6. Aelfwig, abbot of the New Minster at Winchester and Harold's uncle, died at Hastings, and Leofric of Peterborough, nephew of earl Leofric and cousin of earls Edwin and Morcar, died on his return from that campaign (*Anglo-Saxon Chronicle*, 'E', p. 142). Ely was heavily involved in the affair of Hereward and the Isle.

[230] Stenton, op. cit., p. 671. Cf. p. 204, above. Giso of Wells, a second surviving pre-Conquest bishop, was himself a Lotharingian.

[231] Loyn, *Norman Conquest*, p. 156.

unfamiliar chants[232] and liturgical practices, and its weird, un-
pronounceable and ill-authenticated saints,[233] we can see the
same elements of personal unity which are so apparent in the
secular aristocracy of the time.[234] Lanfranc[235] himself,
appointed to Canterbury in Stigand's place, was the friend
and chief adviser of a king who was also a sincere churchman
and convinced ecclesiastical reformer, and between them they
made a partnership of a kind unknown in England since the
days of Dunstan and king Edgar, and not to be known again
for centuries, if ever. With him Lanfranc brought to England a
hand-picked group of pupils and associates from Bec and
Caen, mostly destined for high places, like his nephew, Paul,
who became abbot of St. Albans, Gundulf, subsequently
bishop of Rochester (and surveyor of the king's works at the
Tower of London and perhaps Colchester),[236] and Gilbert
Crispin, abbot of Westminster.[237] The new archbishop established also, through his eminence, his councils and his corres-
pondence, a personal ascendancy over his prelates so rare as
to be unique,[238] and many of these men now set over the
English church, and further united by their common circumstances, must already have been well known to each other
before their preferment, coming not only from the duchy of
Normandy but in many cases also from the great and confident houses within it of Jumièges, Fécamp, Mont St. Michel,
Caen and Bec.[239]

With them these new men brought especially their Norman
genius for order and administration, and, applying it under
the direction of Lanfranc and the king to the reorganisation

[232] An enforced change from their traditional Gregorian chant to that
of Dijon was the immediate cause of the scandal between abbot Thurstan
and his monks at Glastonbury. Knowles, op. cit., p. 115, and below,
p. 258.
[233] Knowles, op. cit., pp. 118–19; Southern, *St. Anselm and his Biographer*, pp. 249 et seq.
[234] Above, p. 211.
[235] For a valuable summary of Lanfranc's career and character, see
Knowles, op. cit., pp. 107–11, 142–3.
[236] See Brown, Colvin and Taylor, *History of the King's Works*, i, 28–31.
[237] Southern, op. cit., pp. 246–7; Knowles, op. cit., pp. 113–14.
[238] Cf. Stenton, op. cit., p. 663.
[239] Cf. Knowles, op. cit., p. 112.

of the English church, gave to that body a new unity which contributed also to the unity of the state. The assertion of the supremacy of the see of Canterbury over that of York not only gave to the church a centralised direction and unified command analogous to that in Normandy but scarcely known in England since the days of Theodore, but also had a political motive as a precaution against the threat of northern separatism.[240] The ecclesiastical unity thus achieved, and the separate identity of the church which was now regarded as a necessary corollary of its dignity, was given further expression by Lanfranc's great series of separate ecclesiastical councils, in 1072, 1075, 1076 and thereafter, of a kind long-since unknown in England, which served not only as occasions to issue and proclaim reforming legislation but also as a means of ending the loose autonomy of pre-Conquest diocesan bishops.[241] The dioceses themselves were reorganised both by edicts for the holding of biannual diocesan synods and the appointment of archdeacons,[242] and by the increasing establishment of secular cathedral chapters on the Norman model,[243] and while these reforms helped to close the undesirable gap between bishops and parish clergy which existed in pre-Conquest England,[244] the accelerated movement of sees from the countryside to new centres of urban population after 1066 brought the church and its organisation into closer touch with contemporary reality.[245]

In England down to 1066 the Old World had survived not least in the complete intermingling of ecclesiastical and secular affairs at all levels.[246] After 1066 the separation of church and

[240] Stenton, op. cit., pp. 656–7; Hugh the Chantor, *History of the Church of York*, ed. C. Johnson, p. 3; cf. p. 77, above.

[241] Cf. p. 105, above; Stenton, op. cit., pp. 657–63; Douglas, *William the Conqueror*, p. 332.

[242] Both edicts promulgated at the council of 1072, Stenton, op. cit., p. 657.

[243] Ibid., pp. 657–8; Douglas, op. cit., pp. 329–30.

[244] Above, p. 105. Cf. also the regulation of the order of precedence for English bishops at future councils drawn up in 1075 (Stenton, op. cit., p. 658).

[245] Stenton, op. cit., pp. 658–9. The removal of the see of Crediton to Exeter had already taken place before the Conquest in 1050.

[246] Above, p. 103.

state implicit and explicit in the Gregorian Reform Movement was recognised in the reorganisation of the English church by the revival of distinct ecclesiastical councils and also by at least the beginnings of a separate system of ecclesiastical jurisdiction exercised through separate ecclesiastical courts.[247] Historians endowed with the advantage of historical hindsight are well aware of the latent paradox involved in these developments, for the more the church became a separate order within society, the more difficult it would become for secular rulers to exercise that control over it to which they were accustomed, while the growing concept of the church as a universal order transcending secular boundaries and centred upon Rome was very shortly to meet the ancient and time-honoured ideas of theocratic, Christian kingship in head-on collision. It may seem, therefore, that in so far as they encouraged the church in England or in Normandy to regard itself as a separate order, and especially by authorising a separate ecclesiastical jurisdiction which stimulated the development of

---

[247] The conventional view is that separate ecclesiastical courts were established as the result of the Conqueror's well-known writ of c. 1072, whose effects were confirmed and perhaps extended by the ecclesiastical council of 1076 (Stenton, op. cit., pp. 661–2. For the writ, see Stubbs, *Select Charters*, 9th edition, pp. 99–100; translation in *English Historical Documents*, ii, 604). The difficulty is that while no full record of the council of 1076 is extant (Stenton, op. cit., p. 659, n. 3), the surviving writ prohibits only the holding of ecclesiastical pleas in the hundred court, and makes no mention of the shire court which probably was more generally used for this purpose and which is still referred to as a court for ecclesiastical purposes in the *Leges Henrici Primi* of the early twelfth century (cf. Barlow, *English Church 1000–1066*, pp. 151–2, 274–6; Matthew, *Norman Conquest*, pp. 193–5). For a casual reference to the bishop in the shire court as late as Henry II's time, see Stenton. *First Century of English Feudalism*, p. 108). Nevertheless, the general tenor of the writ, with its bald statement that the 'episcopal laws' have not been kept properly in England, according to the precepts of the holy canons, before the Conqueror's time, and its provision that in future bishops may summon those accused of any ecclesiastical offence to whatever place they will, may be thought sufficiently clear. The most recent discussion of the subject (C. Morris, 'William I and the church courts', *E.H.R.*, lxxxii, 1967) still seems to regard the Conqueror's writ, with all scholarly qualifications, as the starting point for separate ecclesiastical courts in England.

canon law, which, in turn, in this age increasingly emphasised papal supremacy, William and Lanfranc were undermining that royal authority in ecclesiastical affairs in which they both believed. In the long perspective of history this is true enough, but the paradox only points to the unforeseen results of statesmen's actions in any period, and the necessary distinction always to be made between the view of historians and that of contemporaries. Certainly there was not, nor was there intended to be, any diminution of royal authority over the English church while William and Lanfranc lived, nor was there any investiture contest in England in their time. That control over ecclesiastical affairs which was traditional, to which he was accustomed in Normandy[248] and which he had also inherited from his Old English predecessors,[249] was maintained in England after 1066 by the Conqueror. He, or Lanfranc with his authority, appointed prelates, and while it is possible that the ceremony of investiture with ring and staff, the symbols of spiritual authority, by the king himself only begins in England in his reign,[250] it is certain that bishops and most abbots were more closely bound to the monarch than they were before the Conquest as his vassals by fealty and homage, owing knight-service for their temporalities. The Conqueror himself was accustomed to preside over ecclesiastical councils[251] and his consent was necessary for their decrees.[252] Ecclesiastical jurisdiction was by no means entirely independent of his overriding authority,[253] Odo of Bayeux could be

---

[248] Above, p. 32.
[249] Above, p. 103.
[250] Barlow, *English Church 1000–1066*, pp. 110–11.
[251] Douglas, *William the Conqueror*, p. 334. A glimpse of the system in action is afforded by the Chronicle at Christmas 1085 when the king held his great crown-wearing court at Gloucester, which was immediately and conveniently followed by an ecclesiastical synod – 'Then at Christmas, the king was at Gloucester with his council, and held his court there for five days, and then the archbishop and clerics held a synod for three days. There Maurice was elected bishop of London, and William for Norfolk, and Robert for Cheshire – they were all clerics of the king' (*Anglo-Saxon Chronicle*, 'E', p. 161).
[252] Stenton, op. cit., p. 666, citing Eadmer, *Historia Novorum*, i, 9 (printed in Stubbs, *Select Charters*, p. 96).
[253] Cf. Douglas, op. cit., p. 336.

broken and imprisoned if not as a bishop then as an earl and vassal,[254] and none of his ministers or barons could be excommunicated without his leave.[255] Nor did either William or Lanfranc, men of an older generation in a fast-changing world, approve of the new-fangled Gregorian notions whereby the Papacy should seek to intervene without request in the direction and government of the church within the realm, and such direct papal influence was barred effectively by the dual prohibition of the receipt of papal letters and of visits by his bishops to Rome without the king's permission.[256]

It would, however, be quite wrong to suppose that the achievements of the new and predominantly Norman prelates, and the effects of the Norman Conquest as a whole upon the English church, were confined to organisation and the sphere of ecclesiastical politics. The church on balance profited rather than lost in terms of land and material possessions as a result of the Conquest;[257] it also obtained new blood, and the new men brought with them a new spirit and a revived spirituality as well as organising ability, for they were mostly drawn from the Norman church itself at the apogee of revival and high endeavour.[258] There were, inevitably, some failures or undesirables amongst them. The militant Turold of Fécamp, whom the Conqueror is said to have sent to Peterborough with the comment that since he behaved like a knight he might as well go where he could fight,[259] had a more notorious counter-

---

[254] Stenton, op. cit., p. 608 and n. 3. Cf. *Anglo-Saxon Chronicle*, 'E', p. 164, 'He expelled bishops from their sees, and abbots from their abbacies . . . and finally he did not spare his own brother, who was called Odo.'

[255] Stenton, op. cit., p. 666; Eadmer, ut supra.

[256] Ibid. As for the demand for fealty made of him by Popes Alexander II and Gregory VII, arising in origin from the papal support given to the invasion in 1066 (above, p. 148), it was firmly rebuffed (Stenton, op. cit., p. 667).

[257] Corbett, *Cambridge Medieval History*, v, 509. Cf. Knowles, *Monastic Order*, p. 118.

[258] Above, p. 26; Knowles, op. cit., pp. 124–5.

[259] '*Per splendorem*', inquit, '*Dei, quia magis se agit militem quam abbatem, inveniam ei comparem, qui assultus ejus accipiat. Ibi virtutem suam et militiam experiatur, ibi proelia proludat.*' (William of Malmesbury, *Gesta Pontificum*, p. 420; cf. Knowles, op. cit., p. 105.)

part in Thurstan of Caen at Glastonbury, who set his men-at-arms upon the monks who resisted his attempts to introduce Norman chants and ceremonies in place of their cherished Gregorian practices, the affair culminating in a fight in the abbey church itself.[260] But in the main the appointments made by William and Lanfranc were good, some were outstanding, and almost all were better than the general mediocrity prevailing in the higher ranks of the English church before 1066.[261] Spirit and spirituality are more difficult to measure and assess than the number of archdeacons or the frequency of synods, but we obtain some assistance if we turn to monasticism and the monasteries, still universally regarded in this age as the centres *par excellence* of religious life. For William the Conqueror as for Lanfranc the monasteries were to be the centres of a revival of religious life in England,[262] and the great archbishop, sometime prior of Bec and abbot of St. Stephen's, Caen, was, above all else, 'the father and consolation of monks',[263] and made time amongst his manifold duties in England to compile for his monks at Christ Church his *Consuetudines,* drawn from his own experience at Bec especially and 'from those monasteries which in our own time are of the greatest fame', and which, because of his own influence and fame, spread from Canterbury to many other English houses.[264] The Norman baronage of the first generation were for the most part naturally content to celebrate their victory and give thanks for their new wealth by benefactions to the Norman abbeys of their homeland,[265] but the Conquest nevertheless was followed by a notable increase in the number of monks in England, drawn at least in part from the new Norman ruling classes and their children.[266] It was also followed by the two major foundations in the south, of Battle

[260] Knowles, op. cit., pp. 114–15. Cf. *Anglo-Saxon Chronicle,* 'E', p. 160.
[261] Stenton, op. cit., pp. 663, 664–5; Knowles, op. cit., pp. 113–14.
[262] Knowles, op. cit., pp. 106, 110.
[263] Stenton, op. cit., p. 665; *Anglo-Saxon Chronicle,* 'E', p. 168, *s.a.* 1089.
[264] Knowles, op. cit., pp. 123–4. See also, *The Monastic Constitution of Lanfranc,* ed. D. Knowles (London, 1951).
[265] For this subject, see especially D. J. A. Matthew, *The Norman Monasteries and their English Possessions* (Oxford, 1962), Chapter II.
[266] Knowles, *Monastic Order,* p. 126.

by the king on the field of Hastings as he had vowed,[267] and Lewes by William de Warenne;[268] by an increase in the number of monastic cathedrals from four to nine within the next fifty years;[269] and by the remarkable revival of monasticism in the north beyond Trent and Humber,[270] which began in the Conqueror's reign as the joint endeavour of a Norman knight and two English monks from Winchcombe and Evesham, and which, together with such miscellaneous foundations as that of Robert Malet at Eye in *c.* 1075 as a cell to Bernay,[271] began to redress the geographical imbalance of pre-Conquest English monasticism resulting from the Danish wars.[272] To their English houses, whether new or old, the Norman abbots brought, not always without friction, and sometimes perhaps because of it, a fresh enthusiasm, 'a new discipline and a new, or at least a revitalised, observance'.[273] Many of the new prelates also brought a revival of intellectual activity and something of the new learning from France and Normandy, and, like Lanfranc at Christ Church, Canterbury, the books which were its substance.[274] They brought to England, writes Dom David Knowles, 'an education in letters far deeper and wider than anything they found in possession; above all they brought a culture which gave to those who imbibed it the ability and desire to express themselves with ease in fluent and idiomatic Latin, and thus, while silencing the vernacular literature, made of England a province of the commonwealth

[267] Above, p. 163; *Chron. Monasterii de Bello*, pp. 3–4, 22.
[268] See Knowles, op. cit., pp. 128–9, 151.
[269] Ibid., pp. 129–32.
[270] Ibid., pp. 164 et seq. The Norman knight Reinfrid, who had seen some service, including the grim campaigns in the north in 1069–70, and then became a monk, was not untypical of his class and period. Cf. p. 34, above.
[271] Matthew, *Norman Monasteries*, pp. 46–7; *V.C.H.*, *Suffolk*, ii, 72.
[272] Knowles, op. cit., p. 101.
[273] Ibid., p. 121.
[274] Thus Southern on the books introduced by Lanfranc at Christ Church (*St. Anselm and his Biographer*, pp. 267–8) – 'They embody the ideal of an intellectually well-organised church consciously reproving the casual and miscellaneous interests of the pre-Conquest community: they are the best testimony to the intellectual revolution effected by the Conquest.'

of Latin Europe, which for a century and a half was to form a cultural unit more potent to unite than were racial differences to dissolve'.[275] Whatever may be the final assessment (if one is ever reached) of profit and loss to English culture as the result of the Norman Conquest, this was a rich and noble benefaction.

There also was at least one other benefaction in the realm of culture and of art. To this day the impact of the Normans upon the English church is writ large on the face of England in the shape of great Romanesque churches which no less than the castles are the visible symbols of the Conquest. These monuments deserve emphasis and observation,[276] for they are quite as much the authentic record of a past society as manuscripts and documents. Every major church in England was rebuilt in the decades following 1066 save Westminster and Waltham (the former certainly and the latter presumably because it was already a Norman church in style before the Normans came),[277] and new churches on new sites were added to the existing numbers. The new Norman aristocracy in church and state poured out their new wealth and their pride upon great churches even grander than those upon which they were modelled at home in Normandy, and in so doing gave lasting expression to their faith and piety, their confidence and their vision. 'After their coming to England', wrote William of Malmesbury, 'they revived the rule of religion which had there grown lifeless. You might see great churches rise in every village, and, in the towns and cities, monasteries built after a style unknown before.'[278] Even Wulfstan of

[275] Op. cit., p. 125. One product of the literary culture brought in by the Norman Conquest, paradoxically enough, was a new interest in English pre-Conquest history, exemplified by the monastic historians of the next generation. See Southern 'The Place of England in the Twelfth-Century Renaissance', *History*, xlv (1960), pp. 208–9, and also *St. Anselm and his Biographer*, Chapter VIII.

[276] Much Norman work, of course, was later rebuilt or later ruined, but fine examples of the first generation survive, for example, at St. Albans, Blyth, Tewkesbury, and the transepts of Winchester and Ely, closely followed in date by the splendours of Norwich and, above all, Durham.

[277] For Westminster and Waltham, see p. 103 and n. 190, above.

[278] *Gesta Regum*, ii, 306; translation, *English Historical Documents*, ii, 291. The Normans continued rather than began the process of building

Worcester found it necessary to emulate the standards of the Normans and build a new church, though he wept at the demolition of the old one.[279] There were some who grumbled and took a jaundiced view, as there always are and will be. 'But here', wrote William of Malmesbury, describing the new works, 'I perceive the muttering of those who say it would have been better that the old should have been preserved in their original state than that new ones should have been erected from plunder.'[280] Something of the spirit of the Normans, by contrast, as they built their new Jerusalem, is expressed by Goscelin of St. Bertin, who had seen his bishop plan the new cathedral church at Salisbury – 'He destroys well who builds something better . . . I would not allow buildings although much esteemed to stand unless they were, according to my idea, glorious, magnificent, most lofty, most spacious, filled with light, and most beautiful.'[281] And no one can seriously deny that the Normans did in fact build something better, for their major churches, 'glorious, magnificent, most lofty, most spacious', stand for an architectual revolution in England[282] which fittingly marks the abrupt change from the old world to the new brought about by the Norman Conquest. And here, in the category of major ecclesiastical architecture, which is no bad test of the standard of any civilisation, Anglo-Norman England was to have a substantial contribution of its own to make to the twelfth-century renaissance in the West, for Durham may well be, so far as we can tell, the

new parish churches, and it is at this level chiefly that old and traditional architectural styles survived for some time after the Conquest to produce the so-called Saxo-Norman overlap. But it is the building and rebuilding of major churches that is our present concern, and here the revolution in architectural style and concept, duly noted by William of Malmesbury, is almost complete (see below).

[279] William of Malmesbury, *Vita Wulfstani*, ed. R. R. Darlington, p. 52; *Gesta Pontificum*, p. 283.

[280] *Gesta Regum*, ii, 334.

[281] Quoted by Barlow, *English Church 1000–1066*, p. 167, from Goscelin's *Liber Confortatorius*. For Goscelin, see Barlow, op. cit., Appendix C.

[282] A. W. Clapham, *English Romanesque Architecture after the Norman Conquest*, pp. 1–2, 19; Geoffrey Webb, *Architecture in Britain in the Middle Ages* (London, 1956), p. 26.

first great Romanesque church planned from the beginning (1093) as vaulted throughout in stone, while its pointed arches look towards the achievement of that 'Gothic' architecture which is the triumph of the High Middle Ages.[283]

It is not easy to know how to end any account of the results of the Norman Conquest and thus bring this book to its conclusion. If this chapter has had any one underlying theme it has been the achievement in England after 1066 of a new degree of political unity, symbolised by immediate events as diverse as Domesday Book on the one hand and the plantation of castles on the other, and brought about by the combined agencies of greatly increased and increasing royal power, a new, virile and militant aristocracy, and a reorganised and revived church. To this we must add, if we seek the two most profound results of the Norman Conquest, which between them set the pattern of future English history, a far closer association with the Continent than before, more particularly the breaking of existing ties with Scandinavia and their replacement by stronger bonds with northern France, and this at a crucial moment in history when northern France especially was becoming the centre of a new and rapidly developing medieval civilisation in the West. For the first long-term result, the unity of England at Norman hands was not won without fire and sword and suffering, which had their culmination in the grim campaigns of the Conqueror in the north in 1069–70, but it was achieved, and there is a real sense in which, by comparison with Anglo-Saxon practice, the grip of royal government from the south upon the north begins not so much under Henry II as under William I.[284] On the basis of the unity thus gained the lines of future expansion were marked out, and in some quarters followed up at once. Towards Ireland, intervention and the assertion of authority were

[283] Clapham, op. cit., pp. 38–9; Webb, op. cit., p. 35. Cf. Southern, *History*, xlv, 202.

[284] Cf. above, p. 75, and J. C. Holt, *The Northerners* (Oxford, 1961), pp. 194 et seq. Holt, of course, is dealing principally with the three northernmost counties of Angevin England, Cumberland, Westmorland and Northumberland, which lay largely outside the control of William the Conqueror (ibid., p. 213).

chiefly left to Lanfranc and the church of Canterbury in the Conqueror's generation,[285] though here one must note the curious and enigmatic comment of the 'E' version of the Anglo-Saxon Chronicle (probably itself a Canterbury compilation at this date) – 'and if he [William] could have lived two years more, he would have conquered Ireland by his prudence and without any weapons'.[286] Towards Scotland, if the Conqueror left the problem of the northern border to his successors,[287] he nevertheless obtained the submission of Malcolm, king of Scots, by force of arms in 1072,[288] and established the military lordships of Roger the Poitevin and of Richmond together with the new advanced fortress of Newcastle-upon-Tyne.[289] His son and successor, William Rufus, only a few years after his death, was to roll back the northern frontier on the west to the Solway to take in Westmorland and Cumberland,[290] while in the earlier twelfth century the penetration of southern Scotland by Norman influence and Norman lords can be likened to a peaceful Norman Conquest of the country.[291] On the other landward frontier of the Conqueror's kingdom, there was nothing very peaceful about the penetration of Wales by the new Norman Marcher lords.[292] In the south and centre William fitz Osbern, earl of Hereford, followed by his son, earl Roger of Breteuil, until his fall in 1075, and Roger of Montgomery, earl of Shrewsbury, led the way and established the castle bases, at Monmouth, Chepstow,

[285] See R. W. Southern, *St. Anselm and his Biographer*, pp. 133–4.
[286] *Anglo-Saxon Chronicle*, ed. Whitelock, p. 164.
[287] Stenton, *Anglo-Saxon England*, p. 606.
[288] Ibid, p. 598; cf. above, p. 198.
[289] Ibid., pp. 605–6; Holt, *Northerners*, pp. 213–14; cf. above, p. 215.
[290] W. Croft Dickinson, *Scotland from the Earliest Times to 1603* (London, 1961), p. 73; G. W. S. Barrow, *The Border* (Inaugural Lecture, Durham, 1962), pp. 4 et seq. There, apart from a relapse in Stephen's time, the border on the west was to remain.
[291] Croft Dickinson, op. cit., p. 83. For this subject, see especially R. L. G. Ritchie, *The Normans in Scotland* (Edinburgh, 1954), and G. W. S. Barrow, 'The Beginnings of Feudalism in Scotland', *Bulletin Institute of Historical Research*, xxix (1956).
[292] For what follows, see especially J. E. Lloyd, *History of Wales*, ii, 373 et seq., and J. G. Edwards, 'The Normans and the Welsh March', *Proceedings British Academy*, xlii (1956), pp. 155 et seq.

Montgomery and elsewhere, for the overrunning of south Wales in the next generation; and though in the north the penetration of Hugh d'Avranches, earl of Chester, and his cousin, Robert of Rhuddlan, into Rhos, Rhufoniog and even the principality of Gwynedd was in the event abortive, earl Hugh's motte at Caernarvon was to be carefully incorporated into the great castle which Edward I built there two centuries later, as the symbol not of new conquest but of Norman rights revived.[293] It is not entirely an exaggeration to assert that the conquest of Wales begins in 1066, and the means of the conquest were castles.[294] Nor is it inappropriate to end this essay upon a military note, for the Normans excelled in the art of war, which made them the masters of their world from the Irish Channel to the eastern shores of the Mediterranean and beyond. ('They are', wrote William of Malmesbury, 'a race inured to war, and can hardly live without it'),[295] and warfare brings us back again to the second long-term result of the Norman Conquest of England, that is, the closer integration of this country in the affairs of Western Europe. Part of this revolution, for such it was, in English life and politics is a continuous involvement, as from 1066, in Continental wars, and especially wars in France which, beginning in 1073, scarcely end before 1815. The first inclination of the modern reader may not be to feel gratitude to the Normans for this heritage of blood, but historians must think of war as the catalyst of change. English and European history, social and economic as well as political, including, paradoxically, the history of the growth of English constitutional liberties, would have been very different without it. In the long term as in the short term it seems inevitable to end this book as it began, with Carlyle's unanswerable question – 'England itself, in foolish quarters of England, still howls and execrates lamentably over its William Conqueror, and rigorous line of Normans and Plantagenets; but without them, if you will consider well, what had it ever been?'

[293] Brown, Colvin and Taylor, *History of the King's Works*, i, 369–70.
[294] Cf. *Anglo-Saxon Chronicle*, 'E', p. 164. 'Wales was in his [the Conqueror's] power, and he built castles there.'
[295] *Gesta Regum*, ii, 306; translation *English Historical Documents*, ii, 291.

Select Bibliography

The following bibliography is not intended to be comprehensive but to be merely a list of the principal works consulted in the preparation of this volume and of those most useful for further reading and study. The editions given are those which have been used and cited in the footnotes. Valuable general bibliographies of the subject and the period are to be found in F. M. Stenton, *Anglo-Saxon England*, D. C. Douglas, *William the Conqueror*, and the two relevant volumes of *English Historical Documents*, all cited below.

PRIMARY SOURCES

Aimé of Monte Cassino, *L'ystoire de li Normant*, ed. O. Delarc (Rouen, 1892).

Anglo-Saxon Chronicle, ed. D. Whitelock, D. C. Douglas and S. I. Tucker (London, 1961).

Baudri de Bourgueil, *Les œuvres poétiques de Baudri de Bourgueil*, ed. P. Abrahams (Paris, 1926).

Bayeux Tapestry, ed. F. M. Stenton and others (London, 1965).

Benoit [de Sainte-Maure], in *Chroniques des Ducs de Normandie*, ed. F. Michel, 3 vols. (Paris, 1836–43).

Bishop, T. A. M., and Chaplais, P., *Facsimiles of English Royal Writs to A.D. 1100* (Oxford, 1957).

Brevis Relatio de Origine Willelmi Conquestoris, in *Scriptores Rerum Gestarum Willelmi Conquestoris*, ed. J. A. Giles (London, 1845).

Cartulaire de l'abbaye de la Sainte-Trinité du Mont de Rouen, ed. A. Deville, in *Cartulaire de l'abbaye de Saint-Bertin*, ed. M. Guérard (Documents Inédits sur l'Histoire de France, Paris, 1841).

Cartularium Saxonicum, ed. W. de G. Birch, 3 vols. (London, 1885–93).

Chronicon Monasterii de Abingdon, ed. J. Stevenson, 2 vols. (Rolls Series, London, 1858).

Chronicon Monasterii de Bello, ed. J. S. Brewer (Anglia Christiana Society, London, 1846).

Codex Diplomaticus Aevi Saxonici, ed. J. M. Kemble, 6 vols. (London, 1839–48).

Concilia Rotomagensis Provinciae, ed. G. Bessin (Rouen, 1717).

Dialogus de Scaccario, ed. C. Johnson, A. Hughes and C. G. Crump (Oxford, 1902); also ed. C. Johnson (London, 1950).

Domesday Book (Record Commission, 2 vols., 1783).

Douglas, D. C., *Feudal Documents from the Abbey of Bury St. Edmunds* (London, 1932).

Dudo of Saint Quentin, *De Moribus et Actis primorum Normanniae Ducum*, ed. J. Lair (Société des Antiquaires de Normandie, 1865).

Eadmer, *Historia Novorum in Anglia*, ed. M. Rule (Rolls Series, London, 1884).

——, *Vita Anselmi*, ed. R. W. Southern (London, 1962).

Encomium Emmae Reginae, ed. A. Campbell (Camden, 3rd. Series, lxxii, London, 1949).

English Historical Documents, vol. I (*c.* 500–1042) ed. D. Whitelock, (London, 1955); vol. II (1042–1189) ed. D. C. Douglas (London, 1959).

Eye Cartulary, Essex Record Office, D/DBy Q 19.

Florence of Worcester, *Chronicon ex Chronicis*, ed. B. Thorpe, 2 vols. (London, 1848–9).

Geoffrey Gaimar, *Lestoire des Engles solum la translacion Maistre Geffrei Gaimar*, ed. C. T. Martin, 2 vols. (Rolls Series, London, 1888–9).

Geoffrey Malaterra, *De Gestis Roberti Guiscardi et Rogerii principum Normannorum*, in *Thesaurus Antiquitatrum et Historiaum Siciliae*, ed. J. G. Graevius, v (Leyden, 1723–5).

Guy of Amiens, *Carmen de Hastingae Proelio*, in *Scriptores Rerum Gestarum Willelmi Conquestoris*, ed. J. A. Giles (London, 1845).

Harmer, F. E., *Anglo-Saxon Writs* (Manchester, 1952).

Hemingi Chartularium Ecclesiae Wigornensis, ed. T. Hearne, 2 vols (Oxford, 1723).

Henry of Huntingdon, *Historia Anglorum*, ed. T. Arnold (Rolls Series, London, 1879).

Hugh the Chantor, *The History of the Church of York, 1066–1127*, ed. C. Johnson (London, 1961).

Jordan Fantosme, *Chronique de la guerre entre les Anglois et les Ecossois en 1173 et 1174*, in *Chronicles and Memorials of the reigns of Stephen, Henry II and Richard I*, iii, ed. R. Howlett (Rolls Series, London, 1896).

Lanfranc, *Decreta Lanfranci Monachis Cantuariensibus transmissa*, ed. D. Knowles (London, 1951).

Lanfranci Opera, ed. J. A. Giles, 2 vols. (Oxford, 1844).

Laws of the Earliest English Kings, ed. F. L. Attenborough (New York, 1963).

Liber Eliensis, ed. E. O. Blake (Camden, 3rd Series, xcii, London, 1962).

Magni Rotuli Scaccarii Normanniae sub Regibus Angliae, ed. Stapleton, 2 vols. (London, 1840–4).

Ordericus Vitalis, *Historia Ecclesiastica*, ed. A. Le Prévost, 5 vols. (Paris, 1838–55).

——, Interpolations in William of Jumièges, *q.v.*

Plummer, C., *Two of the Saxon Chronicles Parallel*, 2 vols. (Oxford, 1892–9).

Ralph Glaber, *Raoul Glaber, les cinq livres de ces histoires*, ed. M. Prou (Paris, 1886).

Recueil des actes des ducs de Normandie, ed. M Fauroux (Mémoires de la Société des Antiquaires de Normandie, tome xxxvi, Caen, 1961).

Red Book of the Exchequer, ed. H. Hall (Rolls Series, London, 1896).

Regesta Regum Anglo-Normannorum, 1066–1154, vol. I (*Regesta Willelmi Conquestoris et Willelmi Rufi, 1066–1100*), ed. H. W. C. Davis (Oxford, 1913).

Robert of Torigni, Interpolations in William of Jumièges, *q.v.*

Robertson, A. J., *Anglo-Saxon Charters* (Cambridge, 1939).

Roger of Wendover, *Flores Historiarum*, 5 vols. ed. H. O. Coxe (London, English Historical Society, 1841–4).

Snorre Sturlason, *The Heimskringla or the Sagas of the Norse Kings*, ed. R. B. Anderson, iv (London, 1889).

Vita Edwardi, ed. F. Barlow (London, 1962).

Vita Herluini, ed. J. Armitage Robinson in *Gilbert Crispin* (Cambridge, 1911).

Wace, *Roman de Rou*, ed. H. Andresen, 2 vols. (Heilbronn, 1877–9).

Whitelock, D., *Anglo-Saxon Wills* (Cambridge, 1930).

William of Jumièges, *Gesta Normannorum Ducum*, ed. J. Marx (Société de l'histoire de Normandie, Rouen and Paris, 1914).

William of Malmesbury, *De Gestis Pontificum Anglorum*, ed. N. E. S. A. Hamilton (Rolls Series, London, 1870).

——, *Gesta Regum Anglorum*, ed. W. Stubbs, 2 vols. (Rolls Series, London, 1887–9).

——, *Vita Wulfstani*, ed. R. R. Darlington (Camden, 3rd Series, xl, London, 1928).

William of Poitiers, *Histoire de Guillaume le Conquérant (Gesta Guillelmi ducis Normannorum et regis Anglorum)*, ed. and trans. R. Foreville (Paris, 1952).

SECONDARY AUTHORITIES

Armitage, E. S., *Early Norman Castles of the British Isles* (London, 1912).

Armitage Robinson, J., *Gilbert Crispin, Abbot of Westminster* (Cambridge, 1911).

Baring, F. H., *Domesday Tables for the counties of Surrey, Berkshire, Middlesex, Hertford, Buckingham and Bedford and for the New Forest* (London, 1909).

Barlow, F., 'Edward the Confessor's Early Life, Character and Attitudes' (*English Historical Review*, lxxx, 1965).

——, 'The Effects of the Norman Conquest', in *The Norman Conquest: Its Setting and Impact*, by D. Whitelock and others (London, 1966).

——, *The English Church, 1000–1066* (London, 1963).

——, *William I and the Norman Conquest* (London, 1965).

Barraclough, G., 'The Anglo-Saxon Writ' (*History*, xxxix, 1954).

Barrow, G. W. S., 'The Beginnings of Feudalism in Scotland' (*Bulletin of the Institute of Historical Research*, xxix, 1956).

——, *The Border* (Inaugural Lecture, Durham, 1962).

Beeler, J., *Warfare in England, 1066–1189* (New York, 1966).

Biddle, M., Interim reports on the excavations at Winchester:
Archaeological Journal, cxix (1962).
Antiquaries Journal, xliv (1964).
Antiquaries Journal, xlv (1965).
Antiquaries Journal, xlvi (1966).

Bishop, T. A. M., 'The Norman Settlement of Yorkshire', in *Studies in Medieval History presented to F. M. Powicke* (Oxford, 1948).

Blair, P. H., *An Introduction to Anglo-Saxon England* (Cambridge, 1959).

Bloch, M., *Feudal Society*, trans. L. A. Manyon (London, 1961).

Boüard, M. de., 'De la Neustrie Carolingienne à la Normandie féodale: continuité ou discontinuité' (*Bulletin of the Institute of Historical Research*, xxviii, 1955).

——, *Guillaume le Conquérant* (Paris, 1958).

——, 'Le Château de Caen' (*Caen, Syndicat d'Initiative*).

——, 'Le Duché de Normandie', in F. Lot and R. Fawtier, *Histoire des Institutions Françaises au Moyen Age*, vol. I, *Institutions Seigneuriales* (Paris, 1957).

——, 'Les petites enceintes circulaires d'origine médiévale en Normandie', in *Château-Gaillard, Etudes de Castellologie européenne*, I (Caen, 1964).

Brooke, Z. N., *The English Church and the Papacy* (Cambridge, 1931).

Brooks, F. W., *The Battle of Stamford Bridge* (East Yorkshire Local History Society, 1963).

Brown, R. A., 'A List of Castles, 1154–1216' (*English Historical Review*, lxxiv, 1959).

——, *Dover Castle* (London, Her Majesty's Stationery Office, 1966).

——, *English Castles* (London, 1962).

——, 'The Norman Conquest' (*Transactions of the Royal Historical Society*, 5th Series, XVII, 1967)

Burne, A. H., *The Battlefields of England* (London, 1950).

Buttin, F., 'Le lance et l'arrêt de cuirasse' (*Archaeologia*, xcix, 1965).

Cahen, C., *Le Régime féodal de l'Italie normande* (Paris, 1940).

Chalendon, F., *Histoire de la domination normande en Italie et en Sicile* (Paris, 1907).

Chaplais, P., 'Une Charte originale de Guillaume le Conquérant . . .', in *L'Abbaye bénédictine de Fécamp*, 2 vols. (Fécamp, 1959–60).

Chew, H. M., *English Ecclesiastical Tenants-in-Chief and Knight Service* (London, 1932).

Chrimes, S. B., *An Introduction to the Administrative History of Medieval England* (Oxford, 2nd. edition, 1959).

Clapham, A. W., *English Romanesque Architecture before the Norman Conquest* (Oxford, 1930; re-issued 1964).

——, *English Romanesque Architecture after the Conquest* (Oxford, 1934; reissued 1964).

——, *Romanesque Architecture in Western Europe* (Oxford, 1936).

Clapham, J. H., 'The Horsing of the Danes' (*English Historical Review*, xxv, 1910).

Colvin, H. M., 'Domestic Architecture and Town Planning', in *Medieval England*, ed. A. L. Poole, vol. I (Oxford, 1958).

——, (ed.) *The History of the King's Works*, vols. 1 and 2, *The Middle Ages* (London, Her Majesty's Stationery Office, 1963).

Complete Peerage of England, Scotland, Ireland, Great Britain and the United Kingdom, by G. E. C., 13 vols. in 14 (1910–59).

Conant, K. J., 'Cluny II and St. Bégnigne at Dijon' (*Archaeologia*, xcix, 1965).

Corbett, W. J., 'The development of the Duchy of Normandy and the Norman Conquest of England', in *Cambridge Medieval History*, v (1926).

Croft Dickinson, W., *Scotland from the Earliest Times to 1603* (London 1961).

Darlington, R. R., *Anglo-Norman Historians* (Inaugural Lecture, London, 1947).

——, 'Ecclesiastical Reform in the Late Old English Period' (*English Historical Review*, li, 1936).

——, 'The Last Phase of Anglo-Saxon History' (*History*, xxii, 1937–8).

——, *The Norman Conquest* (Creighton Lecture for 1962, University of London, 1963).

David, C. W., *Robert Curthose, Duke of Normandy* (Cambridge, U.S.A., 1920).

Davis, R. H. C., *A History of Medieval Europe* (London, 1957).

——, 'What happened in Stephen's Reign?' (*History*, xlix, 1964).

Davison, B. K., 'The Origins of the Castle in England' (*Archaeological Journal*, cxxiv, 1967).

Delbrück, H., *Geschichte der Kriegskunst im Rahmen des Politische Geschichte*, iii (Berlin, 1923).

Delisle, L., *Histoire du Château et des sires de Saint-Sauveur-le-Vicomte* (Paris, Caen, 1867).

Dodwell, B., 'East Anglian Commendation' (*English Historical Review*, lxiii, 1948).

Dolley, R. H. M., *Anglo-Saxon Pennies* (London, 1964).

——, (ed.) *Anglo-Saxon Coins* (London, 1961).

Douglas, D. C., 'Edward the Confessor, Duke William of Normandy, and the English Succession' (*English Historical Review*, lxviii, 1953).

——, 'Some Problems of Early Norman Chronology' (*English Historical Review*, lxv, 1950).

——, 'The Earliest Norman Counts' (*English Historical Review*, lxi, 1946).

——, *The Norman Conquest and British Historians* (The David Murray Lecture for 1946, Glasgow, 1946).

——, 'The Norman Episcopate before the Norman Conquest' (*Cambridge Historical Journal*, xiii, 1957).

——, 'The Rise of Normandy' (*Proceedings of the British Academy*, xxxiii, 1947).

——, *William the Conqueror* (London, 1964).

——, 'William the Conqueror: Duke and King', in *The Norman Conquest: Its Setting and Impact*, by D. Whitelock and others (London, 1966).

Edwards, J. G., 'The Normans and the Welsh March' (*Proceedings of the British Academy*, xlii, 1956).

Fliche, A., *Le Règne de Philippe I, roi de France* (Paris, 1912).

Foreville, R., 'Aux Origines de la Renaissance Juridique', in *Le Moyen Age*, lviii (1952).

Fowler, G. H., 'The Devastation of Bedfordshire and the Neighbouring Counties in 1065 and 1066' (*Archaeologia*, lxxii, 1922).

Freeman, E. A., *The Norman Conquest*, 6 vols. (Oxford, 1867–79).

——, See also *Life and Letters of E. A. Freeman*, ed. W. R. W. Stephens (London and New York, 1895).

Fuller, J. F. C., *The Decisive Battles of the Western World* (London, 1954).

Galbraith, V. H., *Studies in the Public Records* (London, 1948).

——, *The Making of Domesday Book* (Oxford, 1961).

Ganshof, F. L., *Feudalism*, trans. P. Grierson (London, 1952).

Garmonsway, G. N., *The Anglo-Saxon Chronicle* (London, 1953).

Glover, R., 'English Warfare in 1066' (*English Historical Review*, lxvii, 1952).

Grierson, P., 'A Visit of Earl Harold to Flanders in 1056' (*English Historical Review*, li, 1936).

——, 'The Relations between England and Flanders before the Norman Conquest' (*Transactions of the Royal Historical Society*, 4th. Series, xxiii, 1941).

Guilhiermoz, P., *Essai sur l'origine de la noblesse en France au Moyen Age* (Paris, 1902).

Halphen, L., *Le comté d'Anjou au xie siècle* (Paris, 1906).

Handbook of British Chronology, ed. F. M. Powicke and E. B. Fryde (London, Royal Historical Society, 1961).

Haskins, C. H., *Norman Institutions* (New York, 1918).

——, *The Normans in European History* (New York, 1915).

Héliot, P., 'Sur les résidences princières bâties en France du xe au xiie siècle', in *Le Moyen Age*, lxi (1955).

Hollings, M., 'The Survival of the Five Hide Unit in the Western Midlands' (*English Historical Review*, lxiii, 1948).

Hollister, C. W., *Anglo-Saxon Military Institutions on the Eve of the Norman Conquest* (Oxford, 1962).

——, *The Military Organisation of Norman England* (Oxford, 1965).

Hollyman, K. J., *Le Développement du Vocabulaire féodal en France pendant le haut moyen âge* (Paris and Geneva, 1957).

Hurnard, D., 'Anglo-Norman Franchises' (*English Historical Review*, lxiv, 1949).

——, 'The Jury of Presentment and the Assize of Clarendon' (*English Historical Review*, lvi, 1941).

John, E., *Land Tenure in Early England* (Leicester, 1960).

Jolliffe, J. E. A., *Constitutional History of Medieval England* (London, 1937).

Keen, M. H., *The Laws of War in the Late Middle Ages* (London, 1965).

Ker, N. R., 'Hemming's Cartulary: a description of two Worcester cartularies in Cotton Tiberias A. xiii', in *Studies in Medieval History presented to F. M. Powicke* (Oxford, 1948).

Kern, F., *Kingship and Law in the Middle Ages*, trans. S. B. Chrimes (London, 1939).

Kimball, E. G., *Serjeanty Tenure in Medieval England* (New Haven, 1936)

——, 'Tenure in Frank Almoign and Secular Services' (*English Historical Review*, xliii, 1928).

Knowles, D., *The Monastic Order in England* (Cambridge, second edition, 1963).

Körner, S., *The Battle of Hastings, England, and Europe, 1035–1066* (Bibliotheca Historica Lundensis, xiv, Lund, 1964).

La Borderie, A. de, *Histoire de Brétagne*, 3 vols. (Rennes, 1896–1900).

Larson, L. M., *The King's Household in England before the Norman Conquest* (Madison, 1904).

Latouche, R., *Histoire du comté du Maine pendant les xe et xie siècles* (Paris, 1910).

——, *Les Origines de l'Economie Occidentale (ive–xie siècle)* (Paris, 1956).

Le Patourel, J. H., 'Geoffrey of Montbray, Bishop of Coutances, 1049–93' (*English Historical Review*, lix, 1944).

Leclerq, J., and Bonnes, J. P., *Un maître de la vie spirituelle au xie siècle, Jean de Fécamp* (Paris, 1946).

Lemarignier, J. F., *Recherches sur l'hommage en marche et les frontières féodales* (Lille, 1945).

Lemmon, C. H., 'The Campaign of 1066', in *The Norman Conquest: Its Setting and Impact*, by D. Whitelock and others (London, 1966).

Lennard, R., *Rural England, 1086–1135* (Oxford, 1959).

Lloyd, J. E., *A History of Wales*, 2 vols. (London, 1912).

Lot, F., *L'art militaire et les armées au moyen âge en Europe et dans le proche Orient*, 2 vols. (Paris, 1946).

Lot, F., and Fawtier, R., *Histoire des Institutions Françaises au Moyen Age*, Tome I, *Institutions Seigneuriales* (Paris, 1957).

Loyd, L. C., *The Origins of Some Anglo-Norman Families* (Harleian Society, ciii, Leeds, 1951).

Loyn, H. R., *Anglo-Saxon England and the Norman Conquest* (London, 1962).

——, 'Boroughs and Mints A.D. 900–1066' in *Anglo-Saxon Coins*, ed. R. H. M. Dolley (London, 1961).

——, 'Gesiths and Thegns from the seventh to the tenth century' (*English Historical Review*, lxx, 1955).

——, *The Norman Conquest* (London, 1965).

Maitland, F. W., *Domesday Book and Beyond* (Cambridge, 1897).

Mason, J. F. A., 'Roger de Montgomery and his Sons (1067–1102)' (*Transactions of the Royal Historical Society*, 5th Series, xiii, 1963).

Matthew, D. J. A., *The Norman Conquest* (London, 1966).

——, *The Norman Monasteries and their English Possessions* (Oxford, 1962).

Miller, E., *The Abbey and Bishopric of Ely* (Cambridge, 1951)

Morris, C., 'William I and the Church Courts' (*English Historical Review*, lxxxii, 1967).

Morris, W. A., *The Frankpledge System* (New York, 1910).

——, *The Medieval English Sheriff* (Manchester, 1927).

Musset, L., 'A-t-il existé en Normandie au xie siècle une aristocratie d'argent?' (*Annales de Normandie*, 1959).

——, 'Relations et échanges d'influences dans l'Europe de Nord-Ouest (x^e–xie siècles)' (*Cahiers de Civilisation Médiévale*, i, 1958).

Navel, H., 'L'enquête de 1133 sur les fiefs de l'evêché de Bayeux' (*Bulletin de la Société des Antiquaires de Normandie*, xlii, 1934).

——, 'Recherches sur les institutions féodales en Normandie (Région de Caen)' (*Bulletin de la Société des Antiquaires de Normandie*, li, 1952).

Oleson, T. J., 'Edward the Confessor's Promise of the Throne to Duke William of Normandy' (*English Historical Review*, lxxii, 1957).

——, *The Witenagemot in the Reign of Edward the Confessor* (London, 1955).

Oman, Sir C., *A History of the Art of War in the Middle Ages*, 2 vols. (2nd edition, London, 1924).

Plucknet, T. F. T., *Edward I and the Criminal Law* (Cambridge, 1960).

Pollock, F., and Maitland, F. W., *History of English Law*, 2 vols. (Cambridge, 1895).

Poole, A. L., *Obligations of Society in the Twelfth and Thirteenth Centuries* (Oxford, 1946).

Poole, R. L., *Chronicles and Annals* (Oxford, 1926).

——, *The Exchequer in the Twelfth Century* (Oxford, 1912).

Porée, A. A., *Histoire de l'abbaye du Bec*, 2 vols. (Evreux, 1901).

Powicke, F. M., *The Loss of Normandy* (Manchester, 1913).

——, See also, *Studies in Medieval History presented to F. M. Powicke* (Oxford, 1948).

Powicke, M. R., *Military Obligations in Medieval England* (Oxford, 1962).

Prentout, H., *Essai sur les origines et la fondation du Duché de Normandie* (Paris, 1911).

——, *Etude critique sur Dudon de Saint-Quentin* (Paris, 1916).

——, *Guillaume le Conquérant* (Caen, 1936).

Prestwich, J. O., 'Anglo-Norman Feudalism and the Problem of Continuity' (*Past and Present*, No. 26, 1963).

——, 'War and Finance in the Anglo-Norman State' (*Transactions of the Royal Historical Society*, 5th Series, iv, 1954).

Quirk, R., 'Winchester Cathedral in the Tenth Century' (*Archaeological Journal*, cxiv, 1957).

Richardson, H. G., and Sayles, G. O., *The Governance of Mediæval England* (Edinburgh, 1963).

Rickert, M., *Painting in Britain – The Middle Ages* (Harmondsworth 1954)

Ritchie, R. L. G., *The Normans in England before the Norman Conquest* (Inaugural Lecture, Exeter, 1948).

——, *The Normans in Scotland* (Edinburgh, 1954).

Ritter, R., *Châteaux, Donjons et Places Fortes* (Paris, 1953).

Ross, D. J. A., 'L'originalité de "Turoldus": le maniement de lance', in *Cahiers de Civilisation Médiévale*, VI (1963).

Round, J. H., *Feudal England* (London, 1895).

——, 'Helion of Helion's Bumpstead' (*Transactions of the Essex Archaeological Society*, New Series, viii, 1903).

——, 'Notes on Anglo-Norman Genealogy' (*Genealogist*, New Series, xvii, 1901).

——, *Studies in Peerage and Family History* (London, 1930).

——, 'The Introduction of Knight-Service into England' (*English Historical Review*, vi and vii, 1891–2; reprinted in his *Feudal England*).

Ruprich-Robert, V., *L'architecture Normande aux xie et xiie siècles en Normandie et en Angleterre*, 2 vols. (Paris, 1899).

Sanders, I. J., *English Baronies. A Study of their Origin and Descent, 1086–1327* (Oxford, 1960).

Sawyer, P. H., *The Age of the Vikings* (London, 1962).

——, 'The Density of the Danish Settlement in England' (*University of Birmingham Historical Journal*, vi, 1957).

——, 'The Wealth of England in the Eleventh Century' (*Transactions of the Royal Historical Society*, 5th Series, xv, 1965).

Schramm, P. E., *A History of the English Coronation* (Oxford, 1937).

Siguret, Ph., 'Trois mottes de la région de Bellême (Orne)', in *Château-Gaillard. Etudes de Castellologie européenne*, I (Caen, 1964).

Simpson, W. D., *Castles from the Air* (London, 1949).

Smail, R. C., *Crusading Warfare* (Cambridge, 1956).

Southern, R. W., 'Lanfranc of Bec and Berengar of Tours', in *Studies in Medieval History presented to F. M. Powicke* (Oxford, 1948).

——, *Saint Anselm and his Biographer* (Cambridge, 1963).

——, *The Making of the Middle Ages* (London, 1953).

——, 'The Place of England in the Twelfth-Century Renaissance' (*History*, xlv, 1960).

——, 'The Place of Henry I in English History' (*Proceedings of the British Academy*, xlviii, 1963).

Spatz, W., *Die Schlacht von Hastings* (Berlin, 1896).

Stenton, D. M., *English Justice between the Norman Conquest and the Great Charter* (London, 1965).

——, *English Society in the Earlier Middle Ages (1066–1307)* (London, 1952).

Stenton, F. M., *Anglo-Saxon England* (Oxford, 1943).

——, *Norman London* (Historical Association, London, 1934).

——, 'The Danes in England' (*Proceedings of the British Academy*, xiii, 1927).

——, *The First Century of English Feudalism* (Oxford, 1932).

——, *The Latin Charters of the Anglo-Saxon Period* (Oxford, 1955).

——, 'The Scandinavian Colonies in England and Normandy' (*Transactions of the Royal Historical Society*, 4th Series, xxvii, 1945).

——, *William the Conqueror and the Rule of the Normans* (London, 2nd edition, 1925).

Stevenson, W. H., 'Trinoda Necessitas' (*English Historical Review*, xxix, 1914).

Stone, L., *Sculpture in Britain – The Middle Ages* (Harmondsworth, 1955)

Stubbs, W., *Select Charters* (9th edition, ed. H. W. C. Davis, Oxford, 1946).

Talbot Rice, D., *English Art 871–1100* (Oxford, 1952).

Taylor, H. M. and J., *Anglo-Saxon Architecture*, 2 vols. (Cambridge, 1965)

Tout, T. F., *Chapters in Medieval Administrative History*, 6 vols. (Manchester, 1920–33).

Van Caenegem, R. C., *Royal Writs in England from the Conquest to Glanville* (Selden Society, lxxvii, 1958–9).

Verbruggen, J. F., 'La tactique militaire des armées de chevaliers' (*Revue du nord*, xxix, 1947).

Victoria County History of the Counties of England (London, 1900–)

Waley, D. P., 'Combined Operations in Sicily A.D. 1060–1078' (*Papers of the British School at Rome*, xxii, 1954).

Webb, G., *Architecture in Britain in the Middle Ages* (London, 1956).

Welldon Finn, R., *An Introduction to Domesday Book* (London, 1963).

——, *The Domesday Inquest* (London, 1961).

West, F. J., *The Justiciarship in England, 1066–1232* (Cambridge, 1966).

White, G. H., 'Companions of the Conqueror' (*Genealogists Magazine*, ix, 1944).

——, 'The Battle of Hastings and the Death of Harold', *Complete Peerage*, XII, Pt. 1, Appdx. L. (London, 1953).

White, L. Jr., *Medieval Technology and Social Change* (Oxford, 1962).

Whitelock, D., 'The Anglo-Saxon Achievement', in *The Norman Conquest: Its Setting and Impact*, by D. Whitelock and others (London, 1966).

——, *The Beginnings of English Society* (London, 1952).

——, 'The Dealings of the English Kings with Northumbria in the Tenth and Eleventh Centuries', in *The Anglo-Saxons. Studies in some Aspects of their History and Culture presented to Bruce Dickens*, ed. F. Clemoes (London, 1959).

Wilkinson, B., 'Freeman and the Crisis of 1051' (*Bulletin of the John Rylands Library*, xxii, 1938).

——, 'Northumbrian Separatism in 1065 and 1066' (*Bulletin of the John Rylands Library*, xxiii, 1939).

Wilmart, A., *Auteurs spirituels et Textes dévots du Moyen-Age Latin* (Paris, 1932).

Wolter, H., *Ordericus Vitalis: ein Beitrag zur kluniazensischen Geschichtsschreibung* (Weisbaden, 1955).

Wyon, A., *The Great Seals of England* (London, 1887).

Yver, J., 'Les chateaux-forts en Normandie jusqu'au milieu du xiie siècle. Contribution à l'étude du pouvoir ducale' (*Bulletin de la Société des Antiquaires de Normandie*, liii, 1957).

——, 'L'interdiction de la guerre privée dans le trés ancien droit normand', in *Travaux de la Sémaine d'histoire du Droit normand*, May 1927 (Caen, 1928).

Zarnecki, G., *English Romanesque Sculpture 1066–1140* (London, 1951).

——'1066 and Architectural Sculpture' (*Proceedings of the British Academy*, lii, 1966).

Index

References to the most frequently mentioned persons (e.g. William the Conqueror) and subjects (e.g. Knights) are selective rather than comprehensive.

Tesson, family, 27
Tewkesbury, Glos., abbey, 260 n.276
Thames, river, 61, 179, 190
Thanet, 142
Thegns, 66, 93 *ter*, 94 *bis*, 96, 166, 207, 227, 229
Thetford, Norf., bishop, *see* William
Thierry, abbot of St. Evroul, 29
Thorkell the Tall, 78
Thurkill of Arden, 186, 204
Tilleul, Humphrey de, 208
Tillières-sur-Avre, Eure, castle, 44 n.132
Tiro, tirones, 47, 170
Tithing, 248
Tonbridge, Kent, honour, 212
Tosny, family, 27, 35, 210; Ralph de, 37, 42, 47, 168 n.132, 212; Robert de, 212; Roger de, 18 n.18, 43
Tostig, earl of Northumbria, son of earl Godwin, 76, 79, 80 n.94, 82, 83, 84, 107 n.218, 108 n.223, 131, 136 n.140, 142-3, 145, 155, 157, 158, 186
Totnes, Judhael of, 209
Toulouse, 11
Towns, urbanisation, 14, 52, 100
Trade and commerce, 14, 23, 51-2, 86, 99-100, 111, 185
Treasurer, Treasury, 69, 70, 247. Cf. *Camera*, Chamber, Exchequer.
Trent, river, 217 n.63, 259
Trimoda necessitas, 64, 89, 90, 91-2
Truce of God, 34, 56. Cf. Peace
Tutbury, Staffs., 210; *castellaria*, 215; castle, 215
Tyne, river, 155, 156

Ulf, bishop of Dorchester, 118, 120
Urban II, Pope, 14, 18
Urbanisation, *see* Towns

Val-ès-Dunes, Calvados, battle, 21, 34, 42, 44, n.135, 45 and n.137, 46 n.147, 56, 58 *bis*, 59
Valognes, Manche, 44 n.136
Varaville, Calvados, battle, 45 n.137, 50 n.164, 51, 58

Vassals, vassalage, 23, 39, 41, 43, 46, 47, 87, 91, 92, 151, 239, 240, 246
Vavasseurs, 40
Vere, family, 210
Vexin, French, 21 n.4, 200; count of, *see* Mantes
Vicomtes, 54, 56, 57
Vicomtés, 22, 52, 54, 57
Vikings, 9-10. *See* Denmark, Norway, Scandinavia
Villein tenure, 240
Vita Herluini, 29 and n.42, 33
Volpiano, William of, abbot of St. Bénigne and Fécamp, 26-7, 28, 29

Wace, 164 n.115
Wales, Welsh, 15, 52, 81 n.98, 83, 97, 108, 115, 190, 195 n.273, 197, 230, 231, 235, 238, 263-4; Marches, 97, 214, 215, 218 n.67, 231, 238, 263-4; Gwynedd, *see* Gruffydd; Powys, *see* Gruffydd; Rhos, 264; Rhufoniog, 264
Wallingford, Berks., 179, 207 n.16, 226; castle, 179, 234 n.142, 235, 237
Walter, bishop of Hereford, 180
Waltham Holy Cross, Essex, abbey, 103, 107, 174, 175 and n.162, 260
Waltheof, earl of Northumbria, 2, 187, 194, 196, 200 n.295, 206
Wapentake, 69; court, 69
Wardship and marriage, 243, 244
Warenne, family, 35, 38; William de, 210, 212, 215, 259
Warfare, 50, 164 n.115, 232, 264; private, 56, 58, 218 n.67; combined operations, 150 n.47; discipline, 51, 151-2, 164 n.115; loot, 174 n.160, 183, 191; reconnaissance, 50, 160, 163; winter campaigns, 51, 185, 191, 195-7. *See also* Archers, *Armigeri, Arrière-ban,* Battles, Battle-axes, Boroughs, Campaigns, *Castellarie,* Castles, Cavalry, *Conrois,* Crossbow-men, England pre-Conquest, England post-Conquest, Feigned flight, Fleet,